VIRGIN ISLANDS
HANDBOOK

allegory of Europe supported by Africa and America by William Blake

VIRGIN ISLANDS HANDBOOK

FIRST EDITION

KARL LUNTTA

MOON
TRAVEL
HANDBOOKS

VIRGIN ISLANDS HANDBOOK
FIRST EDITION

Published by
Moon Publications, Inc.
P.O. Box 3040
Chico, California 95927-3040, USA

Printed by
Colorcraft Ltd., Hong Kong

ISBN: 1-56691-093-5
ISSN: 1092-3357

Editing: Pauli Galin
Map Editor: Gina Wilson Birtcil
Copyediting: Gregor Krause
Production & Design: Carey Wilson
Cartography: Bob Race
Indexing: Diane Wurzel

Front cover photo: scuba diver and coral sea fan by Dean Hulse, courtesy of Rainbow
All photos by Karl Luntta unless otherwise noted.

Distributed in the USA and Canada by Publishers Group West
Printed in China

Please send all comments,
corrections, additions,
amendments, and critiques to:

VIRGIN ISLANDS HANDBOOK
MOON TRAVEL HANDBOOKS
P.O. BOX 3040
CHICO, CA 95927-3040, USA
e-mail: travel@moon.com
www.moon.com

Printing History
1st edition — September 1997

DEDICATION:

To my mother and father,
Anna L. Luntta
and
Hans K. Luntta

CONTENTS

MAPS

MAP SYMBOLS

NUMBERED ROAD	BRIDGE	CHURCH	
MAIN ROAD	○ CITY, TOWN, VILLAGE	CATHEDRAL	
SECONDARY ROAD	▲ MOUNTAIN	WATERFALL	
OTHER ROAD	■ SITE, POINT OF INTEREST	WATER	
TRACK	● ACCOMMODATION	AIRPORT, AIRSTRIP	
PATH	INTERNATIONAL BORDER		

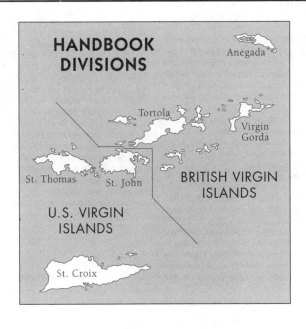

HANDBOOK DIVISIONS

Anegada

Tortola

Virgin Gorda

St. Thomas   St. John

BRITISH VIRGIN ISLANDS

U.S. VIRGIN ISLANDS

St. Croix

CHARTS AND SPECIAL TOPICS

MAKE THIS A BETTER BOOK

The truth is more important than the facts.
      —FRANK LLOYD WRIGHT

Frank Lloyd Wright's sentiment carries a lot of, well, truth. It's a weighty proposition for travel writers; to be sure, the essence of any work is its truth. For travel writing, however, the simple truth about a place may not be enough; facts are what get you there, get you around, and bring you back again.

This book has been carefully researched to provide the most accurate, timely information available, with the hope that it will serve you better, make things easier to discern, and enhance your stay in the Virgin Islands.

Still, things change—good for the Virgin Islands, sometimes not so good for a travel guide. Foreign exchange rates fluctuate, hotels raise their rates, restaurants disappear, new governments are elected, and books take months to get into print. While the general information in *Virgin Islands Handbook* remains constant, specific details may become inaccurate by the time you pick it up. If that's the case, we want to hear from you: about your experiences on the islands and what you've found that can help us in our continuing effort to revise and update *Virgin Islands Handbook*. Jot down observations while you're there—information recorded at the source is always most accurate. When you return, send the information to us; we'll check it out. The most helpful letters will receive an acknowledgment in the next edition.

We would especially like to hear from female travelers, hikers, campers, and outdoor adventurists. If you've run into problems you think other travelers should know of, fill us in. We also encourage long-time island residents to submit comments and opinions based on an insider's view. Be specific; comment on maps, area descriptions, and prices. Include sources where appropriate. Hotel owners are welcome to keep us updated on current rates and other information. Of course, if you found *Virgin Islands Handbook* useful, we'd also love to hear about that.

Address your comments to:

        Virgin Islands Handbook
        c/o Moon Travel Handbooks
        P.O. Box 3040
        Chico, CA 95927-3040 USA

        e-mail: travel@moon.com

You don't take a trip, you let the trip take you.
                    —JOHN STEINBECK
                    (1902-68), novelist

BOB RACE

INTRODUCTION

The U.S. Virgin Islands and British Virgin Islands share similarities beyond their names. The volcanic topography and flora and fauna found in both groups are comparable. Both incorporate dozens of small, uninhabited or private islets off the main islands' coasts. Both share the bright, clear waters of the northern Caribbean Sea. Both boast some of the finest white-sand beaches in all the Caribbean. Both use the U.S. dollar as their official currency. And both share histories as slavery- driven plantation outposts.

Yet the U.S. and British Virgin Islands are, today, diverse in culture and in attitude—perhaps along the same lines as the contrasts between Washington and London. Whereas the U.S. Virgin Islands hum with that distinctly American buzz of activity, the British Virgin Islands seems more sedate, like an older, even wiser brother. The differences are subtle—one feels them rather than sees them, lives them rather than touches them. But they do exist, and your visit to one group will be enhanced by your visit to the other.

The U.S. Virgin Islands enjoy high name recognition among travelers from North America—not surprising, considering that the islands are territories of the United States and heavily promoted stateside. Tourism blurbs announce, "They're Your Islands," and they are—with all the enticements of exotic oddities, but with the com-

forts and, depending on your definition of travel needs, the trappings of familiarity.

The three main islands of the U.S. Virgin Islands group have perhaps higher name recognition than the group itself. **St. Thomas, St. John,** and **St. Croix** share similar histories and cultures, yet, much like the differences between the U.S. and British islands, offer distinct experiences for the visitor. St. Thomas, the islands' urbane social and economic hub, is as dissimilar to sparsely populated, lush St. John as is a lawn (albeit a nice lawn) to a flower garden. To the south, larger and, in places, desert-like St. Croix is the U.S. Virgin Island's museum archive, hosting the islands' historic towns of Christiansted and Frederiksted, as well as forts, ancient storage warehouses, and dozens of structures from colonial days.

Ultimately, however, it's the people of the U.S. Virgin Islands that tie them together, creating the singular territorial entity. With their dual West Indian and American identity, both politically and culturally, you're as likely to see a richly colorful, loud street festival as you are an American fast-food joint; as likely to hear the plaintive plucks and thumps of an island scratch band as the heavy metal wails of rock and roll at the Hard Rock Cafe.

On the other side of the coin—and a thin sea strait called **The Passage**—the British Virgin

THE CARIBBEAN

Islands, sister islands to the U.S. Virgin Islands through history and infrastructure, is one of the last places left in the region where the phrase "getting away from it all" applies more often than not. The main island of **Tortola** hosts the British Virgin Islands' international airport as well as several fine beaches, resort hotels, and the bucolic capital of **Road Town.** But Tortola is as much of the hype the British Virgin Islands will ever offer. Smaller **Virgin Gorda** hosts, again, fine beaches and hotels, as well as the famous rock formation called **The Baths,** but is unencumbered by McDonalds, two-lane highways, and tourism hoopla. On the other two main islands, **Anegada** and **Jost Van Dyke,** each with populations of fewer than 200, you'd be stretched to find much of anything going on save some fine eating and "limin'" (hanging out) at some of the more colorful beachside bars. These four islands—along with several dozen small islets, cays, and rocks, none more than a few miles from the last and all within sight of each other—form a natural playground for day-trippers, sports fishermen, sailors, and other visitors with a yen to escape to a Caribbean

much as it was 30 years ago—genteel, gracious, and sparkling.

A WORD ABOUT TERMS

Throughout this book, several terms are used to describe the Virgin Islands and other geographical groupings of islands in the Caribbean region. First, the phrase "Virgin Islands," or "Virgins," will be used to describe the islands formed by the two political groups, the U.S. Virgin Islands (U.S.V.I.) and the British Virgin Islands (B.V.I.).

The "West Indies" describes the archipelago, some 1,500 miles (2,400 km) in length, constituting a roughly hewn border that divides the Atlantic Ocean and the Caribbean Sea. The total land mass of the hundreds of islands in the archipelago is 91,000 square miles (236,000 square km), about the size of Uganda. The West Indies comprises the Bahamas and Turks and Caicos Islands in the Atlantic Ocean and the islands of the Caribbean. The "Caribbean" islands are, then, technically, all the islands of the West Indies, minus the Bahamas and Turks and Caicos. Bermuda, some 570 miles (917 km) east of the Carolinas in the Atlantic, shares some of the characteristics of weather and culture of the West Indies yet is not considered part of the island group. Ditto, for our purposes, the islands that lie in the Caribbean Sea off the Mexican and Central American coast.

The "Greater Antilles" and "Lesser Antilles" are subgroups of the Caribbean islands and form a bulging arc stretching from Cuba—the northwest tip of which lies between Key West in Florida and Mexico's Yucatán Peninsula, to the southeast, creating a string of islands that ends north of the Venezuelan coast. The body of water encompassed by these islands is the Caribbean

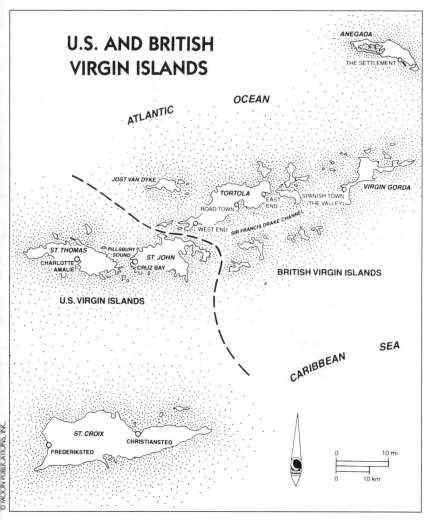

U.S. AND BRITISH VIRGIN ISLANDS

Sea—an area of more than one million square miles (2.6 million square km). The Greater and Lesser Antilles lie south of the Tropic of Cancer, which puts them firmly in the tropics.

The Greater Antilles islands are, in order of descending size, Cuba, Hispaniola (Haiti and the Dominican Republic), Jamaica, and Puerto Rico, plus their smaller adjacent islands. The three Cayman Islands also lie in the waters of the Greater Antilles.

The Lesser Antilles, which were known by the more lyrical name Caribbee Islands in the 17th century, are in turn composed of the Leeward Islands and the Windward Islands.

Farthest north in the Lesser Antilles chain are (grab a map for this) the U.S. Virgin Islands and British Virgin Islands. South of the Virgins is the Leeward Islands group, which consists of Anguilla, Saint-Martin/Sint Maarten, Saba, Sint Eustatius, Saint-Barthélémy, St. Kitts and Nevis, Antigua and Barbuda, Montserrat, Guadeloupe, and adjacent islands (you should be aware, too, that several sources include the Virgins as part of the Leeward Islands, while others do not). Next comes the Windward Islands, comprising Dominica, Martinique, St. Lucia, St. Vincent and the Grenadines, Grenada, and adjacent islands. The remaining Caribbean islands of Barbados, Trinidad and Tobago, the Venezuelan Islands, and Aruba, Curaçao, and Bonaire (commonly known as the ABC Islands) complete the Lesser Antilles roster.

Other divisions among the Caribbean islands rely on politics, not geography. The "French West Indies," sometimes called the "French Antilles" (Guadeloupe, with its dependencies Marie-Galante, Les Saintes, La Désirade, Saint-Barthélémy, and Saint-Martin; and Martinique) and the "Netherlands Antilles" (Bonaire, Curaçao, Sint Maarten, Sint Eustatius, and Saba, plus Aruba as an autonomous member of the Kingdom of the Netherlands) define political groups of islands with past and present affiliations to those countries. Great Britain maintains political ties with the West Indies through direct possessions (Turks and Caicos, the British Virgin Islands, Cayman Islands, Anguilla, and Montserrat) and associations within the Commonwealth. Spain, today, maintains mostly cultural ties with several of its former colonial possessions. The territories of Puerto Rico and the U.S. Virgin Islands have direct political and some cultural ties to the United States. All West Indies islands retain varying degrees of autonomy in their associations with current or former colonial powers and partners.

THE LAND

ISLAND ORIGINS

From the air, the Virgin Islands break the surface of the water like the humped green shells of a family of giant sea turtles moving slowly across the ocean. The islands stretch more or less laterally across the northeast corner of the one-million-square-mile Caribbean Sea, forming a border between it and the open Atlantic Ocean. The archipelago comprises about 130 true islands, although the number is closer to 300 when rocks, sand spits, and uninhabited islets are included. The islands sit, at their western end, about 40 miles (64 km) east of Puerto Rico, just east of its offshore islands Culebra and Vieques, and 1,100 miles (1,771 km) southeast of the southern tip of Florida. South of the Virgins are the islands of the Lesser Antilles, which form a sweeping arc from Anguilla in the north to the southern island of Trinidad, located just miles from the coast of Venezuela.

Most of the Virgin Islands are volcanic in origin, part of a massive system that exploded, literally, through the ocean's surface during a series of violent eruptions millions of years ago. In fact, most of the islands of the Caribbean were born of volcanoes. One look at a map of the region will confirm that its islands do not dot the ocean haphazardly but rather form a neat and consistent arc from north to south, sort of like buoys on the outer edges of a fishing net straining against a current. The reason for this pattern, and for the islands' volcanic origins, involves the weird-but-true theory of plate tectonics.

Plate Theory

Tectonic plates are the large, solid land slabs

Mountain Trunk and Long bays

that compose the earth's crust. These plates (there are an estimated 12 to 20 worldwide) are affected by the seething, roiling inner masses and pressures exerted at the earth's core and are therefore in more or less a constant state of flux. That is, they move—as much as several inches per year—and have been doing so since the formation of our planet, some 4.6 billion years ago.

Tectonic plates average 50 miles in thickness, but several have been estimated to be as much as 100 miles thick. Some correspond to the continents and land masses, others to the floors of the great oceans. Plates do not move in a visible way. Rather, their changes are slow and constant, through entire geological periods. And when they move, they move against each other, bumping and grinding like oversize, aging lambada partners obliged to dance for eternity.

This relentless movement causes changes in the earth's surface, particularly along the boundaries of the plates. The **Caribbean Plate** roughly corresponds to the area we know as the Caribbean Sea, with its eastern boundary along the Caribbean's Lesser Antilles chain of islands. Earthquakes and volcanoes are common throughout this boundary area.

Volcanoes at Work

About 70 to 50 million years ago, a series of violent underwater volcanic eruptions thrust mountains from the floor of the sea, many of which broke the surface of the ocean. The peaks of these mountain chains became the islands of the Caribbean.

In geological terms, the easternmost Caribbean islands are slightly older, having been thrust out of the ocean as part of a series of eruptions that also created the Virgin Islands, the Greater Antilles, and the Andes mountain range of South America. Gradually, these eruptions subsided, and over the course of several million years marine and other life forms developed and lived and died, leaving layers of limestone and sediment on the islands. By the time a second series of eruptions formed an inner arc—the Lesser Antilles—another several million years later, the first islands had become flattened, dead volcanoes. Today, in the inner-arc group of younger islands, active or semi-active volcanoes are still in evidence.

Some Caribbean volcanoes have been recently, and spectacularly, active—the massive 1902 eruption of Mont Pelée in Martinique destroyed the then-capital of Saint-Pierre, killing nearly 30,000 people. The 1977 eruption in of Soufriere (from the French *soufre,* sulfur) in St. Vincent forced the evacuation of a segment of the island. In Montserrat, the volcanic crater of the southern Galways Soufriere has been rumbling and spewing smoke since the summer of 1995. The danger there is imminent—so much so that the island's southern population has been periodically evacuated to the north.

By far, the majority of the region's islands, including the Virgin Islands, belongs to the volcanic group. These islands are characterized by jagged and breathtaking hills, deep valleys, and the remains of current or past volcanic activity, sometimes including volcanic vents, black-sand beaches, and steaming, primordial sulfur springs.

In the U.S. Virgin Islands, St. Thomas and St. John are characteristic volcanic islands, with sharp hills, low valleys, and numerous indents and bays lining their craggy coastlines. St. Croix, located about 40 miles (64 km) south of the main chain and separated from it by a deep ocean trench, is less rugged, with rolling hills and sloping plains and a relatively gentle coast. There is some dispute as to St. Croix's geological inclusion in the archipelago. It's not really part of the Virgin Islands chain, which sits on an elevated submarine shelf called the **Virgin Bank** (which in turn supports the Greater Antilles islands as well as the Virgins). Some geologists contend that the island is not volcanic in origin, although many of its rocks are. Whichever the case, given its history and associations, St. Croix is naturally included as a U.S. Virgin Island.

Tortola, in the British Virgin Islands and also volcanic in origin, is perhaps the most rugged of all the Virgins. Its dips and valleys are vertigo-inspiring and include the chain's highest mountain peak, **Mt. Sage,** at 1,780 feet (541 meters). Even on a bad day, most of the Virgin Islands are visible from Mt. Sage.

A wide range of habitats, generally regulated by amount of rainfall, exist throughout the Virgin Islands: tropical rainforests or semi-rainforests, scrubby savanna-like plains, and, to some degree, mangrove swamps. The exception is Anegada, of the British Virgin Islands; low lying (near the outer edge of the Virgin Bank) and composed of coral limestone, it hosts, for the most part, salt ponds, marshes, sand dunes, and tenacious coastal plantlife such as the sea grape, as well as a magnificent, expansive coral reef.

The Virgin Islands' soil tends to be leached and relatively devoid of nutrients for two reasons: the constant winds and rainfall produce high rates of erosion, particularly in the mountainous regions where runoff is pronounced; and massive man-made deforestation of the last two centuries has accelerated the pace of erosion. Of the Virgins Islands, only St. John—much of it untouched since the 1950s, when the Virgin Islands National Park was created—has soil of

much depth. On the others, topsoil is generally thin and rocky and, consequently, relatively few cash crops are grown in the islands today.

CLIMATE

The Virgin Islands' climate is subtropical. In practical terms for those of us who were occupied during geography class thinking about how we could ask Donna Leibowitz out on a date, this means that it's pretty pleasant most of the time—and certainly a lot nicer than winter in Duluth. Technically, it means that the temperature remains fairly constant, in the 70s and 80s F (20s and 30s C)—with a year-round average of about 78° F (26° C)—tempered by trade winds from the northeast. The tradewinds also help to keep the humidity down to a comfortable level.

The Virgin Islands' seasonal temperature changes, between winter and summer, are limited to less than 10° F (6° C). Additionally, the powerful Caribbean Current, which originates at the juncture of the North Equatorial Current and the Guiana (or South Equatorial) Current and enters the Caribbean Sea at its southeast extremity (and flows northwest), helps to keep the islands surrounded by warm water. The widest variations in island temperature occur with elevation—there's about 1° F (.6° C) of cooling for every 300 feet (98 meters) of ascent. On a windy or rainy day, it can be fairly cool sweater weather in the hills. As well, day-to-night (diurnal) temperatures can drop an average of 10° F (6° C).

Rainfall often occurs in short spurts. Late spring (May and June) and late summer (September and October) are the rainy months, producing an average 50 inches (1,270 mm) per annum.

Of course, to every aspect of paradise there tends to be a dark side—it's the nature of our world. In the case of the Virgin Islands' weather, that dark side comes by way of hurricanes.

HURRICANES

In the Caribbean, the word "hurricane" can bring a tremor to the most stalwart of residents. A hurricane is a wild, high-pressure storm of intense wind that revolves around a low-pressure center (the placid vortex or "eye" of the storm). The shifting eye varies in diameter but can reach 100 miles (160 km) and generally moves in a westward direction. As high-pressure winds revolve around and move toward the low-pressure vortex, they're whipped into a frenzy by centrifugal force and can reach speeds of 120 miles (193 km) per hour or more (severe hurricane winds exceeding 200 mph—321 kph—have been recorded. Thunder, lightning, torrential rain, and turbulent seas usually accompany a hurricane.

Hurricanes tend to travel from the east, often as small storms originating near the west coast of Africa. They move relatively slowly, about 10 miles (16 km) per hour, and gather momentum and destructive force as they make their way across the open ocean. An estimated eight hurricanes per year pass through the Caribbean area, but most do not touch land. Those that do—such as 1988's Hurricane Gilbert, 1989's Hurricane Hugo, and 1995's hurricanes Luis and Marilyn—can cause massive destruction and loss of life.

Hurricanes Luis And Marilyn

Hurricane Luis, with sustained winds of 130 mph (208 kph) and gusts of 160 mph (256 kph), swept from south to north along the outer Eastern Caribbean islands on 5 September 1995. Less than two weeks later, on 15 September, the 110-mph (176 kph) Hurricane Marilyn delivered the second half of the one-two punch.

The two storms bounced from island to island like manic pinballs, and, when all was said and done, caused $3.5 billion in damage in the Caribbean and along the U.S. coast. The human toll was substantial: six died on St. Thomas, the hardest hit of the Caribbean islands. On Antigua, two died, and on St. Martin/Maarten, five deaths were attributed to Luis.

In the British Virgin Islands, Hurricane Marilyn caused major damage to beaches and to the Sir Francis Drake Highway, which runs from the capital of Road Town to the smaller town of West End on Tortola. Several of the British Virgin Islands' major resorts, including the heavily damaged Little Dix Bay and Biras Creek resorts on Virgin Gorda, remained closed until early March of 1996.

The U.S. Virgin Islands fared worse. On St. Thomas, homes, roads, beaches, hotels, and restaurants were destroyed; medical services were disrupted; and the official human toll—six deaths—cast a pall on the island. The U.S. Federal Emergency Management Agency (FEMA), in conjunction with the Army Corps of Engineers, stepped in immediately following the 15 September hurricane. Relief and rebuilding efforts went well, but all services, including phones and electricity, were not completely restored for as long as eight months following the storm.

Many of St. Thomas's homes were gutted and covered with blue tarps issued by FEMA (the blue became a symbol of the hurricane's destructive force) and one of the island's biggest attractions, the huge **Coral World,** a marine park at Coki Beach, remains closed indefinitely.

On nearby St. John, Marilyn's damage to the Hyatt Regency and Caneel Bay resorts was heavy, and the two remained closed for up to nine months following the hurricane. On St. Croix, little damage was reported. In fact, several cruise lines, which had booked St. Croix as an 1996-season alternative to hurricane-damaged St. Thomas, soon "discovered" the island; major lines such as Carnival, Royal Caribbean, and Norwegian announced that St. Croix will remain on their schedules for the near future.

The hurricane season lasts from roughly July through October, though June and November have been visited in the past. A simple island ditty serves as a way to remember: "June, too soon; July, stand by; August, prepare you must; September, remember; October, all over."

A service offered by the National Hurricane Center of the National Oceanic and Atmospheric Administration's (NOAA) National Weather Service will update you on hurricanes whether they're brewing at sea or on top of the area you'd like to visit. The number is in Miami, tel. (809) 494-3286.

FLORA

Terra Firma Flora

Throughout the Virgin Islands, you'll see plantlife evidencing that the islands lie in a sub-arid climatic zone. The islands are neither big enough nor tall enough, even at their highest peaks, to attract enough rainfall to support true tropical rainforests. The result is high-elevation, semi-rainforest areas featuring mahogany, palmetto, lignum vitae (the "tree of life"), and other hardy trees. The trees are often shorter than those found in a true rainforest and harbor a thick undergrowth of mastic, pigeon plum, ferns, and sea grape. At lower elevations, such as the mountain slopes and the rolling, windswept plains of St. Croix, the vegetation becomes even hardier and includes thorny vines, various cacti including turk's cap and pipe organ (also called "dildo"), yucca (also called "Spanish bayonet" for its long, spiky leaves), acacia, turpentine trees, aloe, century plant, rams horn bush, Jerusalem thorn, and guinea grass. The distinctive turpentine tree has been, with some irony, dubbed the "tourist tree" for its bark, which is red and peels from the tree. The century plant, also called agave plant, resembles the medicinal aloe plant—so much so that Columbus mistakenly had 1,000 pounds of it shipped to Spain as a present for Queen Isabella. The century plant will, after a dozen years of growth, sprout a long stem from its center that is covered in sweet, yellow blossoms, a favorite of hummingbirds and bees.

Much of the lower-elevation vegetation is secondary growth, having filled in spaces cleared for sugar and cotton plantations, which ceased to function during the late 19th century due to the lack of a labor pool and the shifting world sugar market.

At sea level, most of the islands feature some swampland abutting beach areas. On St. Croix, St. John, and Anegada, you'll find several large and pungent salt ponds that host their own array of plantlife. Also along coastal areas, one is most likely to find sparse woodlands, coconut and sabal palms, frangipani trees, almonds trees, manchineel trees, sea grape, and marshes and mangrove swamps.

Mangroves are the trees that give the "jungle" look to movies and travel videos shot in the tropics. Several species of mangrove have the ability to drop vertical roots from the branches of the main tree into the mucky swamp, giving it the appearance of a jail cell. As the roots develop, young branches break off from the parent tree to form their own extended growth. Some species of mangrove possess the ability to extract fresh water from salt water, which also allows them to proliferate near the sea. While mangrove swamps support a great amount of life within their own peculiar ecosystems, unchecked mangrove growth can choke the free flow of tidal streams.

A note about the manchineel tree: This tree, also called the poison apple tree, is often found along shorelines, close to the beach. The tree's fruit and milky sap, and even droppings from its leaves, are poisonous and can cause serious burns to the skin. Never eat the tree's fruit, which resembles a small, yellow apple. It's best not to touch any part of the tree, and definitely do not take cover under it during a rain shower—the runoff can cause burns. Most of the islands have taken pains to label these trees wherever possible.

Due to the poor soil and relative aridity of the islands, there are few underground water sources and few freshwater rivers and streams. The Virgins experience a perennial shortage of fresh water, and many of the larger tourist resorts maintain their own desalinization plants to convert sea water to potable water. Visitors can help by limiting their use of fresh water.

The flora of the B.V.I.'s Anegada presents a striking contrast to the rest of the Virgins archipelago. Anegada, a lime and coral atoll far northeast in the chain, has really no elevation at all—its highest point is some 30 feet (nine meters) above sea level. The tiny island is nearly entirely surrounded by extensive coral reefs, and in its center lie several massive fetid salt ponds and flats. The vegetation on the island is universally scrubby, consisting of salt-resistant heath, white cedar, lantana, and sea grape.

Introduced Species

Much of the region's flora has been introduced over the years by various settlers and conquerors. The first direct imports were maize, cassava, sweet potato, cocoa, and tobacco, introduced by the Virgins' original inhabitants, the Arawaks. In some cases, the words for those crops, such as "tobacco" and "cassava," were also Arawak imports.

After the arrival of Columbus, the Spanish brought with them several crops that would become the basis for many West Indian island economies, primarily bananas, cotton, and pineapples. The most significant Spanish introduction

SUGARCANE

Sugarcane is a common name for several species of grass, actually perennial herbs of the genus *Saccharum*. Sugarcane, a long- and thick-stemmed plant, is well suited for cultivation in tropical and subtropical countries and has been an economic bedrock for dozens of emerging nations, particularly the islands of the Caribbean.

Cane was first brought to the West Indies by the Spanish, who grew it with great success in Brazil and, for some time, Cuba.

In the early 17th century, when the Virgin Is-

animal-powered sugar mill

lands were emerging as economic entities, sugarcane farming was a slow and labor-intensive endeavor. Plows and animals were not used; instead, slaves provided the backbone of the labor force and were so inexorably linked to the crop's production that their emancipation throughout the islands during the 19th century ended sugarcane's domination and the plantation society of the day.

Due to the advantageous climate of the islands, sugarcane could be planted year round, but it was best planted during the wet season—June to November. New cane was started from cuttings of old cane and took about 16 months to ripen. The cane was harvested during the drier season, January through May, and immediately sent for milling and processing. Because cane would spoil unless processed within hours of being cut, planters had to stagger the harvesting (and, therefore, planting) over several months. A large plantation with a sizable labor force could expect a yield of about one ton of semi-processed sugar per year per acre of sugarcane.

Milling and processing were done on the plantation, and today on the islands—notably the U.S. Virgins, you'll see ruins of mills. Molasses and rum were also produced on the plantation, and therefore the plantation owner needed mills, boiling houses, distilleries, and storage houses, as well as slave quarters, cooking houses, stables, and his own greathouse. Slaves, in addition to their initial cost, were themselves an ongoing expenditure, needing to be clothed and fed. Yet even given the large initial capital outlays, and even given the whimsies of nature such as hurricanes, droughts, and rodent infestations, or the human obstacles of market fluctuations, wars, and, of course, slave rebellions, a planter's profit margin was healthy.

was sugarcane. Originally from the Far East, the cane produced sugar, molasses and its byproducts, and rum. Sugarcane became so profitable in the Virgin Islands, and in the West Indies in general, that it is almost singlehandedly responsible for the cultural, political, and economic structures that exist today throughout the region.

The Spanish were also responsible for the introduction of ginger, turmeric, tamarind, oranges, limes, and lemons. Indian laborers brought marijuana, or "ganja," and the British

and others contributed flowering plants, garden vegetables, and the ubiquitous breadfruit tree, brought originally to feed slaves in Jamaica and St. Vincent by Captain William Bligh in 1793. (Bligh's first excursion to India and the South Pacific to retrieve the plant, where it is indigenous, was famously unsuccessful. It was during the 1789 voyage that his crew mutinied under the leadership of master's mate Fletcher Christian, reportedly in part because they were denied the very water that was used to nourish the breadfruit seedlings. The crew captured Bligh's ship, the HMS *Bounty,* and cast Bligh and 18 others adrift in a longboat. Bligh survived and went on to transport breadfruit successfully to the West Indies.)

Common trees include the famous poinciana, named after an 18th-century governor of the French Antilles. Its flower is bright red—hence its other popular name, the flamboyant. Also found are the tropical almond tree, *soursop* and *sweet-sop* trees (the pulpy, edible fruits are not sour and sweet but rather sweet and sweeter), and the occasional huge banyan tree. Banyans are easily recognized by their roots, which drop from horizontal branches to take root at the base of the tree, giving them the appearance of dread-locked evergreens. The mahogany tree is a native of the West Indies and produces a dark, hard wood. Not so common is the large cotton (or "silk cotton") tree, which is called "kapok" in the U.S. Virgin Islands. The silk cotton, distinctive for its thick, gray roots that lie above ground like the gnarled and extended fingers of a sleeping giant, can grow to more than 60 feet (18 meters). The papaya tree, sometimes called pawpaw, yields a soft fruit rich in vitamin C.

Mango trees produce their sweet fruit, a favorite in the Caribbean and found in all local markets, from March to October. Date palms, sabal palms, queen palms, royal palms, and coconut palms are found throughout the region. The coconut palm, believed to have originated in the South Pacific, is perhaps the most useful of all. The coconut itself produces food, drink, and oil for cosmetics, and the fronds have long been used to weave mats, hats, and even walls for huts.

Flowering Plants

Thousands of flowering plants and herbs prosper throughout the Virgin Islands. They're called by different local names, many of them downright utilitarian—"jump-up-and-kiss-me" (because of its ruby red flowers), "mother-in-law's-tongue" (sharp leaves and seed pods that rattle), "only-at-night" (it blooms, well, only at night), "painkiller" (the leaves are used to treat arthritis), and the "sensitive plant" (a fern that closes its leaves at your touch). Flowering plants include several hundred species of orchids as well as angel's-trumpet, monkey tail, bird of paradise, hyacinth, and

lobster claw. The ginger Thomas, or yellow elder, is indigenous and is the official flower of the U.S. Virgin Islands (and the Bahamas). The white cedar, the national flower of the British Virgin Islands, produces elegant pink flowers. The tree is not a true cedar but rather a bignonia. Bougainvillea, the ostentatious flowering vine of the tropics, grows everywhere. Its delicate white, rich purple, or orange flowers snake along trees, fences, and other bushes. Added to the striking island scenery are plants familiar to those who travel in the tropics—the multicolored hibiscus, the delicate frangipani, orchids, jasmine, alla-manda, and oleander bushes.

Botanic Gardens

In all, far more species of Virgin Islands native and introduced plants exist than can be enumerated here. St. John alone, perhaps the most fertile of the Virgins, hosts more than 800 species of plants. For a concise treatment of the islands' flora, visit a botanic garden. In the U.S. and British Virgin Islands, you'll find several excellent gardens and walking trails with labeled trees and plants. These are frequently located on resort grounds such as Biras Creek on Virgin Gorda, the Wyndham Sugar Bay on St. Thomas, and Prospect Reef on Tortola. In the British Virgin Islands, Tortola's Road Town is home to the **J.R. O'Neal Botanic Gardens,** which features native and imported plants and an herb garden. At the nearby **Peter Island** resort, you'll find extensive labeled walking trails.

In the U.S. Virgin Islands, St. Croix's **St. George Village Botanical Garden** also features a plantation greathouse, sugar mill ruins, and a blacksmith shop. On St. Thomas, near the capital Charlotte Amalie (A-MAHL-yah), you'll find the small **Estate St. Peter Botanical Gardens,** and on St. John, the many walking trails throughout the national park feature plaques with descriptions of local flora. See the specific island chapters for details.

FAUNA

Birds

The Virgin Islands are home to a large number of bird species, some native to the Caribbean and some visitors from other regions during seasonal changes. In forests, on flatlands, and along the shorelines of the islands, you'll see the big and the small, the luminous and the dull. One difficulty in identifying birds lies with the local custom of using colloquial names for them that differ among islands—but local guidebooks are available that will help identify the more popular species.

Multishaded and shimmering hummingbirds are frequently seen flitting over banana blossoms, century plants, and other nectar-producing flowers. The tiny bananaquit, yellow-breasted with dark plumage, is also called the sugar bird or the yellow bird and is the official bird of the U.S. Virgin Islands. This tiny guy, with wings twitching faster than a Supreme Court nominee at a senate hearing, may be your uninvited guest, feeding at the sugar bowl of your cafe table. The green-throated carib, a hummingbird somewhat larger than others in the species, is also known as the doctor bird. Other indigenous species include the smooth-billed ani (a type of cuckoo, also called the black witch for its color), several types of parakeets, and mockingbirds.

The seagoing brown booby is recognized by its white underbelly and lives the better part of the year at sea, returning to land or small outlying cays to lay eggs. The frigate bird, also called the magnificent frigatebird and the man-o-war, is also seagoing and is recognized by its distinctive forked tail. The frigate has been cruelly slighted by Mother Nature; it lacks the oily film that covers other seabirds' wings and allows them to shed water and resurface after diving. In other words, the frigate will drown if it plunges into the ocean—clearly, this bird never studied Darwin's theories of evolution. Nevertheless, the frigate manages to keep itself fed by skimming the water's surface for fish, or by simply stealing from other birds. The frigate has been slighted in other ways. Its feet are too small to allow it to walk, but its wingspan, as long as eight feet (more than two meters), allows it to remain in flight, soaring and swooping, for great lengths of time. Some believe that frigates are able to sleep while floating on air currents.

The brown pelican, once endangered but on the rebound since the 1960s, can be seen diving—dropping like a stone into shore and harbor waters—fishing for small morsels. The white-tailed tropic bird is distinguished by its long, pencil-like tail, which acts as a rudder for the bird's dramatic swoops and dives.

Other Virgin Islands' birds include several species of egret—snowy, great, and cattle, which are endangered. Herons, a related species, include the great blue, the little blue, and the green and are found in swampy areas throughout the islands.

The ground dove and the mountain dove are also plentiful, particularly in the British Virgin Islands. The mountain dove, called the zenaida from its scientific name, is so prolific that some theorize Columbus named the main island of the chain after the Spanish name for dove or pigeon, *tortola.*

As well, the islands are stopover points for migratory birds, the proverbial North American birds that go south for the winter. These include thrushes, warblers, orioles, blue-winged teals, moorhens, starlings, house sparrows, shearwaters, kingfishers, sandpipers, and the peregrine falcon. Other migratory birds are ocean residents; these include laughing gulls, plovers, and roseate terns. The American kestral, locally called the killy-killy, is a smallish hawk-like bird with a red tail.

For a more thorough treatment of the Caribbean region's thousands of bird species, refer to the seminal *Birds of the West Indies* (Collins), by ornithologist James Bond (whose name was later borrowed by writer Ian Fleming for his Agent 007), or *Birds of the Eastern Caribbean* (Macmillan), by Peter Evans.

Mammals

You won't see much in the way of mammals in either the U.S. or British Virgin Islands. Bats are perhaps the most widespread. Numerous species, including the fisherman's bat and the red fruit bat, inhabit the islands' caves and the cool shade of mangrove swamps, feeding on fruit, fish, and insects.

Occasionally you'll see a mongoose. This ferret-like animal, introduced by sugarcane farmers in the 18th century to help control the destructive cane rat, became notorious soon after its arrival. The prolific rodent turned to feasting on chickens, fish, crabs, insects, turtle eggs, and other harmless island creatures and is still the bane of small farmers and conservationists. However, those who are bothered by snakes may have found a friend; the voracious mongoose considers snakes a delicacy and has all but eliminated them throughout the Virgins.

Amphibians, Reptiles, and Crustaceans

The iguana (some theorize that the word may have found Arawak origins) is a large, seemingly prehistoric lizard indigenous to the Caribbean. You've probably seen iguanas playing the part of dinosaur-like creatures doing battle with Hercules or the Three Stooges in 1950s sci-fi flicks, but don't hold that against them. They were made for the part. With deadish gray, leathery skin and a row of spikes lining their backs from head to tail, the lizards, which can attain lengths of six feet (nearly two meters), do look a bit scary. But they are harmless and feed on vegetation and fruit.

Iguanas, with the oddly redundant scientific name *Iguana iguana,* were once considered a delicacy by some Caribbean peoples and have been hunted for their flesh and eggs for centuries. Over the years, they have also fallen victim to the miscreant mongoose, and their numbers have been greatly reduced, although they can be seen throughout the Virgins.

Other lizards are much more abundant. One of the most common is the small gecko. Geckos tend to live around houses and feed on insects. You'll recognize them by their bobbing heads as they run down window screens or across walls, heading for electric lights and the moths or other insects that flit around them. If you find geckos in your room, remember that they are harmless and try not to hurt them. In fact, they're helpful—they eat mosquitoes.

Also in the lizard clan are tree lizards, members of the anolid family, which include the barred tree lizard and the crested tree lizard. The male of these species, like the male iguana, possesses a dewlap, or throat fan. The dewlap, when inflated with air to the size of a small golf ball, is used to attract females.

There are few snakes in the Virgin Islands, but among them are the indigenous and endangered Virgin Islands tree boa, which is not dangerous to humans.

Several species of sea turtle, both resident and migratory species, are common. Some can grow to lengths of five feet (1.5 meters) or more and weigh as much as 1,500 pounds (nearly

700 kilograms). Turtles are found throughout the islands, and females use isolated beaches to lay as many as 125 eggs during the March to August breeding period. Though sea turtles are protected by law in both the U.S. and British Virgin Islands, it is here, on the beaches, where they are most vulnerable to hunters and poachers. The most common sea turtle is the green turtle, which is actually brown. Other species include the leatherback and the hawksbill, both of which are endangered.

The soldier crab will catch your attention as it ambles slowly and, it seems, with difficulty through the maze of sticks and vines in the forest. These land-based crabs live in the shells of abandoned sea creatures such as whelks and can get quite large—as big as a baseball. They return to the shore by the hundreds each August to deposit their eggs along the beach.

Insects

The Virgins are home to a lively and often voracious array of insects—for many of them, you are destined to be their mealticket. Mosquitoes, of course, and some blackflies and sand fleas, make sleeping nets and repellent necessities when hiking or spending time outdoors.

Coral

One of the great attractions of the U.S. and British Virgin Islands is the accessible submarine life; the clear, unpolluted waters and numerous coral reefs make both diving and snorkeling a joy.

Ocean life originates in and around coral reefs with the smaller, microscopic inhabitants that rank low on the food chain. Coral reefs are actually colonies of living creatures called polyps that exist with the corallite—skeletal remains—of past polyps, creating a life and death cycle that uses past skeletal remains as building blocks. Coral, then, has the appearance of growth, but slow growth—the most prolific corals grow only two or so inches (about five centimeters) per year. When snorkeling or diving a reef, the brilliant colors seen on coral are provided by zooxanthellae, tiny single-cell algae that live within the coral structure itself. The polyps also provide color, but their skeletons are usually white. (The topsoil of some coral atolls is formed, in part, from broken corallite remains.) The organism itself is generally hollow and tubular, with an anterior mouth surrounded by tentacles for gathering plankton and other tiny food particles. Polyps range in size from microscopic to inches across. The coral polyp life-form has been in existence for more than 100 million years.

Ever wonder where the powdery white sand characteristic of some Caribbean beaches comes from? Let's face it, there's a ton of it, and it's constantly washed away, but it's somehow replenished. The answer lies within the the coral reef ecosystem. Various reef fish feed on the colorful algae that lives on coral, and in the process swallow some of the corallite, or skeletons of dead coral. This matter is undigested and passed through their fishy digestive systems, where it is later washed ashore.

Always popular with snorkelers and divers, a coral reef is one of nature's most sublime and remarkable structures. Life within the reef is abundant, if not always evident. A reef accommodates algae, some forms of sea sponge, and sea fans. Small and exotic fish, shrimp, eels, anemone, and the spiny lobster make their homes in and among coral limbs, taking advantage of the rich fare that passes their way. Predatory animals such as crabs, eels, and some sharks use the reef for shelter and for stalking prey.

Coral grows in warm, clear saltwater, generally no deeper than 100 feet (30 meters) below the surface, and the entire reef can grow upward at rates of as much as 40 inches (100 cm) per year. In the case of a fringing or common reef, it often grows in shallow water, closer to shore, aided by the sun. Much of the reef in the Virgins is often directly offshore or within sight of shore.

Coral reefs in the Virgins are generally of three types: common reef, barrier reef, and atoll. A common reef, also called a fringing reef, is actually part of the shore and the main body of the island; it extends outward, like a shelf, from the mainland. A barrier reef rises from the ocean floor farther offshore and is separated from the mainland by open ocean or channels. Coral atolls (such as Anegada in the British Virgin Islands) are in fact entire islands composed of coral remains.

In places, coral brushes the water's surface at low tide. As such, coral is easily threatened by changes in ocean current and weather (particularly hurricanes) and careless divers. Today, the biggest threat to coral reefs is fishermen and divers, both locals and tourists.

Coral life found in local waters includes staghorn and elkhorn corals, so named for their resemblance to the horns of those animals.

Cathedral (also called majestic) coral generally thrives in isolated colonies, away from the main reef. Finger coral, small finger coral, and club finger coral are all common, as is brain coral—named for its resemblance to the outer membrane of the human organ. Great start coral resembles brain coral but has smaller ridges across its surface.

Sea fans, black sea rod, and bent sea rod are notable in that they look like smallish undersea trees or leaves. Lettuce coral, with its bright green color, resembles the vegetable for which it was named.

Soft coral—those with flexible skeletal remains—are mesmerizing as they wave back and forth with the ocean's undulations. Gorgonian coral, named for the snake-hair sisters in Greek mythology, includes sea whips and sea feathers. Commonly found in shades of green, purple, and orange, gorgonian coral is among the prettiest. Sea sponges, including the tube sponge and the purple vase sponge, also make their homes in coral colonies.

Black coral is also common, and striking in its natural state. This coral is a favorite of jewelers and carvers but is a threatened species.

Fish and Other Ocean Dwellers

The fish along the reefs of the Virgin Islands are plentiful and every bit as colorful as their host coral and sponge colonies. About 700 or so species are associated with the coral reef, and while you may not see every one, it'll seem as if you have.

Many types of groupers, snappers, and the red squirrel fish (all good eating) feed on the reef. Flounder, including the common peacock flounder, are plentiful. The multicolored parrot fishes (which feature teeth structures not unlike the beak of a parrot), tiny butterfly fish, hamlets, grunts, doctorfish, porgys, trumpetfish, squirrelfish, and wrasses fill in the spectrum. A number of different types of angelfish, with their wispy fins, are among the most recognizable of reef fish. Some reef fish are unperturbed around divers and will even nibble goodies from their hands. An assortment of nocturnal fish, including the cardinal fish, is visible during night dives.

Game fish and larger fish found in deeper waters include the blue marlin, a favorite of deep-sea fishers for its fighting prowess and its value as a food source. The U.S. and British Virgin Islands offer some of the best deep-sea fishing in the Caribbean region, and you'll find dozens of well-organized fishing charter companies.

Other large fish, many protected by fishing regulations, include the white marlin, wahoo, tuna, barracuda, grouper, tarpon, bonefish, snook, and the blunt-nosed dolphin fish (not the mammal). Bonito and kingfish also run in the deep waters.

Eels and rays also are common among local ocean fauna. The most common eel is the spotted moray, a creature that seems to be all mouth and teeth. They're generally harmless and tend to feed at night. Still, it's best to stay an arm's length away. Morays should not be eaten—they're known to carry toxins that cause food poisoning. The snake eel does resemble a snake and may be handled, but gently. Giant manta rays, in places called devilfish, have been known to allow divers to hitch rides. Mantas are ocean fish and mesmerizing to watch; their pectoral fins propel them with elegant, wavy swells in a fishy version of a slow-motion ballet.

Sharks are not always common in Virgins waters but are seen on occasion. Nurse sharks, up to 14 feet (four meters) long, often lie motionless on the ocean floor. They are not aggressive but they are, after all, sharks and, if agitated or cornered, they will strike. Other sharks found in and around reefs are bull sharks, lemon sharks, blacktips, and sand tigers.

Other reef dwellers include starfish, spiny urchins, sea worms, snails, and shellfish. The conch (rhymes with "honk") is prized for its meat and shell, which can be found for sale at roadside stands throughout the islands.

pelican

BOB RACE

REGIONAL HISTORY

PRE-COLUMBIAN HISTORY

The history of the Virgin Islands mirrors that of the entire Caribbean region. It is a tale of slavers and slaves, of power and impotence, of wealth, poverty, and, ultimately, Europeans and Africans.

For centuries, sugar and slavery fueled each other and the economies of these small islands. The human mix formed the basis for the cultures, art, music, cuisines, and social stratification you'll find throughout the present-day West Indies. Yet before the islands had sugar in common, and before Spain's Ferdinand and Isabella sent Columbus on his way to fame, the islands had known inhabitants for roughly 4,000 years.

The first were Stone Age hunters and gatherers, of whom we know little. We do know, of course, that they hunted and gathered, using tools made of flint and stone. Beyond that, they left no apparent artifacts. We know them today as the Ciboney (sometimes spelled "Siboney"), and that name is reflected in hotel and place names throughout the West Indies.

Arawaks

The Ciboney were followed by the Arawaks, a bold group of seafarers who crossed the Caribbean Sea in two waves—the first estimated sometime between the death of Christ and A.D. 500, the second 350-400 years later—from the Amazon River Valley and Orinoco regions of today's northern Brazil and Venezuela. The Arawaks settled the islands in groups from Trinidad to the Virgin Islands to Cuba, where Christopher Columbus would first encounter them in his late-15th-century voyages. A smaller Arawak subgroup, the Taino, settled areas of the Virgin Islands, Puerto Rico, Haiti, and eastern Cuba.

The Arawaks appear to have been relatively peaceful. They were a fishing and farming culture, fond of ceremony and organized games, and had little history of attacking others.

They settled in large villages of up to 1,000 huts and 3,000 people, generally by the sea or near rivers, yet skilled Arawak artists left paintings on cave walls that indicate they also lived in the central and upland areas of certain islands. On St. John, for instance, hikers can find Arawak rock carvings, or petroglyphs, near the center of the island off the national park's **Reef Bay Trail.**

The Arawaks shaped and milled canoes (the name of which, incidentally, is originally an Arawak word that made its way to English via Spanish). The Arawaks were expert sailors, and their canoes seemed to vary in size and purpose. Some fishing canoes held only one person; traveling vessels held up to 60.

The Arawaks were a diminutive people (averaging five feet, or 1.5 meters, in height), with dark, Asiatic features. They grew cotton with great success, and from that crop we have adopted the Arawak invention (and word) hammock. The Arawaks also crafted jewelry and implements from stone and shell.

The Arawaks grew tobacco (the word derived from the name of their pipe) and used it both socially and ritually. They grew fruit and vegetables, including maize and cassava—called *yucca*—the starchy staple of the tropics. Guava, a fruit that has also taken its name from the Arawak language, was widely utilized. The West Indies' first inhabitants also introduced the words "barbecue," "hurricane," and "manatee" into various languages.

The Arawaks buried their dead in caves, sometimes placing the head and other body parts in large pottery bowls. These bowls and preserved skulls are on display today in several museums in the Virgin Islands.

Caribs

The Arawaks existed unperturbed for centuries—until the arrival of the bellicose Caribs, another seagoing indigenous group who were from the Orinoco region of South America.

. carved stone Arawak figure

BOB RACE

The Caribs were possibly distant relatives of Arawak groups who, over the years, made their way north from South America through the West Indies. Carib raiding parties—estimated at as many as 100 boats to a party—left destruction and conquered islands in the wakes of their war canoes. According to evidence, the Caribs captured and destroyed entire villages and, although it's disputed by some scholars, reportedly their adversaries. In fact, the word "cannibal" is derived from *Caribal,* or perhaps *Caníbales,* the Spanish word for the Caribs.

By the mid-15th century, the Caribs had reached as far north as the Virgin Islands and parts of the Greater Antilles. Their combative nature, in conjunction with the devastation of early Spanish settlement, succeeded in reducing the indigenous Arawak population of the Caribbean from two or three million to a few thousand by the early 16th century. Such was the extent of the Caribs' influence that the waters around them (again via Spanish) acquired their name—the Caribbean Sea.

EARLY EUROPEAN EXPLORATION

Christopher Columbus

Meanwhile, in another part of the world, events began to take place that would change the destinies of the tiny islands of the West Indies.

In his relentless, largely ego-driven quest for riches and a route to the New World, the Italian explorer Christopher Columbus (Cristoforo Colombo in his native language) sailed into both fame and a bit of infamy on his four voyages to the Americas (1492-3, 1493-6, 1498-1500, 1502-4).

The premise of his daring plan, a plan that inspired the Spanish sovereigns Ferdinand and Isabella to provide sponsorship, was that the ever-growing European demand for Asian luxuries necessitated a simpler and more efficient

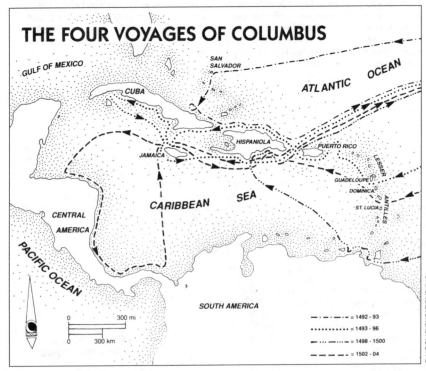

THE FOUR VOYAGES OF COLUMBUS

route to obtain them. Traveling the overland routes of the time was dangerous, time-consuming, and costly. It was part of Columbus's grand scheme, the "Enterprise of the Indies," to find an ocean route west from Spain to Asia and to secure any discovered land for Spain's empire. He did not know, of course, that the Americas lay uncharted between Europe and Asia. It took years and no small effort for Columbus to convince his patrons that he could find this shorter route and thus enrich the Spanish empire and its sovereigns. When he eventually succeeded in convincing the Spaniards to supply his venture, Columbus set sail with the added incentive that, with his success, he was ensured political and property rights for himself and his descendants, as well as 10% of all goods and gold traded or discovered during the voyage.

Columbus, with the title Admiral of the Ocean Sea, Viceroy and Governor and his crew of 90, sailed from Palos, Spain, on 3 August 1492 with a fleet of three caravels, the *Niña,* the *Pinta,* and his flagship *Santa Maria.* Columbus was optimistic that the New World was less than 2,800 miles (4,480 km) to the west. Of course, due to a gross misestimation of the earth's size and an overestimation of Asia's easternmost point, his calculations fell drastically short. The actual (airline) distance between Spain and easternmost Asia is about 10,000 miles (16,000 km).

On 12 October 1492, Columbus and his crew sighted land. It was an island the native inhabitants called *Guanahani.* Renamed San Salvador (Holy Savior) by Columbus, it was most likely today's Watling Island of the Bahamas. Later in this first voyage, Columbus went on to explore Cuba and Espaniola, (Little Spain), today's Hispaniola.

Of the native Arawaks Columbus encountered, he wrote, "They love their neighbors as themselves and their speech is the sweetest and gentlest in the world; and they always speak with a smile." Apparently, this love of neighbors was not adopted by Columbus; he kidnapped six of these sweet and smiling people to serve as guides and to tout as proof of his visit to the New World. His ultimate plan was to enslave the remainder of the Arawaks—and, later, the Caribs—for Spain and convert them to Catholicism. The enslavement of the Arawaks in Hispaniola began almost immediately as Colum-

bus established a garrison there to protect Spain's interests on the island. The Arawaks resisted by fighting and, in instances, committing mass suicide rather than submitting. So began the history of European domination by force in the West Indies.

The Caribs, or at least their reputation, also made an early impression on Columbus. In his journals the explorer wrote, "As for monsters I have found no trace of them except at one point on the second island on the way to the Indies; it is inhabited by a people considered throughout the island to be most ferocious."

It is a small part of Columbus's legacy that when he landed he erroneously believed he was in the Indies, near the coasts of Japan and China. It would be his lifelong belief that he'd discovered islands off the coast of Asia, gateway to the lands traveled by Marco Polo more than two centuries earlier. His lifelong quest was to make contact with the emperor of China, the Great Khan. He would, of course, never succeed. Nevertheless, the islands he discovered came to be known as the West Indies and the people who inhabited them Indians. The momentum of history carries those names today.

Columbus and St. Croix

In his next voyage (1493-96), Columbus bore the title Viceroy of the Indies and commanded an impressive fleet of 17 vessels. Columbus came upon Dominica, located about midway down the Lesser Antilles chain. He made his way north, coming upon Guadeloupe, Antigua, and others, but was blown off course by southwesterly winds. His next sighting and landfall, a small island he named Santa Cruz (Holy Cross), was today's St. Croix of the U.S. Virgin Islands. The island was by then firmly controlled by Caribs— who called it *Cibuquiera* (Stony Land) and important archaeological discoveries at **Salt River Bay** in St. Croix indicate that the area had long been a major cultural center for various Amerindian groups. Columbus sent ashore a landing party which made the mistake of stealing an Arawak slave from the Caribs. Soon after, true to Columbus's recorded impressions of them, the Caribs sent a war canoe out to the *Niña* and engaged the Spaniards in battle. One Carib and one Spanish sailor were recorded dead. The St. Croix landing was and would remain the only documented landing Columbus ever made on what would later become U.S. soil.

Columbus then set sail and charted the Virgins archipelago, notably finding both *San Tomas* (St. Thomas) and *San Juan* (St. John) uninhabited (although archaeological studies have established that most of the larger Virgin Islands supported Arawaks at one time or another). He named today's Tortola from the Spanish word for dove, and Virgin Gorda, literally "Fat Virgin," for . . . well, who knows what went through his mind.

Columbus had some fun in naming the Virgins archipelago. Due to the hundreds of rocks, cays, and islets set among the larger islands, he dubbed the entire group *Las Once Mil Virgenes,* The 11,000 Virgins, in honor of the British 3rd- or 4th-century Saint Ursula and her 11,000 virgin companions murdered at the hands of the Huns at Cologne. Some historians contend that the name was actually *Las Islas Virgenes,* but, whatever the case, parts of the name stuck and the islands became associated with virgins.

Last Voyages of Columbus

On his third voyage (1498-1500), Columbus sailed as far as Trinidad and the Venezuelan coast, charting islands but not necessarily landing on all of them. By the fourth voyage (1502-4), his adventures had taken their toll. The apocryphal Great Khan had remained illusive, and Columbus had discovered no substantial amounts of gold. The sovereigns Ferdinand and Isabella began to question their support, and there were arguments over Columbus's compensation. During this last voyage, his old caravels gave way and sank, and he and crew members were marooned on Jamaica for more than a year. When finally rescued, Columbus returned to Spain a broken and ultimately defeated man. Within two years of his return, he died, at Valladolid, on 20 May 1506.

The early discoveries of Columbus opened the floodgates of European exploration. All this settlement spelled doom for the Amerindian groups, first the hapless Arawaks and then later the Caribs. During the 16th and 17th centuries, they were in turn enslaved, murdered, infected

THE LEGEND OF ST. URSULA

Columbus, in his late 15th- and early 16th-century voyages to the Indies, was fond of naming the islands he charted in honor of saints and religious icons. He diverged only slightly from that custom when he named the Virgin Islands archipelago after the legend of the martyred St. Ursula and her army of 11,000 virgins. But who, precisely, was Ursula, and where did she find 11,000 virgins who were willing to take the martyrdom plunge with her?

According to legend, Ursula was a beautiful princess (princesses, in these legends, just have to be beautiful), the daughter of a 3rd- or 4th-century Christian king of Britain. The kingdom was threatened by a tribe of pagan Huns, whose prince demanded (princes, in these legends, are very demanding) Ursula's hand in marriage. Ursula had no intention of ever marrying, having decided to live a life of serene celibacy (not an oxymoron in her case). Still, in order to save her father's kingdom, she consented to the union. She had one stipulation, albeit a fairly weighty one: she would gather 11,000 virgins from the two kingdoms and live with

them for a period of three years, after which she would marry the prince. The legend contends that Ursula used those three years to train the women into a fighting army. And anyone knows that virginity coupled with weapons of war is a deadly combination.

Buoyed by public support, the army of women made its way to Rome to pledge its allegiance thereto. This made the Hun prince unhappy, and he in turn marched his own army to Cologne, where he awaited Ursula's return. In the battle that followed, Ursula and the 11,000 were killed.

Some versions of the account put the number of virgins at 11, not 11,000—which, let's be frank, is a bit easier to take. Whatever the case, the legend grew after 12th-century citizens of Cologne uncovered bones in an old Roman cemetery. The bones were declared official relics by the Roman Catholic church, and Ursula became the patron saint of maidens. Her feast day was 21 October, the reputed day of the massacre. The feast day is no longer celebrated by the church.

with disease, and zealously converted to death. Many committed suicide rather than submit to European domination. Entire communities were eliminated, and eventually the ruthless process was complete. The Arawaks were killed off completely, but a handful of indigenous Caribs did survive; most live on the islands of St. Vincent and Dominica.

COLONIES

During the 16th and 17th centuries, the European powers established major ports in the West Indies. Charlotte Amalie, on St. Thomas, lay directly on the east-west trade routes and was, due to its accessible deep-water harbor, one of the region's busiest merchant centers.

Tobacco was one of the islands' first cash crops, and small settlements grew larger with the introduction of sugar, cotton, coffee, and other crops. With the absence of Amerindian slave labor, African slaves were imported in increasing numbers, thus ensuring the ethnological and sociological makeup of the Caribbean today.

The European ports and outposts in the West Indies were by no means, however, permanent. Eager to find footholds in the New World, and eager for expansion and commerce (and in some cases religious freedom), principal European countries vied for power and possessions. Spain, which controlled the seas and the major islands of Puerto Rico, Cuba, Hispaniola and, briefly, Jamaica and Trinidad, was the target of French, Dutch, and English ships of war, as well as of privateers and assorted scalawags who roamed the Caribbean in search of easy riches.

In 1648, a group of Dutch colonists landed at Soper's Hole on Tortola in the British Virgin Islands, establishing the first European settlement on the island. By the late 1600s, the British had established claims on some of the British Virgin Islands, but they remained in a continuous state of altercation with the Dutch and Spanish over territorial claims. In 1672, the British governor of the Leeward Islands claimed Tortola for England and sent settlers from Anguilla to appropriate the island. By 1680, the British had established settlements on Anegada and Virgin Gorda and begun to establish sugarcane plantations.

The Europeans in the U.S. Virgin Islands

The rattling of sabers in the Caribbean was part and parcel of the continuing European wars of domination as treaties were signed and alliances rearranged and islands changed hands repeatedly. The islands that eventually became the U.S. Virgins were settled by the Dutch, the English, and the French—often simultaneously. St. Croix proved to be the touchstone, as it was agriculturally profitable and one of the larger islands in the vicinity. By 1645, the Dutch had left St. Croix, and by 1650 the Spanish had reclaimed it and driven off the English. The Spaniards were, in turn, disposed of by the French, who replaced the island's name, Santa Cruz, with St. Croix. In 1653, the French invited the Knights of Malta to settle and manage the island. The Knights in turn sold the island back to the French. Thus continued the schizophrenic history and cultural and linguistic paths that today define the entire Caribbean region.

During this period, the tobacco, cotton, sugar, and indigo plantations of St. Croix went begging for labor. The importation of African slaves commenced in 1673, when 103 slaves were brought to St. Thomas, and accelerated thereafter.

Also during this period, in 1666, the Danes, under the Danish West India and Guinea Company, claimed St. Thomas. The town of Charlotte Amalie, first named *Taphaus* (Tap House), was founded in 1691. The name was later changed to honor the Danish queen. In 1694, the Danes claimed St. John, but continuing hostilities with the British on nearby Tortola prevented them from actually inhabiting the island until 1717. In 1733, two important events took place. First, the French sold St. Croix to the Danish West India and Guinea Company. Then, a massive slave rebellion on St. John—the result of harsh working conditions coupled with a devastating drought and a hurricane that year, put the island in the hands of Africans for six months. The rebellion was put down by the Danes, who were reinforced by French warships and troops.

With the addition of St. Croix, the Danish formed the Danish West Indies colony, and the islands prospered. St. Thomas (named a free port in 1724) had flourished as a center of trade and commerce. St. John was home to large sugarcane and cotton plantations, before and after the slave rebellion. And St. Croix, then

THE ST. JOHN SLAVE REBELLION

By 1733, the island of St. Jan, as the Danes called it, had begun to prosper as a sugar plantation island. Figures show that the number of plantations on the island had increased from 40 in 1721 to more than 100 by 1733. Likewise, the need for slaves to work the plantations had increased during that time, and, by 1733, the slave population numbered nearly 1,100. Slaves greatly outnumbered the whites.

Several factors, beyond the obvious desire of any human being to remove the shackles of bondage, contributed to the 1733 uprising. The island had experienced a severe drought in 1725 and 1726, during which water resources were diverted to the cane fields and the plantation homes. The slaves' food sources—their own corn fields and small garden plots—suffered. The masters were unwilling or unable to part with profits simply to feed slaves and, although some food was imported for the slaves during that time, many were simply left to starve (some to death). Other plantation owners simply let their slaves have days off from field work, which, of course, gave the slaves the opportunity and time to organize. In 1726, slave unrest became palpable, and, as was the custom, panicked reprisals among the outnumbered plantation owners became harsher than ever. Slaves were encouraged to turn in plotters for cash rewards, while alleged conspirators were branded on the forehead and lashed, sometimes to death. Runaways were lashed and killed, or lost limbs, and were pinched with hot irons. The irony, of course, of such brutal behavior on the part of the whites was that the slaves became more, not less, entrenched in their bitterness and need to retaliate.

By November 1733, more natural disasters had struck the hapless island. Another drought, followed by a severe hurricane, in turn followed by a crop-destroying plague of insects, destroyed much of the slaves' food sources. They were again faced with the threat of starvation and planter reprisals. This time, they took matters in hand. They hatched plots—and reckoned they could carry them out.

On the morning of 23 November 1733, a group of slaves approached the garrison at Coral Bay, the island's first and major settlement at the time. With the ruse that they carried firewood, they were allowed in by the fort's soldiers. The slaves then pulled knives and machetes from their wood piles, and dispatched the seven or eight soldiers who held the fort. One soldier escaped, and it was he who later that same day made his way to St. Thomas and informed the governor of the growing rebellion.

The slaves in the garrison then fired the cannon three times, a signal to other slaves throughout the area to pick up arms and do the work of an outright rebellion. This they did, and within hours, groups of slaves roamed throughout the island, murdering plantation owners, overseers, and their families, and picking up other slaves along the way. As they pushed west, word of the rebellion spread, and several owners and loyal (or petrified) slaves retreated to the plantation of a man named Deurloo. There, at the end of Deurloo's cannons, the rebellious slaves met their first real resistance.

For weeks following the initial bloodbath, St. John descended into a state of near anarchy. Slaves holed up in the forests or in the plantation homes of owners they had killed or routed. Yet their victory was short-lived. The fear that the rebellion might spread to neighboring islands drove Governor Gardelin, on St. Thomas, to dispatch 18 soldiers to the island to put down the unrest. They succeeded in routing the slaves from several strongholds and scattering them throughout the island but failed to capture or kill the majority. One report contends that the initial relief parties from St. Thomas managed to execute 32 of the rebels, leaving a remaining force estimated at about 100.

By Christmas, other reinforcements arrived. Danes and Dutch from St. Thomas, English soldiers from nearby Tortola, and French from Martinique to the south arrived on the island with the promised reward that they could keep four-fifths of the slaves they captured in the roundup.

The French, who contributed nearly 600 men to the effort, became the straw that broke the rebels' backs. But the French had motives other than the need for more slaves behind their energetic backing to free St. John. The French government was, at the time, about to embark on a war with Poland with the aim of conquering the country—a result of crossed bloodlines among the commingled European aristocracy of the day. They needed money to do this, and they held St. Croix.

What's more, the French also desired Denmark's neutrality in that war and were more than willing to court her favor. The Danes and French struck a deal. The French sold St. Croix to the Danes, and the Danes in turn promised their neutrality during the war with Poland. The French were more than happy to send several hundred troops to St. John to massage that relationship.

By late winter, the rebel slaves were in bad shape. Scattered, pursued by various reinforcements, out of ammunition and food, and generally lacking anywhere to go, they were demoralized and saw their numbers dwindling. Some simply gave up or were captured. Others committed suicide. Others were killed in battle. By May, the rebellion had run its course. By August, only 15 rebels remained. On promise of a pardon, the 15 gave up and were summarily executed or tortured to death. In total, some 150 slaves had participated in the rebellion. Virtually all were killed in battle or died in jail or by execution.

Source: *Night of the Silent Drums*
by John Lorenzo Anderson

home to the Danish West Indies capital of Christiansted, also had an agricultural economic base.

Buccaneers

The late 16th and early 17th centuries were also a time of unbridled recklessness and, possibly, a smattering of heroics, perpetrated by some of the Caribbean's more colorful malcontents, the buccaneers. Made up of a loose association of sailors, pirates, thugs, and some truly evil people—outcasts who'd given up their nationalities for the lure of the sea and quick wealth—the buccaneers (the name evolved from the French *boucan,* for a wooden rack used to dry meat) were bound together by a unwavering distrust of authority and a particular distrust of Spain. With Spain controlling the trade routes of the West Indies, the buccaneers were also outlaws—and therefore perfect for the job of harassing Spanish possessions throughout the New World.

Nominally employed as privateers by the likes of England, the mercenary buccaneers waged war on the Spanish Main. Names such as Henry Morgan, Captain William Kidd, Black Sam Bellamy, Calico Jack Rackham, Edward Teach (also known as Blackbeard), Mary Read, and Anne Bonney rank among the more well-known—and feared—privateers of the time. One legend claims that the infamous Blackbeard once anchored with his crew off **Deadman's Bay,** on today's Peter Island, while splitting the spoils of a successful raid. An argument erupted and Blackbeard set 15 pirates ashore on the nearby island, called **Dead Chest,** providing one bottle of rum and the men's sea chests for their last days. Hence—and this is where legends always become suspect—the old salt's song lyric "fifteen men on dead men's chest, yo ho ho and a bottle of rum."

The privateer and adventurer Francis Drake, in particular, made use of the secluded Virgin Islands during raids against the Spanish in the late 16th century, and today the ocean passage between Tortola and Virgin Gorda bears his name, the Sir Francis Drake Channel.

End of the Buccaneers

The War of Spanish Succession, fought mainly in Europe, was brought to an end by the 1713 Treaty of Utrecht. During that war, France and Spain, then allies, battled and lost to England and the Netherlands in a familiar skirmish over property and trade rights. With Spain divested of its European possessions and England awarded France's *Asiento* (a contract to supply Spanish New World possessions with slaves), the buccaneers were left without a united front. England no longer needed them, and most buccaneers reverted to their historic roots—they became a small group of marauding pirates, allied with no one but themselves. These were desperate and ruthless and were hunted down like dogs. Others, such as the then Sir Henry Morgan, astutely sensed that the times had changed and changed with them. He disavowed his erstwhile comrades in arms, the pirates and buccaneers, and even helped in their persecution, proving once again that pragmatic hypocrisy has a firm place in world history. Morgan moved on to become a wealthy aristocrat and a titled landholder.

Treaty of Vienna

It wasn't until the period of the Napoleonic Wars, when the 1815 Treaty of Vienna was signed after the defeat of Napoleon at Waterloo, that the West Indies settled down in a semblance of orderly rule. Denmark, a longtime ally of France, had made the unfortunate but historically inevitable choice of siding with Napoleon against the English during the Napoleonic Wars. The British in the Caribbean had seen this as an opportunity to expand their territory, and they attacked and occupied St. John in 1801 and again in 1807, holding it for one and seven years, respectively.

PLANTOCRACY

Emerging from the European rivalries of the 17th and 18th centuries was a Caribbean society economically steeped in agriculture and the slave trade. In the "triangle" of trade, stretching from West African ports, where slaves were bought and loaded onto cargo ships, to various European ports and the sugar-producing ports of the Caribbean (and Brazil), commerce was brisk and profitable. Fortunes were made, often by absentee landholders, and the great plantocracies of the Caribbean created the basis for the multi-tiered, multiracial society we know today.

During the 18th and early 19th centuries, sugar reigned in the Caribbean. More than 10 million African slaves were imported to the Americas, most from western, central, and eventually eastern Africa. Almost all were taken to the Greater Antilles and Brazil where large land masses favored the production of sugar. Still, virtually all the islands of the West Indies, including the Virgin Islands, produced sugar and other crops with slaves providing the labor for building roads, ports, and the infrastructures of the day.

Slave Life

The planter society was characterized by a mishmash of landed plantation owners, overseers, merchants, and, of course, Africans bound by slavery. In white society, the ugliness of brutality, ignorance, and illiteracy was rife, and that was in part the result of years of island colonization by European misfits and criminals. The masters were more often than not unrepentant bigots, and their methods of keeping slaves in line were legendary—beheadings, live burnings, and mutilations were not uncommon. On St. Thomas in 1733, for instance, then-Governor Gardelin issued a number of decrees that display the tenor of the times. Captured runaway slaves would lose a leg or an ear. Runaways who managed to elude capture for six months or more would be killed. A slave or even a free black who raised his hand to a white would be pinched three times with a hot iron and lose the hand. And so on.

Slaves outnumbered their owners by the thousands, and island societies were made up of too few—who were none too lenient—holding too much power—a perfect recipe for tension, rebellion, and, ultimately, failure.

Slave life itself was tragic. Beginning with the infamous Middle Passage from Africa, where captive Africans were chained and relegated to the stench-filled bowels of cargo ships, a slave's

planter, 1791

lot was one virtually without hope. During the 12-week Atlantic passage, many died of starvation or dehydration. On arrival, slaves were typically stripped and exhibited for sale, and even branded—not the last or least affront to dignity they would encounter. Labor in the sugarcane fields was the most difficult and grinding possible, and many slaves died or were beaten to death by overseers. Still more died as a result of suicide, recapture and retribution after running away, or open rebellion. Planters could expect an average of six deaths to occur for every live birth among slaves, and the need to import more Africans increased with the expansion of trade and planter society.

Whites consorted with black slaves—most often by force—producing an unintentional new "brown" layer of society, mixed-race offspring who held a peripheral position between the whites and hapless Africans. In certain cases, the mixed-race class were called "free coloreds," unable to function in a racist white society that saw them as inferior and pretenders, yet considered by whites to be superior to black Africans. The emergence of a brown class so fueled the planters' fears that miscegenation would kick in the door of white supremacy that a bizarre and ultimately futile system of racial classification emerged throughout the islands. A person of mixed race would be, in the English-speaking colonies, classified as musteefino, octaroon, quadroon, mulatto, sambo, and so on, depending on the percentage mix of white and black heritage. Today, though official classifications no longer exist, one needn't look very hard to find that informal color classifications still exist on social and economic levels.

The planter society lived in constant and justified fear of slave uprisings. As if the sheer number of slaves wasn't enough cause for concern, the planters found themselves dealing with a people they had clearly misjudged in terms of intellect and ability to organize. Slaves customarily and relentlessly sabotaged their masters' plantations by ruining farm equipment, holding forbidden meetings, and plotting reprisals. St. Thomas's Governor Gardelin proclaimed that a slave knowingly hiding the details of a slave uprising or plot would be branded on the forehead and receive 100 lashes. Still, rebellions erupted in Barbados, Jamaica, Trinidad,

and, notably, on St. John, where slaves rebelled in 1733. These uprisings were put down with frightening brutality.

Slavery Ends

For years, particularly during the 18th century, many in mainstream European society had been horrified by the spectacle of slavery in the Caribbean. Guided by abolitionist movements and the clergy, protests and calls for an end to the practice were common. During the early 1800s, the reprisals exacted on rebellious slaves by the plantocracy of the New World reached the ears of an already agitated Europe. Finally, after much debate (and ultimately, in the case of the United States, a civil war), the slave trade in the New World began to disintegrate. The Danish West Indies (later the U.S. Virgin Islands) were the first to abolish the practice, in 1792. Great Britain banned trade in slaves in 1808. By 1814, most European countries had followed that lead, and legal trade in slaves had virtually ended. Twenty years later, slavery in the Americas began to end as an institution. The British outlawed the ownership of slaves in 1834, the Danes and French in 1848, the Dutch in 1863, and the U.S. by 1865. The Spanish, who then operated large sugar plantations in Brazil and Cuba, followed in 1886.

POST-EMANCIPATION LIFE

The end of slavery rang the death knell for West Indian planter society. Many former slaves went on to farm small parcels of land, while others remained on the plantations as indentured, paid laborers. Eventually, planters imported more laborers from West Africa, Europe, East India, and other parts of Asia. Yet even this new labor force was not enough to save the large plantations. Rising production costs and competition from other countries, notably Brazil's massive sugar plantations, where slavery remained intact until the late 19th century, forced the hand of the plantocracy, who were not accustomed to either paying their help or even treating them as equals. Some plantations gave way to smaller, more profitable farming activity. Some were gobbled up by emerging production companies. In effect, the great plantocracy of the West Indies became a wistful memory in the colonial mind, and its absence paved the way for the islands' turbulent 20th-century battles for racial equality and viable economies.

THE 20TH CENTURY

The late 19th century and early parts of this century saw a worldwide move in agrarian societies toward forms of industrialized activity. In the West Indies, this shift was first to the industrial centers, the emerging cities of the islands, such as Charlotte Amalie on St. Thomas. Agricultural production had diversified to include coffee, cocoa, bananas, and other profitable crops, and the infrastructures needed for processing and exporting the crops employed thousands.

U.S. Virgin Islands in the Early 1900s

World War I brought profound changes in the international makeup of the world. No longer innocent or isolated, and for the most part shunned by their colonial rulers, the West Indies were caught up in worldwide movements advocating a wide range of human rights, including the all-important voting privilege. Nationalism and universal suffrage were the bywords of the day. The islands and islanders began to define their emerging national identities, and a growing sense of pride in local cultures emanated from this budding nationalism. This was in marked contrast with the prevailing European attitude of the time, which saw the islands as little more than pitiable ghettos and ready-made markets for expensive European technologies. By and large, the typical creole islander of the early 19th century was a disenfranchised worker, a source of cheap labor for foreign-owned industries, yet one whose past and future were linked to the island itself. In the strictest sense of the word, the islanders were true natives. And captive audiences. These imperfect conditions naturally led to conflict between the islanders and the former colonial masters, and to nascent movements for independence.

After the final emancipation of slaves, in 1848, the Danish West Indies, along with most of the Caribbean, entered a period of economic slump and massive migrations that saw freed slaves leave for plantation and construction work in Central America and elsewhere. Additionally, the great sailing cargo ships of the 18th and early 19th centuries were soon obsolete, due to the innovation of steamships. This rendered St. Thomas and other major Caribbean ports less important as stopover points.

Since the 1870s, the Danes had been in a period of protracted negotiations with the United States, seeking to unload their unprofitable and weighty Caribbean possessions. On 31 March 1917, the U.S., fearful of the sort of massive destruction wrought by the first world war and seeking a base from which to guard its new

main street of Charlotte Amalie, St. Thomas circa 1900

canal in Panama, bought the soon-to-be-U.S. Virgin Islands for $25 million in gold.

The U.S. ruled the islands as a naval base until 1927, when citizenship was given to the islanders. The navy and army remained on the islands through World War II (and the U.S. Marine Corps still maintains airfields on St. Thomas and St. Croix). Soon after, universal suffrage was granted, roads and infrastructure were built, and a university was established.

The worldwide depression of the 1920s and '30s plunged the islands into an abyss of economic despair. Islanders, who had migrated in the thousands seeking employment in Central and South America and the U.S., now returned home to find stagnant economies and neglected paradises. Even Herbert Hoover, the U.S. president (1929-33), upon visiting the U.S. Virgin Islands called them an "effective poorhouse."

To an extent, tourism—most often in the form of cruise ships—had existed in the islands during the early part of the century. In the postbellum '50s, many of the islands, having made a shaky shift from primary agrarian to industrial activity, took stock of their natural resources and saw the dollar signs written on the wall, and those dollar signs spelled "tourism." The crystal Caribbean waters and swaying palms were the allure. Today, on many West Indies islands, including the Virgin Islands, tourism earns more foreign currency than any other industry and is both the boon and the bane of the local populace.

Modern Times

The '50s and '60s also saw the ripening of inchoate political movements throughout the Caribbean. Clamor for island self-rule and independence became louder, and colonialism finally began to relinquish its strong grip—sometimes grudgingly, sometimes with great relief. Here, the U.S. and British Virgin Islands share an ironic similarity—today both have degrees of self-rule, but neither is an independent nation.

Through the years, the British had fought attempts to oust them from the islands. Most of these efforts were feeble and short-lived, and the British Virgin Islands have remained a British entity for the entirety of their modern history. They were administered as a colony and part of the Leeward Islands Administration until 1956, when the Federation of the West Indies was in the process of forming. The Federation of the West Indies was the administrative unit comprising British West Indies islands. It collapsed in 1962 due to internecine bickering between, primarily, Jamaica and Trinidad and Tobago. The British Virgin Islands elected not to join the West Indies Federation, instead opting for a form of internal control over their affairs and economic links with the U.S. Virgin Islands. During the 1960s and '70s, constitutions were drawn in the British Virgin Islands that allowed for greater internal government, including the formation of political parties and local elections of a Legislative Council. The system continues today.

In the U.S. Virgin Islands, the 1932 Organic Act introduced U.S. citizenship, suffrage, and a measure of self-government to the islands. In 1956, the U.S. congress, responding to a massive land grant by the millionaire Laurance Rockefeller, established a national park on St. John. In 1968, congress passed an act allowing for greater internal rule and election of a governor by popular vote. Four years later, in 1972, the U.S. Virgin Islands sent their first elected delegate to congress.

PEOPLE AND CULTURE

The blend of European and African cultures in the U.S. and British Virgin Islands is evident in the culture, arts, language, cuisines, and place names of the islands.

Indeed, the majority of the Virgin Islands' combined populations is of African descent. The rest are an increasing number of North American, British, other European, and Caribbean expatriates, many of whom have been attracted by the islands' growing tourism and related service industries.

In the British Virgin Islands, citizens born in the country ("Belongers," as they are called) and naturalized citizens have preference in job and land acquisition over non-islanders. This creates some disparity and a certain degree of resentment among the non-Belongers, who are often seen by locals as interlopers and are denied certain advantages under the law but who are also necessary to fill the increasing number of jobs on the islands.

LANGUAGE

U.S. Virgin Islanders speak English, but with a Creole—sometimes called Calypso—twist. The "h" in many words is simply dispensed with, so that a "thing" is a "ting" and three of those things are "tree tings." If someone gives you three of those things, you say, "Tanks." Likewise, the "t" at the ends of some words is dispensed with, so "what" is pronounced "wah'" and if you don't recognize the thing referred to, you ask, "Wah' dis ting?" The "t" plays tricks when it appears in the middle of a word, so your father becomes your "faddah."

Plurals are often not used but instead replaced by the qualifier "them" (pronounced "dem"). In the end, the phrase above becomes "Tanks for da tree ting dem." On the other hand, some words that are plural by definition in standard English get an "s" anyway—you go to the post office to pick up the "mails."

The pronoun "I" is (not for reasons of humbleness) not often used; instead, it's replaced by "me," as in, "Me goin' downtown." As well, the

pronouns "her" and "him" can be replaced by "she" and "he" as in, "Me goin' wit she." Vowels and consonants in many words are transposed—"film" becomes "flim," for example. And the list of Creole idiosyncrasies goes on.

Likewise, vocabulary in the U.S. Virgin Islands takes on colloquial twists and turns that'd make a linguist's day. Gossip is "melee" (a small weekly humor newspaper out of St. Croix, *Island Melee,* celebrates island gossip), an accident is a "mash-up," and when you're out of cash you are "penny one."

Listen awhile—you'll get the hang of it. Except, of course, when someone doesn't want you to "unnerstan'," in which case he will talk faster than you thought humanly possible.

Here, translate this:

"Wah hap'nin?"
(What's happening?)

"Me jus limin'."
(I'm just hanging out)

"Yeah? Me mash up me car an' me broke me toot dem."
(Yeah? I got into an accident and broke some teeth.)

"You doan say?"
(Get out of town!)

On St. Croix, pockets of expatriate Puerto Ricans (technically, since both Puerto Rico and the U.S. Virgin Islands are U.S. territories, "expatriate" is a stretch of the word) speak Spanish. Spanish influences also affect the English of St. Croix to produce a Creole dialect, and a Creolized culture, called Cruzan (which is also the name of St. Croix's famous rum).

The Danes left a legacy of language in the U.S. Virgin Islands, mainly through place names. In Charlotte Amalie, street names such as Kongens Gade ("King Street"), Dronningens Gade ("Queen Street"), and others reflect Danish heritage.

The British Virgin Islands is still a British Crown Colony and, therefore, a dependent territory. Standard English is used by everyone, although West Indian colloquialisms and the lilting lyricism of the islands' language, as in the U.S. Virgins, is heard throughout. British Virgin Islanders still linger in an Old World approach to human relations—remember, this is a country with the population of a medium-size university, where most people know most everyone else, and if they don't, they at least know everyone else's business. In other words, it's a small town, and politeness helps maintain the order of the society. British Virgin Islanders appreciate a greeting—a simple "Good morning. How are you?" or something along those lines—before getting down to any business at hand.

RELIGIONS

Religions practiced in the U.S. Virgin Islands include Baptism, Methodism, Roman Catholicism, Anglicanism, Moravianism, Episcopalianism, Judaism, and Lutheranism, among others. Several historical churches, including the **Synagogue of Berecha V'Shalom V'Gemilath Chasidim** (Blessing and Peace and Acts of Piety), in Charlotte Amalie, attest to the wide array of religions that have made the U.S. Virgin Islands a home over the centuries. The synagogue, constructed by Sephardic Jews in 1796 and again, after an 1804 fire, in 1833, is one of the oldest in the Western Hemisphere (the oldest synagogue in continual use is in Curaçao). Rounding things out, a small but significant group of Palestinians, primarily businessmen, live and work on St. Croix.

The religion norms among British Virgin Islanders were, likewise, adopted from colonial and missionary days. Methodist, Baptist, Seventh-Day Adventist, Roman Catholic, Anglican, and a variety of evangelical churches pepper the countryside.

On the other hand, as on many Caribbean islands, islanders of both the U.S. and British Virgin Islands hang on tenaciously and often surreptitiously to ancient African beliefs and practices, imported on slave ships. Beliefs in animism (assigning spirits to inanimate objects), ancestor worship, spirit worship, and magic play important parts in Virgin Islands life. *Duppies* and *jumbies* (ghosts) are the bane of schoolchildren and adult believers and are held to cause many of the ills, and even the benefits, that befall individuals. Various forms of *obeah,* or magic, are practiced to entice spirits or ancestors to do good—or bad. Herbal medicines and fetishes are used to sway bodies and minds, and it all melds, somehow, with mainstream religions to produce an odd syncretic belief in both the God of the western world and the spirits of the African world. In other words, Virgin Islanders are not hedging their bets and are cleverly, one thinks, playing both sides of this complicated mystical fence in their earthly quest for spiritual redemption. Fervent prayer and Bible study in addition to casting the bones of a goat may or may not work—but, hey, it probably can't hurt.

MUSIC AND DANCE

The carnivals of St. Thomas, St. John, St. Croix, Tortola, and Virgin Gorda are showcases of local music and dance, not to be missed by anyone with a hankering for truly local scenes. As well as highlighting international reggae, calypso, and soca (a mix of American *soul* and rhythm and blues and Caribbean *ca*lypso) artists, the carnivals present music and dance that is distinct to the Virgin Islands. *Quelbe* music, with a sound reminiscent of "scratch bands," is considered a folk music of both the U.S. and British Virgin Islands. The vocal and instrumental style is a product of western and African influences, and mixes the music of jigs and quadrille dances (see special topic "Quadrille Dancing") of early European settlers, the fife and drum music of their military bands, and the African call-and-response singing of slaves in the cane fields. These call-and-response melodies, an early form of subversive communication among slaves, evolved into the more complex **cariso** melodies of the 19th century. In fact, so subversive was slave music in general that, in the 17th century, Danish plantation owners passed laws forbidding slaves to dance or play drums. Cariso singers still perform at folk festivals and functions, offering commentary on local life and politics. (The cariso style evolved into forms such as the calypso of Trinidad).

Quelbe bands, popular throughout the Virgin Islands, initially imitated the music of their European overseers but later composed and performed original music and developed styles of singing, playing, and instrument construction indigenous to the islands. Instruments were bamboo flutes, steel triangles, guitars, banjos, ukuleles, ribbed squash gourds, tambourines, bass drums, and, today, saxophones. Despite having been considered archaic during the early 20th century, quelbe bands have experienced a revival due to the upsurge of interest in folklore and historical cultural activities. Today, quelbe bands play at traditional functions, carnivals, and dances.

Other African musical influences are strong in Virgin Islands life. *Fungi* bands (the word is pronounced "FOON-ghee," the same as the traditional food made from cornmeal paste), a traditional sort of scratch band consisting of guitars, bass-like instruments such as the one-string bass, African drums, bamboo flutes or recorders, and scratch instruments such as ribbed gourds and washboards, play during carnivals and competitions. *Fungi* bands tend, like traditional calypsonians, to offer sometimes bawdy commentary on local events.

Music Performances

In the U.S. Virgin Islands, *quelbe* festivals are often held at the **Reichhold Center for the Performing Arts** (tel. 809-774-4482) of the University of the Virgin Islands on St. Thomas as well as at venues around the islands. Call for information. Otherwise, look for recordings in local music shops or performances by groups such as

---

QUADRILLE DANCING

Quadrille dancing is a variation on the 18th-century French *cotillion* (petticoat) country dancing. The dance involved partners executing three to five complex sets of movements. Slaves in the West Indies often copied and parodied their owners' customs and adopted quadrille dancing as well as reels, jigs, and other European forms. Accompanied by string bands, these dances soon became part of slave culture and ended up in West Indian-African ceremonies and carnivals. Quadrille dancing is a direct predecessor of the popular North American country square dancing.

Stanley and the Ten Sleepless Nights, Blinky and the Roadmasters, Jamesie and the Happy Seven, and **Bully and the Kafooners.** (With band names like that, can you resist?)

In the British Virgin Islands, catch the annual **Music in Steel—Steel Band Concert** and the **Scratch/Fungi Band Fiesta,** both held in December to showcase local musicians. Call the tourist board (tel. 809-494-3134) for details. As well, several local B.V.I. musicians are a must to catch the feel and rhythm of island life. **Quito Rymer and the Edge** play five nights a week at the lead singer's **Quito's Gazebo** (tel. 809-945-4350), an ocean-edge bar at Cane Garden Bay on Tortola. Quito is a B.V.I. icon and plays a lively set of calypso, reggae, and modern tunes—a good time is always had by all. If you happen to make it to Jost Van Dyke—and you should—stop in at **Foxy's Tamarind Bar** (tel. 809-945-9258), at beachside, where you'll find the internationally renowned and slightly roguish Foxy performing calypso most afternoons. It's just **Foxy Callwood,** his guitar, and his famous graveled voice, making up songs as he goes along.

As on most islands throughout the Caribbean, you'll find local hotel and bar bands proficient on steel drums, an import from Trinidad, and in reggae, Jamaica's most famous export.

Dance Performances

Local dance and cultural troupes are active on the islands, including the St. Croix-based **Caribbean Dance Company** (tel. 809-778-8824), which performs on St. Thomas at the Reichhold Center for the Performing Arts and other venues, and the **Scott West Indian Dance Company** (tel. 809-774-8446).

The **St. Thomas Arts Council** (7B Crystal Gade, Charlotte Amalie, tel. 809-774-8900) and the **Virgin Islands Council on the Arts** (41-42 Norre Gade, Charlotte Amalie, tel. 809-774-5984) can be contacted for a full schedule of St. Thomas folk music and dance-company performances. On St. Croix, contact the **Island Center for the Arts** (tel. 809-778-5272) for schedules and information.

Just outside of Charlotte Amalie, the tranquil **Tillet Gardens Art Center** (4126 Anna's Retreat, St. Thomas, U.S. Virgin Islands 00802; tel. 809-775-1929, fax 809-775-9482) offers the **Arts Alive** and **Classics in the Gardens** programs, with performances by jazz groups, dance groups, string and piano quartets, and others, pretty much year-round. Also at Tillet Gardens you'll find galleries and crafts studios featuring some of the islands' foremost artists.

LITERATURE

The St. Thomas-based University of the Virgin Islands publishes the excellent regional literary magazine *The Caribbean Writer,* and if you're interested in the current state of Caribbean writing, this is the source. The magazine, started in 1987, has published the works of Derek Walcott and poets Marvin Williams and Paul Keens-Douglas, among many others.

As well, look to the university's Reichhold Center for the Performing Arts (tel. 809-774-4482) for readings and appearances by luminaries such as poet Maya Angelou.

University of the Virgin Islands

The university, located on John Brewer's Beach on St. Thomas, should get special mention for its contributions to literature and the arts, as well as education, throughout the Caribbean. U.V.I., a basic liberal arts educational facility, was officially chartered in 1962 as the College of the Virgin Islands. The college began by offering BS and BA degrees in 1970, and in 1976 offered its first masters degree, in education. The college was granted university status in 1986. Also in 1986, the U.S. congress named U.V.I. one of the nation's outstanding black colleges (there are 117 in the U.S.). Today, with campuses on St. Thomas and St. Croix and a research station on St. John, the school enrolls about 3,200 full-time students from throughout the Caribbean.

The university's Reichhold Center for the Performing Arts (tel. 809-774-4482) offers year-round cultural and entertainment programs in symphony, jazz, ballet, and folklore, as well as performances by international luminaries such as violinist Itzhak Perlman. The center is also the venue for the **Caribbean Repertory Summer Festival Theater.** For schedules, write to 2 John Brewer's Bay, St. Thomas, U.S. Virgin Islands 00802-9990.

ISLANDS AT A GLANCE

UNITED STATES VIRGIN ISLANDS

The U.S. Virgin Islands, officially the Virgin Islands of the United States, is an unincorporated territory of the U.S. and comprises an estimated 70 islands, islets, and cays, of which three, **St. Thomas, St. John,** and **St. Croix,** are inhabited and of significant size. The islands lie east of Puerto Rico, at the northwestern corner of the Lesser Antilles chain of islands in the Caribbean. A 1990 U.S. Census Bureau tally put the total population of the U.S. Virgin Islands at 101,809.

St. Thomas

St. Thomas is commercially developed and the home of the U.S. Virgin Islands historic capital, Charlotte Amalie. The island measures 13 miles (21 km) by three miles (five km) at its widest point and is 32 square miles (83 square km) in area. The island is surrounded by fine bays and beaches. Highly developed for tourism, the port receives dozens of cruise ship arrivals each week. St. Thomas's population is 48,166.

St. John

St. John, some four miles (more than six km) east of St. Thomas and seven miles (11 km) west of Tortola in the British Virgin Islands, is the smallest of the U.S. Virgin Islands. Nine miles (14 km) long by five miles (eight km) at its widest point, and 20 square miles (52 square km) in area, with dozens of secluded beaches, it is also the least populated, with 3,504 residents. More than half of the island's land is protected, designated part of the Virgin Islands National Park system.

St. Croix

St. Croix, located some 40 miles (64 km) south of St. Thomas, is the largest of the U.S. Virgin Islands at 84 square miles (217 square km)—28 miles (45 km) long by seven miles (11 km) wide. The island's topography is less dramatic than that of its sister islands, characterized by gently

*1775 map
of the Virgin Islands*

sloping hills, some semi-rainforests to the west, and arid areas to the south and southeast. The people of St. Croix, locally called Crucians (or Cruzans, pronounced "KROO-shans"), number 50,139.

BRITISH VIRGIN ISLANDS

Approximately 60 islands, cays, and tiny volcanic rocks make up the British Virgin Islands archipelago. The islands feature striking beaches, and the crystal waters of the area are a haven for divers and sailors. No hotels reach higher than two stories—about the height of the tallest palm tree. The British Virgin Islands lie in a horizontal chain of islands that begins 40 miles (64 km) east of Puerto Rico, just east of their sister U.S. Virgin Islands. The **Sir Francis Drake Channel** separates the Jost Van Dyke-Tortola group in the north from the Virgin Gorda string in the south. The total British Virgin Islands population is 17,000. The four main islands are:

Tortola

Tortola, a mere 21 square miles (54 square km) in area, is the largest of the British Virgins. The

dramatically hilly island features Mt. Sage, at 1,780 feet (541 meters) the Virgin Islands' highest point, as well as serene beaches and bays along the north shore. The capital—and only real town in the British Virgin Islands—is Road Town, located on Tortola's south central coast. The island's population is 13,200, the majority of the British Virgin Islands' people.

Virgin Gorda

Uneven Virgin Gorda, seven miles (11 km) long and two miles (three km) wide, with an area of eight square miles (21 square km), is the second largest of the British Virgin Islands. The island's one main road passes from **The Valley,** the main settlement, over 1,359-foot (414-meter) Gorda Peak, and ends at secluded **North Sound,** an area of small inlets and fine harbors. The island's famous natural rock formation, The Baths, sits on several beaches to the southeast. Virgin Gorda's population is 2,400.

Jost Van Dyke

Hilly Jost Van Dyke, which received electricity in 1991, hosts one main settlement at **Great Harbour,** where most of the population of 150 live. The four-square-mile (10-square-km) island has

VIRGIN ISLANDS PERSPECTIVES

The combined population of the U.S. Virgin Islands and British Virgin Islands is 118,000, about the same number that live in Abilene, Texas, or Muncie, Indiana.

If each and every student enrolled at the University of Massachusetts at Amherst went to the British Virgin Islands on spring break, the territory's population would double.

Point Udall, on the northeast coast of St. Croix, is the easternmost point of the United States.

If you took all the islands of the U.S. Virgin Islands and British Virgin Islands and plopped them into Luxembourg, their land mass would occupy a mere one-fifth of that tiny European country.

If you head directly west from the Virgin Islands, circumnavigating the globe, here are some of the places through which you'd pass: Negril, Jamaica; Wake Island; Laoag, Philippines; Vientiane, Thailand; Rangoon, Burma; Bombay, India; Bilma, Niger; Timbuktu, Mali.

The U.S. Virgin Islands just might be the most cosmopolitan of all U.S. territories; the islands have been claimed or occupied by the Arawaks, Caribs, Spanish, French, British, Dutch, Danish, and Americans.

several fine beaches and small beach bars and restaurants and is a major attraction for sailors.

Anegada
Anegada, a coral atoll, lies about 16 miles (26 km) north of the British Virgin Islands chain and features a no-nosebleed highest point of 28 feet (8.5 meters). The island is surrounded by a large and treacherous reef, where an estimated 300 wrecks provide fodder for divers. The north shore is nearly 11 miles (18 km) of uninterrupted white-sand beach. Not a large draw for tourists (although a unique one), the handful of small hotels, camping spots, and restaurants serve the island well. The population of 200 lives in **The Settlement,** a small village in the southeast.

tuna

BOB RACE

BOB RACE

ON THE ROAD
OUTDOOR ACTIVITIES

WATER SPORTS

Anyone interested in water-skiing, jet-skiing, parasailing (wherein you are towed by a motorboat while sitting in a sling suspended under a parachute), deep-sea fishing, banana boat riding, kayaking, and windsurfing will find no problem locating numerous water sports centers throughout the islands that will help you fulfill your fantasies. Try your hotel first—if it's seaside, it will most likely have a water sports center. Otherwise, see the specific island chapters in this book for names and addresses of water sports centers.

Surfing and Windsurfing
Note that certain beaches on several of the islands tend to attract people interested in specific water sports. On St. Thomas, just west of Magens Bay is **Hull Bay.** With its somewhat rougher surf and offshore reef, this beach is a favorite with surfers. Also on St. Thomas, **Sapphire Beach,** a wide beach sheltered by a rocky jetty on its south end, is a popular windsurfing spot. **Bluebeard's Beach,** at the far east end of the island near Red Hook (not to be confused

with Bluebeard's Castle Hotel in Charlotte Amalie), features a steady breeze and a bit of a surf and is also frequented by windsurfers.

On St. Croix's north coast, **Chenay Bay** is popular with windsurfers and is home to the **Lisa Neubuger Windsurfing Center** (tel. 809-778-8312), which offers instruction and rentals.

In the British Virgin Islands, Tortola's windy and slightly rough **Apple Bay,** on the northern west coast, attracts surfers. Nearby are water sports outfits where you can rent boards. **Cane Garden Bay,** just down the road, features numerous water sports centers and is a popular windsurfing spot. **Brewer's Bay,** east of Cane Garden Bay, is also popular with surfers. While it's not universal, windsurfing rentals ring in at about $20-35 per hour.

Fishing
Deep-sea sports fishermen and women will find tuna, dolphin, wahoo, kingfish, tarpon, marlin, and dozens of other large game fish in the waters of the Virgin Islands. Fishing excursions are arranged virtually everywhere—start at the local marinas to find charter fishing vessels. On St. Thomas, contact **Sapphire Marina** (tel. 809-775-3690 or 809-775-5889), **St. Thomas Sport-**

DIVING AND SNORKELING SAFETY

Care should be taken to use only certified diving facilities and facilities that will escort only certified divers. It is not unknown for unqualified operations to offer cheap diving packages to neophytes who are unaware of the methods and inherent dangers of scuba diving. These operations are the type that might simply strap a tank on your back and let you have at it—they're a danger to you and to the world of diving.

If diving isn't your cup of sea, then snorkeling will do nicely. All hotels and dive centers rent equipment, and it's inexpensive enough to do as often as you like. Snorkeling is generally safe, but remember to test the equipment first. Get used to your mask and snorkel by practicing first in a pool or shallow water, and don't snorkel or swim alone. Some people like to wear a T-shirt for both protection against the sun and accidental brushes with coral.

Snorkeling in choppy seas is potentially dangerous and probably futile. Visibility is greatly reduced in sloshing, murky water, and waves can push you into rocks and coral. Even though coastlines may have minor tides and gentle currents, it's best to be aware of where currents are if you are snorkeling or diving.

Avoid the porcupinelike sea urchins—especially the black, long-spined urchin. The strong barbs will pierce the skin and break off, resulting in painful swelling. Remove the fragments as soon as possible, soak the affected area in straight vinegar or a strong ammonia solution (urine will do in a pinch), and treat with antiseptic as soon as possible. Then see a doctor. Urchin meat is a table delicacy for some.

Also avoid the green or orange bristle worm, which can also make for a very bad day if its brittle, white whiskers are touched. They detach and become imbedded in the skin. Again, vinegar and medical treatment should follow.

The red fire sponge is also nice to look at but will cause swelling and discomfort if touched. Try to stay clear of all forms of jellyfish, which are not fish at all but primordial globs of membrane and primitive intelligence—again, nice to look at but not to touch. Their tentacles have small, stinging organisms that detach when brushed. Splash the affected area with alcohol but avoid rubbing it or you may activate detached stingers. Talcum powder and other drying agents—sand will work in a pinch—are useful for jellyfish encounters.

Avoid touching any live coral, for the organism's safety and for your own. All corals can be harmful, either by a slow-healing gash or toxins released on touch. Avoid even the smooth-looking coral. Fire corals and stinging corals do what their names suggest and clearly should be avoided. If you accidentally touch them, treat the sting with vinegar and seek treatment. If you want to touch underwater fauna, it's best to wear protective gloves. If you're not wearing fins, wear some sort of protective shoes. Likewise, breaking coral, kicking it with your fins, brushing it with your underwater camera, or other injurious behavior can traumatize the delicate ecological balance of the reef. Think before you act; even turning over seabed rocks might expose the home of a variety of small sea animals.

Snorkeling with a local who can point out reef life is both more rewarding and safer. Many hotels offer guides for snorkelers as well as divers.

For diving emergencies, there is a recompression chamber at the **St. Thomas Hospital** (tel. 809-776-2686). The U.S. Virgin Islands U.S. Coast Guard Auxiliary number is (809) 774-6663, (809) 729-6770 for 24-hour emergencies.

---

fishing Center (tel. 809-775-7990), **Virgin Islands Game Fishing Club** (tel. 809-775-9144), *Bluefin II* (Red Hook, tel. 809-775-6691), or **Fish Hawk II** (Charlotte Amalie, tel. 809-775-9058).

On Tortola, contact **Pelican Charters** (tel. 809-496-7386) at the Prospect Reef Resort in Road Town or **Miss Robbie Charters** (tel. 809-494-3193). On Anegada, where bonefish are the popular catch, contact **Anegada Reef Hotel** (tel. 809-495-8002).

Rates start at about $500 per half day to $900 per full day for a boat of five or so, with lunch and drinks included.

Diving and Snorkeling

If you're a certified diver, you probably don't need to be told that the Virgin Islands offer some of the world's most vibrant and spectacular underwater scenery. Reefs and wrecks, including the famous 1867 wreck of the royal mail steamer,

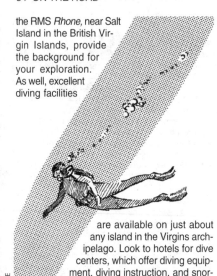

BOB RACE

the RMS *Rhone,* near Salt Island in the British Virgin Islands, provide the background for your exploration. As well, excellent diving facilities are available on just about any island in the Virgins archipelago. Look to hotels for dive centers, which offer diving equipment, diving instruction, and snorkeling equipment. Certified divers should bring their certification cards. Noncertified divers can receive PADI (Professional Association of Diving Instructors) beginner's training, a "resort course," which allows a supervised dive of about 40 feet (12 meters) and is a quick introduction to diving and the world below. If you're interested and have the time and money, more detailed certification is available from various dive centers for an average of $350, which generally includes daily dive fees, manuals, dive tables, a log book, and certification processing fees. Dives start at $25.

Snorkelers can have their pick of spots around the islands, and you can hardly turn a corner and not see snorkeling equipment for rent. Hotels, beach dive shops, and snorkeling cruises rent flippers, masks, and snorkels. Average cost for snorkel gear is about $5 per hour.

It's nearly impossible to say that, as far as snorkeling goes, you'd be hard pressed to find a bad spot in the Virgin Islands. Most water sports centers rent snorkeling gear for about $5 per hour, and you most often can just find a spot at any beach to observe coral formations and fish. Some highlights are **Magens Bay** and **Sapphire Beach** on St. Thomas, **Trunk Bay** and **Watermelon Bay** on St. John, **Buck Island** (officially Buck Island Reef National Monument)

off the north coast of St. Croix, **Smuggler's Cove** and **Marina Cay** on Tortola, and **The Baths** and **Bitter End** on Virgin Gorda.

For non-divers or snorkelers with a yen to stay down a bit longer and farther than snorkeling equipment allows, there's **Snuba,** a sort of cross between snorkeling and scuba diving. The deal is this: You wear masks and fins and are connected by a 20-foot (six-meter) breathing hose to a large, floating air tank above. This allows you to stay down and explore the shallower depths of the ocean floor and reef without lugging around all that diving equipment. Snuba is a St. John operation, tel. (809) 693-8063.

For names and numbers of diving and snorkeling outfits, see the U.S. Virgin Islands and British Virgin Islands chapters.

BICYCLING

Several of the U.S. and British Virgin Islands boast topography conducive to some fine, if vigorous, biking. In particular, St. Croix and St. John in the U.S. Virgins and Tortola and Virgin Gorda in the British Virgins offer rolling hills, brilliant scenery, and off-road trails for excursions. Unfortunately, you'll be a bit harder pressed to find rental companies. Your best bet is to contact your hotel activities desk to find out if the hotel rents bikes to guests (many do). Next, try water sports outfits. On St. John, **Cinnamon Bay Watersports** (tel. 809-776-6330) offers bikes for $10 per hour. The biking on St. John can be difficult at times due to the steep hills, but you'll find several pleasant off-road diversions to places like the Catherineberg Sugar Mill ruins off the Centerline Road, the Annaberg Sugar Mill ruins at Mary's Point, and numerous north shore beaches. As well, the relatively low-lying Coral Bay area is perfect for biking.

On St. Croix, contact **St. Croix Bike & Tours** (5035 Cotton Valley, Christiansted, St. Croix, U.S. Virgin Islands 00820; tel. 809-773-5004 or 809-772-2343). The small company offers bike rentals and guided bike tours of the island, including a northwest coast tour (easy, $35) and a Caledonia Rainforest tour (hard, $45). Tour prices include 21-speed mountain bikes and refreshments. You can also rent bikes and take off on your own for $15 half-day, $25 full day.

Biking on St. Thomas isn't recommended. The hills are steep with sharp curves and the road traffic is hideous just about anywhere on the island.

In the British Virgin Islands, you're sort of out of luck if you want to rent a bike. Several hotels offer bikes for their guests (Biras Creek on Virgin Gorda is one), but in general you'd be better off bringing your bike with you if you want to have that experience.

CAMPING

Camping is most popular on St. John, where you'll find two fine camping sites, one a Virgin Islands National Park camp at **Cinnamon Bay** (P.O. Box 720, Cruz Bay, St. John, U.S. Virgin Islands 00831, tel. 800-539-9998, 809-776-6458, or 809-693-5654, fax 809-776-6458) and the other the private, eco-friendly Maho Bay Camp and Harmony (17 A East 73rd St., New York, NY 10021, tel. 212-472-9453; or P.O. Box 310, Cruz Bay, St. John, U.S. Virgin Islands 00831, tel. 800-392-9004 or 809-776-6240, fax 809-776-6504). The camps offer accommodations ranging from bare sites to small tented bungalows set up on platforms. On St. Croix, the small, beachside campsite at **Cramer's Park** (tel. 809-773-9696) offers few facilities (bring your own tent, water, and food), but it's free. In the British Virgin Islands, your only bet is the small and quiet **Brewer's Bay Campground** (P.O. Box 185, Road Town, Tortola, British Virgin Islands; tel. 809-494-3463), located at Brewer's Bay on the north coast of Tortola.

In general, in the Virgin Islands you are not allowed to simply find a nice bit of beach and pitch a tent. Although this would clearly be romantic and all kinds of beguiling, the problems stem from security and your personal safety, along with private property issues.

GOLF

Duffers will be able to hook a few into the ocean and perhaps some more onto the green on St. Thomas at **Mahogany Run Golf Course** (tel. 809-775-5000 or, in the U.S., 800-253-7103), where President Clinton teed off during his winter

vacation in 1997. The course is an 18-hole, 6,022-yard (1,830-meter), par-70 course and is the pride and joy of the U.S. Virgin Islands. Greens fee is $75 for 18 holes or $40 for nine holes. Clubs and carts are also available for rent.

On St. Croix, golfers will find the **Carambola Golf Club** (tel. 809-778-5638) located at the Carambola Beach Resort on the island's northwest coast. Designed by Robert Trent Jones, the course is 18 holes, par 72, and 6,843 yards (2,080 meters). Greens fees are $77 with cart in the winter season ($43 after 2 p.m.), $48 off-season ($33 after 2 p.m.). A nine-hole course at **The Reef** (tel. 809-773-8844), on the island's east end, is 3,100 yards (942 meters). Fees are $14 for the nine holes, $22 for 18, and rental carts are also available. The nine-hole course at the **Buccaneer Hotel** (tel. 809-773-2100, ext. 738), just outside of Christiansted, sits on the ocean. Off-season, fees for non-guests are $12 for nine holes, $20 for 18; in season, it's $20 for nine holes, $35 for 18. Cart and club rentals are also available.

There are no golf courses on St. John.

In the British Virgin Islands, golfers are out of luck. There is a small "pitch 'n putt" course at the Prospect Reef Resort on Tortola, but chronic golfers will have to content themselves with reflecting wistfully upon the last game they played before they went on vacation. Not that it's impossible to play—a simple reservation and a day trip from the British Virgin Islands to St. Thomas to play at Mahogany Run is possible—and, with a bit of planning, practical.

HIKING

You'll find plenty of opportunities to hike about in the Virgin Islands, particularly on St. John. The National Park headquarters in Cruz Bay (open daily 8 a.m.-4:30 p.m., tel. 809-776-6201) has a pamphlet describing trails that meander to and through plantations ruins, open valleys, thorn bush mountainsides, semi-rainforests, and seaside beaches. The park lists 22 trails in all, constituting some 20 miles of walks. They range from easy (great for kids) to very difficult, from 15 minutes to more than two hours.

On St. Croix, the **St. Croix Environmental Association** (Gallows Bay, Christiansted, St.

Croix, U.S. Virgin Islands 00824; tel. 809-773-1989) offers guided tours of the island's unique environment. Tours include walks of the **East End Beaches, Caledonia Rainforest,** and the **Salt River National Historic Park.** The walks are rated from moderate to strenuous, and the association can advise you on what to wear and bring. The hikes are about three hours each and cost $20 per adult, $12 each for children 6-10.

On Tortola, **Sage Mountain National Park,** at the west end of the island, has three trails that ramble through the 92-acre park toward the peak. The **Henry Adams Loop Trail, Main Trail,** and the **Slippery Trail** are all easy to moderate walking paths. Plan on the better part of a day to hike around Mt. Sage, and bring provisions should you decide on a picnic lunch.

HORSEBACK RIDING

You know those photos you always see on Caribbean hotel brochures, the ones with severely precious couples riding horses along deserted beaches? Well, that could be you—but not in very many places in the Virgin Islands. First of all, the beaches are rarely deserted, but that's another story. Still, horseback riding is a great way to see parts of the island you wouldn't normally see from a car. You can find supervised riding on St. Croix at **Paul and Jill's Equestrian Stables** (tel. 809-772-2627 or 809-772-2880). The stables are located at Spratt Hall, near the Spratt Hall beach north of Frederiksted. On Tortola, horseback tours are offered by **Shadow's Stable** (tel. 809-494-2262) or **Ellis Thomas** (tel. 809-494-4442).

Guided horseback tours can run from two hours to as much as the better part of a day and cost about $25-30 per person per hour.

TENNIS

The larger and even medium-size hotels often have several courts, many lighted for night play, for use by guests or, for a small fee (generally $5-10 per hour), by non-guests. On St. Thomas, two public courts are available on a first-come, first-served basis at the U.S. Sub Base just west

of Frenchtown near Charlotte Amalie. Lights stay on until 8 p.m. Non-guests can swing the racket at the **Sapphire Beach** (tel. 809-775-6100), **Renaissance Grand** (tel. 809-775-1510), and **Wyndham Sugar Bay** (tel. 809-777-7100) resorts, all located on the east side of St. Thomas. Lessons are also available for $35-45 per hour.

On St. Croix, you'll find four free public courts at the **D.C. Canegata Ball Park,** near Christiansted, and two at the **Fort Frederik Park,** behind Fort Frederik in Frederiksted. Non-guests can play at a number of island hotels, including the **Buccaneer** (tel. 809-773-2199, ext. 736), the **Carambola Golf Club** (tel. 809-778-5636), and the **Chenay Bay Beach Resort** (tel. 809-773-2918).

In the British Virgin Islands, you're pretty well limited to hotels for tennis. **Prospect Reef Resort** (tel. 809-494-3311) near Road Town has six courts (two lighted for night use) and charges a small fee for use.

GREEN TRAVEL

In some ways the Virgin Islands look much the same as they did when Columbus happened upon them during his late-15th-century voyages. In other ways, however, the face of the Virgin Islands has changed a great deal since the early days of Amerindian Arawak and Carib settlement. Since the post-Columbian arrival of Spanish colonials, forays into wide-scale agriculture, forestry, light and heavy industry, and even tourism have altered the landscape. Large semitropical rainforests have disappeared; land has been claimed by development; the sea coast has been altered by large reclamation projects—man-made land extensions jutting into the sea—that provide docking space for large ships; and numerous plants and animal species have been introduced by the islands' various settlers. There are few places on any island in the Virgins archipelago that have not been touched by the hand of the human species. This is perhaps more true on an island such as the U.S. Virgins' St. Thomas than on, say, the British Virgins' Anegada, but the pattern is unmistakable—as populations grow and tourism increases, the islands are slowly but surely com-

GREEN TOUR OPERATORS

On St. John and St. Croix, well-informed park rangers offer guided natural history tours and hikes. Other private specialty groups throughout the Virgins exist for birdwatching, biking, hiking, diving, whalewatching, and historical awareness tours and are discussed in the specific destination chapters. The following organizations offer specialized tours to the Virgin Islands and throughout the Caribbean and, though they are not locally owned, are quite sensitive to the needs of the area. Packages may or may not include flights but almost always include lodging or meals and, of course, tour activities. Some are all-inclusive.

American Wilderness Experience (2820-A Wilderness Place, Boulder, CO 80301-5454; tel. 800-444-0099; Web site http://www.gorp.com/awe) offers adventure tours of the Virgin Islands aboard small, shared-sailing yachts or their larger schooner, the *Roseway*. These tours concentrate more on the sailing and available snorkeling and diving experiences than on eco-touring but are known to be responsible.

EarthCorps, the field wing of the nonprofit Earthwatch organization, sends volunteers (no skills necessary) on two-week scientific and conservation projects throughout the world. Past excursions have included helping endangered sea turtles in the U.S. Virgin Islands. You pay for your travel, food, and lodging. Contact Earthwatch at 680 Mt. Auburn St., Box 403, Watertown, MA 02172; tel. (800)

776-0188 or (617) 926-8200, fax (617) 926-8532; Internet address: info@earthwatch.org

Massachusetts Audubon Society (208 S. Great Rd., Lincoln, MA 01773; tel. 800-289-9504 or 617-259-9500, fax 617-259-8899) offers natural history trips, accompanied by field experts. Destinations change every year.

The Nature Conservancy (1815 N. Lynn St., Arlington, VA 22209; tel. 703-841-5300, fax 703-841-4880), a nonprofit organization, sponsors natural history tours worldwide, with in-country naturalists on board. Past trips have included U.S. Virgin Islands cruises and work trips aimed at creating a conservation education center at the site of an 18th-century sugar estate on St. Croix.

Smithsonian Study Tours and Seminars arranges work and study tours worldwide and has in the past included natural history tours in the Caribbean. Tours are led by in-country experts. To be eligible for study tours, you must join the Smithsonian Institution as a member; cost is $22 for a one-year membership. Contact the Smithsonian Associates at Dept. 0049, Washington, D.C. 20073-0049; tel. (202) 357-4700, fax (202) 633-9250.

Unique Destinations (307 Peaceable St., Ridgefield, CT 06877; tel. and fax 203-431-1571) specializes in hiking, biking, diving, kayaking, and historical/cultural and other customized tours and unique accommodations.

---

ing to the realization that conservation of their natural resources is a priority.

During the latter part of this century, the importance of monitoring the world's burgeoning populations and their demands on our natural resources became clear. Thousands of rivers and lakes and entire sections of oceans have been polluted to varying degrees; the air we breathe in our cities has been turned to a sort of sludge; the world's soil and forest reserves have been taxed to what many consider their limits. Whatever your belief regarding the severity of the problems, this much is true: we have rearranged our way of thinking about how we live on this planet. While conservation groups and societies dedicated to natural preservation have existed for centuries, more recent concerns have spawned

highly organized movements (Greenpeace, World Wildlife Fund), political parties (the Greens of Germany), and other groups dedicated to the somewhat loosely defined cause of saving the earth.

Never willing to miss opportunities, the tourism industry has jumped on the bandwagon and introduced an equally loosely defined offshoot industry called "eco-tourism," "eco-travel," or "nature travel."

No doubt, the awareness generated by an ecology-minded travel industry has benefited the preservation of delicate natural resources. We now know that unbridled development of any tourist or recreational facility, be it a megaresort complex or a miniature golf course, can have a deleterious effect on the environment.

We now know that wherever tourists go, whether in great numbers or small, they will affect the environment in some way. And we know that local cultures can be most affected by human activity.

We also know that tourism is a major factor in the world economy in general, and in the Virgin Islands economies in particular. It is clearly here to stay. Tourism is, in fact, partially responsible for the revenue needed to preserve a great many natural resources. The massive national park of St. John, for instance, and other Virgin Islands parks and preserves, are funded in part by admission fees. It appears that a healthy and mutually beneficial relationship between tourism and conservation is possible.

Yet problems exist with eco-tourism, and the problems often involve the word, not the concept. Eco-tourism, for some unscrupulous or merely uninformed tour operators, has become simply an advertising gimmick. A wide range of activities, including tours, forest excursions, and even basic camping, are now touted as eco-tourism activities—simply because they take place outdoors. Such thinking is unfortunately not uncommon and does no good to clear the muddied waters of the eco-tourism industry.

However, there are certainly legitimate opportunities to hook up with responsible ecology- and nature-oriented tours. But since the industry has spawned large lists of eco-travel operations, some research is in order.

What is Eco-Tourism?

A simplified definition might be this: it is any activity that emphasizes and respects the ecological and human cultural aspects of an environment, seeking to leave the ecosystems and cultures unaltered by the presence or acts of visitors to that environment.

Whatever you choose to call it—responsible travel, eco-travel, green travel, or even simply good travel—it need not be the domain of niche tour companies and specialized travel outfits. Good travel probably starts with personal choice. It is a personal choice to try to leave untainted the natural resources and local cultures of any place you visit. This includes being aware of your attitudes and behavior and having some prior knowledge of the balances that need to be maintained in the area.

For instance, the Virgin Islands, as well as many countries throughout the Caribbean, enforce bans on the consumption of green, leatherback, and hawksbill sea turtles, which are designated as either threatened or endangered. Still, confusingly, some restaurants may offer turtle meat on the menus. You can help by not buying it. Several countries disallow the sale of spiny lobsters during their reproductive season, roughly April through June. In the U.S. Virgin Islands, fishermen are not allowed to take spiny lobsters with eggs. Any coral—alive or dead—accidentally broken or deliberately removed from the reef will upset the delicate ecological balance of the life-sustaining reef and thus disturb the food chain. Still, many vendors sell coral jewelry, particularly the highly desirable black coral. Again, the decision to buy or not buy is yours. Whelks should only be taken 1 October through 13 March.

Even seemingly innocuous behavior can directly affect the environment. Riding motorcycles or dune vehicles on a beach can compact sand and therefore contribute to beach erosion. The popular jet skis offered for rent at many resorts cause what many call "noise pollution" and are, principally, annoying.

On the cultural front, you will soon note that the people of the Virgin Islands, in particular the British Virgin Islands, are often conservative in dress, contrary to brochure and popular poster imagery. For both men and women, bathing suits, short shorts, and other revealing clothing are fine for the beach or pool but not in town. You'll also note that nude and topless sunbathing are not publicly practiced in either the U.S. or British Virgin Islands. You will offend sensibilities by not heeding local custom.

Virgin Islanders may object to having their photographs taken without permission. This is true on many of the Caribbean islands, where the indigenous cultures have been poked, prodded, photographed, and displayed in everything from serious scientific magazines to, yes, travel publications. It is always best to ask first. In cases, people may ask you to pay to photograph them—an unfortunate by-product of the times and of tourism. But if the photo means that much to you, pay up.

You can obtain lists of endangered island plant and animal species at information centers in national parks, preserves, and regional tourism offices. They offer the dos and don'ts of behavior regarding use of natural resources, and it is in everyone's interest to follow the rules.

Locally based tour groups offer the best eco-tours, for the obvious reason that their operators are often native and thoroughly familiar with the environment—not to mention that your dollars stay in the local economy instead of supporting some offshore operator. The destination chapters in this book will cover those domestic operators, but the following groups and publications discuss further the issues and concepts of "green tourism" and are worth researching before you depart.

Center for Responsible Tourism is a nonprofit organization dedicated to creating cultural and environmental awareness among travelers, journalists, and those working overseas. The center's take on responsible travel involves codes of ethics for travelers, particularly regarding meeting and learning about host cultures. It also publishes information about responsible cruising. Did you know that many North American cruise ships are registered in Panama or Liberia in order to circumvent U.S. laws regarding seaworthiness, safety of crews, and vessel safety regulations? There's more. Contact the center at P.O. Box 827, San Anselmo, CA 94979; tel. (415) 258-6594, fax (415) 454-2493. Send a self-addressed, stamped envelope.

Directory of Alternative Travel Resources, by Dianne Brause, covers a wide range of adventure and eco-oriented tours and travel possibilities. Cost is about $9. Contact Lost Valley Educational Center, 81868 Lost Valley Lane, Dexter, OR 97431.

The Green Travel Sourcebook: A Guide for the Physically Active, the Intellectually Curious, or the Socially Aware (New York: John Wiley & Sons), by Daniel and Sally Wiener Grotta, is a valuable resource for eco-minded tour and travel opportunities and discusses eco-travel both philosophically and practically. Ask your local bookseller if it's available.

Specialty Travel Index is a U.S.-based magazine that comes out twice a year and lists more than 600 tour operators and outfitters that cater to interests ranging from biking and hiking to diving and archaeology. Entries are thoroughly cross-referenced by geographical region, personal interests, activities offered, and more. This is an important publication for focused travelers. Cost is $6 per copy, $10 for a subscription ($13 in Canada). Contact the magazine at 305 San Anselmo Ave., San Anselmo, CA 94960; tel. (415) 459-4900 or 455-1643, fax (415) 459-4974. You can also contact the staff via e-mail at spectrav@ix.netcom.com, or visit their World Wide Web site at http://www.spectrav.com.

ACCOMMODATIONS

In both the U.S. and British Virgin Islands, a broad range of accommodations is available for all budgets and tastes. You'll find luxury and medium-priced hotels, bed and breakfast inns, guesthouses, camping grounds, and apartments or villas in various price ranges. In fact, some hotels in the Virgins carry so many rates—based on seasons, discounts, and packages—that it can be frustrating to try to determine the best deals. Here are some tips:

Seasons
The busy tourist season in the Virgin Islands lasts, not surprisingly, from mid-December through mid-April (often 15 December through 14 April), roughly the equivalent of the Northern Hemisphere's winter. The summer is off-

season and, as such, priced accordingly. You can count on room rates being lower then, in cases as much as 40% less. During the summer, many small hotels are short of guests, and substantial rate reductions can often be negotiated no matter what your length of stay. Talk directly to the manager or owner. As well, you'll have the added luxury of traveling in uncrowded areas. Some hotels retain the same rate year-round, and others maintain three or more different rates that include "shoulder" seasons—late spring and early fall. Shoulder season rates generally fall between summer and winter rates.

Accommodation Discounts
Many hotels do not fill up, even during the high season. Rather than letting rooms sit empty,

with no money earned, hotels may shift a certain percentage of their business to hotel wholesalers at bulk rates. Wholesalers in turn offer these accommodations to the public at significant discounts. One such wholesaler is the U.S.-based **The Room Exchange**, tel. (800) 846-7000, fax (212) 760-1013. The Room Exchange represents hotels in some 600 locales throughout the world, including the Virgin Islands. Some rooms may be available for as much as 25% off in the high season and up to 50% off in the low season.

A rule of thumb in searching for discounts: it is not *always* best to rely on travel agents; your own research and telephone work will often be rewarded. Avoid calling the toll-free numbers for hotels—you'll often be hooked up to an operator in, say, Des Moines who will not be authorized to offer discounts. Further, toll-free operators in Des Moines may never have been to the hotel in the first place and won't be able to describe its facilities in any more detail than is offered in the hotel brochure. (Sometimes, however—particularly in the U.S. Virgin Islands—the toll-free number is connected directly to the on-island hotel.) In most cases, it is best to first call the hotel or guesthouse directly and ask if it's offering any deals, discounts, or packages. If not, suggest one yourself.

DISCOUNT PACKAGES

A wide range of discount plans is available at hotels and resorts, including package tours sponsored in conjunction with airlines, honeymoon packages, marriage packages, golf packages, scuba diving packages, etc. Most discount packages include ground transfers, inexpensive hotel arrangements (although the hotel might not be the best in its class), and features relating to the theme of the trip (champagne and flowers for honeymooners, discounted greens fees, several "free" dive excursions). When reading brochures and information regarding these packages, note the fine print. Some are offered contingent on midweek travel, Saturday-to-Saturday (or pick the day) stays, or travel during the off-season. Prices are often listed *per person based on double occupancy,* and the single rate, if it exists, may be more than half of the double occupancy rate.

Meal Plans

Of all plans, however, the most common are meal plans. In hotel literature, "EP" means European Plan, which indicates that the rate is for the room only, with no meals offered. "CP" indicates that a continental breakfast is provided. "AP" is American Plan, in which three full meals are offered. This ought to be at least vaguely disturbing to Americans, but probably is not. "MAP" means Modified American Plan and indicates that the hotel will offer two meals, usually breakfast and either lunch or dinner. All these meal plans are offered throughout the Virgin Islands.

All-Inclusive Plans

"All-inclusive" resorts are not yet popular in the Virgin Islands, but several do exist. All-inclusives—a concept pioneered in Jamaica—are just what they say they are: resorts that offer the room, all meals, amenities, tips, and extras for one price. The advantage for many is the simplicity of the exchange. You needn't bother with tipping, arguing over who pays for dinner, or loose change sitting in your shoes on the beach.

The disadvantage is the attitude. There is hardly any incentive to leave the resort for any reason. Meals are prepaid, which means there is no reason to experience local cuisine outside the confines of the resort. The same applies to other activities. The choice to go out and explore, to experience the country, becomes more difficult, and, ultimately, less cost-effective.

Still, all-inclusive resorts can offer financially advantageous packages, particularly when coupled with airfare and transfers, and, for a great many vacationers, are a satisfying experience.

CAMPING

St. John, of the U.S. Virgin Islands, features exceptional campgrounds at Cinnamon Bay—a national park facility—and at Maho Bay and Coral Bay, both private facilities. On St. Croix, a small but nifty campground on the beach at the east end's Cramer Park Bay features few facilities but great get-away-from-it-all appeal. In the British Virgin Islands, you'll find fine campgrounds at Brewer's Bay on Tortola and at a couple of truly isolated spots on the equally isolated island of Anegada. Several small guesthouses also allow camping on their grounds. These campgrounds may provide permanent tent-like structures on platforms, small cabins, or bare spots for setting up tents (your own or one rented from the facility). Prices range from next to nothing to as much as $100 per night in high season for well-equipped platform tents (wood floors, kitchenettes with propane stoves and utensils, furniture, porches, electricity, and wide screens to let in the ocean breezes).

Neither the U.S. nor the British Virgin Islands allow camping outside of approved facilities. That is, you won't be able simply to find a spot on the beach and pitch your tent. This has as much to do with personal safety as with the lack of bathing and toilet facilities.

Camping supplies can be found in specialty stores, such as Wade Enterprises (tel. 809-774-3323) in Charlotte Amalie on St. Thomas, or in chain department stores such as Kmart on St. Thomas and St. Croix. In the British Virgin Islands, camping supplies are limited; try Bolo's Department Store (tel. 809-494-2867) or Pusser's Company Store (tel. 809-495-4599), both in Road Town on Tortola. It's best to bring your own equipment if you're planning on camping—renting camping equipment is not a viable option except from certain campgrounds. (See the destination chapters for campground information.)

VILLA, APARTMENT, AND CONDO RENTALS

Villa or condo rentals are a good bet for families or groups who want a greater degree of autonomy than resorts might offer, and who want to save money to boot. You can cook, eat, see the sights, and sleep at your leisure. Most come equipped with cooks and household help, which gives you the chance to relax a bit and let someone else do the work should that be your choice. For a large group, a villa can be cost effective. The accommodations vary wildly, from apartments and large complexes to near-mansions and even entire private islands. Rates vary according to size, amenities offered, and location. Cost can be as little as $300 per week for a small apartment to as much as $12,000 per week for a luxe villa in the high season. And, if

you've got an extra $11,000 per day (and who doesn't?), you can occupy the luxury villa and all the rest of **Necker Island,** off the coast of Virgin Gorda. Of course, food is included.

Hundreds of companies and private individuals market their villas through publications such as *Caribbean Travel and Life, Islands, Travel and Leisure,* and the U.K.-based *Caribbean World,* as well as other magazines, all available at most magazine stands. Major newspapers, particularly in their Sunday travel sections, list dozens of Caribbean villa rental possibilities. For a start, try these resources:

All About Condos, The Anchorage, 6600 Estate Nazareth #2, St. Thomas, U.S. Virgin Islands 00802, tel. (809) 775-7740, fax (809) 775-9631

At Home Abroad, 405 E. 56th St., Suite 6H, New York, NY 10022, tel. (212) 421-9165

Caribbean Destinations, tel. (800) 888-0987 or (504) 834-7026

Caribbean Escapes, P.O. Box 550, New York, NY 10018, tel. (718) 282-2909, fax (718) 469-4822

Leisuretime Destinations, 905 E. Martin Luther King Dr., Suite 600, Tarpon Springs, FL 34689, tel. (800) 704-2233

Property Management Plus, 5915 Aiken Rd., Louisville, KY 40245, tel. (502) 722-5751, fax (502) 722-8932

Villa Leisure, P.O. Box 209, Westport, CT 06881, tel. (800) 526-4244 or (407) 624-9000

Villas and Apartments Abroad, 420 Madison Ave., Suite 1105, New York, NY 10017, tel. (212) 759-1025

Villas Caribe, 9403 E. Chenango Rd., Englewood, CO 80111, tel. (800) 645-7498, fax (303) 741-2520

Villas International, 605 Market St., Suite 510, San Francisco, CA 94105, tel. (800) 221-2260 or (415) 281-0910

Villas of Distinction, P.O. Box 55, Armonk, NY 10504, tel. (800) 289-0900 or (914) 273-3331, fax (914) 273-3387

West Indies Management Company (WIMCO), P.O. Box 1461, Newport, RI 02840, tel. (800) 932-3222 or (401) 849-8012, fax (401) 847-6290, U.K. tel. (800) 89-8318.

Those hooked into the Internet can visit several Web sites to view and gather information on hundreds of Caribbean villas. One such site is **Resorts and Villas of the Caribbean** at http://www.infi.net/~slm/. The company also offers CD-ROMs (Windows, $29.95) that contain villa photos and information. We haven't seen the CD-ROM and cannot vouch for it, but you can call (804) 784-2693 for information.

ROOM TAXES AND SERVICE CHARGES

You won't encounter sales taxes in the U.S. or British Virgin Islands, but local room taxes will be added to hotel bills. In the U.S. Virgin Islands this tax is added to basic room rates but not meals and extras, and is currently eight percent. Room taxes are applied to villas, apartments, and condos as well, provided the stay is less than 90 days. In the British Virgin Islands, the room tax for hotels, guesthouses, condos, villas, and the like is seven percent. Bare spots in campgrounds—those on which you pitch your own tent—usually don't incur the room tax, though a platform setup would. When booking your hotel, check to see if the room tax is included in the quoted rate or will be added later.

An additional charge you might see on a hotel bill is a 10-15% service charge, which is meant to be a tip for services rendered at the hotel. Ostensibly, this tip is divided among the hotel staff, but if you feel like giving your chambermaid or porter something more, do so. Again, when booking your hotel, check to see if the service charge is included in the rate or is added later.

Most hotels and restaurants in the Virgin Islands gladly accept major North American and European credit cards. American Express, MasterCard, and Visa are most common, and Discover Card is gaining acceptance. Diners Club is still used, though less frequently than during its heyday some years ago. Smaller hotels will accept traveler's checks, but for many small guesthouses throughout the region you will have to pay cash.

FOOD AND DRINK

Your stay in the Virgin Islands will not suffer from a lack of wonderful new things to eat and will certainly be enhanced by trying the local cuisines. You may find that sampling local savories becomes an end in itself. The combination of imported ingredients coupled with West Indian spices, fruits, vegetables, meats, and, of course, seafood, creates an exotic Creole mix. The end result is one of the most tangible cultural exports from the Caribbean (one can find West Indian restaurants and food items in many of the major cities of the world). Into which dark and smoky lounge in the Western world would you walk and not find a daiquiri? Or a piña colada? These rum-based drinks were invented in Cuba and Puerto Rico, respectively.

Virgin Islands cuisine embraces a variety of imports, including imported native West Indian foodstuffs. The islands themselves, due to their poor soil, grow little in the way of vegetables or fruits. Imports come from other Caribbean islands and from Central and North America and can always be found in the busy outdoor markets.

Fruits and Vegetables

Bananas and their starchy cousin, the plantain—both carried by the Spaniards westward from the Canary Islands—are today island dietary staples. Sugarcane and pineapples were also introduced by the Spanish and are part of island folklore as well as diet (sugarcane provides the basic ingredient of rum). Exotic fruits such as the sugar apple, *ginnep* (a plum-like fruit with a large seed), soursop, sweetsop, papaya, and mango are sometimes locally grown, sometimes imported.

African slaves brought with them the literal seeds of future vegetable and fruit crops. Okra, several types of yams, the ackee, and pigeon peas are all African imports. Pigeon peas (also called red peas or gungo peas) play an enormous part in the West Indian diet. When combined with rice, the dish is a staple and side dish in most homes and Creole restaurants. It's often called rice and beans or rice and peas.

Meats

Meat dishes, such as goat water (goat stew), bullfoot soup (tripe and dumplings), mutton stew, pork, and curries, are Virgin Islands favorites, as is the East Indian roti, a thin, pan-baked piece of unleavened bread wrapped around curried meats or vegetables. Pepperpot stew may originally have been an Arawak dish; its base is a meat stock with added spices, vegetables, and the leafy stalk of the eddoe (or *dasheen*) plant. Souse (sowse), often served on holidays or during festivities, is a stew made from the head, tail, and feet of a pig, doused with lime juice. It tastes better than it sounds. A pate (PAHT-tay), a favorite of fast-food joints and roadside vendors, is a flaky pastry filled with spicy meat or fish, often saltfish—the reconstituted version of dried and salted fish fillets. Roadside vendors also serve up the ubiquitous johnny cake, a diet-busting (and therefore tasty like you wouldn't believe) sweetened and fried dough.

Fungi (FOON-ghee), a savory cornmeal paste, is a staple side dish in the U.S. Virgin Islands. Kallaloo has come to mean a spicy gumbo of okra and other vegetables, seafood, and doses of hot pepper.

Seafood

Seafood dishes are, not surprisingly, specialties throughout the Virgin Islands. Large game fish such as mahi mahi, marlin, and tuna are common, as are the smaller yet no less tasty grouper and red snapper. Coconut cream—called "run-down" or some variations thereof—is a favorite sauce on fish. Other sea animals find themselves on Virgin Islands plates no less frequently than fish. Conch (konk) may be grilled, deep-fried to make fritters, or steeped in chowder. Boiled crabs, stuffed crabs, whelks, and even sea urchins, which produce a heavy and gritty sort of meat, are favorite snacks. Lobster—the clawless variety known as the spiny lobster—and shrimp are served simply grilled with butter and garlic.

Spices

Spices perhaps distinguish Virgin Islands cuisine more than anything else. Red pepper, hot sauces, and curries are frequently featured either in the recipe or as a condiment along with the salt and pepper. Common seasonings include ginger, nutmeg, and pimento (called allspice elsewhere), a spice from the fruit of the pi-

LOBSTERS

For those coming from North America, your lobster encounters in the Lesser Antilles will be slightly different from those at home. The lobster you'll see steaming in a puddle of garlic butter or slow-roasting over an open grill will be . . . well, missing something.

Warm-water lobsters—various species are called Florida spiny lobsters, rock lobsters, and slipper lobsters—resemble in most ways the crustacean North Americans have come to know as crayfish. But crayfish they are not; crayfish, which are in fact related to lobsters, are freshwater animals. The spiny lobsters of the Virgin Islands are saltwater creatures. And while North American lobsters are distinguished by their fat front-end pincers or claws—also known as chelae—spiny lobsters are missing those appendages.

Lobster is a common name for the marine decapod (meaning it has five pairs of "legs" on the thorax, or upper body) crustaceans of the suborder Reptantia. The spiny lobster of the Virgin Islands has the fanlike tail and sci-fi antennae you have come to know and expect on a lobster, and, like its northern cousin, is a scavenger of the seas. The female lays eggs about every two years, and lobsters live an average 15-20 years.

Several countries in the Caribbean impose restrictions on catching (usually by pots or by spear-fishing) and consuming spiny lobsters during their reproduction season, April-June. In the U.S. Virgin Islands, spiny lobsters may be captured only by hand or snare, not by spear-fishing, and females with eggs are protected.

mento tree, which tastes of the essentials of cinnamon, clove, nutmeg, and pepper.

Restaurants

Restaurants featuring international cuisine exist throughout the Virgin Islands. This is more the case on the heavily populated islands of St. Thomas and St. Croix than on St. John or the British Virgin Islands. Still, you won't want for fine dining. You'll find Chinese, East Indian, German, Italian, French, and other exotic foods. The language of pizzas is universal. On several islands, local fast-food restaurants serve fried

RUM

Pirates swilled it, slaves distilled it, planters knocked it back with a dash of lime and sugar, and it émerged as one of the West Indies' most enduring icons. It's rum, and it tastes better here than anywhere else in the world.

Rum is, without a doubt, *the* drink of the Virgin Islands. It's served everywhere and anyhow—with fruity, frothy accoutrements in the glitzy tourist resorts, with a cool splash of water in the smoky back-street rum shops of the towns, and every way in between. It's sprinkled in herbalist ceremonies and offered as a gift for redemption in the religious ceremonies of underground sects. And it is, behind calypso and sunburn, the region's most successful export.

The origins of the word are uncertain. Some believe "rum" is derived from the botanical name of sugarcane, *saccharum officinarum,* from which rum is produced. Others believe the word originated among the planters of Barbados, where it reputedly was called "rumbullion," for the escapades it induced.

During Columbus's third voyage of discovery to the West Indies, he planted sugarcane on the island of Hispaniola. The Spanish colonists soon found that a sweet liquor could be made by distilling the heavy residue, molasses, from cane processing. Sailors and buccaneers soon discovered the drink. Cheap to produce and easy to transport, it became identified with life on the seas, as in "yo ho ho and a bottle of rum."

In the 1600s, Europeans began to make excursions into the West Indies, and sugarcane production on massive plantations became a way of life. Rum was produced on a large scale in Barbados and was first produced commercially in Jamaica. It later came to the U.S. Virgin Islands' St. Thomas and St. John and on, a large scale, to St. Croix. In its day, Tortola hosted large sugarcane plantations, but not on the scale that was seen in the larger islands.

Rum was initially considered a drink of ruffians and the lower class and did not gain wide acceptance as proper drink in polite European society for centuries. It wasn't until the early 20th century that rum came into its own as a cocktail ingredient.

The original distilling process is still the basis of rum production today. Pressed, sugarcane produces cane juice, from which both sugar and by-products such as molasses emerge. Water is then added to the molasses to reduce the sugar content, and the mixture is pasteurized. Yeast is added to the molasses mix, and the fermentation produces alcohol. The alcohol in turn kills the yeast, and the result is called "dead wash," which is then distilled to produce rum.

Traditionally, rum was aged in oak casks. The casks produced both the colors and flavor of the various rums you see on the market, although caramel is often added to produce the darkest shades. Today's rum is still aged, for about three years, but often in vats. Premiums rums are aged for as long as 20 years.

For a look at this fascinating age-old process, take a trip to the **Callwood Distillery** at Cane Garden Bay on Tortola, where rum is distilled from pure cane juice.

Rums run the gamut from smooth amber to dark, nearly black varieties, the richest in flavor. Each island produces its own rum, some for local consumption, some for export. The famous Cruzan brand rums of St. Croix are considered by aficionados to be among the best of the region. Export rums are also produced in neighboring islands and, notably, Puerto Rico, which exports the world's most widely consumed rum, Bacardi.

The Virgin Islands' famous "overproof" rums, both white and dark, are the strongest of the lot—you've been warned. The 151-proof rums will put the heartiest of imbibers under the table in a New York minute.

Rum drinks are very popular in the tropics, as much for their attendant fruit mixes and foamy daiquiri-style additions as for the rum itself. One of the oldest mixed rum punches originated during the plantation heydays. Its recipe, in this order, was simple: sour, sweet, strong, and weak. Translation: One part sour, or lime juice; two parts sweet, or sugar; three parts strong, or rum; and four parts weak, or water or fruit juice.

---

chicken, hamburgers, and meat pates. Several American fast-food chains have found their way to the U.S. Virgin Islands and are sometimes, perhaps ironically, favorites of locals. Among them are KFC, Wendy's, Pizza Hut, Domino's, Subway, and McDonald's.

The restaurants of the region run the entire gamut, price- and ambience-wise, from roadside stands to four-star extravaganzas. Stands serve anything from hot dogs and pates to deep-fried fish, and the quality can be good. Luxury restaurants offer superb settings and presentations—and that is what you pay for. The food is also superb, even though it appears that "nouvelle" is French for "light sauces, small portions, too much money." Good deals are the smaller, medium-priced restaurants and cafes that serve authentic Creole and continental cuisine.

Herbal and Local Drinks

Virgin Islands beverages are a treat—and a surprise. The native *mauby* (sometimes rhymes with "Toby"), made from the bark of a tree and mixed with herbs, tastes a bit like sarsaparilla's wayward cousin. Still, it is said to be healthful for pregnant women and especially helpful for men who are having stamina problems. We can safely say that *mauby* is an acquired taste. Much the same can be said about sea moss (also called Irish moss), a drink made from gelatin extracted from seaweed. The gelatin is sweetened and combined with milk or ginger as a restorative tonic, particularly in matters, again (listen up, guys), of sexual potency. Coconut water, the clear, potassium-rich liquid from the center of a green nut, is found in every market throughout the islands. Coconuts are inexpensive, germ-free, and fun to drink. Coconut water is not to be confused with coconut cream or coconut milk, which is derived from the meat of the nut.

Virgin Islanders, like many people with strong connections to their past, practice herbal medicine. Teas are often brewed to cure a variety of ills. Mango tea is said to help arthritis, soursop tea aids in sleep, love bush tea lowers blood pressure, and guava tea helps to calm coughing. These teas are sold today in many of the shops around the islands.

Alcohol

All sorts of alcoholic drinks are available in the resorts and pubs of the Virgin Islands, many of them oddly colored and bristling with those tiny umbrellas that get stuck in your nose. Two beverages are universally available: beer and rum. Several brands of beer are imported from the U.S. (Budweiser, Miller) and from other islands. Most anywhere you'll find Carib and Red Stripe, which is brewed in Jamaica.

However, the true beverage of the islands is rum—in fact, much of the world's rum is produced in the Caribbean. The drink, which is made from sugarcane, originated in Barbados and was first called "rumbullion," presumably for the shenanigans to which it gave rise. Today's rums are varieties of dark, amber, white (overproof—deceptively strong), and spiced. The Cruzan brands of St. Croix are considered to be among the world's best. Other islands, notably Tortola in the British Virgin Islands, are home to small, local rum distilleries.

GETTING THERE

Getting to the Virgin Islands is easier than you might think. Flying is definitely the way to do it. Several North American and European airlines operate regular routes to the major islands of St. Thomas, St. Croix, and Tortola. Keep in mind that airline routes may change with seasons, and some—Northwest Airlines for example—operate Caribbean routes only during the busy high season.

Getting around and between the U.S. and British Virgin Islands is also quite easy. Ferries run regularly between the small and large islands and are often the fastest and least expensive way to travel. Small commercial aircraft also ply the airways among many of the

larger Virgins (St. Thomas, St. Croix, Tortola, Virgin Gorda, Anegada), although that will always entail getting yourself to an airport. Several of the smaller islands, such as St. John and Jost Van Dyke, do not have commercial airstrips and rely instead on private boat and ferry transport.

IMMIGRATION AND CUSTOMS

U.S. Virgin Islands Immigration

U.S. and Canadian citizens should carry proof of identification to enter the islands and will be required to prove citizenship when returning to the mainland. A passport is not required for U.S. citizens, but, let's be frank. Rather than fumbling with the alternatives—birth certificates, drivers' licenses, voter-registration cards, and the like—it is always best to carry a valid passport when traveling *anywhere* outside the mainland. You will be tempted to visit the British Virgin Islands or other Caribbean islands while in the region, and all constitute foreign soil. A valid passport is not required for American citizens to enter the British Virgin Islands but will make entry easier.

Europeans and others generally need a valid passport and visa, the same documentation they would need to enter the mainland, to enter the U.S. Virgin Islands. U.S. entry regulations differ for various countries, so those citizens should check into U.S. visa regulations for their country.

U.S. Virgin Islands Customs

The U.S. Virgin Islands is a shopper's mecca, and customs regulations make it more so. U.S. citizens may bring back with them $1,200 worth of dutiable items purchased in the U.S. Virgin Islands every 30 days. The amount can be expanded for families who live in one household traveling together, so that each family member gets the $1,200 exemption. In other words, a family of five would be able to take home $6,000 worth of goods every 30 days. After the first $1,200, a flat rate of five percent is levied on the next $1,000 worth of goods. Variable rates are levied on items exceeding the first $2,200. Items of island origin, such as original art, crafts, certain foodstuffs, and unset precious gems, are exempt from regulation, but you need to retain and possibly produce sales receipts and certificates of origin for items costing more than $25. Residents 21 and over may take five fifths of liquor home—plus a sixth if it is of U.S. Virgin Islands origin (Cruzan Rum, Chococo, Southern Comfort, and others)—as well as five cartons of cigarettes and 100 cigars.

In addition to the personal exemptions, Americans may *send* $100 worth of goods as unsolicited gifts each day to a friend (you can't send goods to yourself).

When leaving the islands for home, you can, if you have a direct flight to the mainland, clear customs in St. Thomas. If you fly via San Juan, as many do, you'll clear customs there.

Citizens of other countries, upon returning home, will encounter their country's customs policies. Given the vast number of nations in the world, individual policies are too complicated to detail here. However, they will almost always involve the amount of time spent in the islands, the items purchased there, and specifics regarding fruit, animal, and other agricultural products.

British Virgin Islands Immigration

U.S. and Canadian citizens entering the British Virgin Islands will need clear proof of identity, such as a raised-seal birth certificate or voter-registration card, plus a photo ID. Again, a passport is always the better alternative. Travelers from other countries may have to produce a valid passport and visa. A quick check with local authorities or with British Virgin Islands immigration officials will confirm regulations. For all, the approved length of visit is six months, and onward tickets must be produced. Inquiries may be addressed to the Chief Immigration Officer, Government of the British Virgin Islands, Road Town, Tortola, British Virgin Islands, tel. (809) 494-3701, ext. 4961.

British Virgin Islands Customs

The British Virgin Islands is not a duty-free port, but with shopping aplenty and no sales tax, U.S. citizens may find themselves with a load to take home. Here's the deal: you can take home $600 worth of goods as long as your stay has been longer than 48 hours. Family members who live in the same household and are traveling together are allowed the same exemption, and exemptions can be consolidated. A family of four would then have a total of $2,400 worth of goods to carry home. For the next $1,000, U.S. Customs will levy a flat tax rate of 10%. Unsolicited gifts sent to friends (not yourself) can be sent at the rate of one package worth up to $50 per day per friend (no tobacco or liquor is allowed).

Included in your $600 worth of tax-exempt goods is one liter of alcohol for those 21 and over. You can bring 100 cigars home, but, unfortunately, they can't be Cuban cigars. That's a pity, as several British Virgin Islands shops carry numerous fine Cuban brands.

Citizens of other countries should consult their customs regulations for information on the quantity of goods they are allowed to bring home.

In General

For more information regarding customs regulations, U.S. citizens can write for the pamphlet *Tips for Travelers to the Caribbean,* U.S. Government Printing Office, Washington, D.C. 20402, tel. (202) 783-3238. There is a small charge. Or, for a complete list of regulations covering the world, write to the U.S. Customs Service, P.O. Box 7407, Washington, D.C. 20044 for the free pamphlet *Know Before You Go.*

It's a good idea to make two photocopies of important travel documents such as passports, birth and marriage certificates, medical prescriptions, and so on. Leave one copy at home and travel with the other. In the event the original is lost or stolen, photocopies will help the process of replacement.

A note for everyone: The phrase "duty free" most often applies to the vendor from whom you've bought your perfume, jewelry, trinkets, etc. It means that the vendor was not required to pay duty on these items, and, ostensibly, has passed on these savings to you. It has nothing to do with your own country's duty requirements.

AIRLINES

Flying to the Virgin Islands on commercial airlines is easy enough, but it'll take some planning. Here are the basic facts:

For North Americans traveling to the U.S. Virgin Islands, several major airlines offer direct and nonstop flights to St. Thomas and St. Croix. St. John has no commercial airport, and transport to the island is by ferry or private boat. Europeans traveling to the U.S. Virgin Islands have no options for nonstop flights to St. Thomas or St. Croix and will most often fly to San Juan first and then link up with connections to the U.S. Virgin Islands. Travelers from other Caribbean islands have numerous options for direct or nonstop flights to St. Thomas and St. Croix.

North Americans and Europeans traveling to the British Virgin Islands will have to first fly to San Juan or St. Thomas, then make connections to Tortola or Virgin Gorda. You can make further connections to Anegada and Virgin Gorda from Tortola. Travelers from St. Croix or other Caribbean islands can take numerous small airlines to Tortola or Virgin Gorda.

The San Juan Connection

San Juan, Puerto Rico, is an important Caribbean hub and the gateway to the Virgin Islands as well as many of the other Caribbean islands. From major cities throughout North America, travelers can fly to San Juan on a variety of airlines.

American Airlines (tel. 800-433-7300)

Continental (tel. 800-231-0856)

Delta (tel. 800-241-4141)

Northwest (tel. 800-447-4747)

Trans World Airlines (TWA) (tel. 800-892-4141)

United (tel. 800-241-6522)

USAirways (tel. 800-428-4322)

The small **Carnival Airlines** (tel. 800-437-2110) offers connections to San Juan from Los Angeles, Miami, Fort Lauderdale, and JFK International in New York.

Connecting from Other Caribbean Islands

Travelers from North or South America or Europe can access the U.S. or British Virgin Islands from Caribbean islands other than Puerto Rico, most notably Antigua, Sint Maarten, Martinique, and Barbados. A number of airlines fly to those islands, including those mentioned above. Some other options are:

Air Canada (tel. 800-776-3000)

Air France (tel. 800-237-2747)

British Airways (tel. 800-247-9297)

British West Indies Air International (BWIA) (tel. 800-538-2942)

KLM (tel. 800-374-7747)

Lufthansa (tel. 800-645-3880)

Airline Charters and Discount Shops

Charter companies operate a great many flights to Caribbean, and their fares tend to be less expensive than regularly scheduled airlines. That is their advantage. The disadvantage is that charter flights are often coupled with expensive hotel or resort packages. You can, however, in many instances opt to buy the flight and not the entire package. A further disadvantage is that many charter companies operate on a once-per-week basis, departing for the islands on, for example, Saturdays only. This means you must return the

AIRLINES SERVING THE VIRGIN ISLANDS

NORTH AMERICA TO U.S. VIRGIN ISLANDS:

American Airlines (tel. 800-474-4884)
Delta (tel. 809-777-4177 or 800-221-1212)
Prestige Airways (tel. 800-299-USVI)
USAirways (tel. 800-428-4322 or 800-622-1015)

NORTH AMERICA TO SAN JUAN, PUERTO RICO:

American Airlines (tel. 800-433-7300)
Carnival Airlines (tel. 800-437-2110)
Continental (tel. 800-231-0856)
Delta (tel. 800-241-4141 or 800-221-1212)
Northwest (tel. 800-447-4747)
Trans World Airlines (TWA) (tel. 800-892-4141)
United (tel. 800-241-6522)
USAirways (tel. 800-428-4322)

SAN JUAN, PUERTO RICO, OR OTHER CARIBBEAN ISLANDS TO U.S. VIRGIN ISLANDS:

Air Anguilla (St. Thomas tel. 809-776-5789, St. Croix tel. 809-778-1880)
Air St. Thomas (tel. 800-522-3084 or 809-776-2722)
Aero Virgin Islands (tel. 809-776-8366)
American Eagle (tel. 800-474-4884)
Bohlke International Airways (St. Thomas tel. 809-777-9177, St. Croix tel. 809-778-9177)
BWIA (tel. 809-778-9372)
Caribair (tel. 809-777-1944)
Dolphin Airlines (St. Thomas tel. 809-776-9292, St. Croix tel. 809-778-7650)—*Note that Dolphin Airline's finances have been shaky lately, and it may have folded by the time you read this book.*
Leeward Islands Air Transport (LIAT) (St. Thomas tel. 809-774-2313, St. Croix tel. 809-778-9930)
Vieques Air Link (Puerto Rico tel. 809-863-3020, St. Croix tel. 809-778-9858)
Virgin Islands Paradise Airlines (tel. 809-777-8472)
Windward Islands Air (Winair) (tel. 809-775-0183)

PUERTO RICO OR OTHER CARIBBEAN ISLANDS TO BRITISH VIRGIN ISLANDS

Air Anguilla (tel. 809-495-1616)
Air St. Thomas (tel. 800-522-3084 or 809-495-5935)
American Eagle (tel. 800-474-4884 or 809-495-2559)
Caribair (St. Thomas tel. 809-777-1944)
Dolphin Airlines (tel. 800-497-7030)
Gorda Aero Service (tel. 809-495-2271 or 809-495-2261)
Leeward Islands Air Transport (LIAT) (tel. 809-495-1187/8/9)
Virgin Islands Paradise Airways (St. Thomas tel. 777-8472)
Windward Islands Air (Winair) (tel. 809-495-1711)

following Saturday. There are penalties to pay for an added week's stay, and deep-pocket penalties for cancellation. Advance-purchase tickets are often nonrefundable. A final and unfortunate disadvantage is that charter companies may reserve the right to cancel the flight if not enough people have signed on, and refunds can be spotty at best. You be the judge.

One of the larger charter companies flying to the Virgin Islands is **American Trans Air (ATA)** (7337 W. Washington, Indianapolis, IN 46251; tel. 800-382-5892). However, ATA's flights to St. Thomas and St. Croix operate only during the high season, 15 December through 14 April. They fly out of Indianapolis, and if you catch the charter from there it'll be a good deal. In the past, ATA has booked through tour operators out of Boston, Chicago, Dallas, Detroit, Houston, Indianapolis, Milwaukee, New York, and Fort Lauderdale, but fares on charters from those cities have been, in the past, comparable to regular airline travel.

For general package deals, your first and perhaps best contacts are the airlines themselves. Call American, Delta, TWA, and others listed herein to inquire about deals that include flights, hotels, transfers, meals, and rental cars. In some cases, packages can be less expensive than simply booking a flight and hotel. Your second contact should be a reputable travel agent who specializes in Caribbean travel. Bargain houses such as **Vacation Outlet,** of Boston, tel. (617) 267-8100, have consistently provided quality information and services to Caribbean travelers. Again, peruse the travel classifieds of travel magazines or your Sunday paper for deals.

GETTING THERE: U.S. VIRGIN ISLANDS

Two airports service the U.S. Virgin Islands. With a 7,000-foot (2,130-meter) runway, **Cyril E. King Airport** (tel. 809-774-5100) is located a few miles west of Charlotte Amalie on St. Thomas. With a 7,600-foot (2,310-meter) runway, **Alexander Hamilton Airport,** tel. (809) 778-1012) on St. Croix, is located on the southwest coast of the island. St. Thomas is the entry point for most flights and a stopover for flights heading on to other Caribbean destinations, including the British Virgin Islands. St. Croix takes direct flights from

North America and is a stopover for small island-hoppers, particularly flights from Puerto Rico, St. Thomas, and the British Virgin Islands. St. John has no commercial airport and is reached by ferry or private boat.

American Airlines (tel. 800-474-4884) flies into St. Thomas and/or St. Croix several times daily, nonstop, from New York's JFK, Dallas/Fort Worth, Baltimore, Raleigh/Durham, Miami, and San Juan and also makes connections from Toronto. American's **American Eagle** (tel. 800-474-4884) flies daily to St. Thomas and St. Croix from its San Juan hub. **Delta** (tel. 809-777-4177 or 800-221-1212) connects to St. Thomas from Atlanta and Orlando. **USAirways** (tel. 800-428-4322) flies to St. Thomas and St. Croix from Baltimore and Charlotte. **Prestige Airways** (tel. 800-299-USVI), offers nonstop flights from Miami to St. Thomas and St. Croix on Thursday and Sunday and plans to add flights from Flint, Michigan, and St. Louis, Missouri.

There are no nonstop flights from Europe to St. Thomas or St. Croix. Those visitors must fly to San Juan, Antigua, Sint Maarten, or any number of islands and make ongoing connections to the U.S. Virgin Islands on smaller airlines.

St. Croix is reached from St. Thomas by American Eagle, a 25-minute flight, about $55 one-way. The **Seaborne Seaplane** (tel. 809-777-4491, fax 809-777-4502) offers eight flights daily 7 a.m.-5:30 p.m. between downtown Charlotte Amalie on St. Thomas and downtown Christiansted on St. Croix, $50 one-way, $100 roundtrip. Seaborne is a great adventure; the 30-minute flight flies low across the ocean, and the views coming into Charlotte Amalie or Christiansted are spectacular.

A departure tax of $3 is payable when leaving the U.S. Virgin Islands by air, although that amount is usually included in the price of the ticket. When departing by sea, there is no departure tax.

GETTING THERE: BRITISH VIRGIN ISLANDS

Tortola's **Beef Island International Airport** (tel. 809-494-3701, ext. 2103, or 809-495-2525) is the main entry point for those arriving by air. Beef Island, a small splat of land, is connected to Tortola's northeast coast by a one-lane toll bridge.

Virgin Gorda also has an airstrip and is serviced by light aircraft. Since there are no direct or nonstop flights to the British Virgin Islands from North America, South America, or Europe, St. Thomas and San Juan are the main connection points. Several airlines arrive in San Juan or St. Thomas, including **Air Canada, American, Continental, Carnival, Delta,** and **Northwest,** and, from Europe, **British Airways, BWIA, Lufthansa, Iberia,** and **Air France.** Others fly to, primarily, Antigua, Barbados, Martinique, and Sint Maarten, where you can connect to Tortola.

Air St. Thomas (tel. 800-522-3084 or 809-495-5935) flies between St. Thomas, Puerto Rico, St. Barts, and Virgin Gorda. **American Eagle** (tel. 809-495-2559) has seven flights daily from San Juan to Tortola. **LIAT** (tel. 809-495-1187, 1188, or 1189) connects to Tortola nonstop from Anguilla, Antigua, St. Kitts, Sint Maarten, and St. Thomas and has numerous routes throughout the Caribbean. **Caribair** (St. Thomas tel. 809-777-1944) and **Virgin Islands Paradise Airways** (St. Thomas tel. 809-777-8472) connect the U.S. Virgin Islands and British Virgin Islands. **Dolphin Airlines** (tel. 800-497-7030) flies from San Juan to Tortola and Virgin Gorda. Dolphin's finances have been shaky lately, so don't count on its availability at all times. **Gorda Aero Service** (tel. 809-495-2271 or 809-495-2261) schedules flights on Monday and Friday from St. Thomas ($48 one-way) and is the airline to use when flying from Tortola to Anegada ($27 one-way).

The departure tax upon leaving the British Virgin Islands is $10 by air, $5 by sea.

CRUISE LINES

First, a thought: If you really want to explore an island, to experience its culture and milieu, you probably won't do it by arriving on a cruise ship.

Cruising is a wonderful, relaxing experience and a great idea for a vacation. A cruise recalls days of elegance and grandeur, days when traveling was a major and costly undertaking. Today, cruises are within reach of middle-class incomes, and the ships are teeming with the hoi polloi on holiday. All the better still. Yet it is clear that an ocean cruise is not the means to the end, but, for most, the end itself. The cruise is the thing, the port just the icing on the cake.

Still, having said that, we have to keep in mind that cruising on these floating hotels is a wildly popular way of visiting the Virgin Islands (and the Virgins are definitely wired for cruise ships; St. Thomas's Charlotte Amalie is home to the Havensight Mall, a large strip mall of duty-free shops, located right on the cruise ship pier). In 1991, the U.S. Virgins had visits by 1,241 cruise ships—a total of 1,130,978 passengers. This averages to more than 100 ship visits per month or 26 per week, and the trend has continued to the present (allowing for downtime due to hurricanes in 1995). St. Thomas alone had, in a not-so-busy week in April of 1996, four to six cruise ships in port every day. For that reason, St. Thomas is

cruise ship docked in Frederiksted, St. Croix

CRUISE LINES VISITING THE VIRGIN ISLANDS

The cruise lines below visit one or more of the Virgin Islands. Most call at St. Thomas, and several also visit St. Croix, St. John, Tortola, Virgin Gorda, and Jost Van Dyke. Note that some may operate only during the late fall and winter season.

Carnival Cruise Lines, 3655 N.W. 87th Ave., Miami, FL 33178; tel. (305) 599-2600 or (800) 327-9501

Celebrity Cruise Lines, 5200 Blue Lagoon Dr., Miami, FL 33126; tel. (305) 262-8322 or (800) 437-3111

Clipper Cruise Line, 7711 Bonhomme Ave., St. Louis, MO 63105; tel. (800) 325-0010

Club Med, 3 East 54th St., New York, NY 10022; tel. (212) 750-1687 or (800) 258-2633

Commodore Cruise Lines, 800 Douglas Rd., Suite 700, Coral Gables, FL 33134; tel. (305) 529-3000 or (800) 832-1122

Costa Cruise Lines, World Trade Center, 80 S.W. Eighth St., Miami, FL 33130; tel. (305) 358-7352 or (800) 462-6782

Cunard Line, 555 Fifth Ave., New York, NY 10017; tel. (800) 221-4770

Norwegian Cruise Line, 95 Merrick Way, Coral Gables, FL 33134; tel. (800) 327-7030 or (305) 447-9660

Princess Cruises, 10100 Santa Monica Blvd., Suite 1800, Los Angeles, CA 90067; tel. (310) 553-1770 or (800) 421-0522

Radisson Seven Seas/Diamond Cruise Lines, 11340 Blondo St., Omaha, NE; tel. (800) 333-3333

Royal Caribbean Cruise Line, 1050 Caribbean Way, Miami, FL 33132; tel. (305) 539-6000 or (800) 327-6700

Royal Viking Line, 95 Merrick Way, Coral Gables, FL 33134; tel. (305) 447-9660 or (800) 422-8000

Seabourn Cruise Line, 55 Francisco St., Suite 710, San Francisco, CA 94133; tel. (415) 391-7444 or (800) 929-9595

Windjammer Barefoot Cruises, P.O. Box 120, Miami Beach, FL 33119; tel. (305) 672-6453 or (800) 327-2601

Winstar Cruises, 300 Elliott Ave., Seattle, WA 98119; tel. (800) 258-7245 U.S., (800) 663-5384 Canada

often considered the number-one cruise ship destination in the entire Caribbean. St. Croix is also a popular destination, with dozens of large ships calling each week to Frederiksted, and other, smaller ships making their way to Christiansted. St. John's petite harbor accommodates some smaller cruise ships.

In the British Virgin Islands, Tortola is the big draw for cruise ships, although Virgin Gorda, with a smaller harbor, receives some mini-cruise ships. Nearly 63,000 cruise passengers visited the British Virgin Islands in 1993—much less than the U.S. Virgin Islands, but still a substantial shot in the arm for the local economy.

Overall, the Caribbean saw more than nine million cruise ship passengers in 1993 (up from 8.2 million in 1991). Compare that figure to 12 million stay-over visitors and you'll understand the magnitude of the Caribbean cruise ship industry.

Typically, a cruise ship will stop at several ports—as many as one per day—on a one- to two-week cruise. The ship visits each port for a few hours or perhaps the full day—generally, enough time for passengers to disembark and go shopping, have lunch, and maybe visit some sights.

A note of caution: On the days cruise ships pull into port, you can bet that many of the tourist-related items in the craft shops will be inflated in price. Ditto with taxi rates and other services. And hustlers might be out on the streets. The key to getting your money's worth is to be smart and negotiate.

Cruise ships vary in size and capacity as well as in the facilities they offer. You already know the routine: fine dining, shuffleboard, nightly entertainment, romance, and confused celebrities egged on by the vaguely unsettling megawatt smile of Kathie Lee Gifford. If your friends could see you now. The average ship capacity is about 700 passengers, but in today's world of super-cruisers (some so large that they cannot dock in some of the Caribbean's smaller ports), several carry as many as 1,300 passengers. One of the Caribbean's most impressive mega-liners, the *Majesty of the Seas,* of the Royal Caribbean Cruise Line (the largest line in the world), has 14 decks, 11 bars, a casino, and a five-story lobby and carries more than 2,300 passengers—about the same as the population of Virgin Gorda. The largest liner afloat today, the 14-story *Sun Princess,* weighs in at 77,000 tons and stretches the length of three football fields.

Cruise ships from North America depart from New York, Miami, Orlando, New Orleans, San Juan, and other East Coast points as well as Los Angeles and San Francisco. Cost varies, of course, with amenities offered, length of cruise, and type of cabin you choose. Cabins vary in size and location. Another factor in the cruise cost is the addition of roundtrip flights and transfers from your home to the port of departure. An average cabin rate could be as little as $800 per person based on double occupancy for a seven-night cruise, to as much as $4,000. Check with your travel agent for package deals and costs. It's best to find a travel agent that specializes in cruise packages. For further information on the ins and outs of cruising, send a self-addressed, stamped envelope and a request for the pamphlet *Cruising Answers to Your Questions* to the **Cruise Lines International Association,** 500 Fifth Ave., Suite 1407, New York, NY 10110.

GETTING AROUND

ON ISLAND

Buses

Bus transport in the Virgin Islands is quirky at best but will get you to major centers without much trouble. On **St. Thomas,** the U.S. Virgin Islands VITRAN system operates open-air buses, taxi-buses, and closed buses between the Market Place in Charlotte Amalie and Red Hook, on the east end of St. Thomas. Buses also run between the Market Place and the airport and west end of the island, which is designated as "country," and cover the Charlotte Amalie area. Cost is $1-3 one-way (seniors 35-55 cents, students 56-75 cents), and buses operate every day from as early as 5:30 a.m. until 9:30 p.m. Contact VITRAN (tel. 809-774-5678 or 776-4844) for specifics.

On **St. Croix,** VITRAN (tel. 809-773-7746 or 773-1290) runs regular service along the 45-minute route between Christiansted and Frederiksted, with stops along the way, daily from 5:30 a.m. until 9:30 p.m. The buses are large and air-conditioned. Look for VITRAN signs at bus stops. Cost is $1 (seniors 55 cents, students 75 cents), transfers are 25 cents, and exact change is required.

On **St. John,** your best bet is to rent a car. There are no organized bus systems on the island. Some open-air taxi-buses will take you to the beaches from Cruz Bay; cost will depend on how many people get in the taxi.

In the **British Virgin Islands,** a thin line distinguishes buses and taxis. Buses—really open-air trucks with benches or large vans—can take you to some spots on Tortola and Virgin Gorda. You can share taxi-buses to reduce the fare, but all in all, it's easier and more fun to rent a car.

Taxis

In the U.S. Virgin Islands you can identify taxis, either sedan vehicles or vans, by their domed tops and license plates lettered "TP," "CP," or "JP" (for St. Thomas, St. Croix, and St. John, respectively). Taxis are not metered but charge fares per destination and per person depending how many are in the taxi. For instance, on St. Thomas the fare from the airport to Charlotte Amalie is $4.50 for a single passenger or $4 per person for several passengers. From town to, say, Sapphire Resort, a single passenger pays $8.50 while multiple passengers pay $5.50 each. Add $1.50 for services between midnight and 6 a.m., and add a small extra charge for baggage.

INTERNATIONAL TRAFFIC SIGNS

Curves Ahead

Right of Way
Intersection

Stop and Yield

No Parking on
left side

No Parking on
right side

Yield

Dangerous Crossing

School Zone/
Children at Play

No Waiting

No Entrance

Danger

Right of Way
Road

End Right
of Way

No right turn

The same system prevails on St. Croix and St. John. Each driver is required by the Virgin Islands Taxi Association to carry a rate card in the vehicle, and, should there be any question about the fare, ask the driver to produce it. However, drivers are usually honest and will not risk their licenses by overcharging. Several tourist publications, such as *St. Thomas This Week, St. Croix This Week,* and *Virgin Islands Playground,* print updated fares. For complaints or queries, contact the Taxi Commission (St. Thomas and St. John tel. 809-776-8294, St. Croix tel. 809-773-7746 or 773-8294).

Never get into a car with a driver who has no identification as a bona fide taxi driver.

The taxi systems are much the same in the British Virgin Islands. Taxis are unmetered, and fares are set by the Ministry of Communications and Works (tel. 809-494-3701, ext. 2183). Rates per person drop as you add more people to the taxi. On Tortola, for instance, from the airport to Road Town, the fare is $15 each for one to three passengers, $5 each for four or more. The same rate applies from Road Town to West End. On Virgin Gorda, most fares range $2-5 per person. Drivers are required to carry a rate sheet, so ask to see it if you're unsure of the fare.

See specific island sections in this book for taxi companies and island tour rates.

Rental Cars

For those who prefer independence of movement, renting a car is perhaps the best option. Rates across the islands vary with the type of vehicle and the length of the rental, but you can figure on a range of $30-60 per day for a compact or, as it happens often on St. John, a small jeep. For those traveling in groups, splitting the cost of a rental can be an attractive option. Most companies offer unlimited mileage, but you'll pay for gas.

Requirements for rental also vary, but in most cases you'll need a valid driver's license or international license, and, if you're not using a credit card, a deposit. In the U.S. Virgin Islands, you'll also need to be at least 21 years of age—in some cases 25. The U.S. Virgin Islands recognize U.S. drivers' licenses; a valid license from anywhere else is honored for 90 days before the driver must apply for a local license.

The British Virgin Islands require that North Americans and others purchase a temporary visitor's license at a cost of $10. The rental company can issue this license, which is just a matter of paperwork.

In both the U.S. and British Virgin Islands, driving is on the left—a legacy of Dutch and British occupations. An odd situation occurs in that cars tend to be U.S.-manufactured, with the steering wheel also on the left. This puts the driver near the shoulder of the road rather than the center. Practicing in the parking lot before taking the car on the road will help.

Routes are generally well marked on St. Thomas and St. Croix. As for the tiny St. John and all the British Virgin Islands, you'd have to try hard to get lost. In both territories, the speed limit rarely exceeds 35 mph (56 kph).

See specific island chapters for listings of car rental companies.

FERRY SERVICES

It's possible to travel among and between the U.S. and British Virgin Islands by sea rather than air, and, in fact, ferry travel is the preferred mode of travel for many locals and tourists alike. Various ferry services operate between St. Thomas and St. John, St. Thomas and Tortola, St. John and Tortola, St. Thomas and Virgin Gorda, Tortola and Virgin Gorda, and St. John or Tortola and Jost Van Dyke. The boats are generally clean and comfortable (some have even managed to install erstwhile airline seats), and many feature both on-deck and enclosed seating. Ferry transport is wonderful if the weather is good but can be a chore if high winds or rain have kicked up the sea. If you intend to do a lot of inter-island ferry travel and are prone to seasickness, you'll want to bring along your favorite motion-sickness remedy.

In general, you needn't make reservations on ferries (unless you're traveling with a large party or lots of cargo). In fact, at certain ports, ferry operators will fight—not literally, of course—for your business, representatives approaching you and extolling the virtues of their services. But there really aren't many differences among the ferries—the rates are the same, and the departure and arrival times vary little. This gentle caging can be annoying when you're jumping out of a taxi and trying to collect your luggage and pay the taxi fare at the same time. Just tell them to hang on for a minute—they'll listen.

Show up at least 20 minutes before the scheduled departure time.

Some ferries carry cars, but if you're renting, the cost of transporting a car to another island versus renting one on arrival at the second island makes transporting the vehicle a wash. It is illegal to transport rental cars to St. John.

Carriers

A list of the major inter-island carriers follows. See the appendix for detailed schedules and rates along with information about other, smaller ferry companies.

Fast Cat (tel. 809-773-3278).

Inter-Island Boat Services (U.S.V.I. tel. 809-776-6597 or 775-7408; B.V.I. tel. 809-495-4166)

Native Son (U.S.V.I. tel. 809-774-8685 or 775-3111; B.V.I. tel. 809-495-4617)

North Sound Express (B.V.I. tel. 809-495-2271)

Smith's Ferry (U.S.V.I. tel. 809-775-7292 or 775-5532; B.V.I. tel. 809-494-4430 or 495-2355)

Speedy's (U.S.V.I. tel. 809-776-0333; B.V.I. tel. 809-495-5240 or 809-495-5235)

Transportation Services (U.S.V.I. tel. 809-776-6282)

BOAT CHARTERS

The sea, in many ways, defines the Caribbean. Sailing is a fascinating way to get to know a large part of island living, and in the Virgin Islands dozens of options are available for those with a yen to travel on the water. You can charter boats on the mainland of the U.S. or on Puerto Rico or in both the U.S. and British Virgin Islands. Your options when chartering—which is really nothing more than renting—range from day to long-term charters, either with crew or "bareboat" (you crew it yourself), and with a group or by yourself. You can also opt for power yachts over sailing vessels.

Sailors tend to enjoy the British Virgin Islands for their protected waters and the relative closeness of the islands—you'll never leave one without seeing the next. The hundreds of small harbors, inlets, and coves are perfect for dropping anchor for a day.

Crewed yachts come with professional crews and have the options of meals, fishing and sporting equipment, perhaps a bar, and other choices. Costs vary with options, the season, and the number of passengers on board. They can be expensive, from $2,000 per week, without provisions. Others offer all-inclusive packages, from about $1,000 per person per week. Bareboat charters start at about $900-1,500 per week for the boat (off-season, two to eight people) and require the renters to have sufficient sailing and anchoring experience to handle the vessel. In the winter, bareboat charters can range $2,000-6,000 for two to as many as 10 passengers. One option is to charter a bareboat and work as its crew but hire a skipper who knows the ins and outs of the local waters.

Yacht Charter Companies

The Moorings (19345 U.S. 19N, Clearwater, FL 34624, tel. 800-437-7880, fax 813-530-9747; P.O. Box 139, Wickhams Cay, Road Town, Tortola, British Virgin Islands, tel. 809-494-2331, 2332, or 2333, fax 809-494-2226) is perhaps the largest yacht charter company in the Virgin Islands. The Moorings offers complete services from large, luxury, crewed yachts to smaller bareboat charters. Their reputation is solid.

Other yacht and boat charter companies with services in the U.S. and British Virgin Islands:

Admiralty Yacht Vacations, Villa Olga, St. Thomas, U.S. Virgin Islands 00802, tel. (800) 544-0493, Web site http://www.admirals.com

Bajor Yacht Charters, 9602 Estate Thomas, St. Thomas, U.S. Virgin Islands 00802, tel. (800) 524-8292 or (809) 776-1954, fax (809) 776-0460

Nicholson Yacht Charters, 78 Bolton St., Cambridge, MA 02140; tel. (800) 662-6066 or (617) 661-0555

Stewart Yacht Charters, 6501 Red Hook Plaza, Suite 101, St. Thomas, U.S. Virgin Islands 00802, tel. (800) 432-6118 or tel./fax (809) 775-1358

Sunsail, 2 Prospect Park, 3347 N.W. 55th St., Fort Lauderdale, FL 33309; tel. (800) 327-2276 or (305) 484-5246, fax (305) 485-5072

Sun Yacht Charters, 59 B Union St., Camden, ME 04843; tel. (800) 634-8822

VIP Yacht Charters, 6118 Estate Frydenhoj #58, St. Thomas, U.S. Virgin Islands 00802-1402; tel. (800) 524-2015 or (809) 776-1510, fax (809) 776-3801, e-mail 76167.3102@compuserve.com

Virgin Islands Sailing, Ltd., P.O. Box 146, Road Town, Tortola, British Virgin Islands; tel. (800) 233-7936 or (809)-494-2774, fax (809) 494-6774, Florida tel. (800) 382-9666, e-mail visailing@aol.com, Web site http://www.visailing.com.

INFORMATION AND SERVICES

TIME ZONES

The Virgin Islands lie in the Atlantic Standard Time zone, which is four hours behind Greenwich Mean Time (e.g., 4 p.m. in London on a Wednesday is noon on Tortola on that same Wednesday). The Atlantic standard time zone is directly east of North America's Eastern standard time zone and does not make seasonal adjustments; this makes it one hour ahead of Eastern standard time during the winter months, and the same as daylight saving time during the spring and summer months. (In the U.S., daylight saving time begins at 2 a.m. on the first Sunday of April and ends at 2 a.m. on the last Sunday of October.)

More simply: When it's noon in New York on Christmas Day, it's 1 p.m. in the Virgin Islands. But when it's noon in New York on a hot day in July, it's also noon in the Virgins.

ELECTRICITY

Many international travelers have cursed the guys, and we know they must have been guys, who dreamed up the confusing business of 110-120 volts alternating current (AC), which dominates North American households and appliances, and the 220-240 volts direct current (DC), which is Europe's mainstay. Despite the merits of one system or another, it surely has made international travel a challenge. Luckily, those traveling from North America to the Virgins Islands will have few problems. Both the U.S. and British Virgin Islands are primarily on a 110-volt, 60-cycle system.

Travelers from Europe or other Caribbean islands will have to call ahead to check if the hotel has the proper current to run hair dryers, shavers, and laptop computers (note that these days many of these appliances have voltage converters built in). Inquire also whether the hotel has proper outlet configurations for European-style round or three-pronged plugs. Larger hotels carry adapters for use by guests, and you can easily buy the proper adapter set at any electrical store at home.

MAIL

Your hotel will most likely send guest mail and will even sell stamps for postcards and airmail letters, but for specialized package service you'll have to visit the post office.

The U.S. Virgin Islands is attached to the U.S. Postal Service, and rates are the same as on the U.S. mainland. Mail is air-freighted daily, and you can get overnight service to many U.S. cities.

All U.S. Virgin Islands addresses carry a zip code, and letters to the islands should be addressed something like this: Joe Bagadonuts, P.O. Box 555, Charlotte Amalie, St. Thomas, U.S. Virgin Islands 00804 (or the appropriate zip). Post offices are found in all major towns on the three U.S. Virgin Islands, and window hours are Mon.-Fri. 7:30 a.m.-4 p.m., Saturday 7:30 a.m.-noon or 12:30 p.m.

Stamps originating in the British Virgin Islands are bold, colorful, and among the most striking in the world. Philatelists will enjoy them. Airmail package rates to North America are $5 for the first pound, $1.20 per half-pound thereafter. Postcards are 30 cents to North America, and the standard letter rate is 45 cents per half-ounce. Allow about one week for delivery to North America.

The British Virgin Islands' main post office is located on Main Street in Road Town, Tortola, tel. (809) 494-3701, ext. 4996. Several smaller offices are scattered around the islands. Hours are Mon.-Fri. 8:30 a.m.-4 p.m. and Saturday 9 a.m.-noon.

*Park Ranger Carmen
Navarro, St. Croix*

There are no zip or postal codes for the British Virgins, and letters should be addressed something like this: Mary Bonhomie, P.O. Box 555, Road Town, Tortola, British Virgin Islands.

In both territories, a viable, though expensive, alternative for sending packages is **FedEx** (once called Federal Express), which now has offices or representatives on St. Thomas (Havensight Mall, tel. 809-774-4140; airport, tel. 809-774-3393), St. Croix (Ville La Reine Shopping Center, tel. 809-778-8180), and Tortola (tel. 809-494-2297 or 494-4712, fax 809-494-5819). FedEx is convenient for packages containing souvenirs, books, or other items too large to carry home. In the U.S. Virgin Islands, **United Parcel Service (UPS)** has offices on St. Thomas (Alcohens Plaza, tel. 800-742-5877 or 809-776-1700), St. Croix (Builders Yard, tel. 809-773-8466), and St. John (Contant 100 tel. 809-693-8130). **DHL Worldwide Express** (tel. 809-774-6333), on St. Thomas, is also available for international service. Packages to the United States are subject to scrutiny by U.S. Customs agents.

TELEPHONES

Telephone communication in the Virgin Islands is very good and getting better. Both countries use the area code 809, followed by a seven-digit number, which makes direct dialing to and from the Virgin Islands no more difficult than calling anywhere in North America. Toll-free numbers (prefix 800 or 888) are widely used in both territories.

AT&T USADirect Service operates throughout the U.S. Virgin Islands, particularly in larger hotels and airports. This service is for telephone calling-card holders and either bills your home telephone number or allows you to call collect. Sprint and MCI also operate in the U.S. Virgin Islands, and you can tap AT&T service in the British Virgin Islands.

When calling within the British Virgin Islands, you can, due to the small number of phones, drop the first two digits of the phone or fax number and dial just the last five. In fact, all numbers in the telephone book and on business signs contain just five digits. The number 495-1234 becomes 51234, 494-6789 becomes 46789. The "49" occurs in every number.

The U.S. and British Virgin Islands telephone companies (VITELCO and Cable & Wireless, respectively) have created local phone cards meant to take the place of coins in public phones. These magnetized cards come in several denominations and may be purchased at the local phone company, post offices, and shops or convenience stores. The concept is simple: insert the card, make the call, and the cost is deducted from the balance on the card.

U.S.V.I. visitors who need to make calls are best served by public phones located throughout the city and countryside. For more complicated transactions, stop in at public services such as **The Calling Station** (tel. 809-777-8215), located at the Al Cohens Mall, across from Havensight Mall in Charlotte Amalie. Here you can send faxes, use American Express money services, and send mail. Hours are daily 8:30 a.m. until the cruise ships pull out—roughly 5 p.m.

As well, you'll find an **AT&T** calling center (tel. 809-777-8783) at the Buccaneer Mall, across from the Havensight Mall on St. Thomas, open daily 8 a.m.-6 p.m., and another on St. Croix (tel. 809-778-1903), at the Sion Farm Shopping Center in Christiansted.

The U.S.V.I.'s VITELCO offices are located on St. Thomas at the Spenceley Building in Charlotte Amalie (tel. 809-776-9950) and on St. Croix at the Sunny Isle Shopping Center (tel. 809-778-9950); both offices are open daily 8 a.m.-5 p.m. On St. John, The VITELCO office in Cruz Bay (tel. 809-776-6261) is open weekdays 9 a.m.-3 p.m. For hearing- or speech-impaired callers, use VITELCO's Relay Service, which utilizes TTY machines. For hearing-impaired needs, call (800) 440-8477; others call (800) 809-8477.

Use the British Virgin Islands' Cable & Wireless offices to make calls or send faxes, cables, or telexes overseas. Offices are located at Wickam's Cay in Road Town (tel. 809-494-2201) and The Valley, Virgin Gorda (tel. 809-495-5444). Hours in Road Town are Mon.-Fri. 8 a.m.-6 p.m. and Saturday 9 a.m.-2 p.m. The Virgin Gorda hours are Mon.-Fri. 9 a.m.-6 p.m. and Saturday 10 a.m.-2 p.m. Offices are closed on Sunday and public holidays.

Note that telephone calls made from hotels, whether to local or overseas numbers, will usually incur hefty surcharges.

CURRENCY AND MONEY

Both the U.S. and British Virgin Islands use the U.S. dollar as the official currency. This may be surprising to visitors from the U.K. who expect to use pounds in the British Virgin Islands, but the logic is evident. Due to their physical proximity and historical and economic ties, it makes sense that both territories use the same currency.

Traveler's checks are widely accepted in the islands, but don't expect the little johnnycake kiosk to cash one. Major credit cards, such as American Express, Visa, MasterCard, Discover,

and, to an extent, Diner's Club and Carte Blanche, are also accepted in large hotels and many smaller ones. It would be wise to check with your hotel and car rental agency before you leave home to find out what forms of payment are acceptable.

Tipping is common in the Virgin Islands. Think 10-20% at restaurants, but check to see that the gratuity hasn't already been included in the bill (although you are certainly allowed to tip more if you think highly of the service). As well, hotels often automatically add a 10-15% service charge to the bill. In general, taxi drivers, porters, chamberpersons, and skycaps are customarily tipped—for some of them, this is a major source of income.

ATMs
Automatic Teller Machines (ATMs) are slowly making their way to the islands. For U.S.-based ATM cards, such as those compatible with the Cirrus, NYCE, and Plus systems, you'll have no problem in the U.S. Virgin Islands. At least 10 machines are currently available at Chase Manhattan (tel. 809-693-1700) banks, several Citibanks (tel. 809-774-4800), and Banco Popular (tel. 809-693-2777) on St. Thomas. Walk along Veterans Drive on the waterfront in Charlotte Amalie and you'll find several bank branches. On St. John, you'll find an ATM at the Chase Manhattan Bank (tel. 809-776-6881) on Kongens Gade in Cruz Bay. On St. Croix, walk down King Street near the wharf in Christiansted for a Chase (tel. 809-773-1200) ATM. If you're interested in knowing exactly where ATMs are located in the Virgin Islands (and worldwide), you can call the special numbers set up by the Plus (tel. 800-843-7587) and Cirrus (tel. 800-424-7787) systems.

In the British Virgin Islands, you'll find two ATMs in Road Town, Tortola, one at the Banco Popular (tel. 809-693-2777) on Main Street and the other at the Chase Manhattan Bank (tel. 809-494-2662) at Wickam's Cay I.

MEDIA

A plethora of small and large newspapers, cable and local television channels, and radio stations are at your disposal in both the U.S. and the

British Virgin Islands. Most private homes and hotels carry television programming, via local cable companies, from ABC, CBS, Showtime, HBO, ESPN, CNN, and public TV. As well, hotels and newsstands in both territories carry overseas magazines such as *Time* and *Newsweek* and papers such as the *New York Times, Wall Street Journal, Miami Herald, San Juan Star, Times of London,* and *USA Today.* However, overseas news doesn't come cheap-

USEFUL WORLD WIDE WEB SITES

U.S. Virgin Islands Department of Tourism
http://www.usvi.net
You've got to love a Web site with waving palm trees. This biggest single resource for U.S. Virgin Islands information lists useful government, hotel, restaurant, and tourism services addresses on all three islands. It also hosts a diving section, a community calendar, an on-going "win-a-trip" contest, photos, current press releases, fishing news, a current weather site, e-mail, and maps.

Baskin in the Sun
http://www.dive-baskin.com
This site features information about the Baskin in the Sun dive outfit, with contact information, rates, and e-mail address and particulars. The photos are wonderful, and the site links to other British Virgin Islands and diving Web sites.

British Virgin Islands Tourist Board and Hotel and Commerce Association's "Welcome Tourist Guide"
http://www.caribweb.com/
The official tourism Web site features articles on British Virgin Islands culture and events and offers a library of past articles. It also lists tourist board addresses and phones, select hotel and restaurant information, beaches, watersports outfits, and shopping and inter-island transport services. The site features a classifieds section, as well as links to other British Virgin Islands sites.

Caribbean Hotel Association
http://www.caribbeantravel.com
Lists multiple Caribbean destinations, with activities, maps, facts and figures, and accommodations.

Caribbean Tourism Organization
http://www.caribtourism.com
The site is full of graphics and is slow loading but is one of the more comprehensive Caribbean Web sites. It lists a calendar of events, weather updates for most of the islands, a clickable map for navigating directly to the island of your choice, accommodations, events, and tourism office addresses and phone contacts.

CPSCaribNet
http://www.cpscaribnet.com
Presenting limited information on destinations, hotels, and various travel packages (golf, honeymoon) offered by member companies.

Maho Bay Camps/Harmony Resort/Estate Concordia, St. John, U.S. Virgin Islands
http://www.maho.org
Featuring the philosophy of environmentally friendly camp and resorts on St. John, an index of recycled building materials used in constructing the properties, weather updates on St. John, and links to the St. John Web site.

Resort and Villas of the Caribbean
http://www.infi.net/~slm/
While this Web site may be useful for gathering information about the Caribbean in general, it offers little about the U.S. or British Virgin Islands—Tortola is the only island of the Virgins mentioned. The site features photos, villa contacts, CD-ROMs for sale, yacht charter companies, and its newsletter.

Specialty Travel Index
http://www.spectrav.com
Listing more than 600 tour operators worldwide, cross-referenced by geography, activities, and interests. It also features a search utility that didn't seem to work too well at press time—plugging in "U.S. Virgin Islands," for example, fetched references from as far away as Fiji.

St. John
http://www.stjohnusvi.com
St. John activities, restaurants, accommodations, rental cars, Virgin Islands National Park information, real estate, a map, and a short history and description of the island are offered.

DEPARTMENTS OF TOURISM

U.S. VIRGIN ISLANDS
DEPARTMENTS OF TOURISM

CARIBBEAN

P.O. Box 6400
Charlotte Amalie
St. Thomas, U.S. Virgin Islands 00804
tel. (809) 774-USVI (8784) or (800) 372-8784
fax (809) 774-4390
http://www.usvi.net

P.O. Box 200
Cruz Bay
St. John, U.S. Virgin Islands 00830
tel. (809) 776-6450

P.O. Box 4538
Christiansted
St. Croix, U.S. Virgin Islands 00822
tel. (809) 773-0495
fax (809) 778-3101

Strand St.
Frederiksted Pier
Federiksted
St. Croix, U.S. Virgin Islands 00840
tel. (809) 772-0357
fax (809) 778-9259

1300 Ashford Ave.
Condado
Santurce, Puerto Rico 00907
tel. (809) 724-3816
fax (809) 724-7223

UNITED STATES

225 Peachtree St. NE, Suite 760
Gaslight Tower
Atlanta, GA 30303
tel. (404) 688-0906
fax (404) 525-1102

500 N. Michigan Ave., Suite 2030
Chicago, IL 60611
tel. (312) 670-8784
fax (312) 670-8788

3460 Wilshire Blvd., Suite 412
Los Angeles, CA 90010
tel. (213) 739-0138
fax (213) 739-2005

2655 S. Le Jeune Rd., Suite 907
Coral Gables
Miami, FL 33134
tel. (305) 442-7200
fax (305) 445-9044

1270 Avenue of the Americas, Suite 2108
New York, NY 10020
tel. (212) 332-2222
fax (212) 332-2223

The Farragut Building
900 17th St. NW, Suite 500
Washington, D.C. 20006
tel. (202) 293-3707
fax (202) 785-2542

CANADA

3300 Bloor St. W, Suite 3120
Centre Tower
Toronto, ON M8X 2X3
tel. (416) 233-1414 or (800) 465-8784
fax (416) 233-9367

EUROPE

Park Allé 5
DK-8000 Århus C.
Denmark
tel. (45-86) 181933
fax (45-86) 180660

2 Cinnamon Row
Plantation Wharf, York Place
London SW11 3TW
England
tel. (44-171) 978-5262
fax (44-171) 924-3171

Otto-Hahn-Strasse 23
D-50997 Köln
Germany
tel. (069-2236) 841743
fax (069-2236) 43045

Via Gherardini 2
20145 Milano
Italy
tel. (039-02) 33105841
fax (039-02) 33105827

OTHER

Avenida Sao Luis
112 14th Floor
Sao Paulo CEP 010 46-000
Brazil
tel. (11) 257-9877
fax (11) 214-4544

Discover America Marketing, Inc., Suite B234B
Hibiya Kokusai Bldg. 2-3
Uchisaiwaicho 2-chome
Chioyoda-ku, Tokyo 100
Japan
tel. (3) 3597-9451
fax (3) 3597-0385

Also:
St. Thomas/St. John Hotel Association
  tel. (809) 774-6835
St. Croix Hotel and Tourism Association
  tel. (800) 524-2026

BRITISH VIRGIN ISLANDS TOURIST BOARDS

BRITISH VIRGIN ISLANDS

P.O. Box 134
Road Town, Tortola

British Virgin Islands
tel. (809) 494-3134
fax (809) 494-3866

UNITED STATES

370 Lexington Ave.
New York, NY 10017
tel. (800) 835-8530 or (212) 696-0400
fax (212) 949-8254

1804 Union St.
San Francisco, CA 94123-4308
tel. (415) 775-0344
fax (415) 775-2554

EUROPE

FCB Travel and Marketing
110 St. Martin's La.
London WC2N 4DY
England
tel. (44-171) 240-4259
fax (44-171) 240-4270

Sophienstrasse 4
D-65189 Wiesbaden
Germany
tel. (49-611) 300262
fax (49-611) 300766

---

ly; most daily papers are about $3, and Sunday papers as much as $7.

Local newspapers in the U.S. Virgin Islands include the excellent national *Virgin Islands Daily News* (60 cents), a Gannett paper published daily except Sunday. The local *St. Croix Avis* (50 cents), in operation since 1844, is published daily. On St. John, pick up the weekly *Tradewinds* (50 cents) for local news.

Other U.S. Virgin Islands publications include *The Island Trader,* a free paper published on St. Thomas that contains mostly classifieds and adverts and little news. The *Weekly Journal,* also published on St. Thomas, features entertainment and weekly news roundups. The magazine *Pride* is published monthly.

You can find eight local AM and FM radio stations as well as numerous overseas stations on your dial.

In the British Virgin Islands, many hotel televisions carry the same programming as the U.S. Virgin Islands, with added local news and entertainment programs. A national newspaper, *The BVI Beacon* (35 cents), carries a fair amount of international and local news and is published in Road Town, Tortola, every Thursday. *The Island Sun* (35 cents), another weekly, is also published in Road Town.

TOURISM OFFICES

Both the U.S. and British Virgin Islands maintain tourism offices at home and overseas (see chart). In addition to the U.S. Virgin Islands' main tourism office at #78 Constant in the Elainco Building in Charlotte Amalie on St. Thomas (tel. 809-774-USVI or 800-372-USVI, fax 809-774-4390), you'll find a Charlotte Amalie visitors booth at the cruise ship dock at the Havensight Mall and a visitors bureau on the waterfront across the street from the Vendor's Plaza, #2 Tolbold Gade (tel. 800-

372-USVI). On St. Croix, a visitors bureau is located at the cruise ship dock on Frederiksted Pier, in Frederiksted (tel. 809-772-0357), and another is in the Old Scale House in downtown Christiansted (tel. 809-773-0495, fax 809-495-9259). On St. John, find a small tourism office across from the post office and ferry docks in Cruz Bay (tel. 809-776-6450). Offices are generally open Mon.-Fri. 8 a.m.-5 p.m., with extra hours when cruise ships are docked.

Tourism offices in the British Virgin Islands are located on Tortola in the Social Security Building on Waterfront Drive in Road Town (tel. 809-494-3134) and, on Virgin Gorda at Yacht Harbour in The Valley (tel. 809-495-5182). Hours are Mon.-Fri. 8:30 a.m.-4:30 p.m.

If you're set up for Internet access, you can visit the U.S. Virgin Islands Department of Tourism's Web site at http://www.usvi.net. You can also surf the net for a British Virgin Islands on-line publication called "Welcome Tourist Guide" (http://bviwelcome.com) set up by the British Virgin Islands Tourist Board and Hotel and Commerce Association.

barracuda

BOB RACE

SPECIAL TRAVEL SITUATIONS

TRAVELERS WITH DISABILITIES

The tourism infrastructure of the Virgin Islands offers a little bit for everyone, but specialized travel situations need some research.

As a U.S. territory, the U.S. Virgin Islands must comply with provisions of the landmark Americans with Disabilities Act (1990), and some progress has been made. The ADA has decreed that certain businesses and public buildings must incorporate facilities that provide for people with disabilities. These will include parking facilities for the physically challenged, ramps and widened doorways for wheelchairs, lowered light switches and bathroom facilities in hotel rooms declared handicapped accessible, and other accoutrements for people with hearing and sight impairments. Many of the U.S. Virgin Islands' hotels and restaurants, as well as parks and other buildings, do have handicapped accessible facilities. But many do not. This is due to the provisions of enactment of the ADA, which allows a certain amount of time, depending on the size of the facility and other factors, for changes to be made.

Travelers with disabilities will have to do some research to find accessible facilities in hotels and general transport systems throughout the U.S. Virgin Islands. In particular, wheelchair-bound visitors will have to plan well in advance to ensure that their needs are met. Some hotels have accessible first-floor rooms, but not all have appropriate doorways, bathroom facilities, or light switches. Major hotel chains and U.S. Virgin Islands park facilities, particularly the campground at Cinnamon Bay on St. John, do have some handicapped-accessible rooms.

The quickest way to answer your lodging questions is to contact a U.S. Virgin Islands Department of Tourism (see chart) and ask for the *Rates* brochure. In this brochure, hotels indicate, among other items, whether or not they have handicapped facilities. Then call the hotel you'd like to visit and ask direct questions related to your needs about their handicapped accessible units and other facilities.

Transport systems, including ferries, taxis, and buses, are generally not accessible. And beaches are generally not accessible because wheelchairs with oversize tires are not available.

For those with hearing or speech problems, the U.S. Virgin Islands' VITELCO Relay Service utilizes TTY machines. For needs attendant upon a hearing impairment, call (800) 440-8477; for needs connected with impairments of speech and other challenges, call (800) 809-8477.

The British Virgin Islands offer less in the way of hotel, restaurant, and transportation facilities for people with disabilities. The best bet here is to call ahead to the place you'd like to stay.

For more information regarding regional facilities for travelers with disabilities, try contacting **Society for the Advancement of Travel for the Handicapped,** 347 Fifth Ave., Suite 610, New York, NY 10016, tel. (212) 447-7284, fax (212) 725-8253; or **Travel Industry and Disabled Exchange,** 5435 Donna Ave., Tarzana, CA 91356, tel. (818) 343-6339. Both organizations charge fees for membership, and the Disabled Exchange publishes a quarterly newsletter ($15 per year) with information on travel facilities for people with disabilities. Subscribers to *The Itinerary: The Magazine for Travelers with Physical Disabilities* may find occasional articles about Caribbean travel. Contact P.O. Box 2012, Bayonne, NJ 07002-2012; tel. (201) 858-3400.

For an up-to-date regional resource, contact Derrick Palmer, director of **Disabled Persons International,** P.O. Box 220, Liguanea, Kingston 6, Jamaica, West Indies; tel. (809) 929-2073 or 926-6776. Palmer and his organization have worked hard to promote disabled-accessible facilities throughout the Caribbean.

Again, the bottom line: decide on the hotel you would like to visit, then call ahead for information on their facilities. Be specific with your questions.

SENIOR TRAVELERS

Older travelers will find the Virgin Islands an easy and rewarding trip. Since seniors are often unencumbered by job obligations, they can travel at their leisure and take advantage of off-season rates and uncrowded streets.

In the U.S. Virgin Islands, senior discounts are offered by many attractions, hotels, restaurants, and major car rental agencies. The key here is to ask—few will volunteer this information. Some might require AARP membership, but that's not the rule.

By and large, British Virgin Islands hoteliers and restaurateurs have not adopted the custom of giving discounts to seniors. Some do, though, so, again, ask your travel agent or call the facility directly to inquire. And bring identification for proof of age if you intend to seek out senior discounts.

Traveling with senior groups on charters or special cruises organized by senior travel programs may be helpful. In the U.S., contact the **American Association of Retired Persons (AARP)**, 601 E St. NW, Washington, D.C. 20049, tel. (800) 441-2277, (800) 424-3410, or (202) 434-2277 (annual dues $8). Also try the **National Council of Senior Citizens**, 1331 F St. NW, Washington, D.C. 20004, tel. (800) 322-6677 or (202) 347-8800 (annual dues $12).

As well, you might want to contact **Elderhostel**, a group that sponsors seniors with vacationing, learning, living, and volunteering opportunities overseas. Occasionally, trips to the Virgin Islands are offered. This is not your usual sort of trip; accommodations are rustic but comfortable, and you'll spend time in the community working or learning about aspects of the culture that cruise ship passengers won't. Yet the experience is potentially rewarding. Cost is about $1,000 per person for a 10-day trip, not including airfare. Contact Elderhostel at 75 Federal St., Boston, MA 02110-1941, tel. (617) 426-8056.

Many U.S. and international airlines offer a 10% senior discount on normal fares, and several airlines offer larger discounts to seniors for one-trip occasions or through discount coupon books for multiple trips. These trips often involve travel during off-peak times (Monday through Thursday, for example), with 14-day advance booking, based on availability (standby is permissible). The coupon books contain four or eight coupons and sell for about $540 for a book of four. Each coupon book is good for one year from date of issue and is often applicable from any point in the 48 contiguous states. Generally, you must be 62 years or older to qualify. As an example, the American Airlines book of four coupons for flights to San Juan, St. Thomas, or St. Croix costs $541. Since one coupon/ticket is needed each way, your cost will be $270.50 roundtrip. This could be a substantial savings over the average fare of about $400 roundtrip from the U.S. East Coast, and even more of a savings for those traveling from the West Coast. The disadvantages are that you must use the coupons within one year of purchase, and the airlines sometimes run specials that beat the coupon price.

The airlines maintain special telephones numbers for seniors: American Airlines (tel. 800-237-7981), Continental (tel. 800-248-8996), Delta (tel. 800-323-2323), and USAirways (tel. 800-428-4322) are among the better deals for Virgin Islands travelers.

STUDENT TRAVELERS

Full-time students may be eligible for an **International Student Identity Card (ISIC)**, which is available to students through applications at colleges and universities or by application to the Council on International Education Exchange, 205 E. 42nd St., New York, NY 10017; tel. (212) 661-1414. It's a picture identification card entitling you to discounts at certain museums, theaters, attractions, etc., and even some medical insurance benefits. The use of this card is not widespread in the Virgin Islands, but it is worth a try. There is a nominal fee, about $15, for the card. The council also publishes *Student Travels*, which describes overseas travel and work opportunities for students.

TRAVELING FAMILIES

Families are generally accommodated without a problem throughout the Virgin Islands. Many hotels offer free rooms or discounts to families with children under 12 or so, as long as the children stay in the room with the parents. Many offer baby-sitting services and special learning or play programs for kids.

Other resorts do not accommodate children under 18—or, in some cases, 16. Check the destinations chapters for specifics.

Dozens of guidebooks on the market deal specifically with family travel. Recommended is *Best Places to Go,* Vol. I, by Nan Jeffrey (San Francisco: Foghorn Press). A popular newsletter called *Family Travel Times* is published by **Travel With Your Children,** 45 W 18th St., 7th floor, New York, NY 10011; tel. (212) 206-0688. The newsletter does not limit itself to the Caribbean but does have Caribbean features and publishes a Caribbean issue every September.

Villa rentals may be advantageous for families because of the autonomy and, if you do your research, affordability. Most come with household help, including baby-sitters and cooks. The accommodations vary wildly, from apartments to large homes, and the rates vary according to size and location (see "Accommodations," above, for companies listing Virgin Islands villas).

SINGLE TRAVELERS

Singles have a wide range of accommodations possibilities in the Virgin Islands—if they're willing to pay the price. A simple rule of thumb is that single rooms are rarely half the rate of doubles. Sometimes a single will pay only slightly less than a couple, and sometimes the rate for singles and doubles is exactly the same—clearly a cost advantage for couples. The same goes for cabins on cruise ships. Cruise ships want rooms occupied by doubles, who spend twice the amount on meals, drinks, entertainment, etc., not singles, who spend as one. Therefore, most cruise companies levy surcharges for single passengers which may equal the double rate.

Remember, too, that while some hotels give separate rates for single and double rooms, others give rates per person based on double occupancy, which may not be the same as single occupancy. Confusing? Of course it's confusing, which is why a number of organizations have cropped up to make single travel more fun and cost effective.

One such organization is the **Travel Companion Exchange** (P.O. Box 833, Amityville, NY 11701, tel. 516-454-0880 or 800-392-1256, fax 516-454-0170). Owner Jens Jurgens has a philosophy regarding Caribbean travel that he calls Noah's Rule: "Thou must have a travel companion to get a good travel bargain." Jurgens publishes a very useful and concise newsletter with information for travelers, and through it pairs up potential travelers (opposite or same sex). Singles can list their preferences for travel companions, destinations, amount of money they want to spend, and more. It's $99 to list your name and preferences for eight months. A sample copy of the newsletter is $5, and a subscription is $48. The newsletter contains as many as 500 listings of singles looking for travel companions. The Exchange, in operation for more than 15 years, comes highly recommended but cannot screen its listings of travelers. Make sure you meet or talk at length to anyone with whom you plan to embark on a trip, short or extended. If you have to fly from Toledo to Toronto to do so, do it. The small amount of money you spend to make sure your potential fellow traveler isn't an axe murderer could be less than the amount you'd spend on your trip as a single.

NATURISTS

Anyone wishing to doff his or her duds outdoors, at the beach, or on cruises, will have to be discreet in the Virgin Islands. No resorts or beaches sanction clothing-optional activities, and public nudity is against the law.

Having said that, you can find several isolated beaches in both the U.S. and British Virgin Islands where nudity is tacitly practiced. These include Salomon Bay on St. John and the far end of Magens Bay on St. Thomas. Remember, however, that public nudity in both island groups might offend locals—the key here is personal responsibility.

As well, several U.S.-based cruise companies can offer advice on clothing-optional sailing experiences. Start by calling the full-service travel company **Travel Au Naturel,** 35246 US 19 N., Suite 112, Palm Harbor, FL 34684, tel. (800) 728-0185 or (813) 948-2007, fax (813) 948-2832, or the cruise-oriented **Bare Necessities,** 1802 West 6th St., Suite B, Austin, TX 78703, tel. (800) 743-0405, fax (512) 469-0179.

One of the best single sources for information on worldwide clothing-optional activities, with substantial sections on the Caribbean, is Lee

Baxandall's *World Guide to Nude Beaches and Recreation*. Write to N Editions, P.O. Box 132, Oshkosh, WI 54902.

GAY AND LESBIAN TRAVELERS

While facilities for gays and lesbians do exist in the Virgin Islands, visitors will soon find that the island cultures do not always openly embrace homosexuality. No surprise there; it's just that, in general, the Caribbean is no Provincetown or San Francisco. Obviously, homosexuality does exist in the islands, but it is not a lifestyle that is always accepted enough or even tolerated on a level that would make openly gay visitors comfortable in all situations. That said, gays and lesbians will find a number of hotels that are "gay friendly" and others that openly court the gay and lesbian market. One hotel actively advertising for gays and lesbians is the **On the Beach Resort,** near Frederiksted on St. Croix. Gay-friendly hotels include Pink Fancy, in Christiansted on St. Croix, and Blackbeard's Castle, in Charlotte Amalie, St. Thomas.

For more information about gay and lesbian travel in general, a good source in the U.S. is the *International Gay Travel Association* in Key West, Florida, tel. (800) 448-8550. Call them; they might be able to put you in touch with a travel agent in your area who specializes in gay travel.

SPECIALTY TRAVEL INDEX

It seems worth repeating that an extremely useful publication for all travelers is the U.S.-based *Specialty Travel Index,* 305 San Anselmo Ave., San Anselmo, CA 94960; tel. (415) 459-4900, fax (415) 459-4974, e-mail spectrav@ix.netcom.com, Web site http://www.spectrav.com. The magazine comes out twice a year and lists more than 600 tour operators and outfitters that cater to special and not-so-special interests. Entries are thoroughly cross-referenced by geographical region and personal interests. Cost is $6 per issue, or $10 per year ($13 in Canada).

WHAT TO TAKE

Luggage
Consider your clothes laid out on the bed, ready to be packed. Consider your billfold, stuffed with traveler's checks. Conventional wisdom dictates that you put back half the clothes and go out and get some more money—and that is as true in the Virgin Islands as it is elsewhere. It's not that the Virgin Islands are expensive—with effort, and aside from airfare and a rental car, you can cover it on $50 or less per person per day. Of course, you can also spend up to $1,000 per day. It all boils down to elective lifestyles.

Generally, people bring too many clothes, accessories, knicks, and knacks—and get bogged down lugging it all over the islands. Travel lightly and efficiently, particularly if you'll be traveling by ferry between islands. Efficiently means that you are able carry it yourself, be it a backpack or suitcase. For some, that means taking only carry-on luggage, eliminating the risk of lost luggage ending up somewhere in Chechnya and ensuring that you'll be among the first in and out of customs lines. Check with your airline regarding baggage allowance. Most allow two or three checked bags and one or two carry-ons. Typically, the carry-on must be no larger than 45 linear inches in total dimensions (add the length, width, and depth) and up to 70 pounds in weight. Pocketbooks, purses, and small briefcases are not, in practice, considered luggage, so you can take them on as well. Checked bags are typically 62 total inches in size and 70 pounds each. It sounds technical, but in practice these allowances cover just about any standard suitcase or backpack available. Additional bags are charged by weight. But you'd be surprised how much you can fit in a carry-on bag. Remember, in these days of tight airport security, all bags must be tagged with your name and address. It's a good idea to keep an ID label inside the luggage as well for further identification if it's lost or stolen.

Clothes and Toiletries
Think "light" for clothes: light cotton shorts, T-shirts, and tops for both men and women. Take

plaiting hair, circa 1900

sports? dancing? dining in nice restaurants?—and bring the proper footwear.

All basic toiletries are available in both territories, but many are more expensive than at home. You have your own preferences, too, so bring your deodorant, toothpaste, floss, and shampoo, as well as makeup, skin cream, contraceptives, tampons, and other items you'll need to be comfortable.

Also take your prescription drugs, glasses or contacts, vitamins, aspirin, antiseptic cream or spray, sterile strips, lip protection, something for diarrhea, insect repellent, and, if you're prone to it, motion-sickness medication.

Hiking and Camping Supplies

Most campers and hikers have a fair idea of what kind of gear they'll need. Bring it. Several of the islands' camping spots rent tents, but you can't always count on it. Make sure your tent is secure, mosquito proof, and waterproof. If you can lock the zippers or flaps, then do so. You may bring cooking utensils, but keep in mind that many camping areas have kitchen facilities or restaurants nearby. Do bring a can and bottle opener, flashlight, pocketknife, corkscrew, and, if you intend to do some serious hiking, a canteen or water bottle. Of course, your best hiking shoes, shorts, sunglasses, and a sun hat are must-brings. Bring food containers, insect repellent, a small first-aid kit, and a light sleeping bag or sheets.

A day pack is good for shopping and going to the beach. Waterproof matches are important, even when it's not raining; humidity has been known to reduce match heads to useless lumps. A poncho or good umbrella will be very useful. Dried food is your call; there are enough fresh fruits, vegetables, and good restaurants everywhere to warrant leaving the astronaut stuff at home. Extra twine comes in handy for clotheslines and tying things to your pack.

Cameras

It would be a shame not to capture the Virgin Islands' beauty on film. You know your camera, filters, and accessories best, but always pack them with silica-gel bags to beat the occasional humidity. Bring enough film for the entire trip, and consider waiting and having it processed back home. Film is expensive on some of the is-

one set of evening wear (**men, take note:** some, but not many, hotels and restaurants require a jacket and trousers at dinner). Consider prints, which don't show wrinkles readily, and drip-dry-type clothes. Unless you want to take out a series of small loans to pay for hotel laundry services, you'll be doing your own washing. Coin-operated washing machines are readily available on St. Thomas and St. Croix and at various yacht harbors throughout the islands.

Take two bathing suits—unless you actually enjoy putting on a wet bathing suit (in which case we don't want to know).

A lightweight jacket or sweater (flannel shirts work well) may be useful in the cool mountain breezes and even by the beach on some evenings. To save luggage space, wear the sweater on the trip. Airplanes tend to be cool anyway, and if you've just flown out of Toronto in sub-zero weather, you'll need something to get you to the airport—but you'll not want to carry a heavy winter coat to the Virgin Islands.

Flip-flops or light shoes are fine most of the time. Consider your intended activities—hiking?

lands, and although developing is comparable, not all processes are available everywhere. In resort areas, you'll find a fistful of one-hour developing stores.

An instant camera is a great way to give photo gifts to people. If you want to take photos of Virgin Islanders, please ask first. They may want one for themselves, which is where the instant can be fun. They may also want money, and if the photo means enough to you, please respect that. Bring photos of yourself and family if you plan to spend time in rural areas—people love to see and talk about them.

Incidentals

If you have specialized sports gear, bring it along. This includes golf equipment (though the courses do rent), tennis and other rackets, extra balls, and specialty shoes. Scuba divers can bring their regulators and buoyancy compensators, and all divers may want to bring their own masks, fins, and snorkels. Diving equip-ment, however, can be rented at hotels and dive centers. Reef-walking shoes are a nice plus if you intend to spend time walking along the reef and rocky shorelines.

Don't forget your address book at home or at the hotel (it's one of the most commonly left behind items). If you're a big correspondent, bring pens, stationery, envelopes, and, if you're traveling from the U.S. mainland to the U.S. Virgins, stamps. Plastic bags come in handy for storing wet or dirty clothes.

U.S. citizens can carry into the U.S. Virgin Islands an unlimited amount of whatever is legal—it's the same as traveling domestically, from state to state. Foreigners traveling into the U.S. Virgin Islands will find cigarettes and liquor subject to a six-percent duty—there are no exemptions. British Virgin Islands customs charges a minimal tax on anything more than one gallon of alcohol ($2-4 a gallon), but, in the words of a customs official, "We basically don't care about that."

HEALTH AND PERSONAL SAFETY

Local medical professionals, when asked to name the number-one medical problem tourists face, have a stock reply: "The morning after." Indeed, the problems most visitors encounter in the Virgin Islands are overexposure to sun, rum, and spicy foods—all preventable with common sense. It's always wise to increase your intake of nonalcoholic fluids in a tropical environment—you'll lose quite a bit of fluid through sweat. Doctors recommend at least eight large glasses (about eight pints) of water per day. Coconut water is healthy, inexpensive, and a fun alternative to soft drinks (which should not be considered as an alternative to that basic liquid, water, anyway).

Skin Care

It's hot, the water is inviting, and you'd like to get out of doors as soon as possible. But remember, the tropical sun is extremely strong, even when seemingly covered by clouds. If you've got sensitive skin, a wide-brimmed hat and strong sunscreen are in order. Sunscreen is universally available throughout the Virgin Islands, but the prices may be higher than you'd pay at home. It's best to bring your own special brand, and try to take it easy on the tanning process for the first few days. Aloe vera is good for a sunburn, but it doesn't replace the best cure—shade. If you are snorkeling for any length of time, you might want to wear a T-shirt to guard against overexposing your back.

Strange environments and stranger bacteria can affect your skin by contributing to slower healing of cuts and scratches; they become infected more easily, and linger. Scratched mosquito bites are prime offenders, as are small rock scrapes or other skin breaks. Wash, disinfect, and cover all cuts as soon as possible. Try not to scratch bites. It is not true that salt water is a good healer for cuts, especially cuts in their early stages. Salt water carries enough bacteria to give you a nasty infection.

Mosquitos are carriers of the protozoan infections malaria and dengue fever. Malaria is problematic in areas of Haiti, the Dominican Republic, and parts of Venezuela but has not been reported in the Virgin Islands for some time. Dengue fever (symptoms: fever, joint and muscle pains, severe headaches) has been reported in the islands but is not epidemic. The only prevention for dengue fever is mosquito prevention. In mosquito-dense areas, use good repellent and wear clothes that cover your arms and legs. Mosquito nets and screened bedrooms will provide protection. If the smoke doesn't bother you, mosquito coils, which are available locally, are helpful.

Food and Water
Drinking water is generally safe throughout the Virgins, and most is filtered, and/or chlorinated. The exceptions to consider are periods immediately after hurricanes, floods, or other high-water situations, when contaminants may mix in the drinking water supply. Infectious hepatitis, called jaundice or Hepatitis A, can be carried by contaminated water. If you are in a situation where you are wary of the water, drink only bottled water—which is available in most shops and restaurants—or coconut water, which is naturally sterilized. Washing or peeling fruit and paying strict attention to personal hygiene will reduce the likelihood of contracting hepatitis. A commonly available inoculation, gamma globulin, is effective against Hepatitis A. The shot is not required for travel to the Virgin Islands, but if you so choose, doctors can prescribe it. It should be administered as close as possible to your departure date.

Vaccinations, Prescription Drugs, Insurance
Smallpox and yellow fever vaccinations are no longer required of North Americans and Europeans when traveling to the Virgin Islands. Travelers originating from other Caribbean countries, as well as South America, Asia, Africa, and other parts of the world, should check regulations before departure.

If you need prescription drugs, don't count on them being readily available on the smaller islands—bring enough to last your trip. An extra pair of prescription glasses or contacts is also a good idea.

Check your health insurance to see if you're covered overseas, and what the coverage entails. If you want to purchase more, the following offer treatment and evacuation coverage as well as hard-to-find protection for scuba-diving injuries. Payment is determined by the length of time you travel and by the coverage you need.

Price is about $100 per week for a package of medical, evacuation, accident, and loss-of-life coverage. In the U.S., try **American Express Travel Protection Plan,** P.O. Box 919010, San Diego, CA 92191-9010, tel. (800) 234-0375, or **Access America International,** 600 Third Ave., New York, NY 10163, tel. (800) 284-8300.

Sexually Transmitted Diseases
Wherever humans mix in one way or another, sexually transmitted diseases will follow. Herpes, gonorrhea, and other venereal diseases exist in the Virgin Islands. Condoms are available in all pharmacies and hotels shops. *Check expiration dates.*

AIDS has become a problem in the Virgins, as it has throughout the world. Recent estimates put the number of U.S. Virgin Islanders infected with the HIV virus at a rather breathtaking one in eight. Given the number of tourists who move through the region yearly, as well as the number of West Indians who travel abroad, it would be foolish to engage in unsafe sex. However, be aware that even though great strides have been made in public education, some taboos regarding condoms and the use of other safe-sex practices might exist.

Prevention of Seasickness
There are drug-free products on the market to prevent motion sickness. One, a wristband that controls nausea by applying acupressure to specific points on the wrist, costs about $20 for a set of two. They're called Sea Bands and can be found at health-food or sporting-goods stores or through various catalogues.

PERSONAL SAFETY

The issue of visitor safety on all Caribbean islands has become a prime subject for debate in recent years—not surprising, considering that tourism provides major portions of earned foreign exchange on many of the islands. One side of the debate contends that crime in the Caribbean has increased only slightly in recent years, but voracious media coverage has made it appear that major crime waves are sweeping the erstwhile idyllic islands. The other side of the debate contends that crime, including violent

CAR TROUBLE

Businesspeople often speak of the "80/20 rule," which officially refers to the 20% of a company's products that yield 80% of its profits. Unofficially, it means that 20% of the workforce will drink 80% of the eggnog at the annual Christmas party, but that's another story for another time.

I've always thought of travel to the Caribbean in terms of a reverse-80/20 rule: 80% of your meticulous planning will anticipate only 20% of your trip. The rest is in the hands of karma, kismet, fate, God, and airline ticket agents, all of which lie beyond the ken of mere mortals. Despite your best efforts, it's not the planning that determines the success of a jaunt, it's how you handle the unexpected, difficult moments.

Although I've never had an outright Trip from Hell in the Caribbean, I've been at the gates a few times. Yet I've managed to avoid assigning my bad moments to the derogatory stereotypes often applied to the region. Yes, I've encountered incomprehensible ferry schedules and 11 p.m. starts of 9 p.m. calypso concerts, but that to me lends truth to travel. When you're sitting next to a flatulent goat on a crowded bus in the pouring rain, you know you're not in Kansas anymore, Dorothy.

It's generally unfair to blame our Caribbean hosts for our inconveniences, for three main reasons: 1) any American who whines about Caribbean inefficiency has obviously never motored down New York's Hudson River Parkway, which has been, as near as I can figure, under continuous construction since 1898; 2) it's hard to give credence to complaints from those tourists whose idea of the nexus of local experience is to braid their hair and buy straw hats.

Perhaps the most important reason, however, that I haven't blamed my travel troubles on the local milieu has little to do with cultural sensitivity. The truth is, they've often been my own fault.

Consider, for instance, the day I nearly demolished a $60,000 Mercedes-Benz and sent my rental car to the bottom of a marina.

You may be aware that some cars automatically lock when you shut the door. I was not (this has changed). I was on St. Croix and had stopped at a marina to take a few photos. Since the rental car's air-conditioning was on, I left the engine running as I jumped out and slammed the door.

For your information, the sound of four doors simultaneously locking in an idling car with its windows tightly shut resembles thunder. A sonic boom. The sound inside your head after one of the famous Full Moon parties at Bomba's on Tortola.

So I reacted as would any normal person who's just locked himself out of a running car. I kicked the door. The rental, an automatic and an apparently sensitive car, took offense at that and responded by popping itself into reverse.

At this point I should mention that the rear of the car was pointed toward a gleaming, scratchless Mercedes-Benz. I saw my future, such as it was—after the rental had taken out the Mercedes, which no insurance policy I've ever owned would've covered, it would then plow through several more significantly expensive cars and plunge off the dock, bouncing from a luxury yacht into the deep blue water of the marina.

So I took the next logical step. I screamed as if I'd stepped on one of St. Croix's numerous Turk's Cap cacti, which, in fact, I then did as I cleverly ran around the car trying to open unopenable doors. Luckily, I'd pulled the parking brake before locking myself out, but as the straining car inched backwards I suddenly realized, with the crisp clarity of the truly insane, that I'd had better days.

I limped across the way and found a huge rock with which I fully intended to smash the rental's window and thereby safeguard my kids' eventual college educations. But, at the last moment—call it karma—I realized I could instead use it to chock the vehicle's rear wheel and perhaps buy some time.

That I did, and then hobbled to a nearby dive shop where I phoned the rental company.

They had extra keys (score one for Caribbean efficiency), and within minutes a young guy arrived to save the day. Still, when he discovered the scene I'd created he looked at me as if I were missing my straw hat.

The moral of the story? There is none. It might've happened in Boston and I couldn't have blamed Bostonians for it either. Blame it on the 80/20 rule—that unanticipated element that makes travel what it is: a sublime mix of magnificence and sheer terror.

Or call it stupidity. Then help me pull these cactus needles out of my foot.

crime, has indeed increased throughout the Caribbean and is fueled by increased trafficking and consumption of illegal drugs.

As with many prominent social issues, truths can be gleaned from both sides of the debate. No doubt crime has increased in a measurable extent on the islands, and drugs are now more widely available than ever before. And, with the advent of cable television and ubiquitous news organizations such as CNN, these crimes are reported with increasing frequency. The truth, again lying between the two, might be summed up thusly: crime exists throughout the Caribbean, but to a lesser extent than in most major North American or European cities. And visitors and locals alike can avoid crime by taking practical precautions.

So it is in the U.S. Virgin Islands and British Virgin Islands. The U.S. Virgins, with greater populations and ties to the U.S., has reported several high-profile crimes against visitors in recent years, including murder and armed robbery. In 1995, however, according to reports, crime affected only two thousandths of one percent of the U.S. Virgin Islands' two million annual visitors. Even so, the local government has responded decisively and developed several programs to combat crime and allay visitor fears.

Increasingly, police and National Guard troops have been placed on the streets of Charlotte Amalie on St. Thomas—the U.S. Virgin Islands' most troubled spot—and in Christiansted on St. Croix and other selected areas. Among these police are Tourist Oriented Police (TOP), whose job is to keep their eyes on tourists and help them get around. These "TOP-cops" are often bicycle mounted. The tourism department has also produced brochures outlining safety tips for visitors and is scheduled to install street signs indicating "good" areas to explore and "bad" areas to ignore.

In Charlotte Amalie, the bad areas include the **Paul M. Pearson Garden** housing complex, across from the currently abandoned Ramada Yacht Haven hotel; **Harris Court,** near Nelson Mandela Circle by the Havensight Mall; lower **Kronprindsens Gade,** west of downtown; **Hospital Ground,** at Sugar Estate and off Sugar Estate Road north and east of downtown; and **Simmonds Alley.**

In addition, The U.S. Virgin Islands is set to in-

stall more emergency call boxes throughout the islands, urge rental car companies to remove bumper stickers and decals identifying rentals, and, among other measures, increase drug raids and random X-ray inspections at post offices and airports. The results of these measures will be hard to predict, but the government's willingness to address the problem and preserve the major U.S. Virgin Islands' income source of tourism is encouraging.

It's difficult to place the British Virgins in the same category as the U.S. Virgins as far as the prevalence of crime goes. With smaller populations, stringent British laws and punishment codes, and stricter gun controls, the British Virgin Islands are relatively free of violent crime—although petty thefts and break-ins do occur.

Precautions

In general, in both the U.S. and British Virgin Islands, you can take sensible, practical precautions that will limit your vulnerability to bad guys. Women who travel alone are taking a chance of incurring some harassment, most of it verbal. This behavior is as common in the Virgins as it is elsewhere. Staring, whistling, and getting approached might happen. Remember, tourists often represent people out for a good time; that may not be you, but it is some people, and you'll have to put up with the behavioral flotsam left in their wake. Women traveling in groups or with companions are in a better position to avoid it.

The Virgin Islands are more conservative than not, but the abundance of tourist activity

---

APPEARANCE

Among locals in the U.S. and British Virgin Islands, a tradition of covering up remains strong. This is perhaps more the case in the British Virgin Islands. British Virgin Islanders pride themselves on neatness and appearance, and slovenly, tank-topped cruise ship passengers will stand out like, well, slovenly, tank-topped tourists. For locals, long skirts, uniforms for schoolchildren, and modesty are the norm. Bathing attire or skimpy shorts and shirts will offend if worn off the beach.

lends a looseness to the social atmosphere that may be misinterpreted. Beachwear, for instance, is considered just that, and wearing bathing suits or other revealing clothing in public places may send the wrong signals.

Avoid walking along deserted beach stretches at night or getting into unmarked cars declaring themselves taxis. Areas in and around large towns may be dangerous, particularly at night, for locals and visitors alike. If you are unsure, ask the hotel staff or a taxi driver you trust.

Be street-smart, as you would in any major city worldwide. Lock your rental car. Carry your wallet or purse in a pouch or front pocket. Avoid basket-type or open handbags—they're easy targets for pickpockets. Pulling large wads of cash out to make purchases sends a signal as bright as a lighthouse beacon. Don't leave bags unattended at the beach.

Drugs

In the U.S. Virgin Islands and, to a lesser extent, the British Virgin Islands, marijuana, cocaine, crack, LSD—the usual suspects—are available. Drugs are also, of course, illegal according to the laws of the U.S. and Great Britain, respectively. Local authorities are very sensitive to the drug problem, and the police are sophisticated in detecting drug use and trafficking—the U.S. has posted DEA and other federal agents in the islands to help local authorities monitor drug activity. Possession and use are punishable by heavy fines, deportation, and jail sentences. The penalties for smuggling are worse.

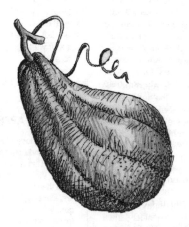

cho cho

UNITED STATES VIRGIN ISLANDS
INTRODUCTION

It is not easy, early in a trip to the United States Virgin Islands, to overcome a vague sense that the islands are large, albeit exotic, side streets off the North American vacation boulevard. From the ubiquitous McDonald's to the surgeon general's warning on cigarette packages, it seems as if the U.S. has come to stay. And it apparently has. The U.S. Virgin Islands, as a territory of the United States, is not likely, in the near future, to eschew the accoutrements of that status. And for some visitors, this is the appeal.

Yet for all the trappings of familiarity for visitors coming from North America, the islands are distinctly West Indian as well. It takes just a bit to scratch the surface to get to those rich roots, reflected in the islands' people, their language and culture, and their history.

Of course, the magnificent countryside and beaches on all three islands also count for something. All are reminders that you have indeed left the mainland behind. This is truer the farther one gets from Charlotte Amalie on St. Thomas, and truer still as one leaves St. Thomas for its sister islands St. Croix and St. John.

There is much to recommend in the U.S. Virgin Islands. The distinctions between the major islands, as well as possibilities for exploring the nearby British Virgin Islands, make for a wide array of choices, and then some.

THE LAND

The U.S. Virgin Islands comprise an estimated 70 large and small islands. Three main islands—St. Thomas, St. John, and St. Croix—are the larger ones and are inhabited. The islands are located just 40-70 miles (64-112 km) east of Puerto Rico and 1,100 miles (1,760 km) southeast of the southern tip of Florida. Geologically, the U.S. Virgin Islands are related in their origins to the British Virgin Islands to the east and to Puerto Rico and the Greater Antilles as part of the extensive underwater shelf called the Virgin Bank.

St. Thomas is the commercial and administrative hub of the three islands, separated from the Puerto Rican islands of Culebra and Vieques

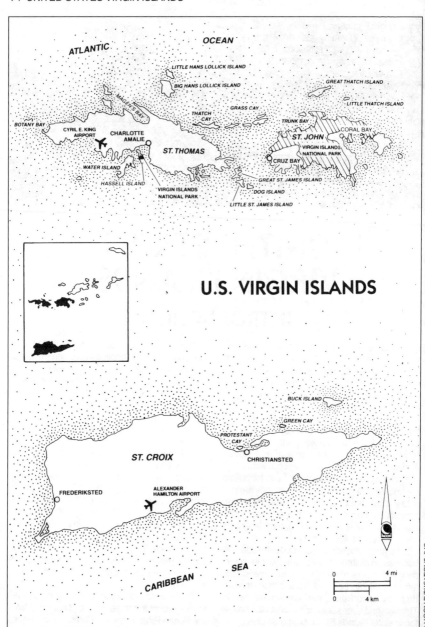

by the **Virgin Passage.** The island is small, measuring 13 miles (21 km) by three miles (five km) at its widest point, and is 32 square miles (83 square km) in area. It is, as are the rest of the U.S. Virgin Islands, a volcanic island—hilly, rugged, and dramatic, with a jagged, irregular coast. Both St. Thomas and St. John are touched by the Atlantic Ocean on their north coasts and by the Caribbean Sea on the south. St. Croix, to the south, sits squarely in the Caribbean Sea.

Crown Mountain on the western end of St. Thomas is the island's highest point, 1,556 feet (473 meters). The rest of the thickly populated (48,000) island is characterized by lesser hills, lowlands to the south and southeast, and a dented coastline of small bays and inlets. Dozens of cays and islets surround the coast and include the National Park entity **Hassell Island,** in **St. Thomas Harbor** across from the south coast's Charlotte Amalie (pronounced A-MAHL-yah). Charlotte Amalie is the largest town on St. Thomas, the cruise-ship center, and the capital and administrative center of the entire territory.

St. John, some four miles (more than six km) east of St. Thomas and seven miles (11 km) west of Tortola in the British Virgin Islands, is—at nine miles (14 km) long, five miles (eight km) across at its widest point, and 20 square miles (52 square km) in area—the smallest of the U.S. Virgin Islands. It is also the least populated (3,500) and unique for having more than 10,000 protected land and offshore acres—part of the Virgin Islands National Park system. The land, donated by the millionaire Laurance Rockefeller in 1956, is one of the oldest of the U.S. national parks. St. John is hilly and lush, with its highest point the central 1,193-foot (358-meter) **Camelberg Peak.** The coast is lined with quiet bays and long beaches, some of the most compelling in the islands. The far western portion of St. John is home to **Cruz Bay,** the island's main center.

St. Croix, located some 40 miles (64 km) south of St. Thomas, is the largest of the U.S. Virgin Islands, at 84 square miles (217 square km)—28 miles (45 km) long by seven miles (11 km) wide. It is less dramatic than its sister islands and characterized by gently sloping hills, some semi-rainforest topography to the west, and dry areas, featuring cacti and scrub brush, in the south and eastern sections of the island. **Christiansted,** on the central north coast, and **Frederiksted,** on the west coast, are home to the majority of the island's population of 50,000.

GOVERNMENT AND ECONOMY

The U.S. Virgin Islands—officially, The Virgin Islands of the United States—is an unincorporated territory of the United States. The head of state is the U.S. president, and the islands combine to elect a non-voting representative to the U.S. House of Representatives. Within the internal government structure of the U.S. Virgin Islands, the executive is a governor (elected every four years), who is supported by a 15-

*Magen's Bay,
St. Thomas*

KEY DATES IN U.S. VIRGIN ISLANDS' HISTORY

(For a more in-depth account of the early days of the Virgin Islands, see "Regional History" in the Introduction.)

A.D. 500: Amerindian Arawaks begin making their way north toward the Virgin Islands from the Orinoco region of South America. They and Amerindian Caribs, also from South America, inhabit the islands until 1500.

1493: Christopher Columbus, blown off course, first sights and charts St. Croix, which he calls Santa Cruz. He later charts the rest of the Virgin Islands, which he dubs *Las Once Mil Virgenes,* The 11,000 Virgins, in honor of the 4th-century martyr St. Ursula and her 11,000 virgin companions.

1625: English and Dutch settlers establish small communities on Santa Cruz.

1650: Spanish marauders capture Santa Cruz, killing or driving off its English and Dutch inhabitants. Later, the lieutenant-general of the French West Indies, de Poincy, claims Santa Cruz for France, renaming it St. Croix. The island is turned over to the French West Indies Company for administration.

1653: St. Croix, bankrupt under the French West Indies Company, is turned over to the Knights of Malta.

1666: Danes, under the Danish West India and Guinea Company, settle St. Thomas.

1671: Fort Christian is built on St. Thomas.

1673: The first boatload of Africans, soon to be slaves, arrives in the Virgin Islands.

1691: Denmark formally founds the town Taphaus on St. Thomas.

1694: Danes claim St. John, but little is done to establish settlements on the island.

1695: The French, due to unprofitable enterprises, abandon St. Croix.

1717: Danish planters from St. Thomas establish plantations on St. John.

1720: St. Thomas conducts its first census; the ratio of slaves to whites on that island and St. John is three to one.

1724: St. Thomas becomes a free trading port.

1730: Following the coronation of the Danish King Christian V, St. Thomas colonists abandon the name Taphaus and rename their town Charlotte Amalie, after his queen.

1733: The Danish West India and Guinea Company buys St. Croix from France, forming, with the islands of St. Thomas and St. John, the Danish West Indies.
   Slaves on St. John rebel, laying waste to several plantations and holding the island for six months before all surrender or are captured to be imprisoned or killed.

1760: Coral Bay, St. John's first town, is established.

1801: The British briefly capture the Danish West Indies and hold the islands for one year.

1803: Denmark abolishes trade in slaves.

1804: Devastating fire sweeps Charlotte Amalie, destroying much of the town.

1807: The British again take possession of the Danish West Indies.

1815: The British return the islands to the Danes.

1848: Slavery as an institution is abolished in the Danish West Indies, and all slaves are freed.

1915: First labor union is established on St. Croix, forming the basis of future political parties.

1917: The U.S. purchases the Danish West Indies for $25 million in gold. The islands become the Virgin Islands of the United States and are administered as a naval base.

1927: U.S. citizenship is conferred on the U.S. Virgin Islanders.

1931: U.S. Virgin Islands administration duties are transferred from the Navy to the Department of the Interior.

1936: The watershed Organic Act transfers a modicum of self-rule to the islands. All islanders are given the right to vote, subject to age and literacy requirements.

1954: A local legislature is elected.

1956: U.S. Congress approves the establishment of the Virgin Islands National Park on St. John.

1968: U.S. Congress passes an act allowing U.S. Virgin Islanders to elect a local governor (previous governors had been appointed by the U.S. president).

1972: U.S. Virgin Islanders elect the first representative to Congress.

1995: Powerful Hurricane Marilyn causes millions in damages and six deaths on St. Thomas and St. John.

1996: Islands are fully recovered from Hurricane Marilyn.

member legislature of senators. The citizens of the U.S. Virgin Islands are also citizens of the United States. The Democratic, Independent Citizens Movement, and Republican parties are the dominant political groups.

There has been agitation in the past regarding the political status of the U.S. Virgin Islands. Some citizens would like to see full independence, some would like greater affiliation, even statehood, while others are happy with the present form of representation. Ongoing debates or referendums, however, do not seem likely to change the islands' status in the near future.

The economy of the U.S. Virgin Islands is reliant on U.S. aid and U.S. Virgin Islanders living abroad as well as on tourism. A Hess Oil refinery and an aluminum plant, both on St. Croix, provide some employment, but by far the main employers are

government, both local and federal, and tourism. Local territorial government and the public sector engage about one-third of the islands' workforce. Tourism and retail trade are the next biggest employers. Agriculture employs few, but outstanding among them are the Senapol cattle breeders of St. Croix. The minimum wage of the islanders is the same as on the U.S. mainland (currently $4.65 and rising), and the standard of living, with a per capita income of $11,000, is higher than on most of the neighboring islands of the Caribbean. Unemployment was about six percent in 1994, in a labor force of approximately 50,000.

Tourism

Tourism, a total of 1,921,000 visitors, accounted for 60% of the U.S. Virgin Islands' gross domestic product in 1994. Of this number, 28%

legislature building, Charlotte Amalie, St. Thomas, built circa 1874

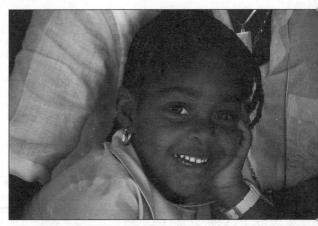

Jonelle-Alexis Jackson, of St. Thomas

were bona fide stayovers, while 72% were day visitors on cruise ships or yachts. Visitors spent $919 million in 1994. St. Thomas is considered to be the number one cruise-ship stop in the Caribbean—an average of five ships per day stop in at Charlotte Amalie (dozens more anchor at St. Croix each month). The islands' hotels have approximately 5,500 rooms available, and this figure is rising. The government and private sector in 1988 launched a $250 million effort to upgrade tourist facilities and island infrastructure to meet the growing demand.

FESTIVALS AND HOLIDAYS

Annual Holidays

Holidays that keep cultural traditions strong include St. Thomas's annual post-Easter **Carnival,** held in late April. The Carnival features African customs such as drumming, dancing the energetic *baboula,* and the exhibition of devils, *jumbies* (spirits or ghosts), and other figures through masquerades. The *mocko jumbi,* a stock comic-grotesque character likely to be found on stilts and wearing a mirror, inhabits many an island festival. Carnival also features masquerade parades, feasts, calypso contests, *quelbe* music, quadrille dancing, and steel bands.

Emancipation Day, celebrating the 1848 end of slavery in the then-Danish West Indies, is celebrated on 3 July. The sounds-like-a-California-thing **Organic Act Day,** in June, celebrates the granting of internal government to the U.S. Virgin Islands. **Transfer Day** (31 March) celebrates the 1917 transfer of the island from Danish to U.S. possession. **Hurricane Supplication Day** is a special day of prayer, held in late July, for delivery from the hurricane season. **Hurricane Thanksgiving Day,** in late October, celebrates the end of the same season. **D. Hamilton Jackson Day** (1 November) celebrates the birthday of an early-20th-century crusader who, in 1915, established a free press and the first labor union in the U.S. Virgin Islands.

St. Croix hosts the two-week **Crucian Christmas Festival,** from Christmas week through the first week in January, featuring feasts, parades, contests, quadrille dancing, and Christmas festivities. The U.S. **Independence Day** (Fourth of July), celebrated throughout the U.S. Virgin Islands, has become St. John's version of Carnival, complete with a week of fireworks and the trappings of St. Thomas's Carnival.

Also celebrated are most U.S. federal and religious holidays such as **New Year's, Three King's Day** (6 January), **Martin Luther King Day, Presidents' Day, Holy Thursday, Good Friday, Easter, Easter Monday, Memorial Day, Labor Day, Columbus Day** (also called **Puerto Rico-Virgin Islands Friendship Day**), **Veteran's Day, Thanksgiving Day** (in November but also the aforementioned additional Thanksgiving Day in October celebrating the end of hurricane season), **Christmas,** and **Christmas Second Day** (26 December).

Annual Events

In addition to annual legal holidays, the U.S. Virgin Islands does not want for yearly special events. The **St. Croix Blues and Heritage Festival,** started in 1996, promises early January performances each year by some of the world's bluesiest artists including Taj Mahal, Earl King, and Al Rapone. Call the seemingly oxymoronic **Blues Hotline** (tel. 800-524-5006) for information.

St. Croix hosts the first race in a series of 11 in the **World Professional Triathlon Tour.** The other 10 running, swimming, and biking races take place around the world. The **St. Croix International Triathlon** is held in April and is preceded by a week of music and food festivities. Call the tourist board (tel. 809-773-0495) for details.

In early February, sailors might want to take part in the **Around St. Croix Race** (St. Croix Yacht Club, tel. 809-773-9531). The **International Rolex Cup Regatta** has been held for more than 23 years at the St. Thomas Yacht Club (tel. 809-775-6320). Other sailing races and tournaments include the **Mumm's Cup Regatta** in May, the **Harvest Moon Race** in October, and the **Veteran's Day Race** in November; call the St. Croix Yacht Club for information on any of these events.

A couple of world-class marlin fishing tournaments are held each August. The **Blue Marlin Tournament** (tel. 809-774-2752) and the **September Moon Classic Blue Marlin Tournament** (tel. 305-599-1583) are favorites with serious anglers.

The **LPGA Pro Am Tournament** is held in mid-April at the Carambola Golf Club (tel. 809-772-2425), on St. Croix.

One Love and his goat, Drake's Seat, St. Thomas

ST. THOMAS

SIGHTS

Downtown Charlotte Amalie

The U.S. Virgin Islands' historic and likable capital, Charlotte Amalie, is an orderly town, laid out in grids, somewhat hilly but easily navigated. The downtown area is congested with both motor and foot traffic, but you'll find the going much easier if you're walking (and it'll be much more fun). The shops, malls, small alleys, cafes, and sights all lend themselves to exploring, and you could easily spend a few hours just roaming the area.

The **waterfront** is the center of town and is bustling with ferries, shops, historic buildings, and government complexes. The busy and often congested two-lane road that runs along the Waterfront is Rt. 30, also called **Waterfront Highway** and, in town, **Veterans Drive** or **Kanal Gade.**

Out in the harbor lie two small islands, **Water Island,** which is privately owned, and **Hassell Island,** which was once attached to the mainland but was separated by the U.S. Navy in order to provide an access channel. Hassell Island (tel. 809-775-6238) is today a Virgin Islands National Park entity and is open to the public, which can explore military fortification ruins and the old shipyard there. A ferry (tel. 809-774-9652) makes the short trip from the mainland's waterfront several times daily.

Much of Charlotte Amalie was destroyed—not once, but twice—in devastating fires in 1802 and 1804. The architecture today reflects Danish, French, and English influences, most dating back to after the fires. The center of the shopping district houses many shops in 19th-century warehouses and shipping centers. Running parallel to the Waterfront Highway, and connected to it by several small roads and alleys, is **Main Street** (Dronningens Gade). Main Street has several examples of the old architecture, including, at its western end, **Market Square,** an iron-roofed structure once used as a slave market and now a produce and trinket market open daily except Sunday. Drop by on Saturday, the busiest day, for fruits and produce from around the islands. Next door to the market is the pastel-peach-colored **Enid M. Baa Public Library.**

A stroll along Main Street is your opportunity to max out your credit cards. This is duty-free shopping heaven, with dozens of jewelry, leather, perfume, and souvenir shops lining the street and tucked in the alleys leading down to Waterfront Drive or up to the city's other Old World road, **Back Street,** which is parallel to Main. It's also a chance to explore the town's historic sights. Head up steep **Raadets Gade** to **Crystal Gade,** where you'll find the **Synagogue of Berecha V'Shalom V'Gemilath Chasidim** (Blessing and Peace and Acts of Piety). The synagogue, sometimes called the St. Thomas Synagogue for short, was first founded in 1796. Jewish settlers from Amsterdam and London had lived on St. Thomas since 1665, and by the time the temple was first constructed, nine families made up its congregation. The temple was destroyed in the citywide fire in 1804, rebuilt in 1833, and is today one of the oldest in the Western Hemisphere (the oldest in continual use is on the Dutch island of Curaçao). Sand covers the floor in memory of the flight over the desert Jews took in their escape from Egypt. Attached to the synagogue is the small **Weibel Museum** (tel. 809-774-4312), which traces the considerable history of Jews in the Virgin Islands. The museum is open weekdays 9 a.m.-5 p.m.

At the eastern end of Main Street is the extension street called **Norre Gade,** with the cream-colored brick gothic **Frederick Lutheran Church.** The Lutheran Church, once the official church of the islands (and of the Danes, since 1536), was lost to fires in 1750 and 1789. The present structure was completed in 1826, gutted by another fire in 1829, and refurbished soon after. The church is open for viewing weekdays and Saturday 8 a.m.- 5 p.m. and for services on Sunday. Call (809) 776-1315 for a schedule.

Head north from the church on Norre Gade to **Government Hill,** where you'll find looming **Government House.** The white structure framed by intricate iron grillwork was built in 1867 and is now the residence of the islands'

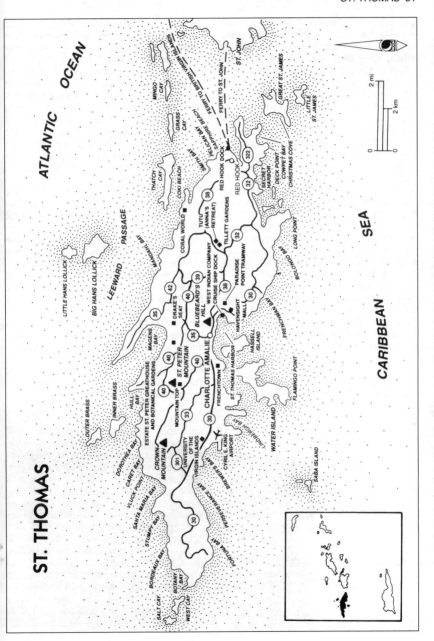

ST. THOMAS

governor. The first floor—with its large reception area—and the second are open to the public. Next to Government House is the foot of the deeply steep **99 Steps** staircase built in the 1700s by the apparently ironic Danes—there are actually 103 steps. The steps were ordered constructed by Danish engineers who, clearly, had never set foot on St. Thomas. Hence, they never realized how heart-attack inspiring the steps turned out to be. The steps were constructed of ballast bricks from Danish ships. The **Lieutenant Governor's Office,** also on Government Hill, is another example of the Danish plantation architecture of the era. Behind the office is the tiny **Seven Arches Museum** (tel. 809-774-9295), which was once a private home and is now fully restored as an example of early Danish life. The attraction here is the furniture; note the detached brick-oven kitchen, the courtyard, and the seven archways throughout the house. The museum is open Tues.-Sat. 10 a.m.-3 p.m. A small donation is requested.

On the other side of the 99 Steps is the **Hotel 1829,** a classic example of that period's architecture. The hotel was originally built as the home of one Captain Lavalette, a French skipper, whose initials are indicated in the iron grillwork above the entrance. The old Lavalette House, now restored, is a hotel, one of the island's better known.

Huff and puff your way to the top of the steps and you'll find **Crown House,** built as a private home in 1750 and once the home of the islands' Danish governors. Also at the top of the steps is the legendary and possibly apocryphal **Blackbeard's Castle.** The tower, now a small hotel with a fine restaurant, was built in 1678 by a Danish governor and originally called Fort Shytsborg. Some historians contend that it is the oldest structure on St. Thomas, beating Fort Christian (see below) by several years. It allegedly later became a hideout of the pirate Edward Teach—Blackbeard—who terrorized the Caribbean seas during the early 1700s. The structure is now a National Historic Landmark.

South from Norre Gade on **Fort Plasden,** across from the main **post office** (tel. 809-774-3750), is **Emancipation Gardens,** where the 1848 emancipation of slaves was officially proclaimed by Governor Peter von Scholten. The small park features a gazebo where you'll often hear bands and concerts at lunchtime. Note the bust of the Danish King Christian V and the small replica of Philadelphia's famous Liberty Bell. A small **Vendors Plaza** is set up on the south side of the park, where you'll find drinks, eats, and trinkets for sale. During the St. Thomas Carnival season, in late April, the Vendor's Plaza and areas surrounding it are converted into **Carnival Village,** the venue for many Carnival events. Across the street from the plaza, on **Tolbold Gade,** is a branch of the **Virgin Islands Tourist Board** (tel. 800-372-USVI).

Queen's Quarter, Charlotte Amalie, St. Thomas circa 1890s

The **Grand Hotel** overlooks the park from the north side. The hotel, which is no longer a hotel but a shopping complex, was built in 1841 and is a fine example of period West Indian architecture. Next door is the **Old Danish Warehouse**, also now a shopping complex.

Cross Fort Plasden from the park and you'll find the rust-red **Fort Christian** (tel. 809-776-4566). The fort, under construction from 1672 until its completion in 1680, is the oldest standing structure in St. Thomas. After the imminent threat from hostile takeovers left the islands, the fort was used as a governor's house, an administrative center, and, more recently (1874-1983), a jail. The clock tower dates back to 1874. The fort now holds historical displays and a small gift shop and is open weekdays 8 a.m.-5 p.m., and Saturday noon-4 p.m. A small donation is accepted.

Across the street from Fort Christian is the 1874 **Legislature Building,** sort of a lime-green regal affair that houses the U.S. Virgin Islands' Legislature. The building was originally built as barracks for the Danish Marines and was later a U.S. troops barracks and a public school. Several major historical events have taken place there, including the ceremony in 1917 that transferred the islands from Danish to U.S. rule. Nearby are the islands' main police department and the Federal Building.

Outskirts of Downtown

At the far west end of town is the small residential area called **Frenchtown.** Frenchtown was settled in the late 18th century by French Huguenot exiles from nearby Saint-Barthélémy, or St. Barts, who fled the island when it was relinquished to Swedish rule. Today, Frenchtown, a fishing village and home to descendants of the original settlers, is also home to several of the island's better bistros and restaurants and a hub of nighttime activity.

At the eastern end of town along Rt. 30, past the **Coast Guard Dock,** is the **West Indian Company Cruise Ship Dock.** Many of the five or six cruise ships that pull into Charlotte Amalie each day dock here, and the area is a center of activity for shoppers and others. The **Havensight Mall,** another shoppers' haven, a string of strip malls, and a tourism booth are located here. Across the street is the **Paradise Point Tramway** (tel. 809-774-9809), a cable car that takes a seven-minute, 660-foot (200-meter) trip up the side of **Slag Hill** overlooking the Havensight Mall and cruise-ship docks. You ultimately reach 700 feet (213 meters) above sea level, and the views of Charlotte Amalie are breathtaking. At the top of the hill is a small resting area with shops, refreshments, and places to sit and take in the view. The tramway operates daily 9 a.m.-5 p.m. (the last cable car up leaves at 4:30 p.m.). Adults pay $10, children under 12 are half price.

Also east of downtown, but west of Havensight, is yet another castle once inhabited by a bearded guy. This one was Bluebeard. The tower sits on the grounds of the Bluebeard's Castle Hotel on **Bluebeard's Hill** (also called Frederiksberg) and allegedly was once the hangout of the pirate of the same name, who built it for his love, Mercedita. Apparently, love was not enough; Mercedita, alas, was unfaithful, and Bluebeard killed her in a jealous rage, then sailed away to other islands and, presumably, other loves. The truth of the tower is simpler. It was built as a watchtower in the late 18th century to help guard Fort Christian and the harbor and later became part of the hotel complex.

Around the Island

St. Thomas's roads are good, the directional signs are adequate, and the getting around is easy if you've got a rental car—just remember to drive on the left. However, you will encounter traffic jams in and around the Charlotte Amalie area and at other places around the island such as **Tutu,** where the Tutu Park Mall creates congestion. If it's a simple island tour you'd like, it may be best to hire a taxi. You won't waste time getting lost, you won't end up in bad sections of town, and the driver can answer your questions. And it's relatively inexpensive: a two-hour tour for two is only $30 (additional passengers pay about $12 each).

Here's an easy scenic drive that takes in many of the island's sights: take Rt. 30 west from Charlotte Amalie, following signs for the airport. This brings you out to the country and heads toward the west end, a relatively uncluttered part of the island. After passing the airport, you'll pass through the **University of the Virgin Islands** complex, a modern pastoral sort

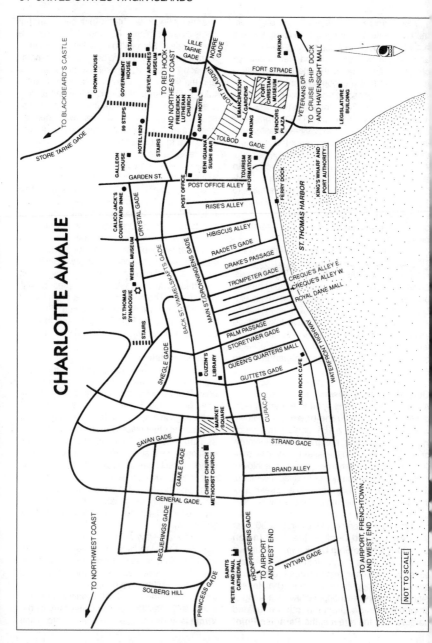

CHARLOTTE AMALIE

TO BLACKBEARD'S CASTLE

CROWN HOUSE

GOVERNMENT HOUSE

SEVEN ARCHES MUSEUM

STAIRS

LILLE TAARNE GADE

NORRE GADE

PARKING

99 STEPS

TO RED HOOK AND NORTHEAST COAST

FORT STRADE

STORE TARNE GADE

HOTEL 1829

STAIRS

FREDERICK LUTHERAN CHURCH

GRAND HOTEL

EMANCIPATION GARDENS

FORT CHRISTIAN MUSEUM

VETERANS DR.

TO CRUISE SHIP DOCK AND HAVENSIGHT MALL

LEGISLATURE BUILDING

GALLEON HOUSE

BENI IGUANA SUSHI BAR

TOLBOD GADE

PARKING

VENDORS PLAZA

GARDEN ST.

POST OFFICE

TOURISM INFORMATION

KING'S WHARF AND PORT AUTHORITY

CALICO JACK'S COURTYARD INNE

CRYSTAL GADE

POST OFFICE ALLEY

FERRY DOCK

WEIBEL MUSEUM

RIISE'S ALLEY

ST. THOMAS SYNAGOGUE

BACK ST./DRONNINGENS GADE

MAIN ST./DRONNINGENS GADE

HIBISCUS ALLEY

ST. THOMAS HARBOR

STAIRS

RAADETS GADE

DRAKE'S PASSAGE

TROMPETER GADE

CREQUE'S ALLEY E.
CREQUE'S ALLEY W.

ROYAL DANE MALL

SNEGLE GADE

PALM PASSAGE

STORETVAER GADE

CUZZIN'S

LIBRARY

QUEEN'S QUARTERS MALL

WATERFRONT HIGHWAY

GUTTETS GADE

HARD ROCK CAFE

CURACAO

MARKET SQUARE

SAVAN GADE

GAMLE GADE

CHRIST CHURCH METHODIST CHURCH

STRAND GADE

BRAND ALLEY

GENERAL GADE

REGJERINGS GADE

PRINCESS GADE

SAINTS PETER AND PAUL CATHEDRAL

KRONPRINDSENS GADE

NYTVAR GADE

TO AIRPORT AND WEST END

TO NORTHWEST COAST

SOLBERG HILL

TO AIRPORT, FRENCHTOWN, AND WEST END

NOT TO SCALE

of setting. The university is the home of the island's **Reichhold Center for the Arts** (tel. 809-693-1559), which offers cultural and folklore performances throughout the year. On the left, right along the road, is long **Brewer's Bay,** one of St. Thomas's more popular beaches.

Bear right at Rt. 301 (West End Road) and you'll be heading into the mountains. Take a left on Rt. 33 (Crown Mountain Road) for further ascent into the hills and sight of **Crown Mountain Peak**—at 1,556 feet (473 meters), the island's highest point. The views to the Atlantic Ocean from points on this drive are striking, and you'll probably want to stop for photos, but don't. Yet. That'll come later. For the moment, your main job is to keep your eye on the road—its twists and turns come up suddenly.

On Rt. 33, look for signs for **Mountain Top** (tel. 809-774-2400), a restaurant and shopping complex located high on **St. Peter Mountain.** Mountain Top has been rated by people who rate these sorts of things as one of the 10 best views in the world. Still, hyperbole aside, the view to the Atlantic is not unlike what it must be to look down from another world. You'll see St. John, Jost Van Dyke, Tortola, and dozens of smaller Virgin Islands. Check them out using the mounted binoculars on the wide viewing deck. Directly below is the majestic **Magens Bay,** possibly the most popular beach in the U.S. Virgin Islands and definitely the most popular on St. Thomas (it is also the beach you see on all the advertising brochures for the U.S. Virgin Islands). At about 1,550 feet (470 meters) above sea level, the views don't get much better. As well, the complex features dozens of funky shops, a photographer whose shtick is to pose you with a parrot, and a bar, which is said to be the birthplace of the banana daiquiri. Birthplace or not, the drink is better here than most anywhere else—maybe it's the altitude. The complex was built as an army lookout more than 40 years ago and has been blown away by several hurricanes but, like your in-laws, it keeps coming back. The shops and bar are open daily.

Leave Mountain Top and head out along Rt. 40 (St. Peter Mountain Road). With the Atlantic still in sight, you'll find the **Estate St. Peter Greathouse and Botanical Gardens** (tel. 809-774-4999). The estate, on 150 acres, was a plantation in the 19th century but was sold to the U.S. Virgin Islands government in 1938. The government developed it as a retreat and sold it to private interests in the 1960s, whereupon it was further developed as an attraction. The entire complex was destroyed by 1989's Hurricane Hugo but was restored soon after. From the observation deck at 1,000 feet (300 meters) above sea level, you'll see Magens Bay, Tobago, Peter Island, Jost Van Dyke, Hans Lollick island, and a number of smaller Virgin Islands. In addition to the huge greathouse, which is a sort of mini-museum of antiques and furnishings as well as local art, you'll find on the grounds a small aviary and an extensive botanical gardens with more than 200 labeled trees and plants, some indigenous, some imported. Other facilities on the grounds include a pool and several private meeting rooms, all of which are designed for corporate functions and weddings. The complex is open for self-guided tours daily 9 a.m.-5 p.m., but come before 4 p.m. to have enough time to tour the entire estate. With your $8 admission ($4 for children 12 and under), you get a rum or fruit punch in addition to the tour.

After leaving the estate, head east on Rt. 40 for a short jaunt to **Drake's Seat.** Drake's Seat is just that, a seat, and a scenic overlook with magnificent views to Magens Bay and the U.S. and British Virgin Islands. The granite seat, with the inscription "The Drake Seat," was reputedly, but probably not, used by the mercenary explorer Sir Francis Drake as a lookout point during his time in the islands in the late 16th century. You'll find several T-shirt and craft vendors selling their wares at the pulloff, as well as a guy with a be-sunglassed donkey or a goat with which you can pose for photos.

From Drake's Seat, head down the hill on Rt. 35 toward Magens Bay, where you can either turn off to the beach or go right on Rt. 42 (Mahogany Run Road). A turnoff from here brings you to the **Mahogany Run Golf Course** (tel. 809-775-5000 or, in the U.S. 800-253-7103), an 18-hole, 6,022-yard, par 70 course, renovated in 1995, which is the pride and joy of the U.S. Virgin Islands. Soon, Rt. 40 meets Rt. 38. A left here and another left on Rt. 388 will bring you to several hotels and **Coki Bay,** another fine beach and the home of **Coral World Marine Park** (tel. 809-775-1555). Coral World is, as of this writing, closed for repairs after 1995's devastating Hurricane Marilyn washed away most of its marine life. In its heyday, Coral World was one of the island's premier attractions—a marine park with nature trails, turtle pools, a baby shark pool, a Touch Pond for kids, an aviary, and changing facilities for the beach. Call the number above or the tourist office (tel. 800-372-8784) for details about its reopening.

Continue along Rt. 38, which soon becomes Rt. 32. This east end of the island is a prime area for resorts, beaches, bays, and tourism activity. Soon, you see signs for **Red Hook,** St. Thomas's "second town," and the jumping-off point for ferries to St. John and the British Virgin Islands. Also in this one-street town are several fine restaurants, hotels, banks, water sports outfits, the **American Yacht Harbor** marina and mall, and the **Virgin Islands National Park** headquarters offices (tel. 809-776-6201).

Continue along the southern coastal road (Rt. 32, then bear left at Rt. 30), where you'll encounter dozens of bays and beaches and some of the island's exclusive resorts. Eventually, the road passes **Morningstar Bay** with its Frenchman's Reef and Morning Star resorts, then on to Havensight and back to Charlotte Amalie.

Take a trip into the interior to the **Anna's Retreat** (also called **Tutu**) section, where you'll find **Tillett Gardens** (tel. 809-775-1929, fax 809-775-9482), an art center with galleries, studios, craft shops, and restaurants. Tillett Gardens, the creation of London-born artist Jim Tillett, was established in the early 1960s and is today one of St. Thomas's showplaces, the best one-stop art center around. It also offers the **Arts Alive** and **Classics in the Gardens** programs, with performances by jazz groups, dance groups, string and piano quartets, and others, year-round.

RECREATION

Tour Companies

You'll have your pick of dozens of professional tour companies that'll take you on anything from island sightseeing tours to mini-cruises to specialized diving or off-island excursions. Some of the better contacts: **Adventure Center** (Frenchman's Reef Hotel, tel. 809-774-2990), **Caribbean Tours** (14 Main St., Charlotte Amalie, tel. 809-776-3650), **Destination Virgin Islands** (19 Norre Gade, Charlotte Amalie, tel. 809-776-2424), **Kelly's Tours** (11b Raphune Hill, tel. 809-777-3979), and **Kon Tiki Party Raft** (tel. 809-775-5055).

For a very specialized tour of underwater activity, contact the **Atlantis Submarine** (Havensight Mall, tel. 809-776-5650 or 800-253-0493). The Atlantis is a true submarine and cruises in depths of as much as 90 feet (27 meters) during its one-hour excursion. You'll see coral reef, fish, turtles, and wrecks on this fascinating narrated dive, which begins in the Charlotte Amalie harbor. The sub's capacity is 46 persons. No children under three feet (one meter) in height or four years of age are allowed. The cost is $72 per adult, $36 for children 13-18 years old, and $27 for children 4-12. The sub operates every day except Sunday, with hourly dives starting at 9:45 a.m. Set aside two hours for the entire trip.

Diving

With all the islands, reefs, wrecks, and reef walls in the surrounding waters, diving is one of the Virgin Islands' most popular activities. And you won't want for dive operations to show you the way to the best spots. These include the **Andreas Reef,** a sloping reef descending from 30 feet (nine meters) to 70 feet (21 meters), covered in tropical fish, stingrays, and multicolored coral. A dive off **Coki Point** is favored by those in love with the many species of warm-water fish found locally. Several wrecks, including those of the *Cartanza Sr.* and the *Witshoal* are favorite deeper-water dives.

Most hotels and resorts are affiliated with a resident dive operation, but for those of you soloing it, contact the following, even before departing for the Virgin Islands.

Admiralty Dive Center (Windward Passage, St. Thomas, U.S. Virgin Islands 00802; tel. and fax 809-777-9802)

Aqua Action Dive Center (6501 Red Hook Plaza #15, St. Thomas, U.S. Virgin Islands 00802; tel. 809-775-6285, fax 809-775-1501)

Arnold's Dive Center (P.O. Box 10894, St. Thomas, U.S. Virgin Islands 00801; tel. 809-775-3333, fax 809-774-3333)

Caribbean Divers (6200 Frydenhoj, St. Thomas, U.S. Virgin Islands 00802; tel. 809-775-6384, fax 809-775-0822)

Chris Sawyer Dive Center (American Yacht Harbor, St. Thomas, U.S. Virgin Islands 00802; tel. 809-777-7804, fax 809-775-9495)

Coki Beach Dive Club (P.O. Box 502096, St. Thomas, U.S. Virgin Islands 00805; tel. 809-775-4220 or 800-474-2654)

Dean Johnson Dive Institute (P.O. Box 6577j, St. Thomas, U.S. Virgin Islands 00801; tel. 809-775-7610)

Dive In (Sapphire Beach Club or P.O. Box 8088, St. Thomas, U.S. Virgin Islands 00801; tel. 809-775-6100, fax 809-775-2403

Dive World (P.O. Box 12140, St. Thomas, U.S. Virgin Islands 00801; tel. 809-774-8687 or 800-467-0488, fax 809-774-7368)

Hi-Tech Watersports (Sub Base or P.O. Box 2180, St. Thomas, U.S. Virgin Islands 00803; tel. 809-774-5650)

St. Thomas Diving Club (7147 Bolongo Bay, St. Thomas, U.S. Virgin Islands 00802; tel. 809-776-2381 or 800-524-4746, fax 809-777-3232)

Sea Trade Ltd. (Crown Bay Marina, St. Thomas, U.S. Virgin Islands 00802; tel. 809-774-2001, fax 809-777-9600)

Underwater Safaris (Marriott Frenchman's Reef Resort or P.O. Box 8469, St. Thomas, U.S. Virgin Islands 00801; tel. 809-774-1350 or 774-4044).

Dives start at $30 per person. For those who prefer snorkeling, the organizations above often also take snorkel groups out, or you can contact the activities desk of your hotel. Average cost of renting snorkel equipment is $5 per hour.

Boating

If you're interested in renting a powerboat for a few hours or a day—be it for exploring, fishing, or swimming—it won't be cheap (from $225 per day for a four-person boat), but it may afford you the luxury of exploring at your own pace. Larger, luxury powerboats are also available for daily or weekly rentals. Contact any of the following.

Aqua Action Watersports (tel. 809-775-6285)

Aqua Blue Powerboats (Sapphire Beach Marina, tel. 809-775-1242)

The Charter Boat Center (Red Hook, tel. 809-775-7990 or 800-866-5714, e-mail cbcboat@ noc.usvi.net, www.usvi.net/vimi/center/)

Island Explorer Rentals (tel. 809-775-5025)

Nauti Nymph Rentals (American Yacht Harbor, tel. 809-775-5066)

See and Ski Power Boat Rentals (Red Hook Dock, tel. 809-775-6265)

Tropical Power Boat Rentals (tel. 809-775-6595)

Virgin Voyages Power Boat Rentals (Sapphire Beach Marina, tel. 809-775-7891)

Watersports Safaris (tel. 809-776-1690)

For day-sails aboard commercial yachts and party boats, as well as sunset cruises and organized snorkeling and picnic excursions, call **Craig's Cruisers** (tel. 809-779-2435) or **Limnos Charters** (tel. 809-775-3203).

If you're into a less raucous sort of boating experience, contact **Virgin Islands Kayak Tours** (tel. 809-777-6200 or 809-779-2155). The tours, led by naturalists, make use of these quiet boats to tour the marine sanctuaries around the island. Kayaks can also be rented at the Sapphire Beach Resort water sports and beach services center.

Sunfish can often be rented at local hotel beach concessions at an average rate of $25 per hour.

Fishing

If you're interested in deep-sea fishing for marlin and other game fish—and the Virgin Islands is the place to do it—start with **Sapphire Marina** (tel. 809-775-3690 or 775-5889), **St. Thomas Sportfishing Center** (tel. 809-775-7990), or the **Virgin Islands Game Fishing Club** (tel. 809-775-9144). The *Bluefin II* (Red Hook, tel. 809-775-6691) and *Fish Hawk II* (Charlotte Amalie, tel. 809-775-9058) also take out fishing groups.

Other Water Sports

Windsurfing, surfing, water-skiing, jet-skiing, banana-boating, parasailing, underwater camera rentals, and a plethora of water activities are handled by full-service water sports outfits, among them **Adventure Center** (Frenchman's Reef Hotel, tel. 809-774-2990), **Caribbean Parasail and Watersports** (Limetree Beach Hotel, tel. 809-775-9360), and **Irie Watersports** (Bolongo Beach Resorts, tel. 809-775-4206).

Land Activities

Tennis players will find that most resorts offer several courts for guests, many lit for play at night. Two public courts are available on a first-come, first-served (so to speak) basis at the U.S. Sub Base just west of Frenchtown near Charlotte Amalie. Lights stay on until 8 p.m. Non-guests can whack a few balls at the **Sapphire Beach** (tel. 809-775-6100), **Renaissance Grand** (tel. 809-775-1510), and **Wyndham Sugar Bay** (tel. 809-777-7100) resorts, all located on the east side of St. Thomas. Cost for non-guests ranges $8-10 per hour. Lessons are also available for $35-45 per hour.

Golf on St. Thomas is summarized in two words: **Mahogany Run.** This 18-hole, par 70 course is the island's finest and only real course and features a difficult set of holes (13-15) called the "Devil's Triangle." Greens fee is $75 for 18 holes, $40 for nine. Carts run $12-15 per person, and clubs rent for $18 for 18 holes $10 for nine; shoes ($10) are also available for rent. After 2 p.m., greens fee ("Twilight Fee") is $60. Call the clubhouse (tel. 809-775-5000 or 800-253-7103) for tee times.

Family Activities

If the kids are old enough and big enough, they'll love the submarine adventure on the **Atlantis.** Just make sure they use the potty before getting on the sub, because once they're aboard there's literally nowhere to go. The **Paradise Point Tramway** is safe and fun for all kids. **Virgin Islands Kayak Tours** offers special excursions for the little ones called **KidsKayak** tours. (See listings above for details on all of these.)

BEACHES

All beaches in the U.S. Virgin Islands are open to the public. Some are fronted by hotels and resorts that offer changing facilities as well as bars and restaurants. Fees are charged on certain beaches for parking or use of the beach; they're usually no more than $4.

On St. Thomas, an estimated 44 talcum-white sand beaches make it one of the better beach islands in the Lesser Antilles. Among the best on the island and, in fact, in the Caribbean is **Magens Bay,** on the north shore. Magens, a public park, is a wide, roomy expanse with a quiet beach sheltered by a long peninsula on its north side. This is a great beach for kids and very popular with tourists and locals, especially on weekends and holidays. The beach has lifeguards, water sports, changing facilities, showers, a boutique, a picnic area, and snack bars.

Magen's Bay Beach

As well, you'll find a small nature trail leading through the coconut grove behind the beach. The park facilities are open daily 6 a.m.-6 p.m., and there's a small admission charge: adults are $1, kids under 12 are 25 cents, and each vehicle costs an additional $1.

Just west of Magens, around the **Tropaco Point** peninsula, is **Hull Bay,** which, with its somewhat rougher surf and offshore reef, makes it a favorite with surfers. A boat ramp for fishermen is located here, and there's a restaurant and bar at the beach to keep you from starving. You can hire local boatmen to take you over to Magens or to nearby **Hans Lollik Island** for a few bucks. The beach itself is long and shaded.

Coki Beach, at Coki Point on the northeast end of the island, is a favorite of snorkelers. The beach is smaller than others, but the water is calm and perfect for viewing coral and fish. You'll find gear for rent, as well as scuba gear and lounge chairs. Also on the beach is a pate and snack cart; bathrooms (but no showers) are nearby. Coral World underwater park is close but currently closed due to hurricane damage. Beach swimming is also available at nearby area resorts such as the Wyndham Sugar Bay Resort, Renaissance Grand Resort, and Point Pleasant Resort.

Heading south from Coki, you'll find a personal favorite at **Sapphire Beach,** at the Sapphire Beach Resort on the island's east end. The wide beach, sheltered by a rocky jetty on its south end, faces St. John and the British Virgin Islands and is a popular water sports and windsurfing spot. Non-guests can rent equipment including lounge chairs and floats ($5 per day), sunfish ($25 per hour), windsurfing boards ($35 per hour), snorkeling gear ($5 per hour), and kayaks. As well, the beach bar and patio restaurant are open to everyone. Go on Sunday and you'll be entertained by the band Deep Unda Kova playing through the afternoon—but go early; the beach is crowded by noon.

Near Red Hook, still on the east side of St. Thomas, is **Vessup Bay** and **Cowpet Bay,** two fine beaches with views to St. John. Both are often uncrowded, as is **Bluebeard's Beach,** nestled between them. Bluebeard's Beach, not to be confused with Bluebeard's Castle Hotel in Charlotte Amalie, features a steady breeze and a bit of surf and is a favorite with windsurfers. Take Rt. 322 at Red Hook.

On the south side of the island, stop in at **Scott Beach, Secret Harbor Resort Beach** (rentals, restaurant), and **Limetree Beach,** at the Bolongo Limetree Beach Resort. Limetree in particular is long and wide and one of the prettiest beaches on the island. You can rent equipment and find refreshments at a variety of locations along the water's edge.

Morning Star Bay beach, fronting the Morning Star Resort, next to the Marriott Frenchman's Reef Resort, is also popular. Here, you can rent beach equipment, including towels, and the resort's Tavern on the Beach bar and restaurant is just steps away. The beach, about a half-mile long (nearly one km), is about 10 minutes from downtown Charlotte Amalie. You'll see cruise ships approaching the harbor and, on a clear day, you might see St. Croix to the south. To get there, you can drive or take a water taxi ($4) from downtown Charlotte Amalie to the Frenchman's Reef Resort.

Lindbergh Bay, near the airport, is a popular and sometimes crowded beach, with plenty of water sports. Stop in at the Emerald Beach Resort (where you can also use the facilities) for access to the beach. There's a small beach-equipment rental place at the hotel. Nearby, just past the university and directly on the road (Rt. 30), is **John Brewer's Bay.** Brewer's Bay Beach is popular and crowded on weekends. Vendors with snack stands show up when the beach gets busy.

Stumpy Bay, at the west end of St. Thomas, requires a short walk (about half a mile, or nearly one kilometer) from the car park down a dirt road off Rt. 30. This is more isolated, but quiet and uncrowded.

In fact, those in need of a beach can pitch up just about anywhere around the island, provided that the hotels fronting the beaches allow access and the beach is safe. Remember: Don't go anywhere that even *seems* off. If it's too isolated, too dark, or just somehow makes you uneasy, forget it. Also, always lock your valuables in the car.

ACCOMMODATIONS

Accommodations on St. Thomas run the full range of large and small resorts, hotels, guesthouses, apartments, and villas. If you can't find it here, you probably can't find it anywhere in the Caribbean. Most of the island's luxury resorts are located on the north and east coasts and front some of its finest beaches and bays. Inexpensive guesthouses and inns are centered around the Charlotte Amalie area.

Remember, room rates are reduced by as much as 40% during the summer season, and, with a little research, are often bargained out through packages and wholesale room discounters. A government hotel occupancy tax of eight percent is charged on accommodations, and often a 15% service charge is added to the bill. Occasionally, an energy surcharge is also added. Most hotels accept major credit cards, but this is not always the case—call ahead if you're unsure. Keep in mind that some properties require a minimum three-night stay, extra persons in the rooms are often charged $10-30 apiece (although as a rule, children are free), and may require a deposit of as much as 50% on the room.

Price categorizations for accommodations listed below are based on the average room rate per night, double occupancy, European plan (no meals), during the 15 December-through-15 April high season, excluding the eight percent room tax. Note: some hotels offer a wide range of rooms, from budget to luxury. **Luxury** rooms run $200 or more, **expensive** rooms range $140-200, **moderate** rooms run $80-140, 'and **budget** rooms cost $80 or less.

Villas, Apartments, and Condos

Private villas, cottages, condos, or apartments—often the best bet for families or large groups—are widely available on all three islands. Real estate agents are often in the villa rental business, and some even specialize in rentals. Rates range from as little as $300 per week for a one-bedroom efficiency apartment (which may not be located near a beach) to as much as $12,000 per week for a freestanding luxury villa with several bedrooms, pool, maid, cook, and beach access. The key is to contact a rental agency, discuss your needs, the size of your party, and your budget, and work with the agency to come up with the best site.

In addition to the rental agencies and Internet sites listed in the On The Road chapter, contact these St. Thomas villa specialists:

Byrne Brown Realty (P.O. Box 7967, Charlotte Amalie, St. Thomas, U.S. Virgin Islands 00801; tel. 809-774-3300, fax 809-774-1556)

Calypso Realty (P.O. Box 12178, Charlotte Amalie, St. Thomas, U.S. Virgin Islands 00801; tel. 809-774-1620, fax 809-774-1634)

Chateu Dolce Villas (P.O. Box 12149, Charlotte Amalie, St. Thomas, U.S. Virgin Islands 00801; tel. 800-843-3566, fax 809-776-4494)

McLaughlin Anderson Vacations (100 Blackbeard's Hill #3, Charlotte Amalie, U.S. Virgin Islands, 00802; tel. 800-537-6246 or 809-776-0635, fax 809-777-4737).

Ocean Property Management (P.O. Box 8529, Charlotte Amalie, St. Thomas, U.S. Virgin Islands 00801; tel. 800-874-7897 or 809-775-2600, fax 809-775-5901) is one of the island's bigger rental agencies. It manages properties at several villa complexes and resorts, among them **Secret Harbourview Villas.** Secret Harbourview, located on the quiet Secret Harbour cove just south of Red Hook, about 15 minutes from Charlotte Amalie, features condo studios ($220 per night) and suites with either one or two bedrooms ($270 and $360 per night). Also in the complex is a pool, fitness room, hot tub, shops, tennis facilities, beach sports center, and several restaurants and snack bars. The attraction is the long, white sand beach and the access to Red Hook. The agency also manages properties near Sapphire Beach, **Sapphire Village** and **Sapphire Bay West,** which range from $160 (studio) to $190 (one bedroom) per night.

As well, call several villas or villa complexes directly for brochures and information. **Blazing Villas** (P.O. Box 502697, Charlotte Amalie, St. Thomas, U.S. Virgin Islands 00801; tel. 800-382-2002 or 809-776-0760, fax 809-776-3603), located at Renaissance Grand Resort on the island's northeast coast, has eight units on Pineapple Beach, and guests have access to all facilities at the Grand. Rates range $100-200 per night. **Pineapple Village Villas** (tel. 800-992-9232 or 809-775-5516, fax 800-874-1786 or 809-775-5516) and **Pineapple Rooms and Villas** (tel. 800-479-1539 or 809-775-0275, fax 809-775-0275), with eight and 11 units respectively, are also located in the Renaissance Grand complex and offer full use of the resort facilities; rates range $100-200. **Jean's Villas** (P.O. Box 11878,

Charlotte Amalie, St. Thomas, U.S. Virgin Islands 00801; tel. 800-874-5326 or 809-775-7078) has 10 units near Coki Beach on the east side of the island. Rates range $150-200 per night.

Resorts and Hotels

Elysian Beach Resort (6800 Estate Nazareth, St. Thomas, U.S. Virgin Islands 00802; tel. 800-753-2554 or 524-4746, 809-775-1000 or 775-2700, fax 809-776-0910 or 779-2844) is set on a winning beach among a grove of coconut palms on Cowpet Bay at the southeast end of the island. The huge resort opened in 1989 and encompasses 175 rooms on five acres, two restaurants (one is gourmet), two bars, the well-equipped Club Elysian fitness center, and an irregularly shaped "fantasy pool" for swimming. Rooms are standard doubles, studio suites, and one- and two-bedroom suites, most with balconies, wet bars, cable, and a/c, and all decorated in a Caribbean style with lots of floral this and that. Also on the grounds are tennis courts and water sports facilities. Across the way is the St. Thomas Yacht Club. Families are encouraged to utilize the Uncommon Family Escape plan, which basically upgrades a one-bedroom suite to two bedrooms for the same price, as long as the stay is for five nights or more. **Expensive.**

Guests can hop the shuttle down to the Elysian's sister resort at Bolongo Bay to stay at the **Bolongo Club Everything Beach Resort** (P.O. Box 7337, Charlotte Amalie, St. Thomas, U.S. Virgin Islands 00801; tel. 800-524-4746 or 809-779-2844, fax 809-775-3208). This resort, slightly less upscale than the Elysian, is on a great south coast beach about 15 minutes from Charlotte Amalie. The hotel, with 160 rooms, has restaurants, a bar, water and other sports, and a choice of all-inclusive or EP rates. This property encompasses other Bolongo properties, once separate but now combined into one long Bolongo conga line of hotels, villas, and sports clubs connected by shuttle. Kids will have fun with the special beach and sports programs set up for them here. The former **Bolongo Bay Beach Villas and Sports Club** and the **Bolongo Limetree Beach Resort,** can be contacted at the numbers above. **Moderate-Expensive.**

Emerald Beach Resort (P.O. Box 340, St. Thomas, U.S. Virgin Islands 00804; tel. 800-233-4936 or 809-777-8800, fax 809-776-3426),

located just behind the airport (and believe me, you'll see and hear the five or six jets that zoom through each day), is a Best Western hotel on the long and wide beach of Lindbergh Bay. The place is, not surprisingly, green, green, green, and boxy in the way beach front hotels can be boxy, but the lush gardens and the beach make up for the building's aesthetic problems. The 90 rooms feature king or pairs of double beds, cable TV, wet bars, a/c, and views of the bay. Also on the grounds is a restaurant and bar, tennis court (not lighted), pool, duty-free shops, and water sports. Just down the waterfront are a couple of small beach cafes. **Expensive.**

Marriott's Frenchman's Reef Beach Resort (P.O. Box 7100, Charlotte Amalie, St. Thomas, U.S. Virgin Islands 00801; tel. 800-524-2000 or 809-776-8500, fax 809-776-3054), on the south coast and east end of St. Thomas Harbor, is one of those resorts in which you can get lost; with 421 rooms (including 18 suites) on 35 acres, six restaurants, bars, shops, a complete sports center, pool, hot tubs, tennis, and a beach at a sister property a few steps away (Morning Star), this is one of the island's biggest resorts. It's also the island's premier business conference center, with 18,000 square feet of meeting space. The resort, built in 1973, became a Marriott property in 1992. Most of the rooms are standard size with either hillside or water views and feature balconies, cable TV and video, mini-bars, coffee makers, hair dryers, and even ironing boards. Check out the resident **Adventure Center** (tel. 809-774-2990) for anything from diving and fishing trips to sunset cruises. This is one of the better one-stop activities centers you'll find. In the hotel's lobby is an ATM; if it's shopping you need, take the shuttle or water taxi ($4) to Charlotte Amalie. Lounge by the pool or in a hot tub and watch the mammoth cruise ships pull into town. Package and all-inclusive rates are available. Several rooms are fully accessible. **Expensive-Luxury.**

Marriott's Morning Star Beach Resort (see address above, or call 800-BEACH CLUB) is located on the beach down a flight of stairs (or you can take a minivan shuttle from the top of the hill) from the Frenchman's Reef Resort. Both properties share facilities, but only the Morning Star has the beach—a long half-mile one. The 96 units in five buildings are designed for luxury—

bathrobes, hair dryers, turn down service, complimentary bottle of champagne on arrival. The location, near Charlotte Amalie, has good access to shopping and historical sights yet is also a good bet for honeymooners and those requiring a comfortable resort with all the amenities—you'll never have to leave. Package and all-inclusive rates are available. **Luxury.**

Renaissance Grand Beach Resort (P.O. Box 8267, Smith Bay Road, St. Thomas, U.S. Virgin Islands 00801; tel. 800-HOTELS-1, 800-322-2976, or 809-775-1510, fax 809-775-3757). This resort, a former Stouffer Renaissance property, sustained a great deal of damage during 1995's Hurricane Marilyn but reopened in late 1996. The resort, on Water Bay near Coki Point on the island's east coast, sits on 34 acres and a fine 1,000-foot (300-meter) beach. The 290 rooms are in standard, superior, or deluxe categories and include some suites, many with ocean views. The marbled and carpeted rooms have cable TV, a/c, bathrobes, coffee makers, and hair dryers, and the suites feature whirlpool spas in the master bedrooms. Plenty of restaurant and bar activity, water sports, six tennis courts, a fitness center, and children's programs complete the picture. Kids under 18 stay free with parents unless extra bedding is required. **Luxury.**

Sapphire Beach Resort (P.O. Box 88088, St. Thomas, U.S. Virgin Islands 00801; tel. 800-524-2090 or 809-775-6100, fax 809-775-4024, www.usvi.net/hotel/sapphire/) sits on one of the island's finest beaches, at St. John's Bay on the northeast coast. The 171 units come in two categories—suites and villas—with views of the beach or of the nearby **Sapphire Beach Marina.** Suites and villas are modern, spacious, and equipped with full kitchens and large refrigerators—great for families. The beach itself is wide and sheltered and comes with a full water sports activities center. Kids under 13 stay free with families, and the hotel offers a **KidsKlub** activities schedule for children 3-12, including fishing at the marina, pool play, arts and crafts, and steel drum playing. The beach is so popular it may get crowded on weekends, particularly on Sunday afternoons when the house band Deep Unda Kova entertains until evening at the alfresco bar. Later, you can eat at the hotel's **Seagrape** restaurant on the seaside patio. This is one of St. Thomas's best resorts for singles and

families alike, and the staff has a deserved reputation for doing their best to meet visitors' needs. (Looking across the bay, the small cay you see is called Lavango, reputedly for "Love and Go," an allusion to a time when it was home to a big cathouse in the 1940s that attracted military personnel.) **Expensive-Luxury.**

Secret Harbour Beach Resort (6280 Estate Nazareth, St. Thomas, U.S. Virgin Islands 00802; tel. 800-524-2250, 800-742-4276, or 809-775-6550, fax 809-775-1501), at Secret Harbour just south of Red Hook, offers 60 units, all studios or suites with one or two bedrooms, overlooking the quiet bay. The beach is long and shaded, the rooms come with kitchens and sunset views, and on the grounds are water sports including diving, duty-free shopping, a pool, restaurant and bar, fitness center, and tennis courts. Kids under 13 stay free with parents. **Luxury.**

Wyndham Sugar Bay Resort (6500 Estate Smith Bay, St. Thomas, U.S. Virgin Islands 00802; tel. 800-WYNDHAM or 809-777-7100, fax 809-777-7200). Though damaged by Hurricane Marilyn in 1995, the Sugar Bay resort has slowly rebounded. The sprawling resort on the east coast's "Resort Row" offers superior, deluxe, and luxury rooms, with either hillside or bay and ocean views, all with cable, a/c, refrigerators, coffee makers, and balconies. The pools are actually three interconnecting poollettes with a cascading waterfall. Also on the grounds are lighted tennis courts, a fitness center (temporarily reduced in size due to the hurricane), shops, and a beach. The $20 Sunday brunch, with the band Starlites providing entertainment is very popular with guests and non-guests alike. Non-guests may use the pool during brunch. **Expensive-Luxury.**

Small Hotels, Inns, and Guesthouses

Admiral's Inn (3700 Villa Olga, P.O. Box 6162, Charlotte Amalie, St. Thomas, U.S. Virgin Islands 00804; tel. 800-544-0493 or 809-774-1376, fax 809-774-8010) is a modern 16-unit inn located at the southern tip of Frenchtown, west of downtown Charlotte Amalie. The inn is seaside on a small beach. The rooms are standard but clean and all have private baths, a/c, cable, and a view of either the open ocean or the harbor. On the grounds is a restaurant and a pool with a poolside bar. Continental breakfast, with homemade breads, is included. **Budget-Moderate.**

Blackbeard's Castle (P.O. Box 6041, Charlotte Amalie, St. Thomas, U.S. Virgin Islands 00804; tel. 800-344-5771 or 809-776-1234, fax 776-4321) is located above Government Hill overlooking Charlotte Amalie. This small hotel, with its signature tower, is reputed to be the lair of the eponymous pirate, whose real name was Edward Teach. Actually, the castle was built in 1678 by Danish governor Iversen to safeguard the harbor after several attacks by the French. The governor called it Fort Skytsborg, and, thanks to his foresight, the castle and its 24-room inn now enjoy one of the best views of the harbor. The rooms are eclectic, incorporating European, Asian, and plantation motifs. Two pools are on the grounds, and the hotel's gourmet restaurant is a treat. Even if you're not a guest, drop in for the Sunday brunch or for live jazz in the evenings every day except Monday. **Moderate-Expensive.**

Bluebeard's Castle (P.O. Box 7480, Charlotte Amalie, St. Thomas, U.S. Virgin Islands 00801; tel. 800-524-6599 or 809-774-1600, fax 809-774-5134) is a 170-room hotel located slightly east of downtown, nestled in the hills above the harbor and bay. The hotel site was one of the town's earliest fortifications and in the 18th century was nameded Frederiksfort after the hill it sits on, Frederiksberg (also called Bluebeard's Hill). It was later, like Blackbeard's Castle, reputed to be a hangout of the pirate for which it is now named. First opened in 1934, the hotel now offers a wide array of rooms, including the older rooms in the tower, which some say have more character. Also on the grounds is a pool, and the hotel provides transport to beaches. One of the hotel's restaurants, **Entre Nous,** is among the best gourmet dining experiences on the island, and the evening views of the lights of town and the harbor are stunning. **Moderate.**

Calico Jack's Courtyard Inne (P.O. Box 460, Charlotte Amalie, St. Thomas, U.S. Virgin Islands 00804; tel. 809-774-7555) is a recently-renovated 17th-century building downtown in the historic district, small—only six rooms—but clean. The pub downstairs is popular. One room is fully accessible. **Budget-Moderate.**

Carib Beach Hotel (Lindbergh Bay, St. Thomas, U.S. Virgin Islands; tel. 800-792-2742 or 809-774-2525). This big, pink 69-unit hotel, located a few minutes west of Charlotte Amalie and near the airport, sits on a fine beach at Lindbergh Bay. The rooms are clean, and most feature views of the bay. On the grounds are a restaurant, water sports, pool, and the beach. It's a good location for those willing to put up with the comings and goings of jet aircraft five or six times per day. **Moderate.**

Danish Chalet Inn (P.O. Box 304319, Charlotte Amalie, St. Thomas, U.S. Virgin Islands 00803; tel. 800-635-1531 or 809-774-5746, fax 809-777-4886). This 15-room inn, located about a five-minute walk west of downtown, is in the hills overlooking Charlotte Amalie (off Solberg Road), and that may be one of its strongest points—the view is remarkable. Some rooms have a/c, others have fans, some have refrigerators. Rooms with shared baths are cheaper. You'll find a small hot tub, but no pool. **Budget.**

Galleon House (P.O. Box 6577, Charlotte Amalie, St. Thomas, U.S. Virgin Islands 00804; tel. 800-524-2052 or 809-774-6952, fax 774-6592) is located up on Kongens Gade on Government Hill, near the Hotel 1829, about a block from downtown Charlotte Amalie's historic district. The 14-unit inn's room's have a/c and cable TV, and some feature refrigerators. The small pool sits surrounded by the rooms, and breakfast is included in the rate. This is a solid, clean hotel in a good location for history and shopping buffs (but not for beach buffs). **Budget.**

Hotel 1829 (P.O. Box 1567, Charlotte Amalie, St. Thomas, U.S. Virgin Islands 00804; tel. 800-524-2002 or 809-776-1829, fax 809-776-4313), the former Lavalette House, the home of a French sea captain, is located on Government Hill near the famous 99 Steps in Charlotte Amalie. From downtown, you can't miss the green awnings and the large "Hotel 1829" emblazoned on the front of the building. The hotel features 15 rooms (two are suites) with a/c, private baths, and TV; some are smaller than you'd like, but that is the character of the place. The general tenor of the Spanish-style hotel is tidy hominess. You can dip in the puddle pool before walking out the door onto Kongens Gade, directly into the town's historic district. **Budget-Moderate.**

Island View Guesthouse (P.O. Box 1903, Charlotte Amalie, St. Thomas, U.S. Virgin Islands 00803; tel. 800-524-2023 or 809-774-4270, fax 809-774-6167) is located in the hills just a few miles west and north of Charlotte Amalie. The family-run guesthouse is clean and small—just nine rooms, some with private baths, some without, some with kitchenettes and others without, some with a/c and some with fans. It's typical guesthouse eclecticism, and that's why you'd go there. It's a good location for those who'd like to be near but not directly in town, and the drive to the beach at Lindbergh Bay is about 10 minutes. Continental breakfast is included in the room rate. **Budget.**

EATING AND DRINKING

Hotel restaurants are a good bet for dining out and often provide evening entertainment as well. However, other island restaurants offer a wide array of fine eats, from West Indian cuisine to Italian to French to Tex-Mex to Chinese to standard American steaks and burgers. Also on the island are various American fast-food joints such as Domino's, McDonald's, Pizza Hut, and KFC (these aren't reviewed here—you already know what to expect, and why eat a McBurger on St. Thomas when you can do that at home?).

Most restaurants accept credit cards, but it's best to call ahead to confirm, as well as to make reservations and inquire about dress codes. While it's rare in the U.S. Virgin Islands to encounter a dress code for evening dining, you will find that most restaurants discourage beachwear, shorts, and flip-flops. It's also best to take a taxi if you're traveling to Charlotte Amalie to dine—you won't want to become lost in a rental car in some sections of town.

Categories used below are based on average entrée price: **expensive:** $25 or more; **moderate:** $10-25; **inexpensive:** $10 or less.

Charlotte Amalie and Environs

Alexander's Cafe (tel. 809-776-4211), on Rue de St.-Barthélémy in Frenchtown serves German and Austrian food and is very chic. **Moderate.** Also located in Frenchtown, again on Rue de St.-Barthélémy, is **Cafe Normandie** (tel. 809-774-1622), a bastion of country French dining. Meals are fixed-price. **Expensive.** Nearby, still in Frenchtown, is **Craig & Sally's** (tel. 809-777-9949), serving French, Italian, and Continental cuisine—great dining in a bistro setting. Ever

heard of eggplant cheescake? You will, if you sample Sally's menu. Closed Monday. **Moderate.** Also in Frenchtown is **Hook, Line, and Sinker** (tel. 809-776-9708), an alfresco cafe on the docks. Breakfast, lunch, and dinner are served daily, and Sunday brunch (10 a.m.-2:30 p.m.) is popular. **Moderate.**

Blackbeard's Castle (tel. 809-776-1234) features daily lunch and dinner at their great little restaurant overlooking the harbor from Government Hill in town. The cuisine is contemporary American. **Expensive.**

The cleverly named **Beni Iguana Sushi Bar** (tel. 809-777-8744) is located in the courtyard of the Grand Hotel shopping court, across from Emancipation Park in the historic district. Sushi lovers know the drill—fish, seaweed, and rice rolls attractively served in wooden boxes. Other menu items, such as salmon (cooked), tuna, and lobster can be had as well. The courtyard setting and a cool Japanese beer are a respite for sweating shoppers. Beni Iguana's is open daily except Sunday 11 a.m.-10 p.m. **Moderate.**

Cuzzin's (tel. 809-777-4711), on Back St., is situated in a historic building and serves up seafood and West Indian cuisine, including curries and light fare. The restaurant is open daily except Sunday for lunch, and Tuesday through Saturday for dinner. **Moderate.**

Entre Nous (tel. 809-776-4050), located at Bluebeard's Castle in the hills on the east side of town, is an experience in fine French dining in an elegant setting. The view of the harbor at night is well worth the slightly expensive menu, and the food is worth it, too. The wine list here is extensive. If you want one exceptional, memorable evening on St. Thomas, this should be your choice. **Expensive.**

Hard Rock Cafe (tel. 809-777-5555) continues in the same tradition as the Hard Rock Cafes you have come to know and love—guitars over the bar, rock 'n roll music, signature "Pig Sandwich" (pork shoulder), and rock memorabilia,which in this case includes a dress worn by Stevie Nicks and sketches by John Lennon. The restaurant doesn't take reservations and is open until 11 p.m. most days, 5 p.m. on Sunday. Alfresco dining overlooks the waterfront, and the location, on Waterfront Drive, is near shopping. If you like your music and burgers big and loud, this is your place. **Moderate.**

Hotel 1829 (tel. 809-776-1829), up on Government Hill, is a great place to have a long before-dinner drink in the cozy bar before dining on the open-air veranda or inside the dining room. The cuisine is a mix of continental and local seafood. Closed on Sunday. **Moderate-Expensive.**

Victor's New Hideout (tel. 809-776-9397) is located just west of town, at the Sub Base (take a taxi). The cuisine is West Indian, highlighting fresh fish dishes, and Victor's is popular with a local crowd. Great eats, great island music on Friday. Lunch is served Monday through Saturday, dinner daily. **Inexpensive-Moderate.**

Out Island

The Agavé Terrace (tel. 809-775-4142), at the **Point Pleasant Resort** on the island's east end, is one of the U.S. Virgin Islands' premier restaurants. The specialty is Caribbean seafood, and the views are tremendous. Open for brunch on weekends. for dinner daily. **Moderate-Expensive.**

Eunice's Terrace (tel. 809-775-3975), located at the east end on Rt. 38, serves some of the better local West Indian specialties, such as conch fritters, lobster, and fresh fish. You'll also find entertainment by a calypso singer or steel pan band every night. The restaurant is open daily for dinner and daily except Sunday for lunch. **Moderate.**

Grateful Deli (tel. 809-775-5160), at the Red Hook Plaza in Red Hook, serves up light fare, including sandwiches with names that grateful Deadheads will appreciate: Sugar Magnolia is ham, smoked turkey, and Monterey Jack cheese; Fire on the Mountain features turkey with spicy pepper-jack cheese. You get the picture. Soups, desserts, espresso, and exotic coffees fill it out. There's even a happy hour for coffee fiends weekdays 4-5 p.m. As well, you can buy deli items and a wide array of ground coffees. **Inexpensive.** Also in Red Hook, stop at the American Yacht Harbor's **MacKenzie's** (tel. 809-779-2261) for fat steaks and fresh seafood. **Moderate.**

Seagrape (tel. 809-775-1600), at the Sapphire Beach Resort on the east end, offers a wide array of local and international dishes. The casual restaurant is right on the water, and the night breezes and bay lights are nice indeed.

Don't miss the Sunday brunch (11 a.m.-3 p.m.), reputed to be the best on the island. The fare is pancakes, Belgian waffles, eggs Benedict, and lunch entrées. **Moderate.**

Polli's (tel. 809-775-4550), inside the Tillett Gardens arts complex at Anna's Retreat, serves up tremendous Mexican food, including chimichangas, enchiladas, and vegetarian chile quesos. It's a good place to grab a bite and a Mexican beer and relax while shopping at the craft center. Open for lunch and early dinner (until 9:30 p.m.) every day except Sunday. **Moderate.**

Romanos (tel. 809-775-0045) on Smith Bay is a fine Italian restaurant. **Expensive.**

Sib's on the Mountain (tel. 809-774-8967) has been serving some of the island's reputedly best steaks and seafood since 1924, but the big, sloppy ribs are a favorite among locals. Sib's is, of course, on the mountain, on Mafolie Road near Mountain Top, so it's best to take a taxi. Lunch and dinner are served daily, and a live band entertains at the popular bar on Wednesdays. **Inexpensive-Moderate.**

NIGHTLIFE

Nightlife is hot and heavy on St. Thomas—particularly (in this order) on weekends, in hotels, and around Charlotte Amalie. Most hotels have house bands or piano bars, usually with no cover charge.

One quick way to tune into what's going on is to pick up the local newspaper, the *Virgin Islands Daily News,* and scan the entertainment section. Listen to the radio for local announcements, or, if you happen to be staying in a hotel with a TV, switch on Channel 4, which features a continuous loop, 24-hour program with tips on nightlife, dining, and shopping.

Nightlife on St. Thomas includes music and dancing but no gambling. Movie theaters are found on the island and show contemporary, fairly recent releases. Most are air-conditioned. **Cinema One** (tel. 809-774-2855), at Estate Thomas, near the Havensight Mall, is a multiplex featuring three theaters. Shows run evenings, with a matinee on weekends and holidays.

Don't forget that the biggest nighttime events of the year, and daytime events as well, take place around April's Carnival, when calypso competitions, big bands (Brass-O-Rama), steel band shows, and more fill the night, primarily in Charlotte Amalie. The venue for larger events is the **Lionel Roberts Stadium.**

For live theater, folklore performances, readings, and concerts, your best bet is the **Reichhold Center for the Performing Arts** (tel. 809-693-1559), at the University of the Virgin Islands. The outdoor amphitheater seats nearly 1,200 and, on a clear night under the stars, is deeply peaceful. Recent performances have included a concert by violinist Itzhak Perlman, a reading by poet Maya Angelou, and the play *I Don't Want to Bathe*. Tickets run $5-30 or more, depending on the show.

Charlotte Amalie and Environs

You can always find canned rock and roll at the **Hard Rock Cafe** (tel. 809-777-5555), on the waterfront in town. Top local and international bands play there as well, most often on weekends. Recently, the band America and the famous Motown girl group the Marvelettes wowed the crowd. Dancing is allowed. **Blackbeard's Castle** (tel. 809-776-1234), on Government Hill, offers live jazz 8 p.m.-midnight Tuesday through Sunday. **Bluebeard's Castle** (tel. 809-776-4050), in addition to its fine dining, has a guy playing lite favorites on piano every Friday and Saturday.

On the waterfront, the **Green House Bar and Restaurant** (tel. 809-774-7998) features happy hours daily 4:30-7 p.m., live music on Wednesday (admission $5), and DJ tunes all other days except Monday.

Marriott's Frenchman's Reef (tel. 809-776-8500) is home to several bars and discos offering DJ-driven dancing Tuesday through Sunday. And, yes, you can join in the karaoke singing as well. The hotel's **Top of the Reef** restaurant features a stage and is the island's only dinner theater, offering plays, comedies, and musicals.

Vincent's on the Bay (tel. 809-776-9830), in Frenchtown, is a great little restaurant and bar where you can listen to a singer/guitarist Thursday and Friday evenings while taking in the breeze and the bay lights.

Out Island

The **Wyndham Sugar Bay** (tel. 809-777-7100) and **Sapphire Beach** (tel. 809-775-6100) resorts, on St. Thomas's east end, features house bands the Starlites and Deep Unda Kova, playing Sunday afternoon until evening—always a popular time with lots of dancing. These two bands are among the island's best and play reggae, rhythm and blues, pop tunes, and their own music.

Iggie's (tel. 809-779-2844) is located at the Bolongo Limetree Beach Resort, on Frenchman's Bay on the south coast. A popular, casual restaurant, Iggie's has music and karaoke at night. Move from Iggies to the **Paradise Club Disco** (tel. 809-776-4470), also a Bolongo property, for live music and DJs.

SHOPPING

St. Thomas, slightly more than St. Croix and definitely more than St. John, offers a wide range of duty-free shopping, art and craft galleries, malls, and hotel gift shops. An estimated 500 shops islandwide carry jewelry, electronic goods, crystal, linens, liquor, leather goods, and the usual suspects. What's more, no sales taxes apply on the islands, so good deals can get even better.

Remember that "duty-free" does not mean the buyer will be exempt from applicable duties and customs regulations when bringing the goods back home. It means the *seller* was exempt from duties when importing the goods for his or her store, which implies that the store will pass on those savings to the consumer. That is often but not always the case. Do a little homework before you go on vacation; price some items in your local shops to get a fair idea of whether you're getting a deal in an island duty-free shop.

Among the reputable stores, and ones that have several island locations are **Boolchands** (tel. 809-776-8890 or 809-776-4110), for electronic goods and linens; **Cartier Boutique** (tel. 800-289-8784 or 809-774-1590), for watches and jewelry; the venerable **Little Switzerland** (tel. 800-524-2010), which has locations throughout the Caribbean, for jewelry, china, crystal, and watches; **Cardow Jewelers** (tel. 800-CARDOWS or 809-776-1140), for jewelry and watches; **AH Riise** (tel. 800-524-2037 or 809-777-4222 or 809-776-2303), one of the better one-stop stores, for perfumes, crafts, jewelry, tobacco, china, crystal, and liquor; **MAPes**

MONDe (tel. 809-776-2886), for a wide collection of fascinating 18th-century prints, lithographs, cards, and books; **The Leather Shop** (tel. 809-776-0290 or 776-0040), for leather goods and luggage; **Mr. Tablecloth** (tel. 809-774-4343), for linens, lace, embroidery, and appliqué; and **H. Stern Jewelers** (tel. 800-524-2024 or 809-776-1939) and **Colombian Emeralds International** (tel. 800-6-NO-DUTY) for jewelry. As well, look to discount stores such as **Woolworth** and **Kmart** for good deals on liquor and tobacco.

Shops are generally open Monday through Saturday 9 a.m.-6 p.m., although larger department stores, grocery stores, and others may be open until 9 or 10 p.m. Many shops open Sunday, particularly to accommodate cruise-ship schedules.

Charlotte Amalie

Charlotte Amalie is the island's main shopping district, due to its cruise-ship traffic. From the Hard Rock Cafe to Fort Christian on the waterfront and two blocks inland on Main Street (Dronningens Gade) and Back Street (Vimmelskafts Gade), this downtown/historic district is ground zero for shoppers. Stores line Main Street, and small malls, shops, and cafes fill the side streets and alleys between the three major streets.

On the waterfront, look for the several malls including the **International Plaza,** near the Hard Rock Cafe and, heading east, **Palm Passage, Royal Dane Mall, Drake's Passage, A.H. Riise Mall,** and **Hibiscus Alley.** These malls connect to Main Street, where you'll find, among many others, **Little Switzerland, C.M. Caron, H. Stern Jewelers, Diamonds International, Amsterdam Sauer, Paradise Jewelers, the English Shop, Parfum de Paris, Boolchands, Cardow's, The Leather Shop, Colombian Emeralds,** and **MAPes MONDe.**

Cross Tolbold Gade east from Main Street at the post office and you'll find the **Old Danish Warehouse,** in the **Grand Hotel Court,** home to several stores such as **the Shoe Box, Cowboys and Indians, Soft Touch Boutique,** and a well-stocked book and magazine store, the **Island Newsstand.** A great place to buy cheap T-shirts and souvenirs is across the way, on the south side of Emancipation Gardens, at **Vendor's Plaza.**

Note that across Tolbold Gade, across from the Vendor's Plaza, is a **tourist information center.** As well, for those in rental cars, **parking** is available in a public lot off Fort Strade, behind Fort Christian. **Public restrooms** can be found on Back Street, at the International Plaza mall, and at the A.H. Riise Mall.

Market Square, on the western end of Main Street, is the place to stop for fresh vegetables, fruits, and crafts.

Havensight Mall

The Havensight Mall complex (tel. 809-777-5313) is located on the waterfront east of downtown on the West Indian Company cruise-ship docks. Don't bother walking—it's a bit of a hike, and the taxi ride is only $2.50 per person. More than 50 shops make up the strip mall, including **Cardow Jewelers, Boolchands, A.H. Riise Gifts, Sea Wench Lingerie, Omni Jewelers, Gucci, Sunglass Hut, Blazing Photos,** and one of St. Thomas's best bookshops, the **Dockside Book Store** (tel. 809-774-4937). As well, you'll find the **Havensight Pharmacy,** (809-776-1235), the offices of **Atlantis Submarine,** a **Scotia Bank** (main tel. 809-777-9373), a **FedEx** office (tel. 809-774-3393), a **tourist information** kiosk, several restaurants and cafes, and a huge parking lot.

Tutu

The **Tutu Park Mall** (tel. 809-774-7144) is located in the area called Tutu, or Anna's Retreat, on Rt. 38 east of Charlotte Amalie. The mall in this often congested area has several large department stores and grocery outlets, including the **Cost U Less** wholesale club, a **Kmart,** and a **Plaza Extra** supermarket. You'll also find about 50 other shops including **Tutu Park Books,** a **McDonald's,** and a **Pizza Hut.** Across the street from the mall is **Tillett Gardens** (tel. 809-775-1929), an arts and craft complex with some of the better galleries on the island.

Red Hook

The sometimes bustling town of Red Hook, the departure site for ferries to St. John and the British Virgin Islands, is also worth stopping in for a bit of shopping. The big kahuna here is the **American Yacht Harbor and Shopping Village** (tel. 809-775-6454), which takes up a big chunk of Red Hook Road, the town's main street. In addition to several banks, yacht rental agencies, yachting and diving outfits, car rental agencies, hairstyling shops, restaurants and pubs (including the popular steak house **MacKenzie's**), the American Yacht Club complex hosts **Little Switzerland, Sunglass Hut, Red Hook Traders, Pusser's West Indian Candy Co., News International, Blazing Photos, Big Planet Adventure Outfitters, Marina Market** (groceries), and **Satori Pottery.** Poke around this tiny town as well for smaller shops and cafes scattered up and down the main road.

Other

The **Al Cohen Mall** on Raphune Hill, immediately past the Havensight Mall on Rt. 38, has several small shops, including **Mahogany Island Style** (tel. 809-777-3060), a shop that specializes in reproduction plantation-era furniture. Also found at Al's are a couple of fine art galleries, **Mango Tango** (tel. 809-775-3995) and **Van Rensselaer Art Gallery** (tel. 809-774-4598).

Mountain Top (tel. 809-774-2400), a restaurant and shopping complex up on **St. Peter Mountain** peak with a scenic lookout, has several shops offering gifts, crafts, spices, and duty-free items.

Galleries

Island art is one of the most popular items to take (or have shipped) home. The vibrant colors of Caribbean paintings and crafts are distinctive and bright, and, in many cases, contradictorily reflect the struggling underside of paradise. The **Camille Pissarro Gallery** (tel. 809-777-5511), on Main Street, upstairs from Amsterdam Sauer, is located in a historic building that is the birthplace of the Impressionist artist Camille Pissarro. The gallery, open weekdays 9:30 a.m.-5 p.m., displays the works of more than 30 local artists.

The frequently mentioned **Tillett Gardens** is home to several galleries and artists' studios, including the **Tillett Gallery & Screen Printing Studio,** which displays the art of Jim Tillett and many local artists.

The **Kilnworks Pottery** center (tel. 809-775-3979), on Rt. 38 at the island's east end, displays the work of owner Peggy Seiwert as well as other local potters and artists.

The **Frederick Gallery** (tel. 809-777-5523) on Trompeter Gade in Charlotte Amalie, offers new and antique art as well as gifty items.

GETTING AROUND

Rental Car Agencies

Rental cars are widely available here. Most companies require that the driver be at least 25 years old. U.S. drivers will need a valid license; others will need to obtain a temporary license through the rental company. Credit cards are almost universally accepted, and rates start at about $30 per day. Most offer free mileage and

tourist jitney

free pickup and drop-off. On St. Thomas, just about any type of car will do as long as it has a trunk where you can lock your valuables.

Even though the U.S. Virgin Islands are a U.S. territory and use left-hand-drive vehicles, remember that driving is on the left—a legacy of Danish rule. The following are reputable rental agencies, and, in many cases, will deliver the car to you at your hotel. Many have several locations around the island, including the airport.

ABC Auto (tel. 800-524-2080 or 809-776-1222)

Avis (tel. 800-331-1084 or 809-774-1468)

Budget Rent-A-Car (tel. 800-527-0700 or 809-776-5774)

Cowpet Auto Rental (tel. 800-524-2072 or 809-775-7376)

Dependable Car Rental (tel. 800-522-3076 or 809-774-2253)

Discount Car Rental (tel. 809-776-4858)

National Car Rental (tel. 809-774-8660)

Sea Breeze Car Rental (tel. 809-774-7200)

Sun Island Car Rentals (809-774-3333)

Thrifty Car Rental (tel. 809-775-7282)

Tri-Island Car Rental (tel. 809-776-2877)

Tours and Taxi Companies

Taxis are probably your best bet for a tour if you've got a short time on the island or if you'd just like to leave the driving to someone else. Most any taxi will do an island tour, and the rate for two hours (plenty of time to see major sights) is $30 for one or two passengers, $12 per passenger for three or more.

Your hotel will most likely have a taxi stand out front or be able to arrange a taxi for you, but for those late-night pickups, call **AAA Taxi** (tel. 809-776-1006), **East End** (tel. 809-775-5555), **Independent** (tel. 809-776-1006), **Islander Taxi** (tel. 809-774-4077), **Tony's Taxi** (tel. 809-775-6494), **VI Taxi Association** (tel. 809-774-9202), or **Wheatly Taxi** (tel. 809-775-1959).

All taxi drivers should carry a rate card, with approved fares set by the Taxi Commission, in the vehicle. They may not have one, but to get a good idea of what it costs to travel around the island by taxi, pick up a copy of *St. Thomas This Week,* a weekly publication (it's bright yellow) found at all shops, hotels, and tourist areas. Sample fares, for one passenger: from the airport to Charlotte Amalie, $4.50 ($4 each for more than one); from Charlotte Amalie to Coki Beach, $7.50 ($5 each for more than one); from Charlotte Amalie to Red Hook, $9 ($5); from Red Hook to the airport, $10 ($6); and from Havensight Mall to Magens Bay, $9 ($6.50).

Remember, never get in a vehicle that doesn't have "TP" on the license plate and a dome light above—it's not an authorized taxi. For questions or complaints, you can call the **Taxi Commission** (tel. 809-776-8294) weekdays 8 a.m.-5 p.m.

INFORMATION DIRECTORY

Police, Fire, Ambulance, tel. 911

Coast Guard, tel. (809) 774-1911

St. Thomas Hospital, tel. (809) 776-8311

American Express Representative, St. Thomas, tel. (809) 774-1855

Chamber of Commerce, tel. (809) 776-0100

FedEx, tel. (809) 774-3393

Havensight Pharmacy, tel. (809) 776-1235

Virgin Islands National Park Service, tel. (809) 776-6201

Department of Tourism, P.O. Box 6400, Charlotte Amalie, St. Thomas, U.S. Virgin Islands 00804; tel. (809) 774-USVI (8784) or (800) 372-8784, fax (809) 774-4390

St. Thomas and St. John Hotel Association, tel. (800) 3GO-USVI or (809) 774-6835, fax (809) 774-4993

ST. JOHN

SIGHTS

Cruz Bay

St. John's main center, and home to most of its 3,500 population, Cruz Bay is located at the island's west end and is the arrival point for ferries from St. Thomas and the British Virgin Islands. The ferry trip to Cruz Bay from Red Hook on St. Thomas crosses **Pillsbury Sound,** a thin strip of water separating the two islands; the crossing lasts a mere 20 minutes and costs $3 one-way. The ferry from Charlotte Amalie to Cruz Bay takes 45 minutes and costs $7 one-way (see appendix "Ferry Schedules"). Whichever one you start from, it makes getting to St. John easy, either for an overnight stay or a day trip. Remember, there are no commercial airports on St. John and no scheduled flights to St. John from any of the Virgin Islands.

The small and cozy town is easily walked—in fact, it's better to walk than drive in town due to its narrow streets—and has everything you'll need: a post office, tourism office, car rental agencies, water sports outfits, shops, groceries, restaurants, inns, hotels, and transportation services. A focal point of the town is the ferry docks area, where you'll find a few small restaurants and taxis lined up along the road between the ferry dock and small **Cruz Park.**

Cruz Bay, although it is now the island's center, was not its first capital. That honor belongs to the east end's **Coral Bay,** which was established as the island's first settlement in 1718, more than 20 years after the Danes took possession of the island in 1694. In the mid-19th century, Cruz Bay was a lonely military outpost filled with Danish soldiers wishing they were back on St. Thomas. By that time, most of the plantation life throughout the Caribbean had died off, and St. John was no exception. Most of its plantations and cultivated land had been abandoned by settlers and reclaimed by forest. Cruz Bay languished until the U.S. purchased the island, in 1917. Tourism hit the scene soon after, and Cruz Bay, with its proximity to St. Thomas, became a population center.

Much of Cruz Bay has given way to semimodern structures, but you'll still see remnants of the colonial era. Those large, white, red-roofed, plantation-style buildings you see on the point to the left of the docks as you approach Cruz Bay by ferry is **The Battery,** a small fortress constructed in 1735. The complex is now used to house the U.S. Virgin Islands' governor when he visits St. John. On the south side of town, off Rt. 104, which heads south to **Great Cruz Bay,** is the **Elaine Ione Sprauve Library and Museum** (tel. 809-776-6359), open weekdays 9 a.m.-5 p.m. The museum and library are

Cruz Bay,
St. John, 1850

COURTESY OF MAPES MONDE Ltd ©

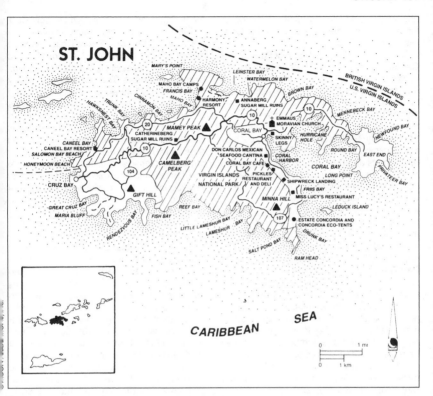

housed in a former plantation greathouse, and today are home to Amerindian artifacts, historical displays of the island's colonial days, and occasional exhibits by local artists.

St. John's **Carnival** festivities begin the last week of June and are capped with 4th of July celebrations including fireworks, parades, feasts, music, and general, all-around nuttiness.

For information about happenings on St. John, stop in at the **tourism office** (tel. 809-776-6450), located across from the customs office and ferry services, and next to the post office on Dronningens Gade. The office is officially open weekdays 8 a.m.-5 p.m., but, in truth, since it's staffed by one person, seems to be open only sporadically.

Virgin Islands National Park

If St. Thomas is the frenetic kitchen and parlor of the U.S. Virgin Islands, then St. John can be considered the lush backyard garden. In the 1950s, years after the U.S. took possession of the U.S. Virgin Islands in 1917, the island came to the attention of wealthy Rockefeller scion Laurance Rockefeller. He purchased large parcels of land and donated about 5,000 acres to the U.S. government, which designated the land a national park in 1956. That makes it one of the oldest national parks of the United States. In 1962, more than 5,500 underwater acres surrounding the island were added to the park, and still more land was added later. Today, 9,500 land acres, plus the underwater reserve—in total about half of this green and hilly island—is protected as part of the Virgin Islands National Park. Aside from the beaches and general lack of bustle, for many the main reason to come to the island is the park, a major attraction. Yet the island itself encompasses some of the finest beaches, camping sites, historical ruins, and ancient Amerindian petroglyphs in all the islands. There is some privately owned property within park borders.

Start by contacting the **National Park Visitor Center** (tel. 809-776-6201, open daily 8 a.m.- 4:30 p.m.) at its dock across from **Mongoose Junction** in Cruz Bay. Rangers will help in planning hikes, walks, and excursions. The park has 22 trails ranging from under one mile to the longest, the 2.4-mile (nearly four-km) **Cinnamon Bay Trail.** Many of the trails, such as the Cinnamon Bay Trail, follow old Danish plantation roads and pass by plantation ruins and buildings. The trails are maintained by the park, yet most are somewhat overgrown and not always well-manicured. The **Brown Bay Trail,** which leads to the **East End Road** at Coral Bay can be difficult; use caution when following this trail. It's not dangerous, just overgrown. The rest of the trails are marked and self-guided, although rangers lead walks on the **Reef Bay Trail,** a five-hour roundtrip excursion that starts at the center of the island and heads south to the sea past Danish plantation ruins and Amerindian petroglyphs. This is the only guided hike that involves a cost—$4 for transportation from Cruz Bay to the trailhead, and another $10 for a boat trip back to Cruz Bay from the trail's end at Reef Bay.

One of the park's more unique trails is an underwater snorkeling trail at the park's **Trunk Bay,** complete with submerged trail markers.

The park visitor center stocks pamphlets that illustrate the trails, as well as books, tapes, videos, and brochures describing and explaining the history and flora and fauna of the park and St. John. Pick up one of the Virgin Islands National Park's *Wha' Happ'nin* program brochures for schedules of historic programs, snorkel trips, and theatrical presentations. Many of the park's programs take place at its **Cinnamon Bay Campground,** located on the north shore.

North Shore Road

Three main roads leave Cruz Bay for the northern, southern, and eastern parts of the island. In fact, there are so few roads on St. John, and the island is so tiny—only nine miles (14 km) long by five miles (eight km) across at its widest point, and 20 square miles (52 square km) in area—that getting lost would be an accomplishment. Figure on a 45-minute drive from Cruz Bay to the eastern settlement at Coral Bay.

Route 20, **the North Shore Road** heads up along the north shore, and it is from here that you'll access most of St. John's tremendous beaches and views. The road ascends quickly from Cruz Bay and skirts the coastline, often at dizzying heights. The views and photographs of the bays below are some of the best-known in the Caribbean. Check out the view of Trunk Bay, with its long, bright white beach. Several other beaches line up along this road, waiting for anyone to jump in and splash. All beaches are free, but remember to watch out for your goods, lock your car, and don't swim in areas that seem isolated or "off." While St. John has experienced little crime in the past, it has had incidents of theft and assault that make precautions important.

After you pass **Maho Bay,** the North Shore Road bears left as a one-way road to become the **Leinster Bay Road.** From here, you can access several beaches, and the **Annaberg Sugar Mill Ruins** high on **Mary's Point.** The ruins, on one of the national park's shorter trails, were part of the thriving sugar plantation era during Danish rule in the 18th century. From the circa-1733 mill ruins—which include an old wattle and daub (sticks and adobe) slave quarters, the mill, and a sugar factory—you'll have views of Leinster Bay as well as the British Virgin Islands' Great Thatch, Little Thatch, Frenchman's Cay, Jost Van Dyke, and Tortola. The park service often conducts historic lectures and craft demonstrations here (for a schedule, call 809-776-6201).

Centerline Road

Route 10 heads out from Cruz Bay and almost immediately ascends into a range of mountains along the spine of the island. This road is the quickest way to get from west to east on St. John. Among these mountains is **Camelberg Peak,** at 1,193 feet (364 meters) one of the island's highest points. You'll also discover, on the north side of the road, the **Catherineberg Sugar Mill** ruins, part of an 18th-century estate. The park's Reef Bay Trail departs from this road and, at the east end, you can stop at **Chateau Bordeaux,** on **Bordeaux Mountain,** for refreshments and some of the more breathtaking views on the island. Bordeaux Mountain is St. John's highest peak, at 1,277 feet (388 meters).

Coral Bay

Just past Bordeaux, the North Shore Road ends at the Centerline Road, and Centerline continues on to the tiny and sleepy settlement of **Coral Bay.** Coral Bay became the island's first settlement, due to its natural, protected harbors at Coral Bay and **Hurricane Hole,** and was infamous as the starting point for the island-wide revolt of slaves in 1733 (see the special topic "The St. John Slave Rebellion"). Today the town is a mishmash of homes, shops, churches, cafes, and a school, sparsely lining the waterfront from Coral Harbor to **Salt Pond Bay** on Rt. 107 (head south off Rt. 10 at the Moravian Church). The salt pond, near the bay, is still harvested by locals when dry weather renders the pond crusty with the salt crystals that form on its surface.

Not a whole lot is going on in Coral Bay except for the tranquil, out-of-the-mainstream ambience of the settlement—if going to St. John is getting away from it all, then going to Coral Bay is *really* getting away. The red-roofed **Emmaus Moravian Church,** built in 1783 and partially reconstructed in 1918, is an example of the style of architecture of the time. The church, the second established mission on St. John and still active today, is registered with the U.S. National Registry of Historic Places.

However, you'll find enough going on in Coral Bay to keep you happy; several small accommodations, including the Estate Concordia campsites (see below), restaurants, cafes, night spots, and water sports outfits are located in the area.

RECREATION

A great deal of St. John's appeal has to do with its relaxed attitude and emphasis on natural attractions. This is not an island where the bays will be buzzing with jet-skis. Nor will the skies be filled with the whooping of swooping parasailors. You won't find a golf course on the island, and tennis is limited to hotels. Still, you'll have plenty of opportunities to play in the water, take side trips to neighboring islands, and have a fine time exploring the island's natural beauty.

Snuba

The word "snuba" hasn't quite yet entered mainstream English, but it soon may; snuba is a sort of cross between snorkeling and scuba diving, wherein you wear masks and fins and are connected by a 20-foot (six-meter) breathing hose and a harness to a large, floating air tank above. This allows you to stay down and explore the shallower depths of the ocean floor and reef without lugging around all that diving equipment. It's designed as a preliminary diving experience, to ease those interested in scuba diving into the underwater environment. The dives take place at the west end of Trunk Bay (not at the underwater snorkeling trail). Cost is $49 for a two-hour dive, which includes some training time. Minimum age is eight years old. Call **Snuba of St. John** (tel. 809-693-8063) for information.

Sailing and Boating

Day-sails in the St. John waters are popular with snorkelers and, of course, irrepressible romantics. Contact the *Jolly Mon* (Cruz Bay, tel. 809-776-6239), a 60-foot (18-meter) catamaran, for snorkeling trips, half-day sails, and Sunday brunch sails. The *Breath* (tel. 809-779-4994 or 809-771-2036), a tall ship with, let's face it, a very strange name, takes day-trips to the British Virgin Islands and to the far ends of St. John (the B.V.I. trips must clear customs). Figure on $60-75 per person, including lunch. The *Sunset Sue* (tel. 809-776-6922) is available for charters to the British Virgin Islands or the far ends of St. John (and picks you up from your hotel). The MY *Cinnamon Bay* (tel. 809-776-6462), a powerboat, takes snorkelers for trips around the island and takes visitors to the British Virgin Islands.

Ocean Runner (Cruz Bay, tel. 809-693-8809) rents powerboats 20-27 feet (6-8 meters) in length by the hour or day. You can also call St. Thomas's **Nauti Nymph** (tel. 809-775-5066) for powerboat rentals (and free delivery to St. John). Boat rentals start at $200 per day for a smaller boat capable of carrying four. **Noah's Little Arks** (Wharfside Village, Cruz Bay, tel. 809-693-9030) rents dinghies for $50 half-day, $80 full day.

Prior to the destruction of Hyatt Regency resort on St. John by Hurricane Marilyn, the *Atlantis Submarine* (Havensight Mall, St. Thomas, tel. 809-776-5650 or 800-253-0493) made once-a-week departures from the hotel's docks. The

Atlantis has suspended those trips until the hotel is completely refurbished. The construction is, as of this writing, ongoing. When it does resume operation, the *Atlantis* will cruise in depths up (or down) to 90 feet (27 meters) during its one-hour, narrated excursions, and you'll see fish, coral reef, and wrecks in the waters of St. John and St. Thomas. The sub's capacity is 46 persons; no children under three feet (one meter) or four years of age are allowed. The cost is $72 per adult, $36 for children 13-18, and $27 for children 4-12. Call to inquire about the submarine's St. John schedule.

Full-Service Water Sports

Scuba diving, night dives, snorkeling, windsurfing, sportfishing, water-skiing, boating, kayaking, underwater camera rentals, trips to neighboring islands, and a plethora of other water activities are handled by full-service water-sports outfits, among them **Coral Bay Watersports** (Coral Bay, tel. 809-776-6850), **Cruz Bay Watersports** (Cruz Bay, tel. 809-776-6234), **Low Key Water Sports** (Cruz Bay, tel. 800-835-7718 or 809-693-8999), **Paradise Watersports** (Chocolate Hole, tel. 809-693-8690), and **St. John Water Sports** (Mongoose Junction in Cruz Bay, tel. 809-776-6256).

Hiking

Stop in Cruz Bay at the Virgin Islands National Park headquarters (tel. 809-776-6201, open daily 8 a.m.-4:30 p.m.) for a pamphlet describing the 22 trails that meander to and through plantation ruins, open valleys, thorn bush mountainsides, semi-rainforests, and seaside beaches. The park boasts 22 trails in all, amounting to some 20 miles. They range from easy to very difficult, 15 minutes to more than two hours. Just remember to wear sturdy hiking shoes—flip-flops will not make it over rocks and thorny scrub—and bring a hat or sunscreen. It's best to hike (and swim) with a partner, and when you encounter historic ruins, which are located all over the island, please remember to leave them alone. Climbing on them or removing stones and other artifacts will only contribute to their disintegration. Also, since the trails often intersect with main roads, remember to walk facing the traffic, which is on the left.

Family Activities

St. John is the sort of island that lends itself to family activities, from swimming to exploring easier walking trails with kids. Visit the Virgin Islands National Park headquarters in Cruz Bay for a full schedule of park activities; several programs feature puppet shows, hands-on crafts demonstrations, and theater designed for kids. As well, there's a small playground at the park headquarters.

BEACHES

If St. John is singled out for one particularly appealing aspect, it is often—and rightfully so—the island's beaches. Miles of coastline and small bays have produced some of the most striking beaches in the Caribbean, many used as backdrops for brochure and fashion photography. Look to the north coast for dozens of beach stops, but you'll find both popular and isolated beaches from north to south and east to west. Many are accessible by car, and parking is free, but for several you'll have to park and hike a bit.

Near town, take the national park's **Lind Point Trail** to isolated **Salomon Bay Beach** and the long **Honeymoon Beach.** Salomon is often used by nude bathers. On the North Shore Road heading out of town, you'll come across **Caneel Bay,** on which the Caneel Bay resort sits. A series of beaches is accessible through the hotel grounds. The entire coastline from Caneel Bay to **Turtle Bay** is fine for swimming and snorkeling. **Jumbie Bay,** between Hawksnest and Trunk Bay, is isolated and often used by au naturel sunbathers.

Continuing along the North Shore Road, you'll soon pass, in succession, **Hawksnest Bay, Trunk Bay,** and **Cinnamon Bay.** All three are part of the Virgin Islands National Park system and have lifeguards, snack bars, picnic tables, showers, and changing facilities. These three are wide and clean and are the island's more popular beaches. Trunk Bay's underwater snorkeling trail will take you past coral and colorful parrotfish, snappers, tang, and many more species. Cinnamon Bay, a long beach, is good for night snorkeling. Keep your things locked or with someone, however—petty thieves have been known to roam the beaches.

The long and narrow beach at **Maho Bay** sits right on the road. Park anywhere you find a spot on the shoulder. Maho is a good beach for the kids, as it's shallow and usually calm. Bear left after the one-way section of the North Shore Road for the Maho Campground and Harmony Resort, as well as **Francis Bay**, which has parking, picnic areas with grills and toilets, and a long, narrow beach with good snorkeling.

Leave Francis Bay, passing by the Annaberg Mill on an unpaved road, and you can access **Watermelon Bay.** Or you can hike in on the park's **Johnny Horn Trail.** At Watermelon, and its offshore islet **Watermelon Cay,** you'll find great snorkeling and swimming and a calm bay.

The island's east end sports rough surf and rocky ocean bottoms—few good swimming spots are found here. Better to head to the south shore and south of Coral Bay on Rt. 107, where you'll find **Salt Pond Bay,** another park beach. The beach is a 10-minute walk from the carpark and offers a picnic area. Leave the Salt Pond parking area and bear left on a windy and hilly road, which then turns into a gravel road, and you'll soon come to **Little Lameshur Bay.** This tiny beach has a picnic area and parking and is isolated. The bay is also accessible from the Bordeaux Mountain Trail. **Europa Bay** and **Genti Bay,** both accessible only on walking trails, have small beaches.

Also on the south shore, south of Cruz Bay, are several bays not maintained by the Virgin Islands National Park. **Great Cruz Bay,** on which the Hyatt Regency resort sits, has a nice beach but is currently not easily accessible to the public.

ACCOMMODATIONS

Accommodations on St. John, as in the rest of the U.S. Virgin Islands, run the full range of large and small resorts, hotels, guesthouses, apartments, and villas. The island currently has two ultra-luxury resorts, located on the north and south coasts. Both, however, **Caneel Bay** and the **Hyatt Regency St. John,** were heavily damaged by Hurricane Marilyn in 1995 and are still recovering. In particular, the Hyatt ran into ownership problems after the hurricane, and it is unclear under which name the resort will reopen.

Most guesthouses are in the Cruz Bay area, but villa rentals dot the island. St. John stands out among the other Virgin Islands for its great camping sites, along the north and east coasts.

Room rates are reduced by as much as 40% during the summer season, and, with a little research, are often bargained out through packages and wholesale room discounters. A government hotel occupancy tax of eight percent is charged on accommodations, and often a 15% service charge is added to the bill. Occasionally, an energy surcharge is also added. Most hotels accept major credit cards, but this is not always the case—check beforehand. Keep in mind that some properties require a three- to seven-night minimum stay, extra persons are often charged $10-30, and the hotel may require a deposit of as much as 50% on the room.

The accommodations listed below are categorized based on the average room rate per night (double occupancy), European plan (no meals), during the high season of 15 December through 15 April, and excluding the eight percent room tax. A designation of **luxury** indicates that rooms run $200 or more; **expensive** rooms are $140-200; **moderate** indicates a range of $80-140; and **budget** rooms cost $80 or less. Keep in mind some hotels offer a wide range of rooms, from budget to luxury.

Villas, Apartments, and Condos

In addition to the rental agencies and Internet sites listed in the Introduction, contact these St. John villa and home rental specialists. The villas represented by the following tend to fall in the luxury category.

Caribbean Villas (P.O. Box 458, Cruz Bay, St. John, U.S. Virgin Islands 00831; tel. 800-338-0987 or 809-776-6152, fax 809-779-4044)

Caribe Havens (P.O. Box 455, Cruz Bay, St. John, U.S. Virgin Islands 00831; tel. and fax 809-776-6518)

Catered To (P.O. Box 704, Cruz Bay, St. John, U.S. Virgin Islands 00831; tel. 800-424-6641 or 809-776-6641, fax 809-693-8191)

Destination St. John (P.O. Box 8306, Cruz Bay, St. John, U.S. Virgin Islands 00831; tel. 800-562-1901 or 809-779-4647)

St. John Properties (P.O. Box 700, Cruz Bay, St.

John, U.S. Virgin Islands 00831; tel. 800-283-1746 or 809-693-8485, fax 809-776-6192)

For properties in the moderate category, contact:

Caribe Havens (P.O. Box 455, Cruz Bay, St. John, U.S. Virgin Islands 08031; tel. and fax 809-776-6518)

Cruz Bay Realty (P.O. Box 66, Cruz Bay, St. John, U.S. Virgin Islands 00831; tel. 800-569-2417 or 809-693-8808, fax 809-693-9812)

Pastory Estates (P.O. Box 458, Cruz Bay, St. John, U.S. Virgin Islands 00831; tel. 800-338-0987 or 809-776-6152, fax 809-779-4044)

Samuel Cottages (P.O. Box 123, Cruz Bay, St. John, U.S. Virgin Islands 00831; tel. 809-776-6643)

Vacation Homes (P.O. Box 272, Cruz Bay, St. John, U.S. Virgin Islands 00831; tel. 809-776-6094, fax 809-693-8455)

Vacation Vistas (P.O. Box 476, Cruz Bay, St. John, U.S. Virgin Islands 00831; tel. 809-776-6462)

Villa Portfolio (P.O. Box 618, Cruz Bay, St. John, U.S. Virgin Islands 00831; tel. 800-858-7989 or 809-693-9100, fax 809-693-5423)

Resorts and Hotels

Caneel Bay (P.O. Box 720, Cruz Bay, St. John, U.S. Virgin Islands 00831; tel. 800-928-8889 or 809-776-6111, fax 809-693-8280) is luxurious in the Old World sense of the phrase. The resort was created by philanthropist Laurance Rockefeller, who also bought and donated much of the island's land to the U.S. Interior Department and park service. The sprawling resort has 171 luxury rooms and cottages spread out over a property that incorporates seven beaches. The rooms have no phones or television and fans instead of air conditioning—clearly, you get a sense of being closer to the air and water around you. Sports, especially tennis, are big at the resort and include water sports and a pool. You'll find three restaurants or terrace dining areas and all the personal attention that this sort of place demands. **Luxury.**

Hyatt Regency St. John (P.O. Box 8310, Cruz Bay, St. John, U.S. Virgin Islands 00831; tel. 800-233-1234 or 809-693-8000, fax 809-693-8888), south of Cruz Bay, is the largest hotel on the island, with nearly 300 rooms and suites, numerous amenities, and a swimming pool that could swallow a small county. At the time of this writing, the hotel had suffered extensive hurricane damage and was also in the process of selling its property to a European firm. It may reopen under a different name, but one would hope that they'll keep the same address and phone numbers. **Luxury.**

Small Hotels, Inns, and Guesthouses

Small **Cruz Inn** guesthouse (P.O. Box 566, Cruz Bay, St. John, U.S. Virgin Islands 00831; tel. 800-666-7688 or 809-693-8688, fax 809-693-8590) is just a few blocks from the center of town (from the ferry dock, walk up Prindsen Gade three blocks, then take a right at the Julius Sprauve Elementary School, then take your second right). Cruz Inn encompasses a couple of West Indian-style homes that offer a combination of 14 simple rooms, efficiency apartments, apartments, or suites, sleeping two to six people. Some share baths, some have air conditioning. This is a great location from which to explore town and the surrounding areas. Air-conditioning incurs a surcharge, and, to keep costs down, no daily maid service is offered, but linens are changed once weekly. **Budget.**

Frank Bay B&B (P.O. Box 408, Cruz Bay, St. John, U.S. Virgin Islands 00831; tel. 800-561-7290 or 809-693-8617), also small, opened in 1995 and can be found just down the hill from Ellington's Restaurant at Gallows Point. The three-room home, a West Indian house built in the 1940s, sits on an acre of land amidst a Japanese-flavored garden. The home has a veranda for gazing out over the water and a large greatroom for guest interaction. Of the three rooms, two share a bath; one of these has a/c, the other is cooled by a fan. The Garden Room has a private bath and entrance. All rooms are decorated in muted batik fabrics. Across the street is a small, rocky waterfront area where you can snorkel, but this is no place for swimming. The owner, Joshlynn Crosley, also owns the **Cafe Roma** in town. This is a fine place for quietly doing nothing. If you're in a taxi looking for the place, tell the driver to go to Dr. Tobacco's old house. Don't ask. You can visit the hotel at its Web site, www.teaminteract.com/stjohn/frankbay. **Moderate.**

Gallows Point Suite Resort (P.O. Box 58, Cruz Bay, St. John, U.S. Virgin Islands 00831; tel. 800-323-7229 or 809-776-6434, fax 809-776-6520), with 15 buildings of four units each, sits on a point on the south side of the Cruz Bay harbor, a five-minute walk from downtown. Note the ancient cemetery on the right as you walk to the hotel. Whether or not this has something to do with that "gallows" in the name of the area is unclear. According to local legend, Gallows Point was an area where rebellious slaves were executed.

Whatever the case, the complex is currently pleasant, surrounded by lush gardens and views of St. Thomas and other islands. The resort comprises suites, with harbor views or ocean views, decorated in that island-chic floral pattern seen so often in Caribbean hotels. They are spacious, comfortable, and come with full kitchens (large stoves and fridges), balconies, and big beds. You'll find a pool and sun deck on the premises. The small beach is good for a quick splash, but don't get your hopes up—it's pebbly and good for snorkeling but pales in comparison to other St. John beaches. You won't find water sports here. Also, one of the island's more elegant restaurants, **Ellington's** (tel. 809-693-8490), is located here. Ellington's serves continental cuisine and seafood specials and has music nightly—and wonderful sunset views as well. **Luxury.**

Inn at Tamarind Court (P.O. Box 350, Cruz Bay, St. John, U.S. Virgin Islands 00831; tel. 800-221-1637 or 809-776-6378, fax 809-776-6722), an informal, 19-room B&B, is located on the Southside Road (Rt. 104) just a few blocks from the ferry docks, across from the Elaine Ione Sprauve Library and Museum. It's a great location for exploring town, and the simple rooms are clean and safe. There's no pool on the grounds. The courtyard restaurant, **Etta's**, serves up West Indian specialties. **Budget.**

Oscar's Guest House (P.O. Box 117, Cruz Bay, St. John, U.S. Virgin Islands 00831; tel. 888-672-2784 or 800-854-1843, and 809-776-6193 or 809-776-6232) is a seven-room guesthouse located on top of Oscar's Convenience Market on Kongens Gade (two blocks up from the ferry dock, near the Chase Manhattan Bank). All rooms are simple but do include cable TV, a/c, fans, and private baths. You won't find a bar, restaurant, or kitchen for guest use on the property, but the location, smack in the center of things, won't leave you wanting for places to eat. **Moderate.**

Popular **Raintree Inn** (P.O. Box 566, Cruz Bay, St. John, U.S. Virgin Islands 00831; tel. 800-666-7449 or tel. and fax 809-693-8590), owned by the same folks who own the nearby Cruz Inn, is a small, clean guesthouse with eight guest rooms and three efficiency apartments. The apartments sleep up to six and are equipped with full kitchens and private baths. The eight rooms also have private baths. To keep costs down, no daily maid service is offered, but linens and towels are changed once each week (and, of course, after you check out). Note that Raintree is a *nonsmoking* guesthouse. The on-premises restaurant, **The Fish Trap** (tel. 809-693-9994) serves up local West Indian and seafood specialties on an outdoor patio. The place is central to town (next to the Catholic church one block away from the ferry docks), and a good deal, especially if you've got two or more people staying in an efficiency apartment. Air-conditioning incurs a surcharge of $5 per day. **Budget-Moderate.**

Camping

It could be argued that the campgrounds on St. John are among the finest in the Caribbean. It can also be argued that they aren't exclusively campgrounds, given the strictest definition of the word. The campgrounds themselves offer everything from inexpensive bare sites to luxury tents or cottages with kitchenettes.

Cinnamon Bay Campground (P.O. Box 720, Cruz Bay, St. John, U.S. Virgin Islands 00831, tel. 800-539-9998 or 809-776-6458 or 809-693-5654, fax 809-776-6458) is terrifically located and managed by the Rosewood Resorts company. The Virgin Islands National Park campground offers a full range of semi-roughing-it accommodations along the half-mile white sand beach—the longest on the island. Found on Cinnamon Bay along the north shore, in addition to the beach, the campground includes several of the national park walking trails, and the grounds are the home of the national park's amphitheater, where many of the scheduled lectures and demonstration take place. As well, there's a water sports center, a snack bar, the

T'ree Lizards Restaurant for evening meals, a small museum, a general store, and a place of worship in the campgrounds.

The range of accommodations covers some 28 bare sites, 44 tented sites, and 40 small airy cottages (15 feet—4.6 meters square). The cottages have electricity, fans, charcoal grills and propane stoves, water containers, and kitchen utensils. Large screened panels front a small deck with chairs, and each cottage comes with a small desk and four twin beds. You can get fresh linens and towels from the front desk twice each week. Rates in winter for beachview cottages are $105 d, plus $15 for each additional person. Regular cottages run $95 d per night, plus $15 for each additional person. The eight percent accommodations tax applies.

The tents are generous by tent standards, 10 by 14 feet (three by four meters), and sit on a wooden platform. They come equipped with cots and include bed linen and towels, picnic tables, grills and propane stoves, water containers, cooking utensils, and gas lanterns. Guests can turn in their linens and towels for fresh ones twice a week. Rates in winter are $75 d, $15 for each additional person. Taxes apply.

The bare sites come with grills and picnic tables, and campers bring their own tents, utensils, towels, and bedding. Rates in winter for bare sites are $17 d, plus $5 for each additional person. No taxes are charged on bare sites.

All guests use one of four ablution blocks, which include toilets and cold-water showers (some have facilities for guests with disabilities).

Visitors can select special packages including meal plans (MAP $22 per adult per day, $16 for children 12 and under; AP $28 for adults, $22 for kids), weeklong all-inclusive plans including some water sports activities, or MAP plans including snorkeling.

In addition to its attractive rates, the scheduled park activities, the beach, and nature walks make this one of the best places on the island to take kids. Book early; the campsites are in great demand.

Just up the road from Cinnamon Bay is the privately owned **Maho Bay Camps** (17 A East 73rd St., New York, NY 10021; tel. 212-472-9453 or P.O. Box 310, Cruz Bay, St. John, U.S. Virgin Islands 00831; tel. 800-392-9004 or 809-776-6240, fax 809-776-6504). The camp, owned and operated by eco-tourism pioneer Stanley Selengut, is dedicated to preserving the land, meaning that all sites are elevated and hand-constructed from mostly recycled materials so as to leave the natural environment as undisturbed as possible. The camp features 114 "tent-cottages," of the type you might see in the film *Lawrence o. Arabia,* each with rooms separated by screens wood floors, kitchenettes, propane stoves, utensils, furniture, porches, electricity, and wide screens to let in the ocean breezes. Each has two beds plus extra mattresses. The campsites are built into the side of the hill overlooking Maho Bay, set in and among natural gardens and trees. The beach below is one of the more popular on the island, and other beaches at Little Maho Bay and Francis Bay are within walking distance.

Toilets and pull-chain showers are communal, and water sports facilities, a store, and a restaurant serving breakfast and dinner can be found on the grounds. Cost is $95 d in the winter season plus $15 for each additional person. No credit cards are accepted.

To get to Maho, take the North Shore Road past Maho Bay, follow the signs to the Annaberg Mill, and bear left toward Francis Bay. You'll see the sign. Maho Bay Camps is extremely popular, particularly in the winter months, so contact them well ahead for reservations.

Up the hill, overlooking the Maho Bay camps, is another Stanley Selengut property called **Harmony Resort** (same address). Harmony opened in 1995 and is more upscale than the Maho property, featuring six buildings, with upper and lower units, built using theories of sustainable development. The resort features passive solar energy and wind energy units, recycling systems, and construction materials made of items most people consider refuse (waste rubber made into floor tiles, glass from discarded light bulbs incorporated into ceramic tiles, cardboard made into roofing shingles, etc.). The units contain high-efficiency refrigerators, and several have mini-computers mounted by the beds which are used to monitor energy use and efficiency and which can be used to call up descriptions of products used in the building's construction.

Harmony's rooms are efficiency apartments with queen-size or pairs of twin beds, kitchens with appliances, private baths, and decks overlooking the bay and hill. Guests can use the failities at Maho Bay Camps. **Expensive.**

Over at the far east end of the island, south of Coral Bay on Rt. 107, is **Estate Concordia and Concordia Eco-tents** (same address as Maho, tel. 809-693-5855). This is another Stanley Selengut property, dedicated to ecologically sound construction and sustainable development. The entire 52-acre property, a former cotton plantation, abuts national park land and sits on a hill overlooking Salt Pond Bay, Ram Head, and the open ocean. The vistas are stunning.

The Estate Concordia property includes comfortable studios and loft duplexes, cooled by breezes and overhead fans, with large kitchens, verandas, and private baths. Definitely luxurious. **Expensive.**

The Eco-tents, located next door to the villas, are "tent-cottages" in much the same style as the tents at Maho—elevated platforms, constructed so as not to disturb the ground cover, all with fabric walls, lots of open-air screening, kitchenettes, and solar panels with battery banks. The difference is that each unit has a private bath (with a composting toilet) and shower. Each unit sleeps four to six. Additional people are $25 per person per night. **Moderate.**

The entire complex is connected by planked boardwalks, and you'll find a large swimming pool at the base of the property. You'll be alone out here—it's a perfect place to relax and listen to the wind whistle through the trees. At nearby Coral Bay, you'll find restaurants, shops, and grocery stores.

You can visit the Maho Bay Camps, Harmony, and the Concordia properties at their Web site, www.maho.org.

EATING AND DRINKING

Unlike St. Thomas and St. Croix, you won't find a lot of American fast-food chains on St. John. The restaurants are generally small, intimate, and varied, and most are located in Cruz Bay and Coral Bay. Frequently restaurants accept credit cards, but it's best to call ahead to confirm.

Categories used below are based on average entrée price: **expensive** is $25 or more; **moderate** is $10-25; **inexpensive** is $10 or less.

Cruz Bay

Asolare (tel. 809-779-4747), perched up a hill on the North Side Road overlooking town, serves Asian specialties. The views from here are of the town and harbor. **Moderate.**

The Back Yard (tel. 809-693-8886), on Kongens/Vesta Gade across the street from Joe's Diner, is a small, squeezed-in-an-alley restaurant and bar, great for a quick drink. **Inexpensive-Moderate.**

Bad Art Bar (tel. 809-693-8666), an upstairs joint next to Woody's across the street from the Chase Manhattan Bank, serves burgers, sandwiches, and drinks. The art decorating the interior, by the way, is indeed bad—very cheesy. Velvet-Elvis bad. It's all in fun, and you've got to

fish market, Cruz Bay, St. John

admire their stance on art: even if it's bad, it can entertain. **Moderate.**

Cafe Roma (tel. 809-776-6524), upstairs on Kogen's Gade a few doors down from the Chase Manhattan Bank, serves Italian and vegetarian specialties. Open daily for dinner only, from 5 p.m. **Moderate.**

Chilly Billy's (tel. 809-693-8708) is just up from downtown, between the North Shore Road and the Centerline Road. The small restaurant is open daily, a great place for breakfast. Lunch too. **Inexpensive-Moderate.**

Ellington's (tel. 809-693-8490), at the Gallows Point Resort, offers continental and seafood specials and views to live for. Dinner only, daily. **Moderate.**

Etta's (tel. 809-776-6378), at the Inn at Tamarind Court, serves West Indian specialties. **Moderate.**

The Fish Trap (tel. 809-693-9994), at the

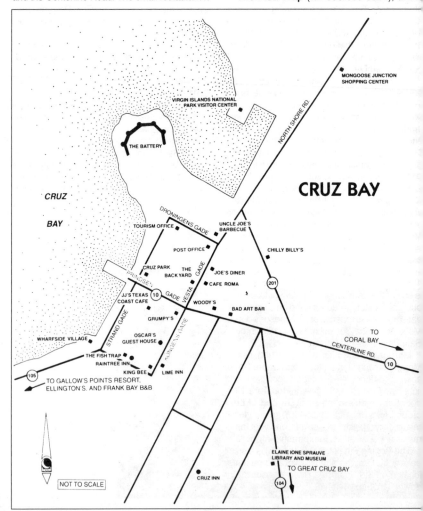

Raintree Inn downtown, does the seafood dinner thing and does it well. It also serves pastas and a variety of meat dishes. Closed Monday. **Moderate.**

Fred's (tel. 809-776-6363), across the street from the Lime Inn on Kogen's Gade, serves breakfast, lunch, and dinner and specializes in West Indian treats. It's also one of Cruz Bay's happening dancing spots. **Moderate.**

Grumpy's (tel. 809-693-8775), across the street from the Wharfside Village, serves breakfast, lunch, and dinner every day 7 a.m.-1 a.m. The fare is burgers, seafood, pizza, sandwiches, and more. Also, you'll find live music every night from 9 p.m. **Moderate.**

JJ's Texas Coast Cafe (tel. 809-776-6908) is the place for Tex-Mex, and it's located in the park, across from the taxi stand. **Moderate.**

Joe's Diner (tel. 809-776-6888), in the middle of town behind the post office, is a Cruz Bay landmark serving simple, fast burgers, sandwiches, and fried chicken on an outdoor patio overlooking the street. And, let's be frank, you've got to love a place named Joe's Diner. **Inexpensive-Moderate.**

King Bee (tel. 809-693-7270), next to Sutton's Jeep Rental on Kongens Gade, serves West Indian specialties such as conch fritters, fungi, souse, kallaloo, and fresh fish. Open Monday through Saturday for lunch and dinner, Sunday for brunch only (11 a.m.-3 p.m.). **Inexpensive.**

The **Lime Inn** (tel. 809-776-6425 or 809-779-4199), on Kogen's Gade, is set in a garden and is one of the town's more popular spots, serving burgers, lobster, grilled fish, and an all-you-can-eat shrimp feast special on Wednesday. Open Monday to Friday for lunch and Monday through Saturday for dinner. **Moderate.**

Morgan's Mango (tel. 809-693-8141), next to Mongoose Junction on the North Shore Road, serves seafood, West Indian specialties, and light fare. Open daily for dinner. **Moderate.** Next door to Morgan's is the small **Garden of Luscious Licks** (tel. 809-693-8400), serving three meals daily. Health food, salads, and vegetarian meals are specialties. **Inexpensive-Moderate.**

The **Rolling Pin** (tel. 809-779-4775) is a small bakery that serves sandwiches and pastries, located on the Southside Road just outside of downtown. **Inexpensive.**

Saychelles (tel. 809-693-7030), at Wharfside Village by the docks, is an elegant evening dining spot. Specials are seafood, pasta, and continental cuisine. You can dine alfresco over the beach or in an air-conditioned dining room. Open daily for dinner. **Moderate-Expensive.** Nearby is the **Paradise Cafe** (tel. 809-779-4810), where you can grab a drink before dinner or a coffee during the day. Open daily 10 a.m.-6 p.m. **Inexpensive.** Also at Wharfside Village is the oddly named **Pusser's Wharfside Village** (tel. 809-693-8489). Pusser's, a set of bars and restaurants including a beach bar, takes its somewhat unappetizing name from a corruption of the word "purser." The establishment, which has branches throughout the U.S. and British Virgin Islands, serves famous Pusser's Rum, a rum that was issued to sailors of the British Royal Navy until 1970—by, of course, the purser. The fare is burgers and steaks, and the famous drink is a Painkiller—Pusser's Rum, pineapple, and coconut cream. You'll also find a travel-clothing and -accessories shop. **Moderate.**

Uncle Joe's Barbecue sits on the docks and serves up barbecued chicken, ribs, and steaks with beans and rice, corn on the cob, and all the fixings. The open-air restaurant has only three or four tables, but you can grab an order and head to the park to eat. Open Monday through Saturday for lunch and dinner, Sunday 3:30-8:30 p.m. **Inexpensive.**

Woody's (tel. 809-779-4625), a bar and restaurant across the street from the Chase Manhattan Bank, serves lunch and dinner daily, with a bar menu and a happy hour (3-6 p.m.). Seafood is the specialty. **Inexpensive-Moderate.**

Several restaurants located in the Mongoose Junction shopping complex are also fine for a quick bite or drink while strolling. **St. John Books** (tel. 809-779-4260), upstairs, has a cappuccino bar and is a great place to buy a newspaper and hang out for a while. The **Mongoose Restaurant** (tel. 809-693-8677) serves breakfast, lunch, and diner daily, is also a deli, and has music nightly; the **Gecko Gazebo** (tel. 809-693-8340) serves drinks in the courtyard; **Paradiso Restaurant** (tel. 809-693-8899) is open daily for dinner and serves Italian specialties; and the **Sun Dog Cafe** (tel. 809-693-8340) serves light lunches and takeout. All **Inexpensive-Moderate.**

Coral Bay

Coral Bay Cafe (tel. 809-693-5161) is located on a small turnoff from the main road, Rt. 107, south of Coral Bay. The small outside eatery serves breakfast, sandwiches, coffee, cakes, cookies, pies, and lighter fare. Great place for a quick snack. Martha Matthias, the owner, is a wonderful source for goings-on around Coral Bay. Open Tues.-Sat. 8 a.m.-8 p.m. **Inexpensive-Moderate.** Next door is **Joe's Discount Extra** grocery store and liquor shop, where you can grab the morning paper.

Don Carlos Mexican Seafood Cantina (tel. 809-776-6866) sits on the bay, on Rt. 107, and serves Mexican and seafood specials for lunch and dinner every day. The restaurant is open to the ocean breezes. This is your chance for the best Mexican on the island. The happy hour, weekdays 4:30-6 p.m., is popular, and the 46-ounce margaritas are not for the faint of heart. Their sister restaurant in the States, also named Don Carlos, holds the world record for burrito excess for having produced a mile-long burrito beast in 1992. With credentials like that, who could resist? **Moderate.**

Miss Lucy's Restaurant (tel. 809-779-4404) is located seaside at Friis Bay, on Rt. 107. The simple restaurant specializes in authentic West Indian foods, and is open every day except Sunday for lunch and dinner. **Inexpensive-Moderate.**

Pickles Restaurant and Deli, on the main road, is open daily 10 a.m.-6:30 p.m. for take-out sandwiches and meals. **Inexpensive-Moderate.**

Shipwreck Landing (tel. 809-693-5640) is a seafood restaurant in the small Shipwreck Landing shopping complex. **Moderate.**

Skinny Legs (tel. 809-779-4982) bar and restaurant, just past the Moravian Church and fire station on the East End Road, serves burgers and seafood and has entertainment some nights. It's also got a satellite dish, a horseshoes setup, and a dart board. This is Coral Bay's happening sports bar and night spot. The restaurant opens daily at 11 a.m. **Moderate.**

Other

Several restaurants at the island's two hotels have been, in the past, recommended. The Hyatt Regency's **Cafe Grand, Splash Bar & Grill,** and **Ciao Mein** Italian and Asian restaurant were open to the public before the hotel's de-struction by Hurricane Marilyn. Call (809) 693-8000 to check if they've reopened. Ditto with Caneel Bay's **Equator** (tel. 809-776-6111), which offers seafood and West Indian and Thai cuisine. All **Moderate-Expensive.**

Chateau de Bordeaux (tel. 809-776-6611), near the far end of the Centerline Road, serves fine French cuisine at a unique setting high up in the mountains. It's worth the 35-minute drive from Cruz Bay just for the views of the hills and ocean below. You'll need to make reservations for this one. **Moderate-Expensive.** Several shops and a smaller bar and cafe are attached to the Chateau Bordeaux complex.

NIGHTLIFE

In many ways, the nightlife on St. John is like the day life—relaxed, quiet, pretty well down with the sun. However, if you want to boogie, you've got a few options. Several Cruz Bay restaurants and hotels offer live music with some regularity, including **Chilly Billy's** (live reggae or steel pan music on Fridays) and **Grumpy's** (live music every night from 9 p.m. to midnight). **Ellington's,** at Gallow's Point Resort, has live music every night until 10 p.m., usually a steel pan band. Mongoose Junction's **Mongoose Restaurant** has live bands and music on weekends.

Skinny Legs, in Coral Bay, has occasional live music, a TV, and is the town's number-one nighttime hangout.

SHOPPING

Little in the way of shopping exists on St. John outside of Cruz Bay. You'll find gift shops in some of the local hotels and at some of the campsites, and you'll find a smattering of shops in Coral Bay at **Shipwreck Landing** and **Coral Bay Watersports,** but by and large, for locals and for visitors, Cruz Bay is the only game in town.

Shops are located all about Cruz Bay, but the town is no duty-free shopping haven. Rather, its shops are smaller and specialize in local crafts and art. However, a couple of malls are worth a stop. **Wharfside Village,** near the ferry dock, has **Jeweler's Warehouse, Blue Carib Gems, Isola Furniture,** and **Freebird Creations.**

Freebird sells jewelry and watches; Isloa carries furniture inspired by Indonesian design.

A short walk from the National Park Visitor Center, on the North Shore Road, you'll find **Mongoose Junction**, with the artisans galleries **Batik Kitab, Under The Sun/Bajo El Sol,** and **World View Graphics.** Also look for **Bamboula, Big Planet Adventure Outfitters, Island Galleria, The Fabric Mill,** and the gem shops **Best of Both Worlds, Caravan Gallery, Colombian Emeralds International,** and **R&I Patton Goldsmithing.** You'll find a half-dozen other shops, real estate agencies, and several cafes and restaurants at Mongoose Junction.

For books and periodicals, stop at **Sparky's** (tel. 809-776-6284), at Meada's Plaza behind the visitor center (at Cruz Park across from the dock taxi stand). Sparky's also carries U.S. newspapers. **St. John Books** (tel. 809-779-4260) and the always entertaining **MAPes MONDe** (tel. 809-779-4545), both at Mongoose Junction, carry wide selections of prints, cards, books on local history and culture, and best sellers. St. John Books, a second-floor shop, also carries newspapers and has a small, outdoor coffee bar overlooking the road.

For groceries, stop in at the **Marina Market** (tel. 809-779-4401) on the Southside Road near the Sprauve Museum. They've got a fine deli with meats, cheeses, barbecued chicken, drinks, and more. The market is open weekdays and Saturday 6 a.m.-9 p.m. and Sunday 8 a.m.-8 p.m. **Nature's Nook** (tel. 809-693-8695), at the docks, is good for fruits and vegetables. **Our Place,** a tiny hole in the wall near the docks, sells produce and herbs. **Jayma Discount Grocery** (tel. 809-693-8700) is a full-service grocery, located at the area called Enighed, a couple of blocks up from the ferry docks. Near Jayma is the **Star Fish Market** (tel. 809-779-4949), also a grocery store and deli. For fresh fish, you can also find the local fishermen bringing in their catch to a small market behind the customs and immigration building, near the Battery across from the tourism office. The fishermen toss the fish out onto a small table and, if you trust your instincts about fresh fish, you can bargain away. Make sure the fish doesn't smell worse than it should, and check the eyes—cloudy eyes mean old fish.

GETTING AROUND

Rental Car Agencies

Most rental car companies require that the driver be at least 25 years old. U.S. drivers will need a valid license; others will need to obtain a temporary license through the rental company. Credit cards are almost universally accepted, and rates start at about $45 per day—less for weekly rentals. Most offer free mileage and free pickup and drop-off. On St. John, jeeps or vehicles with high clearance are recommended and are, in fact, the typical rental vehicle offered.

Remember that even though the U.S. Virgin Islands are a U.S. territory and use left-hand-drive vehicles, driving is on the left side of the road, a legacy of the Danish system.

The following are all in the same ballpark when it comes to rates and service and are based in Cruz Bay.

Conrad Sutton Car Rental (tel. 809-776-6479, fax 809-693-8099)

Cool Breeze Rentals (tel. 809-776-6588, fax 809-693-8078)

Hertz (tel. 800-654-3131 or 809-776-6412)

Hospitality Rent-A-Car (tel. 809-693-9160)

Spencer's Jeep Rentals (tel. 809-776-6628 or 809-693-8784, fax 809-693-8399)

St. John Car Rental (tel. 809-776-6103, fax 809-693-8711)

It seems strange that the rental companies don't offer motorcycles or moped-type scooters for rent—St. John is an island that lends itself to putting along on a bike. Perhaps the issue is one of insurance. Whatever the case, you'll have to make do with a car.

Taxis and Organized Tours

Most taxis on St. John are of the safari-jitney type, meaning open-air flatbed trucks with benches set up for passengers. Most any taxi will take you on an island tour. The rates, for a two-hour tour of the island, run $30 for one or two passengers, and $12 each for three or more.

Taxis can always be found at the ferry docks, but if you'd like to arrange a tour before your arrival, call the reliable and informative **Derrick Thomas** (tel. 809-693-7530). This is also the number of St. John Taxi Services, a central taxi dispatch office.

Typical rates for getting from Cruz Bay to selected island sites are: to Annaberg Mill, Maho Bay, or Coral Bay, $10 for one, $12.50 for two, and $5 each for three or more; to Cinnamon Bay, $5.50 for one, $8 for two, and $3.50 each for three or more; to Trunk Bay, $5 for one, $7.50 for two, and $3 each for three or more.

There is no organized bus service on St. John.

MISCELLANEOUS

In Cruz Bay, clean **public restrooms** can be found in a green and white structure next to the Customs and Immigration building (also a ferry departure dock), across from the tourism office. Two **public phones** are located in front of the post office. The **post office** (tel. 809-779-4227) is open weekdays 7:30 a.m.-4 p.m. and Saturday 7:30-noon. An **ATM** is located at the Chase Manhattan Bank on Kogen's Gade. Best bet for film and developing is **Cruz Bay Photo Center** (tel. 809-779-4313), next to Wharfside Village. **Paradise Laundry** (tel. 809-693-8848), in Cruz Bay, has coin-operated machines.

INFORMATION DIRECTORY

Police, Fire, Ambulance, tel. 911

St. John Community Health Clinic, Cruz Bay, tel. (809) 776-6400

St. John Drug Center, Cruz Bay, tel. (809) 776-6353

United Parcel Service, tel. (809) 693-8130

Department of Tourism, P.O. Box 200, Cruz Bay, St. John, U.S. Virgin Islands 00830; tel. (809) 776-6450

St. Thomas-St. John Hotel Association, tel. (809) 774-6835

ST. CROIX

SIGHTS

St. Croix is somewhat removed from St. Thomas and St. John, in terms of both distance and character. The island is located 40 miles (64 kilometers) south of St. Thomas and, on a clear day, visible through the haze from the highest points on St. Thomas and St. John. Due to its former status as the premier plantation center of the old Danish West Indies and as the first of the Virgin Islands sighted by Columbus during his second voyage to the West Indies (he named it Santa Cruz), the flavor of the island is one of quiet, historical encounters and laid-back shopping, dining, and sightseeing. The fading yellow Danish government buildings of Christiansted speak volumes of the old days; most are on the U.S. National Registry of Historic Places. The island towns themselves, Christiansted and Frederiksted, are small jumbles of rarely crowded streets, easily navigated, with side streets and alleys harboring shops and small cafes.

St. Croix, though the largest of the three U.S.

Virgin Islands, measuring 84 square miles (217 square km)—28 miles (45 km) long by seven miles (11 km) wide—can easily be covered in a couple of days if you're energetic and want to see the entire island. Alternately, pick a few quiet adventure days and select some of the more intriguing sites, such as Buck Island, Estate Whim Plantation, and Cramer's Park, which this dry, somewhat scrubby island has to offer.

Christiansted
The northern coast's **Christiansted** is St. Croix's hub and commercial center. The town is compact and can appear busy in that small-town sort of way—traffic jams at busy hours, a few honking horns, and shops overflowing when cruise ships are visiting this town and Frederiksted, on the island's west end. It's also home to about 2,500 of the island's 50,000 population and no more than a half hour's drive from just about any point on the island.

The downtown area features narrow one-way streets and architecture with a heavy Danish influence. All roads lead to the harbor area,

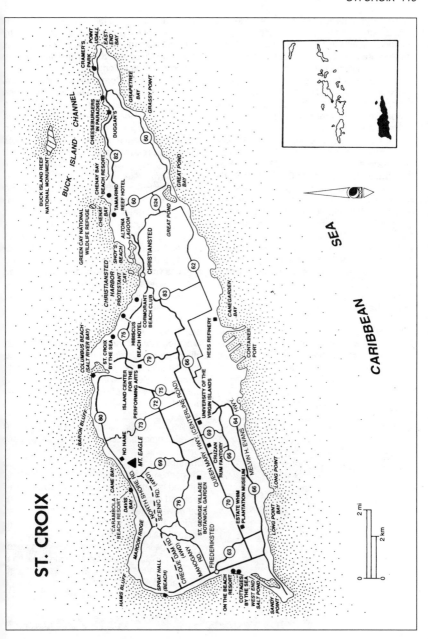

ST. CROIX

called **Kings Wharf,** where many of the town's hotels, duty-free shops, and a little shopping boardwalk face the ocean and the small, off-shore **Protestant Cay.** Protestant Cay is home to a resort called, cleverly, Hotel on the Cay, which is popular for day trips and has the only beach in town. A small shuttle boat runs to the cay from the docks near **Fort Christiansvaern.**

Fort Christiansvaern is among a group of buildings that make up the centerpiece of Christiansted. Now maintained by the U.S. National Park Service (tel. 809-773-1460), the buildings are collectively the **Christiansted National Historic Site.** They include the **Old Danish Scale House,** the **Old Customs House,** the **Steeple Building,** the **Danish West India and Guinea Company Warehouse, Government House,** and the fort. The buildings were constructed during the Danish heyday in the islands, circa 1730-80, and are distinguished by their pale yellow or pink paint and red roofs.

Fort Christiansvaern is one of five Danish forts in the U.S. Virgin Islands and is built on the site of an old French fort called Fort Saint Jean. The Danish edition was completed in 1749 and used by the military until 1878. It has served as a courthouse and police station since then and is now open for self-guided tours weekdays 8 a.m.-5 p.m. and weekends 9 a.m.-5 p.m. Visitors will find the battlement wall with cannon still mounted, a kitchen, magazine room, a couple of rooms furnished in the style of the day, soldiers' cells, and a military museum display. You'll also find a gift shop here (open until 4:30 p.m.), and a park ranger's station. Nearby is a small carpark. Admission is $2 for ages six and up and is collected at the fort (the only site that collects admission).

The nearby Customs House, with its wide, sweeping staircase, was completed in 1751 and today houses the national park offices. The Old Danish Scale House, across the street, was once used to weigh and assess goods for import and export taxes. It now houses the **St. Croix Visitors Bureau** of the tourism department (tel. 809-773-0495). Visitors are welcome to stroll in and have a look.

The white Steeple Building on Company and Hospital Streets was built as a Lutheran Church in 1753 and in later years became a bakery and a hospital. Today it is maintained by the park service and houses a small museum of Amerindian artifacts, sugarcane industry displays, and a small section on the life of the American statesman Alexander Hamilton, who spent 10 years of his boyhood on St. Croix. The museum is open Tuesday, Wednesday, and Thursday 9-11 a.m. and 1-4 p.m.

Across the street from the Steeple Building is the Danish West India and Guinea Company Warehouse, which now houses the central post office, police station, and, not insignificantly, public restrooms. The warehouse was constructed in 1750, and the courtyard behind the post office once served as the town's slave market.

Christiansted,
St. Croix, 1837

THE ALEXANDER HAMILTON CONNECTION

Alexander Hamilton (1755-1804), the American statesman, author of the Federalist papers, and tragically famous bad shot, is legendary in the West Indies.

Hamilton was born on Nevis, an island south of St. Kitts in the Lesser Antilles. He was the second illegitimate son of a Scottish trader and sailor named James Hamilton, and his mother was Rachel Levine. In 1763, the small family moved to St. Croix, where James promptly abandoned them and returned to Nevis. After his mother's death of yellow fever, when Hamilton was just 13, the young boy became an accountant of sorts, entering the counting house of trader Nicholas Cruger. He exhibited great ability—so much so that when it was clear it was time to further his education, Cruger volunteered to finance a trip to the colonies. There, Hamilton intended to enter Princeton College, in New Jersey. Princeton rejected him because of his illegitimacy, but, by 1773, he'd ended up at King's College in New York, an institution now known as Columbia University.

Hamilton served with distinction in the War for Independence, later became a lawyer, and, after the establishment of the government, in 1789, with George Washington as president, was appointed secretary of the treasury. Hamilton later became the leader of the Federalist Party and supported John Adams in his bid for the presidency.

Hamilton's fate was sealed with the presidential election of 1800, during which the candidates, Thomas Jefferson and Aaron Burr, received equal numbers of electoral votes. Hamilton lobbied the House of Representatives on behalf of Jefferson, incurring the wrath of Burr. Several years later, Hamilton engineered Burr's defeat in a gubernatorial election in New York State, and Burr challenged him to a duel. Hamilton reluctantly accepted (his son had been killed in a duel three years earlier) and was shot and killed.

The buildings where Hamilton lived and worked in Christiansted were replaced in the mid-19th century. Hamilton is honored today with a small display in the National Park Service's Steeple Building.

Government House, an imposing structure on Kongens Gade (King Street), once housed the government of the entire Danish West Indies and was the residence of the Danish governor. The main building was built by a merchant in the 1740s and was purchased by the Danish government in the early 1770s. The grand ballroom, at the top of the streetside stairway, is the building's centerpiece, with mirrored walls and a giant candelabra. Today, Government House still houses the St. Croix government offices. Visitors can see the ballroom and other parts of the building on an intermittent basis, depending on staffing.

If you're interested in historic churches, you'll find, next to Government House and across Queen Cross Street, the **Lord of God Sabaoth Lutheran Church** (tel. 809-773-1320), built in 1740. At the far end of King Street, several blocks up from the wharf, is **St. John Anglican Church** (tel. 809-778-8221), built in 1849 on the site of the town's original Anglican church (circa 1775). Note the intricate woodwork of the ceiling support beams.

On Company Street, you'll find an open area called **Market Square,** the traditional site of produce and fruit vendors. Today the market is still active and you'll find dozens of vendors selling their wares. The market is particularly busy on Saturdays.

The historic sights of Christiansted can be seen on guided walking tours sponsored by **Take-A-Hike** (tel. 809-778-6997). The short version is about two hours and costs $5.50 per person. An extended tour is also available. Call ahead for times and days of departure.

For a different sort of experience, stop in at the small **St. Croix Aquarium,** located in the Caravelle Arcade on Strand Street. This nonprofit marine education center, formerly located in Frederiksted, has small aquariums and, for the kids, a touching pond and children's discovery room. Tours are led by marine biologist Lonnie Kaczmarsky, who personally catches the aquarium's fish and their food, and—in an appropriate gesture for a conservationist—releases fish as new ones are brought in. This means the fish on display are constantly rotating in and out of the aquarium. As well, all the fish are released once every year for tank cleaning and because, hey, it's a nice thing to do. The largest tank is 500 gallons, and the largest fish on display is usually a nurse shark. The center is open Tuesday through Saturday 11 a.m.-4 p.m. (school groups only 9-11 a.m.), and admission is $4.50 for adults and $2 for kids 12 and under. Call center director Sonia Kulyk (who is married to Lonnie) at (809) 773-8995 for information.

Frederiksted

The small town of **Frederiksted,** on St. Croix's west end, has always lived in the shadow of the larger Christiansted but is important in the history and commerce of the island even today. Its deep-water port is, unlike Christiansted Harbor, able to receive large cruise ships, which makes Frederiksted the arrival point for most cruise passengers—who are then often shuttled to Christiansted.

The town has its own charm, however, in its easily navigated size and its small waterfront shopping and strolling area. The architecture of the shopping district—the old warehouse area—reflects Victorian sensibilities, due to an almost complete rebuilding of the town in 1878.

Frederiksted was originally founded in 1752 as a port of commerce and a military garrison to service the island's western-side farmers and plantation owners. The town and its fort were named for Danish then-king Frederik V. In 1867, a large, strong tidal wave wiped out the warehouses along Strand Street. Soon after they were rebuilt, the island's sugar plantation economic base began to crumble. Plantations had been on the decline since the emancipation of slaves in 1848, and, by 1878, a series of bad crops and natural disasters found farmers and planters ill equipped to pay their already straitened laborers. Contract negotiations broke down, and laborers rioted, first in Frederiksted, burning most of the town. Christiansted sent in troops to quell the uprising, but the rioters moved out and into the countryside, where for the next five days they burned and looted across the island. The riot was dubbed the great "fireburn" and is credited, not surprisingly, with being one of the instigating factors in bringing better working conditions to the Virgin Islands.

Today, the waterfront **Strand Street** area reflects post-1880 Victorian architectural influences. Strand runs along the waterfront's **Verne Richards Memorial Park,** its northern end meeting the **Frederiksted Pier,** the cruise-ship dock. On the pier is the **visitor's center** (tel. 809-772-0357) and the **Old Customs House,** once used to assay merchandise for duties and customs. On the north side of the pier is the centerpiece of town, **Fort Frederik** (tel. 809-772-2021). The blood-red fort, completed in 1760 (note the date over the entrance) has six rusted cannon perched over the sea wall, cannon that fired the first salute to the new United States flag in October 1776. The fort was also the site at which the governor of the Danish West Indies declared slaves free in 1848. Since the purchase of the island by the U.S. in 1917, the garrison has been a police station, jail, courthouse, fire department headquarters, and telephone exchange. You'll find exhibits throughout portraying the history of military life and, interestingly, hurricanes that have hit the island. The fort is maintained by the Division of Libraries, Archives, and Museums, and admission is free, although donations are accepted; hours are weekdays 8:30 a.m.-4:30 p.m.

Next to the fort is the small **Buddhoe Park,** and near the gazebo in the park is a small information kiosk with a map of town and a nearby craft market.

On Market Street, you'll find the old **Market Square,** the heart and soul of town in the old days and today still an operating outdoor market.

Other historic buildings in town, many rebuilt after the fire, include the **Old Apothecary Hall,** on King Cross Street, and the **Athalie MacFarlane Petersen Public Library** (tel. 809-772-0315), on the south end of Strand. The library was built in 1880 by an American. The three-story **Victoria House,** also on Strand, has fine examples of Victorian gingerbread embellishments on its exterior. **St. Paul's Anglican Church** (tel. 809-772-0818), on King Cross Street near the cemetery, is built in the Georgian style, and parts of the structure date back to 1812.

On the north side of Fort Frederik is a small public beach with public tennis courts. Often called Frederiksted Beach, it's a fine place to cool off and meet locals.

If you're staying in a villa near town, you can find fresh fish at the local **fish market** at the end of Fisher Street, off Strand.

The historic sights and buildings in Frederiksted can be seen by guided walking tours offered by **Take-A-Hike** (tel. 809-778-6997). The tour of Frederiksted is $6.50 per person.

Out Island

St. Croix's roads are in good shape and fairly well marked, making it easy to navigate the island. The area immediately around Christiansted is a bit congested, but once you get out of town traffic flows smoothly. As you tour the countryside, you'll note many pre-fab-type houses and other buildings; these are legacies of past hurricanes. Just south of town is the giant, belching **Hess Refinery** and its container port. The refinery provides hundreds of island jobs and has the added result of driving gas prices down on the island, as much as 40 cents less per gallon than on the mainland.

Head west from Christiansted on either of two main roads. Route 66, the **Melvin H. Evans Highway**, dips to the south and passes the Hess Refinery and the island's airstrip, the **Alexander Hamilton Airport** (tel. 809-778-0216). Also near the airport is the island's horserace track, the **Flamboyant Race Track** (tel. 809-778-7179).

The **Centerline Road,** also called the **Queen Mary Highway** (Rt. 70), passes west through shopping malls and residence areas as well as the St. Croix branch of the **University of the Virgin Islands** on its short trip from Christiansted to Frederiksted. Guided tours are conducted through the **Cruzan Rum Factory** (tel. 809-772-2080), west of the university, where you get a nip after the 20-minute walk. St. Croix's Cruzan Rum is known worldwide and has won awards in the past. A small admission is charged; tours are conducted weekdays 9-11:30 a.m. and 1-4:15 p.m.

West of the rum factory, you'll find the **St. George Village Botanical Garden** (tel. 809-692-2874), a 16-acre park built on the ruins of a sugarcane plantation that operated from 1733 until 1917. There are self-guided trails through the park, which includes the ruins of an old rum factory, an aqueduct, a blacksmith shop, a cactus garden, tropical orchard, rainforest, an educational center, and a gift shop. In all, you'll find more than 800 species of plants here. Some evidence indicates that the grounds were also once an Arawak village. Admission is $5 for adults, $1 for children 12 and under. The garden is open daily 9 a.m.-5 p.m. in winter and Tuesday through Saturday 9 a.m.-4 p.m. in summer.

Just down the road toward Frederiksted is the **Estate Whim Plantation Museum** (tel. 809-772-0598), another restored sugarcane plantation, with a magnificent old greathouse complete with period furniture, a mill, a village of slaves' quarters, and various plantation structures. And, of course, a gift shop and museum store. The greathouse is often used for concerts and cultural events. Admission is $5 for adults and $2 for children, and the plantation is open daily 10 a.m.-4 p.m. in summer, closed on Sundays in winter.

Take the **Mahogany Road** (Rt. 76) northeast from Frederiksted and you'll pass through a high-elevation semi-rainforest area with lush foliage and tall trees, including the namesake mahogany, yellow cedar, royal palms, and cotton trees. The rainforest is not a true one but rather a subtropical forest—and the only area on St. Croix where fresh water is found year-round. From the hills, the views of the coast and open ocean are among the island's best. Stop in at **St. Croix Leap** (tel. 809-772-0421), an open-air workshop and gallery where you'll find woodcarvers and other artisans working. St. Croix Leap is supported by the St. Croix Life and Environmental Arts Project and is open every day.

If you branch left on Rt. 763, you'll pass a couple of turnoffs, the **Scenic Road** and **Creque Dam Road,** which bring you to the northwest coast and the Caledonia Rainforest. These roads are suitable for 4WD vehicles only.

If you don't have a 4WD, stay on the Mahogany Road and take a left on Rt. 69, which will bring you north to the shore and the **North Shore Road.** This area is dotted with exclusive resorts, golf courses, restaurants, and beaches. The road soon brings you to the north shore's **Salt River National Park** historic area. The spot is believed to be the site of Columbus's landing and was dedicated as a park and ecological reserve in 1993, the quincentennial of that event. Three-hour tours by foot of the marshes and ecosystems in the area are conducted by the

St. Croix Environmental Association (tel. 809-773-1989). Cost is $20 for adults, $12 for kids under 10 (children under six are not allowed). The association also conducts a number of weekly nature hikes to important environmental and wildlife sites throughout the island.

East of Christiansted, on **East End Road** (Rt. 82), you'll pass a number of hotels, restaurants, bays, and beaches, including **Chenay Bay** with its nearby **Green Cay Marina.** The ride is a relaxing one, and you'll pass upper-end residences festooned with decorative frangipani, bougainvillea, and hibiscus. Ultimately, you'll arrive at **Cramer's Park.** The park, with a beach, changing rooms, and camping facilities, is the easternmost part of the island accessible by two-wheel-drive vehicles. You can drive a 4WD vehicle farther east, or hike the two miles (three km) to **Point Udall,** the easternmost point in the United States. Along the way you'll pass thorny scrublands, cactus, and small bays.

green turtle

The big thing behind Cramer's Park, the one that looks like the Jolly Green Giant's satellite dish, is a telecommunications radio telescope. Actually, it's part of a series of 10 similar telescopes set up at various places around the U.S. which together make a single, huge, radio telescope capable of transmitting vast amounts of data over the world's Internet systems. This device was funded by the National Science Foundation at a cost of $5 million dollars, is 82 feet (25 meters) in diameter, and weighs in at 260 tons. Sometimes guides are about, and they can explain the dish's functions and capabilities.

Backtrack from Cramer's Park and head south on Rt. 60, the **South Shore Road.** Soon you'll notice that the terrain becomes hilly, rocky, wide open, and covered in short scrubby bushes and tough grass. The south side of the island is the leeward side and gets less rain than the north. You won't find many pleasant beaches here as the shoreline is rocky and dangerous in places, but the views from the hills—particularly at **Grapetree Bay, Grassy Point,** and **Great Pond Bay** (where you'll find a large salt pond), are worth the drive. Bring your camera.

Buck Island

The **Buck Island Reef National Monument,** as it is officially known, is one of St. Croix's premier attractions and one of the most unique spots in the Caribbean. The wooded, uninhabited island almost two miles off the northeast shore of St. Croix is a nature preserve administered by the **U.S. National Park Service** (P.O. Box 160, Christiansted, St. Croix, U.S. Virgin Islands 00821; tel. 809-773-1460). The preserve is large—880 acres, 176 of land and 704 of clear water and coral reef. It's the reef that is the main attraction, for snorkelers and divers alike. It extends nearly all the way around the island and on the eastern end is marked by an underwater snorkeling trail with plaques and directions. On the reef, you'll likely see massive elkhorn and other types of coral, as well as dozens of species of tropical fish and other reef dwellers. The reef also supports brown pelicans, terns, and lobsters as well as hawksbill, leatherback, and green turtles. This is easily one of the best snorkeling spots in the Caribbean—set aside some time, at least a day, to see it all. Remember, avoid touching coral; you'll upset the delicate and long-suffering ecosystem if you knock bits off and will upset yourself if you touch one of the more nasty varieties, such as fire coral.

Buck Island itself is more than a mile long by a half-mile wide and rises to 304 feet (92 meters) at its highest point. A walking trail covers the west side of the island, and visitors will also find a long, white sand beach, picnic areas with grills, and pit-toilet restrooms. You're allowed to cook on the grills and to pick up dead wood for that purpose. Remember, however, to avoid sticks from the manchineel tree; its sap is poisonous and can burn. The manchineel, also called the poison apple tree, grows to 50 feet (15 meters) and bears long, leathery green leaves and a small yellowish fruit resembling an apple. The entire tree, including the sap, fruit, and smoke from its burning wood, is, to varying degrees, poisonous. The British and the U.S. Virgin Islands have made inroads in labeling these coastal trees wherever possible, but don't count on it in all cases. The tiny, yellow fruit is the giveaway—stay away from it.

A special area is set aside for boaters to dock, and scuba divers are also directed to a diving area set aside for them. Buck Island is a great day-trip for families (bring sunscreen), and the park service has contracted with several companies in Christiansted to bring people out to the island. **Mile Mark Watersports** (tel. 809-773-2628), located at the King Christian Hotel on the wharf, is one of them; see below for others. Mile Mark will organize diving charters ($50 per person), Buck Island beach barbecues ($50 per person), glass-bottom-boat trips ($35 per adult, $25 per child), and sailing trips. Note that when cruise ships come into town—currently Wednesday is a heavy day—most Buck Island charter companies have been contracted ahead of time to take cruise passengers to the island and will be full, so plan around that.

RECREATION

Tour Companies
St. Croix Bike & Tours (5035 Cotton Valley, Christiansted, St. Croix, U.S. Virgin Islands 00820; tel. 809-773-5004 or 772-2343) offers bike rentals and guided bike tours of the island. Currently, they offer two tours—a northwest coast tour (easy, $35) and a Caledonia Rainforest tour (hard, $45). The Caledonia Rainforest is at the northwestern end of the island, within an area of the Mahogany Road rainforest not accessible by ordinary cars. Tours include refreshments and the use of 21-speed mountain bikes. Simple bike rentals are $15 for a half-day, $25 for a full day. Despite the address, they're located in Frederiksted, in an alley called Inter Passage, across the street from the cruise ship pier.

Eagle Safari Tours (tel. 809-778-3313, fax 809-773-1672) gives guided, narrated tours aboard a safari bus—an open-air truck outfitted with benches and a canopy. Basically, it's an island tour passing through the St. George Botanical Gardens, the rum distillery, Whim Plantation, Frederiksted, and the Mahogany Rainforest. Tours leave from Christiansted at 9:15 a.m. every day except Sunday and return at 1:30 p.m. Cost is $25 per person.

A full-service tour group called **Island Attractions** (tel. 809-773-7977) will organize Buck Island trips, safari tours, sports including water sports, car rentals, and even weddings and hotel reservations. This group also runs Big Beard's Adventure Tours and is located at the Pan Am Pavilion across the street from the Caravelle Hotel downtown .

Diving
One of the island's larger diving outfits is **Virgin Islands Divers** (tel. 800-544-5911 or 809-773-6045, fax 809-773-2859, e-mail vidivers@aol.com), located at the Pan Am Pavilion on the waterfront in Christiansted. Virgin Islands Divers is a full PADI facility, offering instruction and certification ($185-300), one- and two-tank dives ($50-70), night dives ($55), dive packages, and snorkeling trips ($25-35) to island reefs, including the reef at the small offshore **Green Cay.**

Also contact **Dive St. Croix** (tel. 800-523-DIVE or 809-773-3434, fax 809-773-9411), a division of Mile Mark Charters offering instruction and certification, including resort certification ($75 and you're allowed to do shallow, supervised dives; cost includes one dive), night dives ($50), and a full range of diving experiences. Other diving outfits are **Anchor Dive Center** (Salt River National Park, tel. 800-532-3483 or 809-778-1522), **Dive Experience** (Strand St., Christiansted, tel. 800-235-9047 or 809-773-3307), and **Island Snorkel Excursions** (tel. 809-773-6733). In Frederiksted, contact **Cruzan Divers** (Strand St., tel. 800-352-0107 or 809-772-3701) or **Cane Bay Dive Shop** (tel. 809-772-0715, or, in Cane Bay, tel. 773-9913).

Boating
The *Teroro II* (tel. 809-773-3161), a trimaran, takes trips out of the north coast's Green Cay Marina to Buck Island. The *Diva* (tel. 809-778-4675), a sailboat also out of Green Cay Marina, makes excursions to Buck Island and other island sites. **Bilinda Charters** (tel. 809-773-1641) organizes snorkeling and sailing excursions. **Big Beard's Adventure Tours** (tel. 809-773-4482), at the Pan Am Pavilion on the waterfront, takes half- and full-day sailing trips to Buck Island. Cost usually ranges from $35 per adult for a half-day trip to $55 for the full day, which includes a beach barbecue. Kids' rates are $25 for the half-day and $40 for the full day.

Call **St. Croix Marine** (tel. 809-773-0289), **Salt River Marina** (tel. 809-778-9650), or **Green**

Cay Marina (tel. 809-773-1453) for general information about boating and fishing excursions.

Fishing

The season for sportfishing is September through June. You'll find kingfish, wahoo, swordfish, marlin, and yellowfin tuna abundant in St. Croix's waters. Call the aptly named **Fishaholic Services** (tel. 809-690-8570) for custom trips. Also try **Lisa Ann Charters** (Green Cay Marina, tel. 809-773-3712), **Capt. Pete's Sportfishing** (tel. 809-773-1123), and the **Ruffian** and **Shenanigans** (St. Croix Marine, tel. 809-773-7165 or 773-6011, evenings 773-0917). Half- and full-day trips, including bait, tackle, and drinks, are the norm and run on average $375 per person for four hours to $600 per person for eight hours. Boats carry six or more persons.

Other Water Sports

The Hotel on the Cay in Christiansted Harbor is where you'll find the **St. Croix Water Sports Center** (tel. 809-773-7060). The benefit of this place is not only that it's a large water sports outfit renting windsurfers, jet-skis, snorkeling equipment, and more and offering parasail rides, but also that the cay is the place to do it. At the north coast's Chenay Bay, the **Lisa Neubuger Windsurfing Center** (tel. 809-778-8312) offers rentals and instruction.

Land Activities

One of the leading community organizations on St. Croix, the **St. Croix Environmental Association** (Gallows Bay, Christiansted, St. Croix, U.S. Virgin Islands 00824; tel. 809-773-1989), in addition to being a vocal proponent of environmental causes on the island, offers guided **walking tours** of the island's unique environment, from the pretty to the mundane (but necessary). Tours include walks of the east end beaches, Caledonia Rainforest, and the Salt River National Historic Park. The walks are rated from moderate to strenuous, and the association can advise you on what to wear and bring. The hikes are about three hours each and cost $20 per adult, $12 for children 6-10 (they're not recommended for kids under six). Contact the association for meeting times and places for each walk.

Anyone fancying a bit of **golf** will find plenty of action at the **Carambola Golf Club** (tel. 809-

778-5638), located at the Carambola Beach Resort on the island's northwest coast. The course, designed by Robert Trent Jones, is 18 holes, 6,843 yards (2,080 meters), and par 72. Greens fees are $77 including cart in the winter ($43 after 2 p.m.) and $48 ($33) off-season. Club and shoe rentals are also available. A nine-hole course at **The Reef** (tel. 809-773-8844), on the east end, is 3,100 yards (942 meters). Fees are $14 for the nine holes, $22 for 18; cart rentals are $6 per person for nine holes, $12 per person for 18. You'll also find a driving range at the course. The nine-hole course at the **Buccaneer Hotel** (tel. 809-773-2100, ext. 738), just outside of Christiansted, sits on the ocean. Fees for nonguests off-season are $12 for nine holes, $20 for 18; in season, it's $20 and $35. Cart rentals are $9 per person for nine holes and $13 per person for 18. Club rentals are also available.

Tennis buffs will find four free public courts at the **D.C. Canegata Ball Park,** near Christiansted, and two at the **Fort Frederik Park,** behind Fort Frederik in Frederiksted. Nonguests can play at a number of island hotels, including the Buccaneer (tel. 809-773-2199, ext. 736), the Carambola Golf Club (tel. 809-778-5636), and the Chenay Bay Beach Resort (tel. 809-773-2918). Fees range $5-8 per person per hour.

Horseback riding is best organized through **Paul and Jill's Equestrian Stables** (tel. 809-772-2627 or 809-772-2880), located at Sprat Hall, near the Sprat Hall beach north of Frederiksted. Paul and Jill and company will take riders on tours of the rainforest and through the hills and beaches of the very pretty northwest corner of the island. They only offer one or two rides per day, so reservations—one day in advance—are necessary.

Family Activity

The **St. Croix Aquarium** (tel. 809-773-8995), at the Caravelle Arcade on Strand Street in Christiansted, is a nonprofit marine education center that has small aquariums and more, including a touching pond with shells, starfish, and blunt-tipped sea urchins. A new children's discovery room has recently been added. Tours of the aquarium, which houses mostly reef fish, are lead by a marine biologist. The largest tank is 500 gallons, and the largest fish on display is a nurse shark (usually). The center is open Tuesday through Saturday 11 a.m.-4 p.m. (school groups only 9-11 a.m.). Admission is $4.50 for adults and $2 for kids 12 and under.

BEACHES

St. Croix is an island known for many things, but beaches are not among them. While the island has several fine spots for swimming and snorkeling, and its coastline is stunning in places, it sports fewer pristine, white sand beaches than the other islands. The best are found along the north shore. **Cane Bay,** on the northwest shore along Rt. 80 (North Shore Road), is a popular snorkeling spot with water sports facilities and restaurants nearby. The beach is rarely crowded, and the reef is close to shore.

On the island's west end, south of Frederiksted, is **Sandy Point,** a long, pretty, isolated beach. There are no facilities here, and the area, designated the **Sandy Point Wildlife Refuge,** is protected as a nesting environment for marine turtles. In Frederiksted itself, you'll find a public beach with facilities in the Fort Frederik Park behind Fort Frederik. North of Frederiksted, on the west end, are several long beaches including **Sprat Hall** and **West End Beach Club,** both with facilities and water sports rentals. About a half-mile south of Frederiksted is another long, sandy beach fronted by a couple of hotels. Stop in at **On the Beach Resort** where you can have a drink at the beach bar.

On the north side of the island, connect up with the North Shore Road and you'll find some of the best beaches on the island. At the west end of the road, the **Carambola Beach Resort** starts off the chain of beaches. Nearby is **Cane Bay Beach,** where you'll find several beachside restaurants and bars, as well as water sports facilities. This is one of the island's more popular spots; the beach is long, shaded in spots, and its reef is not far from shore. **Columbus Beach (Salt River)** is the site of Columbus's 1493 landing on St. Croix. There are few facilities here, but the historical value is a draw.

In Christiansted itself, your best bet for splashing the day away is **Hotel on the Cay,** located on small Protestant Cay in the harbor. A shuttle at the wharf runs people back and forth all day long. On the cay, you'll find water sports, bars, and restaurants.

East of Christiansted, still on the north shore, you'll find several fine beaches along the East End Road. **Buccaneer Resort,** about three minutes out of town, allows non-guests to use their beach and changing facilities for a fee of $4, which seems sort of ridiculous, but there you have it. Also located here are beach bars and water sports. Nearby is **Shoy's Beach,** a free and wide but not extremely long beach of fine, honey-colored sand. To get to Shoy's, turn in at the entrance to Buccaneer, then bear right at the guard station and follow that road straight for just under a mile, until you see an archway and gate—the entrance to a residential community—and a sign reading No. 10 Estate Shoy Beach. Park there and walk the path to the left of the sign. You won't find changing facilities here; it's just the beach and you.

Farther east on East End Road is **Chenay Bay,** which features bars and restaurants at the **Chenay Bay Beach Resort,** as well as water sports. At **Reef Bay,** stop in at **Duggan's Beachside Bar** (tel. 809-773-9800), where you'll find a bar, beach chairs, changing facilities, and even a tennis court.

At the near end of the road and island is **Cramer's Park,** a camping facility with grills, changing rooms, and bathrooms, but no running fresh water. You'll also find a small concession stand, but it may be closed, so bring your refreshments. The beach here isn't large, but it's inviting and rarely crowded. Great beach—a personal favorite.

Off the northeast shore, visit **Buck Island,** part of the national park system and designated a national monument. The island is protected, and the snorkeling, which includes underwater trails, is tremendous. The island is reached by boat only, with departures from Christiansted or from the Green Cay Marina on the north shore. See "Tour Companies," above, for companies that are authorized to make island trips, or call the **National Park Service** (tel. 809-773-1460) for information.

ACCOMMODATIONS

Accommodations on St. Croix range from large and small resorts to hotels, guesthouses, apartments, villas, and camping facilities. Many of the island's hotels are located in Christiansted and along the north shore, where beaches are located east and west of the town. As well, Frederiksted is home to several small, intimate properties—the type that remind you that you are removed from the bustle of it all. Remember, room rates are reduced by as much as 40% during the summer season and are often bargained out through packages and wholesale room discounters. A government hotel occupancy tax of eight percent is charged on accommodations, and often a 15% service charge is added to the bill. Occasionally, an energy surcharge is also added. Most hotels accept major credit cards, but this is not always the case—call ahead and check. Keep in mind that some properties require a minimum stay of three to seven nights, may require a deposit of as much as

50% on the room, and often add $10-30 to the rate for any extra persons staying in the room.

The accommodations listed below are categorized based on the average room rate (some hotels offer a wide range of rooms, from budget to luxury), double occupancy, European plan (no meals), per night, during the 15 December-through-15 April high season, excluding the eight percent room tax. A designation of **luxury** indicates that rooms run $200 or more; **expensive** rooms are $140-200; **moderate** indicates a range of $80-140; and **budget** rooms cost $80 or less.

Villas, Apartments, and Condos

Private villas, cottages, condos, and apartments are often the best bet for families or large groups and are widely available on St. Croix. Real estate agents are often in the villa rental business, and some specialize in rentals. Rates range from as

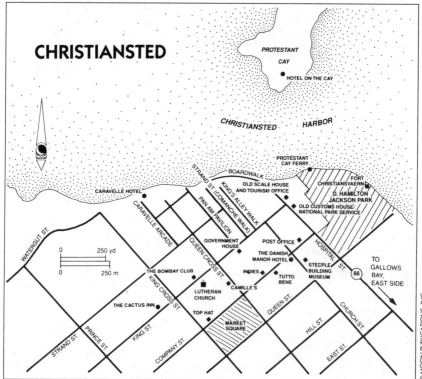

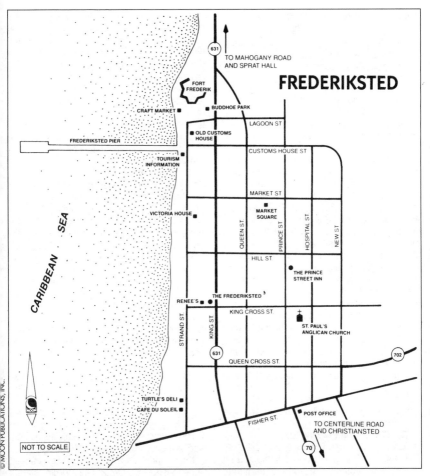

little as $300 per week for a one-bedroom efficiency apartment that may not be near a beach to more than $10,000 per week for a freestanding luxury villa with several bedrooms, a pool, a maid, a cook, and beach access. The key is to contact a rental agency; explain your needs, the size of your party, and your budget; and work with the agency to come up with the best site.

American Rentals and Sales (2001 Old Hospital St., Christiansted, St. Croix, U.S. Virgin Islands 00820; tel. 809-773-8470, fax 809-773-8472)

CMPI (P.O. Box 26160 G.B.S., St. Croix, U.S. Virgin Islands 00824; tel. 800-496-7379 or 809-778-8782, fax 809-773-2150)

Island Villas (6 Company St., Christiansted, St. Croix, U.S. Virgin Islands 00820; tel. 800-626-4512 or 809-773-8821, fax 809-773-8823)

Seaview Farm (Bay Road, 180 Two Brothers, Frederiksted, St. Croix, U.S. Virgin Islands 00840; tel. 800-792-5060 or 809-772-5367, fax 809-772-5060)—rents cottage units

Teague Bay Properties (tel. 800-237-1959 or 809-773-4850, fax 809-773-5868)

Tropic Retreats (P.O. Box 5219, Christiansted, St. Croix, U.S. Virgin Islands 00823, tel. 800-233-7944 or 809-778-7550, fax 809-778-3557)

Resorts, Hotels, Inns, and Guesthouses

Many of St. Croix's hotels and resorts are located along the central north shore east and west of Christiansted, but quite a few are located in the island's two main towns. Both towns are good bases for shopping, entertainment, eating out, and exploring the rest of the island.

In Christiansted, the small **Anchor Inn** (58 King Street, Christiansted, St. Croix, U.S. Virgin Islands 00820; tel. 800-524-2030 or 809-773-4000, fax 809-773-4408) sits on the downtown waterfront facing the boardwalk that wraps around from the wharf. The hotel's rooms are simple and non-frilly, and each has cable TV and a/c or ceiling fans. The upstairs restaurant, the **Anchor Inn Restaurant,** overlooks the water, and you'll find a small pool on the grounds. **Moderate.**

The **Breakfast Club** (18 Queen Cross St., Christiansted, St. Croix, U.S. Virgin Islands 00820; tel. 809-773-7383) is a nine-room B&B located on one of the busy downtown streets, about four blocks from the waterfront. The rooms all have private baths and kitchens with stoves and fridges. Outside, on the deck, is a hot tub for guest use. The room rates include all taxes, service charges, and full breakfast. This is a very good deal. **Budget.**

The **Cactus Inn** (48 King St., Christiansted, St. Croix, U.S. Virgin Islands 00820; tel. 809-692-9301) is not elegant—it's actually a bit seedy, with fading paint and indeterminate smells emanating from somewhere—but is a good deal in a good downtown location. The 11 rooms have private baths with hot and cold water and TVs—some also have refrigerators. The place could be cleaned up a bit, but you'll spend less per day here than in most places on the island. **Budget.**

The **Caravelle Hotel** (44A Queen Cross St., Christiansted, St. Croix, U.S. Virgin Islands 00820; tel. 800-524-0410 or 809-773-0687, fax 809-778-2966) is a small, 43-room hotel located on the harbor near the wharf—a clean, mod-

ern establishment with a great location downtown close to pretty well everything you'd want. The rooms come in three categories (budget, deluxe, and superior), and all but budget have water views. The hotel's one suite has a full-size refrigerator and a kitchenette with utensils, two baths, an exercise bike in the room, and a telescope. Yikes. The hotel also has a pool, a restaurant, and a popular seaside pizza joint and bar. **Moderate.**

Club Comanche, (1 Strand St., Christiansted, St. Croix, U.S. Virgin Islands 00820; tel. 800-524-2066 or tel. and fax 809-773-0210), located on the downtown waterfront, is one of the island's older continuously operating hotels. In fact, it's said by some to be the oldest inn in the Caribbean. Sections of the building the hotel occupies are more than 250 years old, and the pool—definitely one of the oldest in the Caribbean—dates back to 1948. The caged elevator in the lobby sounds a note of the past. Notice the old sugar mill tower behind the pool on the waterfront—*that's* how old the place is. Today, though the inn indeed has seen better days, it is one of the best buys in town. The 40 rooms are eclectic, decorated with antiques, poster beds, and 1970s-style kitschy carpeting and funky lamp shades. Many of the rooms are airy, with plantation-style window shutters and lots of rich woods inside. The hotel restaurant and bar are popular with locals and visitors alike. Overall, it's a clean hotel, well located, and the owner, Mary Boehm, is one of the nicest people in town. She's been around forever, so she'll be able to give you inside information. You couldn't get a nicer reception if you tried, and the hotel is a good deal. **Budget-Moderate.**

The **Danish Manor Hotel** (2 Company Street, Christiansted, St. Croix, U.S. Virgin Islands 00820; tel. 800-524-2069 or 809-773-1377, fax 809-773-1913) is located a couple of blocks from the waterfront on one of Christiansted's busier streets. The hotel has 34 modern, simple rooms, each with a/c, cable TV, and a fridge. Outside, there's a courtyard pool and a bar. Continental breakfast is included with the rates, but an added 10% "energy charge" is not. The downtown location and reasonable rates make this a good bet for Christiansted. **Budget-Moderate.**

The **Pink Fancy Hotel** (27 Prince St., Frederiksted, St. Croix, U.S. Virgin Islands 00840; tel.

800-524-2045 or 809-773-8460, fax 809-773-6448) is located just three blocks from the waterfront and is a small, seven-room hotel in a historic building, with a pool and clean, comfortable rooms. **Moderate.**

Hotel on the Cay (P.O. Box 4020, Christiansted, St. Croix, U.S. Virgin Islands 00821; tel. 800-524-2035 or 809-773-2035, fax 809-773-7046) is a small resort on an offshore cay in the harbor and has the only beach in town, pool, tennis, restaurants, and regular ferry service to the wharf. **Luxury.**

King's Alley Hotel (57 King St., P.O. Box 4120, Christiansted, St. Croix, U.S. Virgin Islands 00822; tel. 800-843-3574 or 809-773-0103, fax 809-773-4431) is one of the newer additions to downtown Christiansted. The hotel is part of the Kings Alley Walk harborside shopping and restaurant complex in the downtown historic area. The complex itself holds 20 stores, three bars, a restaurant, and the hotel, which features a dozen new suites and rooms done in Danish West Indies plantation replica furniture. The new suites were added to the existing King's Alley Hotel, which has undergone major refurbishment in the past year. The hotel is basically new, modern, and in a convenient downtown location. **Moderate-Expensive.**

The **King Christian Hotel** (P.O. Box 3619, Christiansted, St. Croix, U.S. Virgin Islands 00822; tel. 800-524-2012 or 809-773-2285, fax 809-773-9411), located right on King's Wharf downtown, is directly in the thick of it all. The small hotel has just 39 rooms, all basic but clean, with phones, TVs, fridges in the rooms, and a/c and ceiling fans. Most of the rooms have harbor views from balconies, and you'll find a small pool and patio in the interior courtyard. The hotel's restaurant was closed at the time of this writing. **Moderate.**

In the Frederiksted area, you have numerous choices for accommodations. **The Frederiksted** (20 Strand St., Frederiksted, St. Croix, U.S. Virgin Islands 00840; tel. 800-524-2025 or 800-595-9519 or 809-772-0500, fax 809-778-4009) is a 40-room downtown hotel, a few blocks from the pier on the waterfront. You'll find a pool and restaurant on the grounds, and the rooms all have TVs and a/c. **Moderate.** Nearby is **The Prince Street Inn** (402 Prince Street, Frederiksted, St. Croix, U.S. Virgin Islands 00840; tel. 809-772-9550), a six-room inn located in a historic old Lutheran parsonage. The rooms are simple, and the location in town is perfect. Note the ancient baobab tree in the yard—a tree originating in Africa. **Moderate.**

Just outside of Frederiksted are several fine hotels that'll keep you near the beaches and things to do on the western side of the island. **Sprat Hall Plantation** (P.O. Box 695, Frederiksted, St. Croix, U.S. Virgin Islands 00841; tel. 800-843-3584 or 809-772-0305) situated north of town, overlooks the ocean. The old plantation estate has rooms and efficiencies all wrapped up in a serene colonial milieu. Sports are available including horseback riding. A nice place to get away for quiet time. **Moderate-Expensive.** A couple of minutes south of town is **On the Beach Resort,** (P.O. Box 1908, Frederiksted, St. Croix, U.S. Virgin Islands 00841; tel. 800-524-2018 or 809-772-1205, fax 809-772-1757) which is, well, on the beach, with a pool, beach bar, and restaurant. The rooms range from "minimum" to deluxe suites and apartments—meaning that they have kitchens and a lot of space. But, hey, you're on the beach, so the smaller rooms should do. The hotel is gay-friendly, and actively advertises to the gay market. **Moderate.** Nearby is **Cottages by the Sea** (P.O. Box 1697, Frederiksted, St. Croix, U.S. Virgin Islands 00841; tel. 800-323-7252 or tel. and fax 809-772-0495), a group of, well, cottages by the sea. (You've got to love truth in advertising.) The 20 units sit on a fine sandy beach good for snorkeling and splashing. Rooms have kitchens and TVs. **Moderate.**

Along the north shore are the island's large (and small) beach resorts. The **Westin Carambola Beach Resort** (P.O. Box 3031, Kingshill, St. Croix, U.S. Virgin Islands 00851; tel. 800-228-3000 or 809-778-3800, fax 809-778-1682) is one of the island's biggest resorts (150 rooms) and is located on striking Davis Bay. The attraction here is the resort life—full water sports, tennis, restaurants, beach bars, fitness rooms, golf at the island's premier championship course, and luxury villa-style rooms with oversize bathrooms and stocked mini-refrigerators. **Luxury.**

Just west of Christiansted are a load of smaller, 40- to 65-room hotels and resorts on sandy beaches, including **Hibiscus Beach Hotel** (4131 La Grande Princesse; Christiansted, St.

Croix, U.S. Virgin Islands 00820; tel. 800-442-0121 or 809-773-4042, fax 809-773-7668), **St. Croix by the Sea** (P.O. Box 248. Christiansted, St. Croix, U.S. Virgin Islands 00821; tel. 800-525-5006 or 809-778-8600, fax 809-773-802), and the **Cormorant Beach Club** (4126 La Grande Princesse; Christiansted, St. Croix, U.S. Virgin Islands 00820; tel. 800-548-4460 or 809-778-8920, fax 809-778-9218). All are in the **moderate-expensive** range. The Hibiscus, in particular, is small, intimate, and appealing.

Two miles (three kilometers) east of Christiansted, along Rt. 82, you'll find **The Buccaneer** (P.O. Box 25200, Gallows Bay, St. Croix, U.S. Virgin Islands 00824; tel. 800-255-3881 or 809-773-2100, fax 809-778-8215). The Buccaneer is one of the island's older and larger resort complexes (150 rooms, 300 acres) and is set on a wide sandy beach dotted with palms. You'll find tennis, a nine- or 18-hole golf course, water sports, a fitness center, jogging and nature trails, boutiques, two pools, four restaurants, and rooms ranging from standard to beachside suites. All rooms feature balconies or patios, cable TVs, small fridges, and hair dryers. This is pretty well the last word in luxury on St. Croix, the sort of place you can enter and need never leave for the entirety of your vacation. **Luxury.**

East of The Buccaneer, near Green Cay Marina, is the smaller **Tamarind Reef Hotel** (5001 Tamarind Reef, Christiansted, St. Croix, U.S. Virgin Islands 00820; tel. 800-619-0014 or 809-773-4455, fax 809-773-3989). The Tamarind has 46 rooms ranging from standard to deluxe suites, 19 with kitchenettes. There are two beaches here, one called a "shell beach," meaning it's somewhat rocky, and the other a small swimming beach. The hotel guests use the facilities at the marina, including its dive shop and water sports outfits. This is a perfect spot for taking off to explore Buck Island or the closer Green Cay. **Moderate.** By the way, at the marina entrance you'll see a sign reading, To Beach. Do not use this beach—it's foul with detritus from the marina, full of garbage, and unsavory.

East of the Tamarind is **Chenay Bay Beach Resort** (P.O. Box 24600, Gallows Bay, St. Croix, U.S. Virgin Islands 00824; tel. 800-548-4457 or tel. and fax 809-773-2918), a small cottage resort. The cottages are equipped with kitchens,

a/c, and TVs, and the beach is one of the island's better. The **Lisa Neubuger Windsurfing Center** (tel. 809-778-8312) is there to offer windsurfing lessons and rentals. Other water sports are also available, as are tennis, a swimming pool, and a restaurant on the grounds. **Expensive.**

Camping

Small **Cramer's Park** (tel. 809-773-9696) is located on the far east end of the island—where the road ends (at the junction of Routes 82 and 60, head straight on 82 for a few hundred yards). The spot offers bare site camping directly on the beach. You'll find bathrooms and changing rooms, and cooking grills for general use, but no freshwater showers—you'll have to carry in your own water as well as your tent. The buildings on the grounds are maintained by the island's Department of Housing, Parks, and Recreation, and some remain damaged by 1989's Hurricane Hugo. Still, the beach is fine, the camping is free—yes, free—and there aren't many better deals than that. The beach can get crowded on weekends, and security may be an issue. Lock up your goodies in a car rather than the tent. A lifeguard is on duty daily 9 a.m.-5 p.m.

EATING AND DRINKING

Apart from the hotel restaurants—and many of St. Croix's hotels offer fine dining—St. Croix has a bit less to choose from than St. Thomas but more choices than St. John. You won't go hungry on the island. Most restaurants accept credit cards, but it's best to call ahead to confirm—as well as to make reservations and inquire about a dress code. While it's rare in the U.S. Virgin Islands to encounter dress codes for evening dining, you will find that most restaurants discourage beachwear, shorts, and flip-flops.

You'll find plenty in the way of fast food chain restaurants such as Wendy's, Pizza Hut, Subway, and McDonald's scattered around the island, particularly in the shopping malls around Christiansted.

Categories used below are based on average entrée price: **expensive** is $25 or more; **moderate** is $10-25; **inexpensive** is $10 or less.

Christiansted

Antoine's (tel. 809-773-0263), on the wharf at the Anchor Inn, serves fine seafood and West Indian specialties. **Moderate.**

The Bombay Club (tel. 809-773-1838), on King Street, has a pub atmosphere and serves fresh seafood, pastas, steaks, fajitas, and sandwiches. Fun place. Lunch and dinner daily. **Moderate.**

Camille's (tel. 809-773-2985), on Queen Cross Street near the Lutheran Church, is, bar none, the best place in town for breakfast. The fare is omelettes, bagels and lox, waffles, pancakes, muffins, hair-raising coffee, and a whole lot more. Breakfast is 7:30-10 a.m. daily except Sunday. Lunch and dinner are also served. **Inexpensive.**

Comanche Club (tel. 809-773-2665), at the Club Comanche hotel, is a popular dinner spot, serving roast lamb, pork, and duck as well as seafood, steaks, ribs, and lamb chops. The open-air restaurant overlooks the waterfront and has been serving fine food for a long time. Lunch and dinner are served daily except Sunday. **Moderate.**

Indies (tel. 809-692-9440), on Company Street, serves West Indies-inspired seafood dishes (the menu changes nightly) on a colorful open-air patio. Pastas, conch fritters, quesadillas, and (personal favorites) island pumpkin ginger soup with coconut followed by dolphin run-down, are likely to be found on the menu. A sushi bar is open (at the bar) Wednesday and Friday 5-8 p.m., lunch is served weekdays, and dinner is nightly. Look for live jazz on Saturday evenings. This is a fun place to start, or end, a night out. **Moderate.**

King's Landing Yacht Club (tel. 809-773-0103), on the boardwalk at the King's Alley Hotel, is a popular bar and restaurant serving sandwiches, light fare, and seafood dinners. **Moderate.**

Morning Glory (tel. 809-773-6620), in Gallows Bay at the Gallows Bay Market Place just east of town, serves breakfast and lunch (lunch only Sunday). Munch on muffins and waffles, slam down some espresso, and head for the beach. **Inexpensive.**

Stixx (tel. 809-773-5157), next to the Club Comanche overlooking the waterfront, has a raw bar, pizzas, and sandwiches and is a great place to down a few brews or a Cruzan rum punch. Sunday brunch is also served. **Inexpensive-Moderate.**

Top Hat (tel. 809-773-2346), on Company Street, is the town's favorite steak house and also serves some Scandinavian specialties, courtesy of owner and chef Bent Rasmussen. **Moderate.**

Tutto Bene (tel. 809-773-5229), next to the Danish Manor Hotel on Company Street, is an Italian bistro specializing in provincial cuisine, with pastas, meats, seafood, desserts, and espresso. **Moderate.**

If you're in a hurry or just want a couple of sandwiches for a picnic, stop in at **Alley Galley** (tel. 809-773-5353), located under the Comanche Walk on Strand Street. They've got deli sandwiches, munchies, gourmet items, cheeses, beer, wine, and, yikes, pina coladas on tap. **Inexpensive.**

Frederiksted

Café du Soleil (tel. 809-772-5400), on Strand Street's waterfront, specializes in local seafood dishes, steaks, and lamb. Open for dinner daily except Thursday and Sunday, brunch on Sunday. **Moderate.**

On the Beach Cafe (tel. 809-772-4242), at the resort of the same name, is your bet for a great sunset from its beachside location. The cafe serves lunch and dinner daily, as well as Sunday brunch. **Moderate.**

Renee's (tel. 809-772-0500, ext. 300), at the Frederiksted Hotel, serves pastas, seafood, and steaks. Dinner is served Tuesday through Saturday, lunch Tuesday through Friday. **Moderate.**

Turtle's Deli (tel. 809-772-3676), on Strand Street across from the waterfront, serves sandwiches, fresh breads, and deli specialties. Open daily. **Moderate.**

Out Island

Cheeseburgers in Paradise (tel. 809-773-1119) is not owned by Jimmy Buffett, as far as we know, but serves large burgers, burritos, salsa and chips, and, of course, margaritas. Located about three miles (five km) east of Christiansted, it's open daily from 11 a.m. Count on live music Friday, Saturday, and Sunday nights. **Inexpensive-Moderate.**

Duggan's (tel. 809-773-9800) is located on the water at Teague Bay, a few miles east of

Christiansted. The fare is seafood, pastas, and steaks; lunch is lighter. This is a great getaway for a day on the beach or for dinner. Lunch is served daily, dinner nightly, and brunch on Sunday. **Moderate.**

The Galleon (tel. 809-773-9949), at Green Cay Marina, serves dinners daily except Sunday. The fare is French, continental, with local seafood specialties. **Moderate.**

No Name (tel. 809-778-0035) is located on the North Shore Road at the Cane Bay Reef Club. The fare is seafood and burgers, and the seaside location is a big draw. Go for the sunset, slide into dinner. **Moderate.**

NIGHTLIFE

Live music from steel bands to rock to jazz fill the night air all about St. Croix, mostly on weekends. Hotels and restaurants, as well as nightclubs, offer music and dancing, and there is often no cover charge at hotels. For those with a taste for theater and the performing arts, you'll have plenty from which to choose, particularly in the Christiansted area. For ideas of what to do, listen to local radio or pick up copies of the local newspaper, the *St. Croix Avis,* or the tourist publication *St. Croix This Week.*

Recently, the issue of gambling has come up in the pages of local newspapers. St. Croix has decided to break from U.S. Virgin Islands tradition and allow limited casino gambling on the island. (St. Thomas and St. John still do not allow it.) Some sectors of the community abhor the idea, while others, particularly many in the tourism industry, feel gambling will provide an added draw to visitors. The issue has been debated and contested in various referenda, and it appears that the green light has been given. Look to larger hotels to introduce casinos in the near future.

The **Caribbean Dance Company** performs every Friday at the Hibiscus Hotel, a few miles west of Christiansted. The company incorporates African and Caribbean folk music, dancing, and storytelling in high-energy, evocative performances. Call (809) 778-8824 for schedules and information.

Various international artists and performing groups are hosted by the **Island Center for the**

Performing Arts (tel. 809-778-5272), located on Rt. 79 near the hospital. The center has in the past hosted the Harlem Spiritual Ensemble, the Boston Pops traveling group, the Temptations, and various cabaret and local performers, including the **Caribbean Community Theatre** (tel. 809-778-3596), which performs plays and musicals, both locally written and imported.

The Estate Whim Plantation, on Centerline Road, hosts regular performances of classical music and cultural events presented by **The Landmarks Society** (tel. 809-772-0598), a group dedicated to preserving and promoting the arts.

If you're not satisfied with the hotel's cable TV selections, you can head out to seven-screen **Sunny Isle Theatres** (tel. 809-778-5620) or the two-screen **Diamond Cinemas** (tel. 809-778-5200), at the Sunny Isle Shopping Center just west of town.

Christiansted and Environs

The **Buccaneer** (tel. 809-773-2100), east of town, offers nightly entertainment, usually steel and calypso bands. **Indies** (tel. 809-692-9440), on Company Street, has live jazz performances every Saturday and some Fridays. **Moonraker Bar** (tel. 809-773-9581), on Queen Cross Street, offers live music and karaoke singing most weekends. We recommend karaoke for all honeymooners—it'll test the mettle of your new marriage. For extra fun, choose "Having My Baby," by Paul Anka. Anyway, **King's Landing Yacht Club** (tel. 809-773-0103), on the waterfront, has live West Indian-style music on weekends, including steel bands and calypso singers. **Club Comanche** (tel. 809-773-2665) and **Top Hat** (tel. 809-773-2346) restaurants feature piano bars most evenings. **Lizards** (tel. 809-773-4485), an upstairs restaurant on Strand St. between King Cross and Queen Cross Streets that serves burgers, steaks, ribs, and seafood, also offers live bands every night (no cover). On Saturday, dinner is served until midnight. This is one of the town's happening night spots.

Hotel on the Cay (tel. 809-773-2025) has live steel bands Tuesday evening and Sunday afternoon. The steel band also accompanies a floor show featuring the Mocko Jumbi carnival character (he's the tall guy, on stilts) and those obligatory but apocryphal staples of Caribbean shows, the fire eater and the limbo master. How low can you go? Keep your chiropractor's number handy.

Frederiksted
Blue Moon (tel. 809-772-2222), on Strand Street, offers live jazz on Friday and Saturday night, and, interestingly, poetry readings on Sunday afternoons. Weekdays, look for blues, jazz, and other live entertainment. **Pier 69** (tel. 809-772-0069), a restaurant and bar on King Street, features live music and dancing. The restaurant offers Mexican dishes, burgers, and light fare.

Just north of town, on Mahogany Road, stop in at **Hut Domino Club** (tel. 809-772-9914) on Sunday nights for live music. Domino is also a restaurant specializing in barbecue and local West Indian dishes. Keep a lookout for their logo—a pig.

Out Island
Cheeseburgers in Paradise (tel. 809-773-1119) has live music, usually guitar, starting at 7 p.m. Thursday through the weekend

On the north shore, you'll always find steel bands and calypso or reggae at the **Westin Carambola Beach Resort** (tel. 809-778-3800). Down the road, back toward Christiansted, you'll find the **No Name** at Cane Bay Reef Club (tel. 809-778-0035) and **The Waves at Cane Bay** (tel. 809-778-1805), which, aside from being great places to have a cool one and watch the sun set, often offer live entertainment on weekends.

SHOPPING

Cruise-ship passengers tend to make their way from Frederiksted, where the ships dock, to Christiansted, where they fulfill their shopping needs. The downtown area of Christiansted, in and near the historic district, is filled with duty-free shops carrying jewelry, leather, china, perfumes, electronic goods, and crafts.

The phrase "duty-free," remember, does not mean the buyer will be exempt from applicable duties and customs regulations when bringing the goods back home. It means that the seller was exempt from duties when importing the goods for the store and implies that the store is passing on those savings to the consumer. That is often true but not always the case. Do a little homework before you go on vacation; price some items in your local shops to get a fair idea of whether you're getting a deal in an island duty-free store.

Christiansted
Stroll down **King Street** toward the wharf and you'll find shops such as **St. Croix Perfume Center** (tel. 809-773-7604). **Little Switzerland** is also on King Street, as are entrances to the shops at **King's Alley Walk.** Turn the corner from King to the wharf area and you'll see **Ay Ay Gold** and several other small shops and markets. From here you can step onto the **Board-**

Whim Plantation, St. Croix

walk that circles around to the back entrances of the hotels and King's Alley Walk.

On Queen Cross Street, you'll find dozens of shops, galleries, and arcades, including the **Caravelle Arcade,** at the Caravelle Hotel, and the **Pan Am Pavilion.** On **Company Street,** you'll find smaller shops such as **Frontier Duty-Free Shops, Urban Threads,** and **Sonya Jewelry** (tel. 809-778-8605). Also on Company is the open-air **Market Square,** where you'll find fruits and vegetables, T-shirts, carvings, and curios.

For newspapers, books, magazines, and stationery, stop at **Island Newsstand** (tel. 809-773-9109), on Company Street, or **The Bookie** (tel. 809-773-2502), on Strand.

Frederiksted

In addition to the T-shirt and craft vendors that set up along the waterfront park whenever a cruise ship pulls into town, you'll find shopping along Strand Street. The choices for duty-free shopping are not as numerous here as in Christiansted, but you'll find branches of **Larimar** jewelers, **Gems Direct, Little Switzerland,** and **Colombian Emeralds International** on the waterfront. As well, walk along the cross streets connecting to **King** and **Queen** Streets, both parallel to Strand, for shops such as **JIA Liquor, Cecelia's Gifts,** and **La Femme Amour.**

Out Island

Several malls lie outside Christiansted and Frederiksted and comprise stores such as Kmart, Woolworth, and large supermarkets. The **Sion Farm Shopping Center, Sunny Isle Shopping Center, Villa La Reine Shopping Center,** and **Sunshine Plaza,** all on Centerline Road or just a turnoff from it, should answer just about all your needs. This sometimes unsightly stretch of road is chockablock with small strip malls and shopping centers.

GETTING AROUND

Rental Car Agencies

Often, rental car companies require that the driver be at least 25 years old. U.S. drivers will need a valid license; others will need to obtain a temporary license through the rental company. Credit cards are almost universally accepted, and

rates start at about $30 per day. Most offer free mileage and free pickup and drop off. On St. Croix, just about any type of car will do as long as it has a trunk where you can lock up your valuables. A nice plus about driving on St. Croix is that gasoline is cheap—as little as $1.05 per gallon, due to the proximity of the large Hess oil refinery.

Even though the U.S. Virgin Islands are a U.S. territory and use left-hand drive vehicles, driving is on the left side of the road—a legacy of the Danish system. If you're unsure how this works, go slowly; it takes time as a driver to get used to seeing the shoulder of the road rather than the center.

Contact any one of the following agencies.

Avis (tel. 809-778-9355)

Budget Rent-A-Car (tel. 800-527-0700 or 809-778-9636)

Caribbean Rentals (tel. 809-773-7227)

Centerline Car Rentals (tel. 809-778-0450)

Green Cay Caribbean Car Rental (tel. 809-773-4399)

Hertz (tel. 809-778-1402 or 773-2100)

Midwest Auto Rental (Frederiksted, tel. 809-772-0438) **Thrifty** (tel. 809-773-7200)

Tours and Taxi Companies

Your hotel should be able to call or arrange a taxi for you, but if that isn't the case, call in Christiansted **Caribbean Taxi** (tel. 809-773-9799), or **Cruzan Taxi** (tel. 809-773-6388), or **St. Croix Taxi** (tel. 809-778-1088). In Frederiksted, call **Combine Taxi** (tel. 809-772-2828) or **Frederiksted Taxi Service** (tel. 809-772-4775). Calling a taxi will automatically add one-third to the standard fare.

Taxi stands can be found in Christiansted at the wharf or in Frederiksted next to Fort Frederik. For those interested in island tours, it's easy to find an accommodating driver. A two-hour tour for one or two people should run $30, a three-hour tour $40.

All drivers are required to have rate cards in their vehicles. Since this isn't always the case, pick up a free copy of *St. Croix This Week* at just about any hotel or shop. You can't miss it—it's the pink publication. Inside, you'll learn that the rate from the airport to Christiansted for one or two people is $10; from the airport to Frederiksted is $8; from Christiansted to Frederiksted is $20, and pretty much everything else is less than that. Minimum charge in town is $2.

Remember, for questions or complaints, you can call the **Taxi Commission** (tel. 809-773-8294) weekdays 8 a.m.-5 p.m.

INFORMATION DIRECTORY

Police, Fire, Ambulance, tel. 911

Gov. Juan F. Luis Hospital, Christiansted, tel. (809) 776-6311

Ingeborg Nesbitt Clinic, Frederiksted, tel. (809) 772-0750

American Express Representative, St. Croix, tel. (809) 773-9500

Chamber of Commerce, tel. (809) 773-1435

FedEx, tel. (809) 778-8180

Virgin Islands National Park Service, tel. (809) 773-1460

Department of Tourism, P.O. Box 4538, Christiansted, St. Croix, U.S. Virgin Islands 00822; tel. (809) 773-0495, fax (809) 778-9259, Frederiksted, tel. (809) 772-0357

St. Croix Hotel and Tourism Association, tel. (800) 524-2026 or (809) 773-7117

St. Croix Hotel Association, tel. (800) 497-7030 or (809) 773-7117

BOB RACE

BRITISH VIRGIN ISLANDS
INTRODUCTION

The British Virgin Islands have been and remain happily unencumbered by what often appears to be a Caribbean-wide scramble for the tourist dollar. This does not mean visitors are unwelcome—the British Virgin Islands receives more than 300,000 visitors every year, many of whom are on yachts—or wishing they were.

Neither does it mean that the British Virgins is the only group of islands in the region that has maintained a relatively quiet serenity in the face of rapid regional growth. It is just that they do it well. The express policy of the tourism authorities, and of most British Virgin Islanders, is to maintain the integrity of the natural environment—which has everything to do with the sea around the 60 or so islands, cays, rocks, and volcanic blips that make up the striking archipelago. It is the sea, the sailing, the diving, and the uncanny beauty of the beaches and shores that attract visitors to the islands. No hotels reach much higher than two stories—about the height of the tallest palm tree. The islands are home to no casinos, no large nightclubs, and, for that matter, no large towns. Indeed, they're home to little more than a small and unaffected population and the land and sea—the extremely comely land and sea—that surrounds them.

THE LAND

The origins of the place names in the British Virgin Islands tell the story of the islands' settlement. Various explorers, from the Amerindian Arawaks to Columbus to the 17th- and 18th-century European settlers, have come up with monikers such as **Tortola, Virgin Gorda, Jost Van Dyke,** and **Anegada,** the four main and populated islands, as well as **Norman Island, Peter Island, Ginger Island, Great Thatch, Fallen Jerusalem, the Dogs, Beef Island, Eustatia Island, Great Camanoe,** and more. Many names and their meanings have been obscured by history, while others reflect the vagaries of European colonization and whimsy.

The British Virgin Islands lie in a horizontal chain beginning 50 miles (80 km) east of Puerto Rico, just a few miles east of their sister islands, the United States Virgin Islands. The archipelago comprising the U.S. and British Virgin Islands as well as the Puerto Rican islands of Culebra and Vieques, lies on the **Virgin Bank,** a huge underwater shelf that encompasses the islands and waters stretching east of, and geologically related to, Puerto Rico and the Greater Antilles.

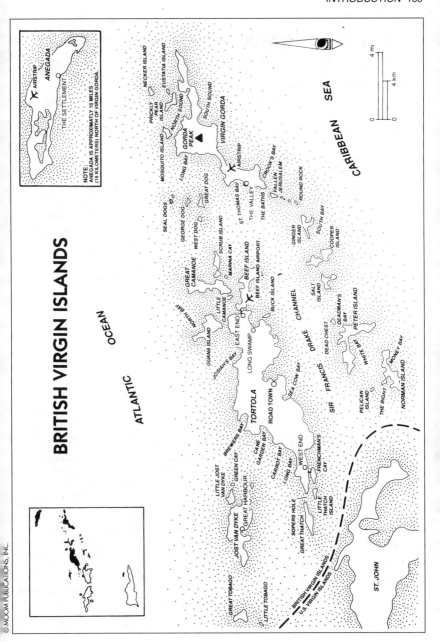

BRITISH VIRGIN ISLANDS

ATLANTIC OCEAN

CARIBBEAN SEA

NOTE:
ANEGADA IS APPROXIMATLY 10 MILES
(16 KILOMETERS) NORTH OF VIRGIN GORDA.

ANEGADA
AIRSTRIP
THE SETTLEMENT

NECKER ISLAND
EUSTATIA ISLAND
PRICKLY PEAR ISLAND
MOSQUITO ISLAND
NORTH SOUND
SOUTH SOUND
LONG BAY
GORDA PEAK
VIRGIN GORDA
SEAL DOGS
GEORGE DOG
GREAT DOG
WEST DOG
AIRSTRIP
ST. THOMAS BAY
THE VALLEY
CROOK'S BAY
FALLEN JERUSALEM
THE BATHS
ROUND ROCK
SOUTH BAY
GINGER ISLAND
COOPER ISLAND

GREAT CAMANOE
LITTLE CAMANOE
SCRUB ISLAND
MARINA CAY
BEEF ISLAND
BEEF ISLAND AIRPORT
BUCK ISLAND
SALT ISLAND
DEAD CHEST
DEADMAN'S BAY
PETER ISLAND
WHITE BAY
MONEY BAY

GUANA ISLAND
NORTH BAY
JOSIAH'S BAY
EAST END
LONG SWAMP
DRAKE CHANNEL
SIR FRANCIS

TORTOLA
BREWERS BAY
ROAD TOWN
SEA COW BAY
CANE GARDEN BAY
CARROT BAY
LONG BAY
WEST END
FRENCHMAN'S CAY
PELICAN ISLAND
THE BIGHT
NORMAN ISLAND

JOST VAN DYKE
LITTLE JOST VAN DYKE
GREEN CAY
GREAT HARBOUR
SOFERS HOLE
LITTLE THATCH ISLAND
GREAT THATCH

GREAT TOBAGO
LITTLE TOBAGO

ST. JOHN

BRITISH VIRGIN ISLANDS
U.S. VIRGIN ISLANDS

4 mi
4 km
0

© MOOM PUBLICATIONS, INC.

KEY DATES IN BRITISH VIRGIN ISLANDS' HISTORY

A.D. 500: Amerindian Arawaks begin making their way north toward the Virgin Islands from the Orinoco region of South America. They are followed by Amerindian Caribs, also from South America. The groups inhabit the islands until 1500.

1493: Christopher Columbus, blown off course, first sights and charts nearby "Santa Cruz" (St. Croix). He charts the rest of the islands, which he dubs *Las Once Mil Virgenes*—The 11,000 Virgins—in honor of the 4th-century martyr St. Ursula and her 11,000 virgin companions. Tortola, Virgin Gorda, and Anegada all receive Spanish names (Turtledove, Fat Virgin, and, approximately, Place of Drowning, respectively).

1595: Sir Francis Drake, the legendary British explorer and mercenary, passes through what is now Sir Francis Drake Channel on his way to engage the Spanish Armada.

1648: Dutch colonists establish a settlement at West End, on Tortola.

1672: The British governor of the Leeward Islands claims Tortola for Britain and sends planters from Anguilla to settle the island.

1673: The first boatload of Africans, soon to be enslaved, arrives in the Virgin Islands.

1680: The British establish settlements on Virgin Gorda and Anegada.

1724: Nearby St. Thomas becomes a free port.

1733: Slaves on nearby St. John rebel, and Tortola sends reinforcements to help put down the insurrection, which lasts for six months.

1801: The British briefly capture the Danish West Indies. They hold the islands for one year.

1807: The British again take possession of the Danish West Indies.

1815: The British return the islands to the Danes.

1834: Slavery as an institution in the British West Indies is abolished, and all slaves in the British Virgin Islands are freed.

1871: British Virgin Islands are administered as part of Britain's Federation of the Leeward Islands, later Federation of the West Indies.

1917: The U.S. purchases the Danish West Indies for $25 million, and the islands become the Virgin Islands of the United States.

1956: British Virgin Islands are administered as part of Britain's Federation of the West Indies, which collapses in 1962.

1960's: Through a series of internal referenda, British Virgin Islanders are given more say in the running of their affairs via the election of local executive and legislative councils and a chief minister elected from the ruling party.

1995: Powerful Hurricane Marilyn sweeps through Tortola, Virgin Gorda, and the U.S. Virgin Islands. The islands recover within six months.

The **Sir Francis Drake Channel** separates the Jost Van Dyke-Tortola group in the north from the Virgin Gorda string in the south. Virtually the entire group is of volcanic origin, save for Anegada, a flat coral formation at the far northeast end of the chain.

Of the four main islands, **Tortola** is the largest at 21 square miles (54 square km). This is the main entry point for visitors and the economic and administrative center of the islands, with a population of about 13,000—nearly four-fifths of the population of the entire British Virgin Islands. Tortola is mountainous, with an irregular coast characterized by fine white sand beaches. The central spine of mountains culminates at

Mt. Sage, a national park in the southwest, which is the island's highest point at 1,780 feet (534 meters). Quasi-rainforest flora covers the mountainside. The natural harbor at **Road Bay,** on the southern side of the island, is host to **Road Town,** the capital and business center of the British Virgin Islands, population 2,500. Tortola is connected by a toll bridge to Beef Island, site of the islands' **Beef Island International Airport.**

Virgin Gorda is an extremely irregular island—really three islands connected by isthmuses—with a total area measurement of eight square miles (21 square km). The eastern section is low-lying and home to several beaches and outlying cays. The middle section is hilly, rugged, and dominated by **Gorda Peak,** another national park and, at 1,359 feet (408 meters), Virgin Gorda's highest point. The island's southern section is flat and somewhat arid, with several beaches and attractions, including **the Baths,** a popular rock and cave formation. The population of the island is 1,500, almost all of whom live in **the Valley,** which incorporates **Spanish Town,** in the south.

Smallish **Jost Van Dyke**—the "j" is often pronounced as a "y"—named after a reputed pirate, is four square miles (10 square km) of mostly rugged hills, the highest at just over 1,000 feet (300 meters). The settlement at **Great Harbour** is home to much of the population—total 200—who are engaged primarily in tourism and related services.

Anegada, flat and 15 square miles (39 square km), is composed of coral limestone and sandy hillocks that rise no higher than 27 feet (eight meters) above sea level. The coast is smooth, and natural reefs—particularly along the western, leeward side—protect the beaches. The reef is not only beautiful, but also dangerous; nearly 300 shipwrecks lie offshore, more than anywhere else in the Caribbean. In fact, the name Anegada may have come from the Spanish *anegar,* literally "to drown." The attraction here is diving, obviously. Through National Parks Trust (tel. 809-494-3904) regulations, much of the island has been set aside as a reserve for birds and other wildlife. Several large salt ponds, one of which is set aside as a flamingo reserve, stretch inland. The island is 20 miles (32 km) northeast of Virgin Gorda, somewhat isolated from the main group, and most of the population of less than 200 lives in **the Settlement,** on the island's west side.

Another dozen or so islands of the group, some privately owned, are inhabited, bringing the British Virgin Islands' population up to 17,000.

GOVERNMENT AND ECONOMY

The British Virgin Islands are a Crown Colony, with an appointed governor representing the Queen of England. British Virgin Islanders are, at least on the surface, proud of their British ties and enamored of the queen. The islands' crown-appointed governor presides over an Executive Council comprising the chief minister, an attorney general, and several ministers of government. The governor changes at the request of the British government and can therefore serve for years. The head of local government today is Chief Minister Ralph T. O'Neal. The Legislative Council comprises elected members plus a governor-appointed member and a speaker of the council. Elections are held every five years.

The economy of the islands is reliant on British aid and EEC and associated aid grants, as well as the tourism industry, in which yachting, boating, and charters play large roles. More

350-year-old Callwood Rum Distillery, Cane Garden Bay, Tortola

than 325,000 visitors fly in or sail through the British Virgin Islands each year, of which about two-thirds are overnight visitors. The rest are day-trippers or cruise passengers. More than half of the overnight visitors take up some form of yacht activity for at least part of their vacations. The overnight visitors have at their disposal some 50 hotels and 160 guesthouses or villas, most on Tortola. Tourism is also the single most significant sector of the British Virgin Islands' economy, contributing, in the latest estimates, some $185 million per annum to the gross domestic product.

The British Virgin Islands offer incentives, through laws passed in the mid-1980s, for businesses to set up offshore companies. Foreign-owned but locally registered companies benefit from tax exemptions and the strong B.V.I. currency—the U.S. dollar. Nearly 20,000 offshore companies are registered in the British Virgin Islands, providing, through registration fees and some taxes, substantive revenue for the islands.

The farming and fishing industries remain small, and the British Virgin Islands imports much of its food and other needs.

An interesting although small source of local income comes from the **B.V.I. Film Commission** (tel. 809-494-4119), which promotes island locations for motion picture and television shoots. Commercials for products such as such as Coors Beer and Frito-Lay snack chips have been shot on the island.

British Virgin Islanders enjoy one of the region's highest per capita incomes, with the standard minimum wage at about $3 per hour.

FESTIVALS AND HOLIDAYS

Sailing and Water Events

Festivals and local events attest to the blending of the European and African cultures. The British love of sailing has been influential—virtually no month goes by without a sailing race or regatta. These include the **Sweethearts of the Caribbean Classic Yacht and Schooner Regatta** (Jolly Roger Inn, tel. 809-495-4559) and the **Hearts & Flowers Race** (B.V.I. Yacht Club, tel. 809-494-3286), both in February; the **Tides of March Sailing Race** (B.V.I. Yacht Club, tel. 809-494-3286), in March; the **British Virgin Is-**

lands Spring Regatta (B.V.I. Yacht Club, tel. 809-494-3286), in April; the **Pusser's Marina Cay Regatta** (B.V.I. Yacht Club, tel. 809-494-3286), in May; the **B.V.I. Match Racing Championship** (B.V.I. Yacht Club, tel. 809-494-3286), in July; **Foxy's Wooden Boat Regatta** (Foxy's Tamarind Bar, tel. 809-495-9258), in August; **Women's Sailing Week** (Bitter End Yacht Club, tel. 809-494-2746) and the **Pro-Am Regatta** (Bitter End Yacht Club, tel. 809-494-2746), both in October; the **Pusser's Round Tortola Sailing Race** (B.V.I. Yacht Club, tel. 809-494-3286), in November; and the **Commodore's Race** (B.V.I. Yacht Club, tel. 809-494-3286), in December.

Windsurfers and aficionados might want to look up the **Bud Open Windsurfing Competition** (Jolly Roger Inn, tel. 809-495-4559), held in January, or the **Bacardi Rum HIHO** (tel. 809-495-4148), held in June.

Carnivals

The **B.V.I. Summer Festival Days** is the islands' nod to West Indian and African influences and amounts to a raucous midsummer carnival. Held in late July or August, it features two weeks of nightly music, steel pan bands, quelbe bands, calypso and *soca* (another indigenous Caribbean music form, a blend of American rhythm and blues-based *soul* and island-wide *calypso*) competitions, prince and princess shows, feasts, parades, and arts and crafts shows. The festival usually takes place in Road Town, Tortola.

The **Virgin Gorda Easter Festival** is yet another carnival-influenced event and is held in the days leading up to the Roman Catholic period of atonement, Lent. The four-day fete features a festival village full of vendors' booths, a food fair, the Rise and Shine Tramp (a J'ouvert-like early-a.m. march) complete with local bands and calypsonians, and the final Grand Parade, with floats and stock carnival characters like the stilt-legged *Mocko Jumbi*. Fungi bands, reggae shows, and calypso competitions are held throughout the festival.

In late July, the British Virgin Islands celebrate the end of slavery with the **B.V.I. Emancipation Festival Celebrations** (tourist board, tel. 809-494-3134), two weeks of calypso, fungi, quelbe, and steel bands, arts and crafts, and food fetes. Festival Village is set up in Road Town on Tortola.

Other annual musical events are the **Music in Steel—Steel Band Concert** and the **Scratch/Fungi Band Fiesta,** both held in December to showcase local musicians. Contact the British Virgin Islands tourist board (tel. 809-494-3134) for information.

Regular Events

While it's an event, it's anything but "regular": once each month on the appropriate day, the infamous and bombastic Bomba hosts a **Full Moon Party** at his **Surfside Shack** (tel. 809-495-4148), on Carrot Bay on Tortola. This party is wacky, to say the least—no frat-house party has ever had anything on Bomba. "Very celubrious" barbecues, music, various degrees of inebriation, and dancing are the party's mainstays, which keep going until the weest of hours. At midnight, Bomba serves up his entirely unwholesome but wildly popular "magic tea," a drink lightly laced with hallucinogenic mushrooms. This is not for the faint of heart, so be warned.

One of the year's biggest and most popular parties takes place on New Year's Eve at **Foxy's Tamarind Bar** (tel. 809-495-9258), on Jost Van Dyke. From throughout the U.S. and British Virgin Islands, sailors drift in for the festivities, which include pig roasts, music, dancing in the sand, and generally heavy partying. Foxy, a local and international legend, sings calypso and plays the gracious host. This is another wee-hours event, and hundreds of people have been known to attend. Plan to sleep on your boat.

Public Holidays

Public holidays in the British Virgin Islands include **New Year's Day, Commonwealth Day** (second Monday in March), **Good Friday, Easter, Easter Monday, Whit Monday** (July), **Territory Day** (1 July), **St. Ursula's Feast Day** (21 October), **Christmas Day,** and **Boxing Day** (26 December). True to its modern-day British roots, the British Virgin Islands celebrates the **Queen's Birthday** (second Saturday in June) and the **Birthday of the Heir to the Throne** (Prince Charles's birthday, 14 November).

TORTOLA

Long and lush, with dramatic rises and deep dips into valleys, Tortola (from the Spanish for "dove") is the British Virgin Islands' population and administrative center and, at 21 square miles (54 square km), the largest island of the group. The island is also a center of activity, restaurants, and accommodations, and one could happily spend a vacation on Tortola alone. It is not a place of trendy bistros and raucous nightlife (in general, that is—exceptions can always be found), but rather maintains a sort of quietly proper British gentility. It's an island where a "good morning" or a "how are you?" goes a long way and where the pace of life is, or seems, well in tune with the taciturn dignity of the surrounding mountains and sea.

SIGHTS

All telephone numbers below are listed with full area code and exchange. However, within the

British Virgin Islands, you need only dial the last five numbers. The phone number (809) 495-6789, for example, can be locally rung up as 56789.

Road Town and Environs

Road Town, on large **Road Bay** on the island's south-central coast, is a small, functional center, with a shop-laden **Main Street,** government offices, and a busy waterfront. Here you'll find a post office, banks, churches, a prison, the tourist board, Cable and Wireless offices, a police station, shops, the ferry dock, hotels and, of course, several marinas up and down the waterfront. The town's style is quaint and modern West Indian. The style of the brightly painted wooden and stone buildings, particularly along the old Main Street—an attraction in itself—is the architecture of the turn-of-the-century Caribbean.

Main Street runs parallel to the thoroughfare **Waterfront Drive,** which is a main link between the eastern and western ends of the island. A ride on Waterfront through Road Town will take

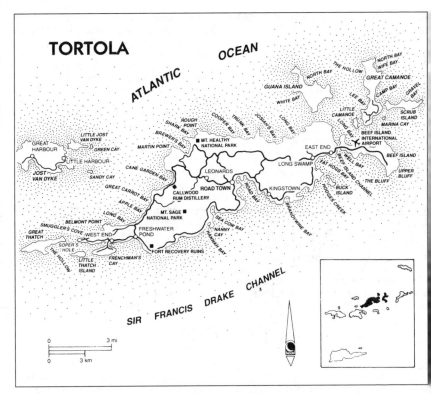

you anywhere you want to go in town and beyond. A focal point on Main Street is the **Sir Olva George's Plaza,** which sits between Waterfront Drive, where the ferry docks are located, and the main post office on Main Street. The square, just a sitting area really, sits beneath several large ficus trees and is lined with government offices—including the customs office—and shops. This area was once a market center for island produce and is named for a British Virgin Islands politician and businessman.

The post office building, with its dramatic gothic-style arches, dates back to 1866. The original flooring and walls are still visible on the ground floor. (Post office hours are weekdays 8:30 a.m.-4 p.m. and Saturday 9 a.m.-12 p.m., tel. 809-494-3701).

Stroll down Main Street for shopping, and take in some of the more colorful West Indian-style homes and buildings in the islands. The stark white **HMS Prison,** which is not open to the public unless you manage to get yourself incarcerated, was built in the 18th century and still maintains many of its original architectural features. On either side of the prison are **St. George's Anglican Church** (tel. 809-494-3894), rebuilt after a hurricane damaged it in 1819, and the **Methodist Church** (tel. 809-495-9619), built in 1924. Inside the Anglican church is a copy of the 1834 Emancipation Proclamation that freed slaves in the islands. These two churches represent two of the main religions of the British Virgin Islands.

Also on Main Street is the unfortunately currently closed **Virgin Islands Folk Museum.** The museum presented stone artifacts from the early Amerindian presence on the islands, displays from plantation slavery days, as well as bits and pieces salvaged from the wreck of the

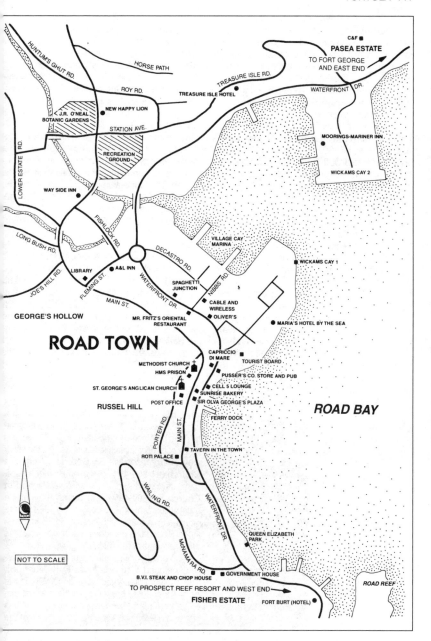

RMS *Rhone,* a British mail ship that sunk off the coast of Peter Island in the 1800s. A small gift shop carried several good books about island history and lore. There is no telling when the museum will reopen, if ever, but hours (variable with season) were 9 a.m.-4 p.m. weekdays except Wednesday, Saturday 9 a.m.-noon. The museum was closed Sunday. Admission was not charged in the past.

A 15-minute walk from the center of town (north, on Main Street) is the **J.R. O'Neal Botanic Gardens** (tel. 809-494-4557), one of the showpieces of Road Town. The four-acre gardens, built on the grounds of the old Government Agricultural Station, is home to a wide array of local and imported tropical plants, a pond with a waterfall, and a small gift shop, all explored on self-guided walks. Royal palms, Norfolk pines, banana trees, gingers, orchids, bougainvillea, and various species of cactus are just a few of the plants housed here and labeled with descriptive placards. The gardens also feature a small Fern House and Orchid House and an Herb and Medicinal Garden, with descriptions of local herbs and remedies. The gardens are named after Joseph Reynold O'Neal (a name you'll see on businesses throughout town), who, among other endeavors, was a chairman of the National Parks Trust, which administers the gardens through the Botanic Society. The gardens are open daily during sunlight hours, and admission is free, although a $2 donation is recommended.

The J.R. O'Neal Botanic Garden is located in a section of town near **Wickam's Cay,** a busy shopping area and intersection—the town's large traffic rotary is here—where you'll find many of the town's department stores, supermarkets, and small malls, as well as the massive cruise-ship dock. Farther east along Waterfront Drive, past the traffic rotary, is **Wickam's Cay II,** which holds several marinas. Both cays are built on reclaimed land.

Several forts and historic ruins dot the countryside near Road Town. **Fort Burt** is now a hotel—one of the islands' first—but was constructed by the Dutch and later rebuilt by the British. The foundation is all that remains of the original structure. The ruins of **Fort George,** and **Fort Charlotte,** both built in 1794, can be found on strategic hills overlooking the harbor.

Out Island

You'll find **Mount Sage National Park** off steep **Ridge Road** at the island's west end. At 1,780 feet (541 meters), it's Tortola's highest point, and the views are stunning. Three trails lead from the parking area through the park's 92 acres and up to the peak—an easy walk. The semi-rainforest hosts a variety of rainforest flora and fauna, including a wide array of birds. Many of the trees are marked, and you'll have views below of the Sir Francis Drake Channel and nearby islands. There is no admission, and you'll find several shops and a restaurant at the park entrance.

Main Street,
Road Town, Tortola

At the far west end of the island, in the town of **West End,** is **Soper's Hole,** believed to be the site of the first Dutch landing on the island, in 1648. The harbor has a ferry landing with customs and immigration facilities, as well as a marina, restaurants, and shops. The shopping center and marina at Soper's Hole is one of the best on the island and is done up in bright, West Indian colors—always a great photo.

Nearby, on the south coast road, is **Fort Recovery,** in the Fort Recovery Estates villas complex. The ruins of the fort consist of a tower and a few crumbled remains. There are no tours, but you can clamber around.

On the **North Coast Road** up from West End, you'll pass **Apple Bay,** the beginning of a series of hotels and restaurants that sit on the bays and beaches of the north shore. At the crowded and popular **Cane Garden Bay,** lined with hotels and shops, you'll find the **Callwood Rum Distillery** in a 350-year-old stone plantation building. It's not a big distillery, but rum is still produced from pure cane juice in copper vats using a method called pot distilling and still aged in casks. The building is dark, smoky, and chockablock with copper vats and distilling paraphernalia. You can buy rum here—it's called Arundel, after the first family that operated the distillery (the Callwood family has operated it for the last 200 years). Rum is $5 per bottle for the white and $6 for the dark. Tours are conducted on the outside of the building—no one gets to go deep into the works. Check it out Monday through Saturday from 8:30 a.m. to 6 p.m. The tour costs $1, and you can take photos if you first buy a bottle of rum.

Just past Cane Garden Bay, heading east, you can branch down to **Brewers Bay,** which features a long, shaded beach and a campground. Back up in the hills you'll see a turnoff to **Mt. Healthy,** another small national park. The turnoff starts as a cement road and quickly turns into a rough dirt road, which may be impassable after a heavy rain. The highlight here is an old stone windmill, once part of a sugar plantation. You can walk around it, but that's about it. The view below is of Brewers Bay. For more information about national parks on Tortola, or in the British Virgin Islands, contact the **British Virgin Islands National Parks Trust** at P.O. Box 860, Road Town, Tortola, British Virgin Islands; tel. (809) 494-3904, fax (809) 494-6383.

At the east end of the island, just past a town named **East End,** is the confusingly named **Beef Island,** which is the home of the British Virgin Islands' **Beef Island International Airport** (tel. 809-495-2525). Many visitors are confused by the reference—when they're flying into Tortola, they're surprised to hear that they'll be landing at Beef Island. No worries; Beef Island is indeed an island, separated from Tortola by the narrow Beef Island Channel, but is connected by a tiny toll bridge. The toll bridge is majestically named the **Queen Elizabeth Bridge,** in honor of the queen's visit in 1966. The toll, 50 cents, is collected by a guy who will hold out a cup.

Besides the airport, Beef Island is the home of several notable hotels and restaurants and has a couple of pleasant bays and beaches for those staying at that end of the island. Off the shore of Beef Island, near **Great Camanoe Island,** is **Marina Cay,** a small islet with a marina that is the home of **Pussers,** a hotel/restaurant/pub/shopping complex.

RECREATION

Diving

Scuba diving is very popular in the British Virgin Islands, at least for those who dive. With the plethora of reefs surrounding the many islets and cays, as well as reefs and wrecks off the shores of main islands, divers won't want for a new dive spot every day. Most all outfits can arrange diving trips, advanced dives, night dives, and resort certification, as well as snorkeling and diving packages coupled with hotel stays. Cost for one-tank dives averages $70-80. Resort certification, which includes initial instruction and a shallow supervised dive, averages $100.

Baskin in the Sun (P.O. Box 108, Road Town, Tortola, British Virgin Islands, tel. 800-233-7938 or 809-494-2858, fax 809-494-5853, e-mail baskindive@usmall.com) is one of the bigger operations in the Virgin Islands; its trips start at $80 for a one-tank dive and go up to $320 for packages of 10 dives. They also organize snorkel trips twice per day, at 8:30 a.m. and 2:30 p.m., for $25 and $20 respectively, and rent a wide array of diving and snorkeling equipment. Baskin's offices are located at the Prospect Reef Resort in Road Town, Soper's Hole in West End, and the

Village Cay Marina in Road Town. Check out their Web site at www.dive-baskin.com.

As well, contact:

Blue Waters Divers (P.O. Box 846, Road Town, Tortola, British Virgin Islands, tel. 809-494-2847, fax 809-494-0198)

Trimarine (P.O. Box 362, Road Town, Tortola, British Virgin Islands, tel. 800-648-3393 or 809-494-2490, fax 809-494-5774)

Underwater Safaris (P.O. Box 139, Road Town, Tortola, British Virgin Islands, tel. 800-537-7032 or 809-494-3235, fax 809-494-5322)

Snorkeling

Caribbean Images Tours (P.O. Box 505, East End, Tortola, British Virgin Islands; tel. 809-494-1147, fax 809-494-3966) specializes in snorkeling tours of Tortola, Jost Van Dyke, Peter Island, Virgin Gorda, and even the RMS *Rhone,* the sunken mail boat off Peter Island. They'll stop at smaller islands along the way. The company is located at Prospect Reef Resort in Road Town, and departures are daily at 9:30 a.m. for the full day's tour and half-day morning trips at 1:30 p.m. for half-day afternoon trips. Trips are $40 per person half-day, $60 full day. Snorkeling equipment and drinks, but not lunch, are included in the rate. Note that credit cards are not accepted.

Boating

Many visitors will elect to charter a boat and sail their way around the British Virgin Islands, living on the boat and seeing the sights at their leisure. Not only is this a wonderful way to see the islands, but it is, in some ways, also the most convenient. The type of boat and/or crew you charter will depend on your sailing skills and your budget. Dozens of charter outfits in the British Virgin Islands offer everything from organized sailing to bareboat and crewed charters. If you're up for it and have the experience, try the variation where you hire a skipper and you serve as the crew. You'll find about 15 marinas scattered throughout the island group providing water, electricity, and shopping for boat visitors, as well as anchorages scattered throughout the bays and inlets. Boat charter rates depend on how many passengers are involved, the size and make of the boat, whether it's a sailboat or a powerboat,

the size of the crew, and amenities offered. Figure a minimum of $2,500 per week for a bareboat in high season to as much as $17,000 per week for a crewed charter for 10 persons. On average, a party of four for a week in high season on a crewed sailing yacht will run $9,500. Rates may be significantly reduced during off-season. The original and largest charter company in the British Virgin Islands is **The Moorings** (P.O. Box 139, Road Town, Tortola, British Virgin Islands or 19345 U.S. Hwy. 19 North, 4th floor, Clearwater, FL 34624; tel. 800-535-7289 for bareboat charters, 800-437-7880 for crewed charters, or, in the B.V.I., tel. 809-494-2331 or 2333, fax 809-494-2226). The Moorings, which has yachts in harbors throughout the Caribbean and the South Pacific, is a full-service travel company and maintains hotels at their yacht marinas throughout the world. The Moorings' Web site is www.interdu.com/moorings.

For a bit less hype and possibly a more personal touch, these small companies offer bareboat, crewed, and skippered charters and motor yacht charters:

Virgin Islands Sailing (Mill Mall, Road Town, Tortola, British Virgin Islands or 2216 Lakeshore Dr., Nokomis, FL 34275, tel. 800-233-7936, B.V.I. tel. 809-494-2774, fax 809-494-6774)

Discovery Yacht Charters (P.O. Box 281, Road Town, Tortola, British Virgin Islands, tel. 809-494-6026, fax 809-494-6035, Canada, tel. 416-891-1999, fax 416-891-3623)

Marine Enterprises Boat Rentals (P.O. Box 3069, Road Town, Tortola, British Virgin Islands; tel. 809-494-2786, fax 809-494-4744)

North South Yacht Vacations (P.O. Box 281, Road Town, Tortola, British Virgin Islands, tel. 809-494-0096, fax 809-495-7543)

Seabreeze Yacht Charters (P.O. Box 528, East End, Tortola, British Virgin Islands; tel. 800-668-2807 or 809-495-1560, fax 809-495-1561)

Sunsail (P.O. Box 609, Frenchman's Cay, Tortola, British Virgin Islands or 2 Prospect Park, 3347 N.W. 55th St., Fort Lauderdale, FL 33309; tel. 800-327-2276 or 305-484-5242, fax 305-485-5072; B.V.I., tel. 809-495-4740, fax 809-495-4301)

Tropic Island Yacht Management (P.O. Box 532, Maya Cove, Tortola, British Virgin Islands, tel. 800-356-8938 or 809-494-2450, fax 809-495-2155)

Day Sails

Hop on a boat for a day, let someone else do the driving, have some drinks and lunch, and you've just experienced one of the pleasures of being a tourist. Day-sailing boats, from power yachts to tall ships and catamarans, are found in Tortola's many marinas and are all in the business of taking visitors on tours of the many cays and diving and snorkeling spots around the islands, including **The Baths,** at Virgin Gorda; Peter Island; **The Caves,** at Norman Island; Jost Van Dyke; and several of the smaller British Virgin Islands. The routine is often this: an early morning start, sunbathing, swimming and snorkeling, lunch (often with complimentary drinks), and general relaxation as the waves slap against the hull of the boat. Rates for day sails vary with the trip and offerings, but you should count on at least $50 per person and perhaps as much as $100. The *Goddess Athena* (tel. and fax 809-494-0000), a large ketch, makes day sails to neighboring islands and evening twilight sails. It also hosts theme sails, such as pirate trips. Other day-sailing outfits or vessels include the *Classique* (tel. 809-494-3623), the *Dual Bliss* (tel. 809-496-7149), **King Charters** (tel. 809-494-5820), **No Fear Day Sailing** (tel. 809-494-4000), the *Patouche II* (tel. 809-494-6300), the *Ppalu* (tel. 809-494-0608), *Take Two* (tel. 809-494-5208), and the *White Squall* (tel. 809-494-2564). Call; they will often pick you up from your hotel and return you later, at no extra cost.

Fishing

Tuna, dolphin, wahoo, kingfish, and marlin all make their homes in British Virgin Islands waters, and you can get at them through a number of sport fishing outfits. **Pelican Charters** (tel. 809-496-7386), at the Prospect Reef Resort in Road Town, takes anglers out on the optimistically named M/V *Whopper,* a 45-foot Chris Craft Tournament Sportsfisherman. The boat holds five persons and heads out for full-day ($900) or half-day ($600) excursions. Drinks and lunch or, for the half-day trips, drinks and snack are included. They'll also organize overnight trips out

to Anegada and conduct tours of the marine environment for $90 per person.

Miss Robbie Charters (tel. 809-494-3193) also organizes deep-sea fishing excursions.

Other Water Sports

A full range of water sports, including windsurfing, kayaking, water-skiing, snorkeling, small powerboat rentals, and more are handled by several outfits: **Baby Bull Water Sports** (tel. 809-495-9627) at Cane Garden Bay, **Boardsailing BVI** (tel. 809-495-2447) at Nanny Cay and Trellis Bay, and **Splash Sports** (tel. 809-495-4558) at Carrot Bay.

Land Activities

You won't find public courts in town, and **tennis** players will have to rely on hotels for their facilities. Prospect Reef Resort near Road Town has six courts (two lighted for night use) and charges a small fee for use.

Horseback tours of the island are offered by **Shadow's Stable** (tel. 809-494-2262) and **Ellis Thomas** (tel. 809-494-4442).

Need a **massage** or, what the heck, a facial after all that tennis or horseback riding? I would. (Not the facial—the massage.) Anyway, call Cynthia Elmore at **Solé Massage and Spa Services** (tel. 809-494-5999, fax 809-494-1473), in Road Town, for a range of therapeutic treatments. She also has an office at Peter Island. You won't be in better hands anywhere on the island.

If **golf** is your game, you're pretty much out of luck on Tortola; no full 9- or 18-hole courses are to be found, although there is a small "pitch 'n putt" course at the Prospect Reef Resort. As of this writing, plans to develop an 18-hole course on Beef Island were on someone's desk but had hit a snag due to issues surrounding water use—the British Virgin Islands has little in the way of extra water, and the amount it would take to keep an 18-hole course green could be prohibitively expensive, or even impossible to set aside.

Hiking

Mount Sage National Park, at the west end of the island, has three trails that wend their way through the 92-acre park toward the peak. The **Henry Adams Loop Trail, Main Trail,** and the **Slippery Trail** are all easy-to-moderate walking paths. Allow the better part of a day to hike around Mt. Sage, and bring provisions should you decide on a picnic lunch.

BEACHES

Tortola's best beaches are found along its north and northwestern shore. Some are accessible by car, others by boat or by short hikes. All beaches in the British Virgin Islands are open for public use; some have facilities and yacht moorings in secluded bays, others have few facilities or nothing at all. Generally, the only facilities for changing are at nearby hotels.

Among the best are **Smuggler's Cove,** at the far west end, a small, pristine beach with good snorkeling. Occasionally there is a small, self-serve, honor-system refreshment stand set up at the beach. To get there, take the North Shore Road to Long Bay Resort and follow an extremely rough dirt road into the hills and down to the shore. Beware of this road after heavy rains—it's not for the faint of heart.

Long Bay, where the resort is located, is, not surprisingly, long. The surf here is generally calm but can be rough on windy days. Heading east, the rougher **Apple Bay,** lined with palm trees, is a favorite spot with surfers. Next up are **Little Carrot Bay** and **Great Carrot Bay,** where you'll find **Bomba's Surfside Shack** (tel. 809-895-2148). Bomba's is famous for its weekly barbecues and its monthly Full Moon Party, a wildly popular island event showcasing all sorts of debauchery. Several other small restaurants and bistros are located on this beach. Heading north and east, **Cane Garden Bay** is wide and long and popular with swimmers—there are plenty of beach bars, water sports, etc. This section is perhaps the most popular beach on the island. Stop in at the seaside **Quito's Gazebo** (tel. 809-495-4837) for a drink and a live performance by **Quito Rymer and the Edge.** Quito is the owner of the pub and one of the British Virgin Islands' more popular recording artists. Or, stop in at the large and pink **Rhymer's Cane Garden Bay Beach Hotel** (tel. 809-495-4639)—Rhymer is a big name in these parts—where you can hang out at the beach bar and use the showers ($1) and other facilities.

Up over the hill, and left down to the water,

you'll find **Brewer's Bay.** The beach here is protected, calm, and shaded. Brewer's Bay was once the site of several sugar mills and distilleries and is now home to beach bars and a campground. The beach is most often used by campers but is rarely crowded.

Heading farther east on the North Shore Road, you find a turnoff to **Josiah's Bay,** a long, uncrowded beach.

Elizabeth Bay, on the eastern end, is small and secluded. Just north of the airport on Beef Island is another beach named **Long Bay,** which is long and rarely crowded. The nearby salt pond is home to nesting terns and other sea birds. Also on Beef Island is **Trellis Bay,** a wide beach with water sports outfits.

ACCOMMODATIONS

Tortola's accommodations include large and small, pricey and inexpensive. Few large resorts are found on the island; rather, the norm is small hotels and inns, guesthouses, apartments, and villas. In fact, renting villas is popular in the extreme on Tortola, due to the large number available and their relatively reasonable rates.

Most of the island's hotels and villas are located on the northwest coast, fronting the island's finest beaches and bays. Hotels and inexpensive guesthouses and inns are also found in and around Road Town.

Remember, room rates are reduced by as much as 40% during the summer season; with a little research, you can often find them bargained out through packages and wholesale room discounters. A government hotel occupancy tax of seven percent is charged on accommodations, and often a 10-15% service charge is added to the bill. Most larger hotels accept major credit cards, but this is not always the case—call ahead and check. Keep in mind that some properties require a minimum three nights stay, extra persons in the rooms are often charged $10-30 (although, as a rule, children are allowed in free), and may require a deposit of as much as 50% on the room.

The accommodations listed below are categorized based on the average room rate (some hotels offer a wide range of rooms, from budget to luxury), double occupancy, European plan (no meals), per night, during the 15 December-through-15 April high season, excluding the eight percent room tax. A designation of **luxury** indicates that rooms run $200 or more; **expensive** rooms are $140-200; **moderate** indicates a range of $80-140; and **budget** rooms cost $80 or less.

Villas, Apartments, and Condos

In addition to the villa rental companies mentioned in the Introduction to this book, the following local villas and villa rental services are available at average rates of $100-200 per day.

Bananas on the Beach (P.O. Box 2, West End, Tortola, British Virgin Islands, tel. 809-495-4318, fax 809-495-4299)

CGB Cottages (Cane Garden Bay, Tortola, British Virgin Islands, tel. 809-495-4871)

Heritage Villas (P.O. Box 2019, Carrot Bay, Tortola, British Virgin Islands, tel. 809-494-5842, fax 809-495-4100)

Icis Vacation Villas (P.O. Box 383, Road Town, Tortola, British Virgin Islands, tel. 809-494-6979, fax 809-494-6980)

Lloyd Hill Villas (P.O. Box 3310, Road Town, Tortola, British Virgin Islands, tel. 809-494-2481)

Mt. Sage Villas (P.O. Box 821, Road Town, Tortola, British Virgin Islands, tel. 809-495-9567, fax 809-494-1562)

Rockview Holiday Homes (P.O. Box 263, Road Town, Tortola, British Virgin Islands, tel. 809-494-2550, fax 809-494-5866)

Sunset Vacation Apartments (Cane Garden Bay, Tortola, British Virgin Islands, tel. 809-495-4751)

Resorts and Hotels

Fort Burt Hotel (P.O. Box 243, Road Town, Tortola, British Virgin Islands, tel. 809-494-2587, fax 809-494-2002) sits in the hills just south of downtown Road Town, overlooking the ocean. The hotel features a restaurant, pool, and water sports, and the location is fine for exploring the island. The entire complex is built on the remains of an 18th-century fort. **Moderate.**

Fort Recovery Estates (P.O. Box 11156, St. Thomas, U.S. Virgin Islands, tel. 800-367-8455 or 809-495-4467, fax 809-495-4036), on the south shore near West End, consists of villas located on the grounds of a 17th-century Dutch fort. The villas are modern and well equipped, you've got the ocean and a beach directly outside your door, and the price is right if you can get a small group together to rent a villa (which accommodate four to eight people). Rates include continental breakfast. **Expensive.**

Frenchman's Cay Resort Hotel (P.O. Box 1054, West End, Tortola, British Virgin Islands; from U.S., tel. 800-235-4077; from Canada, tel. 800-463-0199; local tel. 809-495-4844, fax 809-495-4056) is a small, elegant resort on a small cay connected by a bridge to the southwestern town of West End. The resort comprises nine self-contained luxury villas on the beach, all with kitchens, patios, sitting areas, and stunning views of the ocean and St. John and St. Thomas to the west. As well, you'll find a restaurant, a tennis court, a pool, and water sports on the grounds. Villas are one- or two-bedroom and fit four to six people. Meal plans are available at a cost of $45 per day per person. **Expensive-Luxury.**

Long Bay Beach Resort and Villas (P.O. Box 284, Larchmont, NY 10538, North America tel. 800-729-9599 or 914-833-3300, fax 914-833-3318, U.K. tel. 0800-898-379) is one of the island's premier resorts. It sits on a hill overlooking the seriously pretty Long Bay, located about five minutes from West End. The accommodations are in airy, spacious rooms or villas, and all sit on the ocean or have views to the ocean below. The sound of the surf at night rolls up the hillside. All rooms and villas have a/c, phones, large refrigerators, full kitchens, and hair dryers. As well, most have balconies or patios. You'll find several bars and restaurants, including the elegant Garden Restaurant, as well as shops on the grounds. A shuttle runs daily to nearby Smuggler's Beach. The resort can organize golf, horseback riding, and water sports, and there is a freshwater pool at one of the beachside restaurant bars. A tennis court is also on the grounds. Since many of the resort's rooms and villas are located on a steep hillside, heavy walking may be required—not for the faint of heart. Small golf carts buzz about picking people up here and there, but if you want independence of movement, get a room or villa on the beach or at the base of the hill. **Luxury.**

Maria's Hotel by the Sea (P.O. Box 206, Road Town, Tortola, British Virgin Islands, tel. 809-494-2595, fax 809-494-2420) is located at Wickam's Cay I, near the cruise ship dock. The large, white block building holds 20 rooms, most with kitchenettes, and each room has a phone, TV, and a small balcony over the harbor. There's no beach here, but the hotel has a pool, and **Maria's Restaurant** is known locally for its West Indian fare. The hotel is basically uninspiring, but the town location is good, and the place is safe and comfortable. Maria's has another small hotel, **Hotel Castle Maria** (same address, tel. 809-494-2553, fax 809-494-2111), with 30 rooms, located south of town at Fisher Estate, near the Fort Burt Hotel. Both are **moderate.**

The **Moorings-Mariner Inn** (P.O. Box 139, Road Town, Tortola, British Virgin Islands, tel. 800-535-7289 or 809-494-2332, fax 809-494-2226), located at Wickam's Cay II near the outskirts of Road Town, serves mainly as a departure and return point for guests who have chartered with the Mooring yacht charter company, whose yacht fleet is docked at a marina right outside the doors of the hotel. The 40-room hotel (36 standard, four suites) offers basic amenities, clean rooms, a pool, restaurant, bar, and tennis court. The location is fine for exploring the island, and you get a chance to hang with yachties, who can tell you a bit about the islands. **Expensive.**

Prospect Reef Resort (P.O. Box 104, Road Town, Tortola, British Virgin Islands, tel. 800-356-8937, from Canada 800-463-3608, local 809-494-3311, fax 809-494-5595, e-mail prr@caribsurf.com). This 130-unit resort, set on 44 acres just south of Road Town, may be one of the nicest places to stay on Tortola. The resort, which manages a small harbor and marina, is one of the better places to launch a diving excursion—more than 50 dive sites lie within 20 minutes of the hotel. The rooms are eclectic, from oceanview suites and villas to loft studios and suites overlooking the ocean or hills behind. Many of the rooms have been recently refurbished; at least half feature a/c, all have fans, most also have cable TV, phones, and kitchenettes. The resort is children-friendly and offers kids' activities including a hunt for several turtles that live in a tidal channel that flows through the resort grounds. You'll also find a kids' activities center and a wading pool. The adult freshwater pool is Olympic-size, and there's a diving pool nearby. Even though the beachfront is rocky, the resort has fashioned two "sea pools"—an environmentally friendly way of allowing seawater and small sealife to gather in pools protected from the surf by a sea wall. The resort also has two restaurants, two bars, shops, courtesy buses to Cane Garden Bay, a health center, deep-sea fishing aboard the M/V *Whopper,* and the Baskin in the Sun dive shop. Dive, honeymoon, and health-center packages are available. **Expensive.**

Rhymer's Cane Garden Bay Beach Hotel (P.O. Box 570, Cane Garden Bay, Tortola, British Virgin Islands, tel. 809-495-4639 or 495-4215, fax 809-495-4820) sits on the northwest coast's Cane Garden Bay, one of the nicest beaches on Tortola. This hotel—you can't miss its effervescent blue, green, and pink exterior (sort of the colors of a sun-baked tourist)—has 21 rooms, each with a/c, TV, and a kitchenette. The rooms are simple, the long, wide beach is the attraction. You'll also find a restaurant and bar, beauty salon, shops, and a small grocery store on the grounds. A good deal for the person who is beach-bound. **Moderate.**

Sebastian's on the Beach (P.O. Box 441, Road Town, Tortola, British Virgin Islands, tel 800-336-4870 or 809-495-4212, fax 809-495-4466), is medium-size—26 rooms—located right on the beach at Little Apple Bay. The rooms are bright and cheery, done up in Caribbean floral patterns, and many have balconies overlooking the beach. The hotel restaurant is renowned for its seafood. Dining is at oceanside and a delight. Surfboards (Apple Bay is known for its big waves) and snorkeling gear are available for rent. A meal plan is available for $35 per day per person. **Expensive.**

Sugar Mill Hotel (P.O. Box 425, Road Town, Tortola, British Virgin Islands, U.S. tel. 800-462-8834, Canada tel. 800-209-6874, local tel. 809-495-4355, fax 809-495-4696) is located on the beach at Apple Bay. The 18-room inn sits on the grounds of a defunct 360-year-old sugar plantation and is one of the island's more luxurious spots. The rooms are elegant and made for comfort, and the restaurant, set in a stone building that was once a rum distillery, is world renowned for its local and continental cuisine. You've got the beach, you've got a pool, you've got gourmet dining—the best small hotel on the island. No children under 10 are allowed in the winter season, and the hotel is closed August and September. **Luxury.**

Treasure Isle Hotel (P.O. Box 68, Pasea Estate, Road Town, Tortola, British Virgin Islands; tel. 800-437-7880 or 809-494-2501, fax 809-494-2507) is one of the older hotels on Tortola and was once affiliated with the Moorings yacht charter company. Located at the eastern end of town, between Wickam's Cay I and Wickam's Cay II, the 40-room hotel is bright and cheery. You'll find a pool, restaurant, bar, and water sports, including a sailing school and charter sailing activities. The rooms are all floral and rattan in the way that Caribbean hotels tend to be, and the location, on a busy road just outside of town, is fine for exploring. The hotel offers transportation for guests to nearby beaches and water sports areas. Meal plans are available for $40 per day per person. **Expensive.**

Small Hotels, Inns, and Guesthouses

A&L Inn (P.O. Box 403, Road Town, Tortola, British Virgin Islands, tel. 809-494-6343 or 494-6345, fax 809-494-6656) is a new second-floor downtown inn (on Fleming St., between Main and Wickam's Cay I) with 14 comfortable rooms, all with a/c, refrigerators, and TVs. There's also a small bar that serves snacks downstairs. There is a great location for exploring Road Town and a very good deal. **Budget.**

Beef Island Guesthouse (P.O. Box 494, East End, Tortola, British Virgin Islands, tel. 809-495-2303, fax 809-495-1611) is a small guesthouse on Trellis Bay, near the airport on Beef Island. The four rooms are comfortable and have private baths, and the beach is okay—there are better beaches elsewhere, but for the price it's a fine place to base yourself for exploring, or if you've got an early-morning flight. A small bar and restaurant next door, the **Loose Mongoose**, is a popular hangout and often features live entertainment. **Moderate.**

Jolly Roger Inn (West End, Tortola, British Virgin Islands, tel. 809-495-4559, fax 809-495-4184), a five-room guesthouse, sits at the end of the ferry dock road at West End, the entrance to Soper's Hole. The ocean is just outside the door

(no beach). The restaurant is a local hangout and serves inexpensive West Indian food as well as barbecues and Sunday brunch. Live music is on the menu Friday and Saturday nights. Three of the simple but clean rooms share baths (hot and cold water), the other two have private baths. **Budget.**

New Happy Lion (Road Town, Tortola, British Virgin Islands tel. 809-494-3909) is a bar and restaurant with a few attached apartments, located near the Botanical Gardens. The apartments are one- or two-bedroom, with kitchens, TVs, and private baths. There's nothing spectacular about the place, but it's clean and the price is right. **Budget.**

Ole Works Inn (P.O. Box 560, Cane Garden Bay, Tortola, British Virgin Islands, tel. 809-495-4837, fax 809-495-9618). This eight-room inn sits on the site of a sugar mill estimated to be about 300 years old. The beach is just a stone's throw away, and you'll find the Gazebo Restaurant, home of the singer Quito Rymer, on the bottom floor. The rooms are modern, not large, but come with fans and refrigerators. **Moderate-Expensive.**

Pusser's Marina Cay (P.O. Box 626, Road Town, Tortola, British Virgin Islands; tel. 809-494-2174, fax 809-494-4775) is located on a small cay off the Beef Island coast, east of Great Camanoe Island. The Pusser's Company, purveyors of rum, island-chic clothing, and other items, bought this tiny islet in 1960, some years after the writer Robb White lived there. White wrote the 1953 book *Our Virgin Island,* which was later made into a film starring Sidney Poitier and John Cassavettes. The cay now has a small hotel that accommodates 16 in single rooms and villas. You'll find a pool, water sports, a restaurant and bar, and pretty much total isolation out here; if that's what you want, this is a good place to do it. The hotel runs regular free ferries to and from Trellis Bay every hour or so from 10:15 a.m. until 10:15 p.m. (call the number above for special requests). **Moderate-Expensive**

Serendipity House (P.O. Box 509, East End, Tortola, British Virgin Islands, tel. and fax 809-495-1488) is a small guesthouse at Josiah's Bay, on the north coast. Accommodations are provided in a series of one to three bedrooms, either communicating or private, and the rooms all have private baths, kitchens, and TVs. You'll also find a pool on the grounds. The beach is just down the road. **Budget.**

Tamarind Club Hotel (P.O. Box 509, East End, Tortola, British Virgin Islands, tel. 800-313-5662 or 809-495-2477, fax 809-495-2858, e-mail rcg550@aol.com) is a nine-room inn at Josiah's Bay on the north coast, about 20 minutes from Road Town. The beach itself is about a mile from the hotel, but on the grounds you'll find a pool and a restaurant, and the small, clean rooms have fans, small fridges, and telephones. Some rooms have a/c and TV. This is a good deal if you like to be somewhat far from the crowd. **Moderate.**

Turtle Dove Lodge (P.O. Box 11, West End, Tortola, British Virgin Islands; tel. 800-223-4483 or 809-495-4430, fax 809-495-4070) overlooks Long Bay at the west end of the island and features cabins with 12 beds. The place is spartan but tidy, the cabins have kitchens, and the beach is nearby. No credit cards are accepted. **Budget.**

Way Side Inn (P.O. Box 258, Road Town, Tortola, British Virgin Islands; tel. 809-494-3606). This small inn, on a far end of Main Street, has seen better days—some walls are cracked, and the roof leaks in places. The rooms are small, sparsely furnished, and some share baths, which have cold water only. You get a fan in the rooms, a towel, and soap. But the price is right for those who want this sort of adventure in living. No credits cards here. **Budget.**

Camping

Brewer's Bay Campground (P.O. Box 185, Road Town, Tortola, British Virgin Islands, tel. 809-494-3463), located at Brewer's Bay on the north coast, is reached by a winding and steep road that branches off from the main Ridge Road down a steep hill to the coast, and then back up again. The campground has 21 prepared sites, meaning that you get a large tent on a raised wooden platform under a canopy, plus beds, linens, a gas stove, an ice chest, a lantern, rainwater for drinking, and cooking and kitchen utensils. A shared ablution block is used for bathing, toilet, and washing clothes or utensils. Bare sites, meaning that you bring your own tent, are also available. Snacks and drinks are sold, and several local restaurants, including **Nicole's Beach Bar,** are within walking distance. The campground is located on Brewer's Bay Beach, a long and secluded swimming spot. This is a great deal for campers. **Budget.**

EATING AND DRINKING

Local Tortola specialties are seafood and West Indian dishes such as *fungi*—a pasty cornmeal starch—and fresh fruits and vegetables. You won't find much in the way of exotic restaurants on the island, nor will you find fast-food chain restaurants, but you'll be pleased with the quality of the local fare—some is outstanding. Hotel restaurants often accept credit cards, but don't count on it in every case. Smaller restaurants, particularly beach bistros, are not as likely to accept plastic.

Categories are based on average entrée price: **expensive** is $25 or more; **moderate** is $10-25; **inexpensive** is $10 or less.

Road Town

Brandywine Bay Restaurant (tel. 809-495-2301) near Road Town is seaside dining, elegant, continental and Florentine cuisine, dinner only. **Expensive.**

The Butterfly (tel. 809-494-3606), on Main Street, specializes in seafood and West Indian. It's located near the Sunday Morning Well, the spot where the emancipation of slaves was declared in the 19th century. **Inexpensive-Moderate.**

B.V.I. Steak and Chop House (tel. 809-494-5433) is located above the Hotel Castle Maria at Fisher Estate, south of downtown, with views of the harbor. If you like your steaks, ribs, lamb chops, veal chops, and more thick and, in this case, imported, this is the place. They also serve Italian dishes such as eggplant parmigiana, fettuccine alfredo, and baked stuffed shells, and are open daily for breakfast, lunch, and dinner. **Moderate.**

C&F (tel. 809-494-4941), at Purcell Estate (take a taxi; you'll never find it in your rental car) is named for chef/owners Clarence and Florena Emmanuel. If the adage is true that the best food is where the locals eat—and it is—then this is the place you'll want to go for superb West Indian and seafood specialties. It's always crowded, and that's good sign. The decor is sort of cheesy, velvet Elvis mixed with a vague nautical motif (plastic fish and nets hanging about), but the overall effect is kitschy and warm. The specialty here is barbecue, and Clarence does it right inside the restaurant, slapping whole snappers and lobsters on the sputtering grill. Overhead fans and an open patio keep the smoke out of your eyes, but the mildly acrid smell is of an endless fish fry. Try the wahoo or conch with rice and peas on the side, and finish it off with key lime pie. C&F is open for dinner from 6:30 p.m. every day, until 11 p.m. on weekdays and midnight on weekends. You won't be sorry you dined here. **Moderate.**

Capriccio di Mare (tel. 809-494-5369), on Waterfront Drive downtown, serves pastries, sandwiches, pizzas, pastas, Italian desserts, and the best coffees and espressos in town. It's open weekdays 8 a.m. until 9 p.m. and Saturday until 5 p.m. No credit cards. **Inexpensive-Moderate.**

Cell 5 Lounge (tel. 809-494-4629), on Waterfront Drive across from the ferry dock, has a sign out front that states, "Sorry, we do not cater to persons in a hurry." Refreshingly honest, one thinks. Cell 5 obtained its odd and, let's face it, unpleasant name via some legal troubles owner Walter de Castro—now known as Rasuhuru—once had that he believes were unjust (ask him; the story concerns the government's attempts to usurp reclaimed land rights from local people and is full of nefarious skullduggery—definitely worth sipping a couple of beers over). The point is that the name honors the location in the local hoosegow that Rasuhuru once spent some time while fighting the government. Anyway, the place is a bar, but the small restaurant area serves breakfast, lunch, and dinner. The fare is local seafood, saltfish, whelk, souse (spicy pigs' feet), and sandwiches. The bar sits in a great location from which to watch Road Town amble by. Open daily from 7 a.m. until late; no credit cards. **Inexpensive.**

Fort Burt Hotel (tel. 809-494-2587) serves a wide array of West Indian seafood and traditional English dishes. **Moderate-Expensive.**

Oliver's (tel. 809-494-2177), at Wickam's Cay I, serves West Indian specialties and is open daily 8 a.m.-11 p.m. for breakfast, lunch, and dinner and often throws live entertainment into the mix. **Inexpensive-Moderate.**

Pusser's Co. Store and Pub (tel. 809-494-2467), on Waterfront Drive downtown, serves sandwiches, pizzas, burgers, fish and chips, and meat pies. Pusser's gets its name from "purser," the man responsible for the weekly ration of rum handed out to members of the Royal Navy until the 1970s. Rum drinks mixed with Pusser's brand rums are the specialties of the bar. The place is all dark wood and brass, much like the quarters of a ship, and behind the bar and restaurant is the Pusser's Co. Store, which sells nautical items and L.L. Bean-like yachtie clothing. They'll also deliver pizzas to area hotels; call (809) 494-3897. The restaurant is open daily 8:30 a.m.-11 p.m. (no breakfast is served, but you can have a sandwich). **Inexpensive-Moderate.**

Somehow, we would have been happier if **Mr. Fritz's Oriental Restaurant** (tel. 809-494-5592) were called, say, Mr. *Wong's* Oriental Restaurant, but, as it turns out, Fritz is a first name, not a surname. This is basic Chinese food, with takeout standards, but it's the best game in town if you like Asian cuisine. The restaurant is open Monday through Friday for lunch and dinner, weekends for dinner only. **Inexpensive-Moderate.**

Roti Palace, a very tiny palace indeed, is located on Abbott Hill off the south end of Main Street. The fare consists of *rotis,* those flat, unleavened bread disks wrapped around savory meats and vegetables and spiced with curries and other East Indian additions. *Roti* fillings here are often conch, lobster, goat, and okra. The small restaurant seats 12 and is open daily except Sunday 11 a.m.-9 p.m. Cash only. **Inexpensive.**

Spaghetti Junction (tel. 809-494-4880), on Waterfront Drive, serves Northern Italian specialties and is open Monday through Saturday for dinner only. **Inexpensive-Moderate.**

Sunrise Bakery (tel. 809-494-2425) is located in a small alley off Main Street across from the ferry docks. This is a great place to stop for turnovers, muffins, cake squares, rolls, bread, meat patties, drinks, and more. Open Monday through Saturday 6 a.m.-6 p.m. **Inexpensive.**

The creatively named **Tavern in the Town** (tel. 809-494-2790) is a small English tavern located on Main Street in town—oddly enough—and serves meat pies, fish and chips, grilled steaks, and pub fare. The tavern is all brass and dark wood. Open daily except Saturday for lunch and dinner. **Moderate.**

Around the Island

Clem's by the Sea (tel. 809-495-4350), at Carrot Bay in West End, serves local dishes and seafood. **Inexpensive-Moderate.**

Jolly Roger Inn (tel. 809-495-4559) serves up seafood, barbecue, and pastas at the small harborside restaurant and hotel. Expect live music on Friday and Saturday nights. **Moderate.**

Mrs. Scatcliffe's Bar and Restaurant (tel. 809-495-4556) is another one of those restaurants where the adage "If locals eat here, you should, too" rings true. This popular West Indian restaurant at Carrot Bay is popular and often crowded on weekends—make reservations. The cuisine is West Indian, as local as it gets, with souse, conch, johnnycakes, barbecue, and local vegetable creations as specialties. Mrs. Scatcliffe serves dinner daily and lunch on weekdays. Dinner is from 7-8:30 p.m. **Inexpensive-Moderate.**

Sebastian's on the Beach (tel. 809-495-4212), at Little Apple Bay, serves seafood seaside and West Indian and continental fare and is open daily. **Moderate.**

Skyworld (tel. 809-494-3567) is one of the island's more unique restaurants. Located 1,300 feet (about 400 meters) in the hills off the Ridge Road, the location provides panoramic views of the Tortola highlands, Brewer's Bay, and neighboring islands. You can even see St. Croix on a clear day. A small observatory is set up here, and you can drop a quarter into a telescope for a better view. The restaurant serves basic West Indian and international fare, but the views are the attraction. Don't miss sunset from here. You'll also find a small gift shop in the back. Open daily from 10 a.m., it serves dinner from 6:30 p.m. (reservations requested). Credit cards are allowed for bills exceeding $35. **Moderate.**

Struggling Man's Place (tel. 809-494-4163) is just south of town, at Sea Cow's Bay, and serves authentic West Indian specialties. **Inexpensive.**

The Sugar Mill (tel. 809-495-4335), at Apple Bay, is one of the island's best, serving an eclectic range of creative West Indian and continental dishes. The setting is a 17th-century stone building once used as a rum distillery. **Moderate-Expensive.**

At Cane Garden Bay, a series of restaurants and beach bars are worth a stop. **Myett's** (tel. 809-495-9543), **Stanley's** (tel. 809-495-9424), and **Netty's Diner** (tel. 809-495-4633) all serve seafood and West Indian specialties and are great places to hang out at the beach and have a drink and a snack, or maybe catch the sunset and stay for dinner. Live music and weekend barbecue buffets are the norm. **Moderate.**

NIGHTLIFE

Tortola is, by and large, a quiet place, but you will find local bands and entertainment, particularly on weekends, often in hotels or restaurants. Nightclubs and discos, sui generis, are rare. Your best bet to try to tap into local goings-on is to pick up a copy of a newspaper or grab a copy of *Limin' Times,* a weekly entertainment guide.

Here's a sample of local entertainment options: **Clem's by the Sea** (tel. 809-4954350), at Carrot Bay, features Clem himself on steel pan with his band the Starlights on Saturday and Monday during his big barbecue buffet. **Myett's** (tel. 809-495-9543), in Cane Garden Bay, often features live bands on weekends during *its* barbecue buffets. **Mrs. Scatcliffe's** (tel. 809-495-4556), the West Indian restaurant at Carrot Bay, features *fungi* and scratch bands most evenings after dinner. **Treasure Isle Hotel** (tel. 809-494-2501), in Road Town, offers steel pan music by the Shooting Stars during *its* Saturday-night barbecue blowout. **Quito's Gazebo** (tel. 809-495-4837), at Cane Garden Bay, features local recording artists Quito Rymer and the Edge five nights a week. **Sebastian's by the Sea** (tel. 809-495-4212), by the sea at Apple Bay, has steel pan and *fungi* bands on weekends. **The Last Resort** (tel. 809-495-2520), a bar and restaurant on small Bellamy Cay in Trellis Bay, features cabaret performances by the owner, as well as local bands, nightly.

Any mention of nightlife on Tortola must include the name of the infamous bar owner, raconteur, philosopher, and very large man Bomba. Bomba owns the bar **Bomba's Surfside Shack** (tel. 809-495-4148), on Cappoon's

Bay, just down the road from Sebastian's by the Sea at Apple Bay. The shack is truly a shack, made from flotsam and jetsam that has washed up from the sea just feet from the back of the ramshackle but wholly interesting building. You see hubcaps, broken wood, bicycle parts, flags, just about everything (including the kitchen sink) tacked up on walls around the bar and barbecue grill. At first glance, the place looks like a colorful junkyard office. You'll also see bras, panties, wrapped condoms, and other items hanging about—testament to some salacious good times at Bomba's. Bomba encourages people to write messages on the walls—some of these are not printable in family travel guides. Bomba himself has contributed "Bomba Shack, where white girls' legs get red hot," and "Bomba created all things but one: God created Bomba." I like a man with a healthy ego. Bomba's is open every day and has special entreaties: Monday is Lover's Night, where single women drink $1 beers; Wednesday is a barbecue buffet ("all you can eat on one plate") of ribs or chicken for $7; Sunday is also barbecue fare from 3 p.m.; and live music is offered on Monday, Wednesday, and Friday.

As if that weren't enough, Bomba offers—and this is what he's famous for, aside from his distinct take on life—his monthly Full Moon Party. Check the astrology charts for the exact date. The Full Moon party is a huge blast, with bands, food, drinks, and, at midnight, Bomba's notorious "magic tea." Bomba's tea—make no mistake about this—is hallucinogenic, made from local mushrooms of the psilocybin variety. It is, according to Bomba, not illegal to possess the mushrooms, only to sell them. So, cleverly, Bomba sells souvenir cups to imbibers for $5 and offers the tea for free. He claims the tea isn't very strong. No matter. The legality is of little consequence; police are on hand to provide security for the party and never seem to mind.

SHOPPING

The British Virgin Islands offer no real duty-free shopping, but you'll see some fun things to buy and take home, particularly in the way of local crafts and art. Remember, shops and most other businesses are open Monday through Saturday from 9 a.m.-5 p.m. and are closed on Sunday. Your best bets for shopping are **Main Street** in Road Town and **Soper's Hole,** in West End; both offer dozens of small crafts and souvenirs shops.

On Main Street, stop at **Sunny Caribbee Spice Company** (tel. 809-494-2178) for herbs, spices, soaps, cosmetics, and local art and crafts. **Samarkind** sells local jewelry. **Kaunda's Kysy Tropix** (tel. 809-494-6737) sells VCRs, stereos, cameras, and electronic equipment. **Little Denmark** (tel. 809-494-2455), one of the town's more interesting shops, carries

Tortola's famous Bomba's Surfside Shack, Carrot Bay

souvenirs, fishing equipment, jewelry, knicks and knacks, and much more. Check out its humidor for fine cigars, including Havanas. **Pusser's Company Store** (tel. 809-495-4599) sells yachtie, yuppie sorts of clothing as well as colognes, watches, and some books. Your best bet for books and magazines in town is **Esme's Shop** (tel. 809-494-3961), at Sir Olva George's Plaza between Waterfront Drive and Main Street. Here you'll find local newspapers and magazines as well as the *New York Times* ($4) and other international papers.

For gourmet meats, wines, caviar, pastries, and cheeses, among other items, stop at **Fort Wines Gourmet** (tel. 809-494-3036), on Main. For regular groceries and bakery items, your best bet is **Rite Way** (tel. 809-494-2263), at Wickam's Cay II, or **Bobby's** (tel. 809-494-2189), at Wickam's Cay I. Next door to Bobby's is **Bolo's Department Store** (tel. 809-494-2867), where you can get, well, things you get in department stores, including film, sandals, and that extra luggage you'll need to carry everything home.

Maya'a Ethnic Vision (tel. 809-495-5711), at Wickam's Cay I, sells Afrocentric and international paintings, sculpture, pottery, and gift items from Thailand, Australia, and all around the Caribbean.

For a pure tourist experience, visit a small market called **Crafts Alive,** near the cruise ship pier at Wickam's Cay I. Here you'll find T-shirts, bags, hats, and all manner of craft items.

At colorful **Soper's Hole,** at West End, you'll find a dozen or so souvenir, clothing, and craft shops.

GETTING AROUND

Car Rentals

Driving on Tortola is a piece of johnnycake, in a manner of speaking. The roads are well marked, and you'll find few traffic jams, no traffic lights, and breathtaking views from the hills of neighboring islands floating in the sea. You'll need to produce your valid license to purchase a temporary British Virgin Islands driving license ($10), which you obtain through the rental company. Car rental rates start at $35 per day. On Tortola, most companies are located in Road Town. Try:

Alphonso Car Rentals (tel. 809-494-3137)

Avis (tel. 809-494-3322)

Budget (tel. 809-494-2531)

Caribbean Car Rental (tel. 809-494-2595)

Del's Jeep and Car Rental (tel. 809-495-9356)

Denzil Clyne Jeep and Car Rental (Cane Garden Bay, tel. 809-495-4900)

Hertz (West End, tel. 809-495-4405)

Honey Bee Auto Rental (tel. 809-494-3667)

International Car Rentals (tel. 809-494-2516)

National (tel. 809-494-3197)

Those with a yen for biking—and it would have to be a strong yen to want to navigate the hills of Tortola—can call **Last Stop Sports** (tel. 809-494-0564, fax 809-494-0593), at Nanny Cay, near Road Town, or **Boardsailing BVI** (tel. 809-495-2447), at Nanny Cay or Trellis Bay. Bike rentals start at $20 per day ($120 per week) and include helmets.

Motor scooters start at about $30 per day and are found in Road Town at **DJ's Scooter Rentals** (tel. 809-494-5071).

Remember, driving is on the left (British style) and cars are left-hand-drive (U.S. style), so take care and practice a bit before you take the car on the road.

Taxis

You'll find taxis on Tortola at the airport and at the ferry docks in Road Town and West End, as well as at a stand on Wickam's Cay I. Taxi rates are set by the government, and virtually all will be able to offer island tours as well as simple point-to-point transportation. Fares are based on three passengers, and most times you will not be the sole person in the taxi—particularly for a long trip. If you do hire the taxi for yourself, you'll pay the full fare. For example, a taxi from Road Town to West End is $5 each for three people, but if you want to ride alone, you'll pay the $15. Sample fares per person in shared taxis: from Road Town to Wickam's Cay II, $2; from Road Town to Brewer's Bay, Cane Garden Bay, West End, or Carrot Bay, $5; from Beef Island Airport to Road Town, $5.

On Tortola, island tours start at $45 for one to three people for a three-hour tour.

If you need to call a taxi, let your hotel recommend one or call **B.V.I. Taxi Association** (tel. 809-494-2322 or 494-3942), **Style's Taxi Service** (tel. 809-494-2260), or **Turtle Dove Taxi Service** (tel. 809-494-6274 or 494-4301)

Buses
Buses on Tortola are inexpensive—fares are no more than $3—but the schedules not always discernible. Nevertheless, **Scato's Bus Service** (tel. 809-494-2365), in Road Town, is the one to call. Scato's offers island tours as well.

MISCELLANEOUS

Remember that the currency of the British Virgin Islands is the U.S. dollar. U.S. dollar traveler's checks are widely accepted, as is cash. Credit cards are accepted by many businesses, but not all, particularly smaller hotels, guesthouses, and restaurants. Currency is best changed at banks, which are located in Road Town and include **Barclays** (tel. 809-494-2171), among others. Bank hours may vary but are generally Monday through Thursday 8 a.m.-4:30 p.m. and

Friday until 5:30 p.m. You'll find outside ATMs at **Banco Popular** (tel. 809-494-2117), next to the customs office on Main Street in Road Town and at **Chase Manhattan Bank** (tel. 809-494-2662), at Wickam's Cay I.

Cable and Wireless is available to make phone calls and to send faxes, telexes, and cables. Hours are weekdays 7 a.m. -7 p.m., Saturday 7 a.m. -4 p.m., and Sunday 9 a.m. -2 p.m.

INFORMATION DIRECTORY

Police, Fire, Ambulance, tel. 999

Peebles Hospital, tel. (809) 494-3497

J.R. O'Neal Drugstore, tel. (809) 494-2292

Chief Immigration Officer, tel. (809) 494-3701

National Parks Trust, tel. (809) 494-3904

British Virgin Islands Tourist Board, P.O. Box 134, Road Town, Tortola, British Virgin Islands; tel. (809) 494-3134 or 494-3489, fax (809) 494-3866

British Virgin Islands Hotel and Commerce Association, P.O. Box 376, Road Town, Tortola, British Virgin Islands; tel. (809) 494-3514

VIRGIN GORDA

Virgin Gorda is strung out over seven miles (11 km) from east to west, comprising a hilly middle section, a flatter east end, and a populated southwest end. The island's main center, **The Valley,** which incorporates the island's original center of **Spanish Town,** is in the southwest. Virgin Gorda was once a major commercial center but today is better known as an excellent anchorage for yachts and for its secluded beaches. A road connects the west end of the island with **North Sound,** a large bay separating the east end of the island with the offshore islets of **Mosquito Island, Prickly Pear Island, Necker Island,** and **Eustatia Island.** Prickly Pear Island has been declared a protected national park.

Transport to Virgin Gorda is by ferry (see the appendix "Ferry Schedule") or by shuttle flight from Tortola. The airstrip is located in The Valley.

SIGHTS

Virgin Gorda isn't an island chockablock with historical sites, botanical gardens, zoos, or attractions. It is, mostly, a very small, very quiet, and very unpretentious place to kick back, swim a little, do some diving or snorkeling, and eat too much. After all, Virgin Gorda is an island that didn't get a telephone system until 1968 and didn't get electricity until 1971. It isn't even a place where you'd want to hire a taxi to take a tour of the island. You can rent a car and see pretty much all there is to see in a day or two. In fact, if you do rent a car and tour the island, you'll find that you can drive from one end to the other in about a half-hour, tops. And, if you keep the car for the day, you'll probably pass several people more than once.

The island's center and capital is **The Valley,** which is mainly a few roads and small settlements situated around the **Virgin Gorda Yacht Harbor.** The Yacht Harbor complex is where you'll find shops, eateries, supermarkets, banks, and the tourism offices (tel. 809-495-5181). The offices, to the right of the building from the parking lot, are open Monday through Friday 8:30 a.m.-4:30 p.m.; they'll be able to help you with brochures, maps, and questions you have about the island.

The road that passes in front of the Yacht Harbor is one of the town's main roads—south leads to Spanish Town (a section of The Valley), which sports a post office and some restaurants, and then on to The Baths, which are really part of The Valley; north leads out of town first past a small park next to the Yacht Harbor (you might see some sheep grazing in the park), then past the ferry docks, then past Little Dix Bay and on to Gorda Peak and North Sound.

This road wasn't constructed until 1969 and wasn't paved until 1980. The airstrip is located to the east of the Yacht Harbor. And that's just about it for The Valley.

Just south of the Yacht Harbor in The Valley is **Little Fort National Park,** once the site of a Spanish fort. The fort is in ruins, and you can see part of the old Powder House. The park is now a 36-acre wildlife sanctuary. On the eastern shore of the western tip of the island is **Copper Mine Point,** reached by a dirt road at the south end of The Valley. You'll know you're on the right track if you pass the **Mine Shaft Café and Pub** (which also has a miniature golf course). The mine was worked by Cornish miners from 1838 to 1867 and probably by Spanish miners 300 years before that. Remains of stone buildings, a cistern, and green-tinged mineshafts and rocks can be seen looming out over the thundering surf.

One of Virgin Gorda's most popular attractions, and most photographed places, is **The**

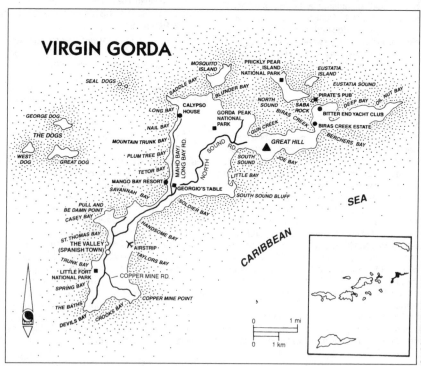

*The Baths,
Virgin Gorda*

Baths. The Baths, at the south end of the island, are a series of giant (meaning really big) boulders that sit at the water's edge creating caves, caverns, sunlit shafts, and small tidal pools within. The geological origins of the rocks and how they ended up here are unclear. The name allegedly came from the practice of bringing newly arrived slaves here—slaves who'd managed to survive the treacherous journeys from Africa and other islands—to clean them up before offering them for sale. The Baths' immense rocks are so tightly packed and formidable that escape from the area was virtually impossible.

Visitors can park at the entrance, where they'll find **The Top of The Baths** restaurant (with a swimming pool) and several small snack bars and gift shops. Park and follow the signs to The Baths (about 350 yards down). Another path leads to the far side of The Baths, a small bay and beach called **Devils Bay** (600 yards). At the bottom of The Baths path, you'll find picnic tables, T-shirt vendors, and the small **Poor Man's Bar,** selling drinks, hot dogs, and snacks. You can wend your way through The Baths to Devils Bay—you'll find ropes and other devices to help you clamber over some of the more slippery bits. Wear a bathing suit for this small hike—some of the cave pools, where you'll see small tropical fish and coral, are at least waist deep.

Gorda Peak National Park is located in the central section of Virgin Gorda and encompasses 265 acres, all of the island's land starting 1,000 feet (300 meters) above sea level. The peak, at 1,359 feet (408 meters), is the island's highest point, and the hike to the top is a wonderful way to spend a morning. To get to the paths that lead to the peak, drive up the main road from The Valley toward Gun Greek. After a few minutes' drive from town, you'll see two paths marked with Gorda Peak National Park signs pointing the way up to the peak. The first path is the longer hike, about a 45-minute trek up the side of the mountain. The second path, about a mile farther down the road, is moderately difficult—it's about 800 yards (800 meters) to the summit, a 15-minute hike at an easy pace. You'll pass through heavy bush and forest with mahogany and semi-rainforest flora. At the top of the path are three picnic tables and a port-a-potty, and another five minutes' walk will bring you to a small observation platform (look for the sign pointing the way). Climb up and you'll be treated to a view unique on the island. You'll be able to see all the Virgin Islands, including St. Thomas and St. Croix, and will no longer question, if you ever did, your decision to vacation here. Take a look to the south and west of the island and you'll see a string of small cays, including **Fallen Jerusalem,** just by The Baths, **Ginger Island, Cooper Island, Dog Island, Salt Island, Peter Island,** and **Norman Island.** Several of the islands are available for mooring and are frequently visited by nesting sea birds. Norman Island, accessible by boat only, is thought to be the inspiration for Robert Louis

Stevenson's *Treasure Island.* Fallen Jerusalem and Dog Island are protected by National Park Trust regulations. Others are frequented by day-trippers looking for isolated beaches and quiet repose. Cooper Island, Peter Island, and Mosquito Island to the north are privately owned and host resorts and hotels.

At the town of **North Sound,** where the road from The Valley sort of ends, you'll find a few small shops, a post office, and a police station. Nearby is **Gun Creek,** where you'll find a small slip from which transport ferries depart to Biras Creek, Bitter End, Necker Island, and Drake's Anchorage (all private resorts or islands with resorts, with complimentary transport for guests). Here you'll find some taxis hanging about, a convenience store, the **Last Stop Bar,** and not much else.

RECREATION

Water Sports

In general, head to the island's marinas for a full range of water sports, boat charters, boat rentals, and other aquatic adventure information. The marinas at **Yacht Harbor** (tel. 809-495-5500 or 495-5500, fax 809-495-5706), **Leverick Bay** (tel. 809-495-7365 or 495-7421, fax 809-495-7367) and **Bitter End** (tel. 800-872-2392 or tel. and fax 809-495-9636) can organize dinghy rentals (about $65 per day), whaler rentals (about $100-150 per day), sailboards (about $25 for two hours), kayaks (about $15 per hour), water-skiing (about $75 per hour), Sunfish (about $20 per hour), and snorkel gear (about $5 per day).

Diving

Dive B.V.I. Ltd. (P.O. Box 1040, Virgin Gorda, British Virgin Islands, tel. 809-495-5513, fax 809-495-5347, U.S. tel. 800-848-7078) has outlets at Virgin Gorda Yacht Harbor, Leverick Bay, and Peter Island. **Kilbride's Underwater Tours** (P.O. Box 40, Bitter End, Virgin Gorda, British Virgin Islands, tel. 809-495-9638, fax 809-495-9639) is located at Bitter End, near Biras Creek.

Boating

For day cruises to neighboring islands, including Anegada, and short charters, contact **Euphoric Cruises** (tel. 809-495-5542, fax 809-495-5818),

or, at Bitter End (tel. 800-872-2392 or 809-495-9636), the **Prince of Wales** and the **Paranda.** For renting boats, you can also contact, in addition to the marinas mentioned above, **Speedy's** (tel. 809-495-5240, fax 809-495-5755), one of the ferry services of the British Virgin Islands (it also rents cars).

Fishing

The **Classic** (Biras Creek, Virgin Gorda, tel. 809-494-3555) costs $650 per day, $450 per half-day. As well, call **Island Boyz Charters** (tel. 809-495-5511) and **Mahogany Watersports & Tackle** (tel. 809-495-5070, fax 809-495-4080), across the street from the Yacht Harbor, for charter fishing and boating.

Family Activities

Rent a small boat or dinghy for the day, make sure it has life jackets, and buzz around the islets and small cays of North Sound, stopping at beaches and several small beach pubs for refreshments and a splash in the water.

If the kids have long enough legs to make it over some big roots and rocks, take a walk up to **Gorda Peak** at Gorda Peak National Park. The lower path is relatively short, about 800 yards (800 meters), and you find plenty to see and explore on the mountaintop. Bring a picnic lunch.

BEACHES

The British Virgin Islands' most well known beach is **The Baths,** south of The Valley, a natural formation of colossal boulders that form pools, caves, and oddly lit, shimmering grottos. Walking trails—slogging trails, actually—ramble through the boulders and pools. This is an enormously popular attraction and is likely to be swamped with visitors during cruise-ship stopovers, or, actually, most of the time. Still, The Baths are unlike most beaches you've seen. Plan to go early in the morning or later in the evening to avoid the crowds. At the south end of The Baths is small **Devils Bay,** which you can reach via a path from The Baths' parking area or a path near the rock formation. North of The Baths, just around the corner, is a small snorkeling beach called **Spring Bay,** and next to that is **The Crawl,** which is good for snorkeling. Both these beaches, just south of The Valley, can also be reached by road. **Trunk Bay,** a series of secluded beaches north of Spring Bay, is accessible by boat or by hike from Spring Bay. **Savannah Bay,** on the narrow isthmus between the west and central sections of the island north of The Valley, is wide and expansive and one of the island's nicer beaches. There are no facilities here, and entrance to the beach is littered with other people's garbage, but once you hit the water you'll forget about it. Near Savannah Bay you'll see a small dirt road that bears to the left (west). Along this road are several small hotels and villas and some isolated, clean beaches at **Pond Bay, Mountain Trunk Bay** and **Long Bay.** You'll have to park your car wherever it seems convenient and walk down to some of the bays, as the roads can be steep, rocky, and treacherous for cars.

You'll also find beaches at **Bitter End, Biras Creek** (for guests), and on several of the small islands in North Sound. **Prickly Pear Island,** for example, has a small beach bar at **Vixen Point.** In order to get to Bitter End, Prickly Pear, or any of the smaller islands of the group, your best bet is to rent a small boat or dinghy at one of the marinas and putter around to the islands. Leverick Bay's water sports center rents four-person dinghies for $65 per day, less for weekly rentals. If you can make it out to Bitter End, the marina there has numerous rental opportunities.

In total, Virgin Gorda has nearly 20 beaches, many secluded, some easily accessed aboard shuttle boats.

ACCOMMODATIONS

Accommodations on Virgin Gorda are somewhat limited, if only because the island itself is small and sees little in the way of visitors who are not on their own yachts. Still, you'll find a full range of resorts, hotels, guesthouses, apartments, and villas.

Remember, room rates are reduced by as much as 40% during the summer season, and are often bargained out through packages and wholesale room discounters. A government hotel occupancy tax of seven percent is charged on accommodations, and often a 15% service charge is added to the bill. Occasionally, an energy surcharge is also added. Most, but not all, hotels accept major credit cards. Keep in mind that some properties require a minimum three-night stay, extra persons in the rooms are often charged $10-30 apiece (although, as a rule, children are allowed in free), and may require a deposit of as much as 50% on the room.

The accommodations listed below are categorized based on the average room rate (some hotels offer a wide range of rooms, from budget to luxury), double occupancy, European plan (no meals), per night, during the 15 December-through-15 April high season, excluding the eight percent room tax. A designation of **luxury** indicates that rooms run $200 or more; **expensive** rooms are $140-200; **moderate** indicates a range of $80-140; and **budget** rooms cost $80 or less.

Villas

The British Virgin Islands Tourist Board will assist in making contacts and reservations with dozens of property management companies throughout the island. Sometimes, however, it's better to consult villa agencies on the island itself. One of the largest Virgin Gorda agencies is **Virgin Gorda Villa Rentals, Ltd.** (P.O. Box 63, The Valley, Virgin Gorda, British Virgin Islands; U.S. tel. 800-848-7081, Canada tel. 800-463-9396, local tel. 809 495-5201, fax 809-495-7367). This agency deals directly with more than 25 villas and condo units scattered around the island. Rentals start at about $1,100 per week in the winter for a one-bedroom villa and go as high as $5,000 per week for a four-bedroom villa in the high season—plus 19% tax and service charge. Other contacts: **Diamond Beach Villas** (P.O. Box 69, Virgin Gorda, British Virgin Islands; U.S. tel. 800-871-3551, Canada tel. 800-487-1839, local tel. 809-495-5452, fax 809-495-5875), located at Mountain Trunk Bay; **Guavaberry Spring Bay Vacation Homes** (P.O. Box 20, Virgin Gorda, British Virgin Islands; tel. 809-49495-5227, fax 809-495-5283), at The Baths; **Leverick Bay Resort and Marina** (P.O. Box 63, Virgin Gorda, British Virgin Islands; U.S. tel. 800-848-7081, Canada tel. 800-463-9396, local tel. 809-495-7421, fax 809-495-7367), at Leverick Bay; **Property Management Plus** (P.O. Box 1072, Virgin Gorda, British Virgin Islands; tel. 809-495-5867); and **Kanaka Property Management** (P.O. Box 25, Virgin Gorda,

British Virgin Islands; tel. 809-495-5201). Cost ranges $600-2,400 per week during the high season.

Hotels and Resorts

Biras Creek Estate (P.O. Box 54, Virgin Gorda, British Virgin Islands; tel. 800-608-9661 or 800-223-1108 or 809-494-3555, fax 809-494-3557) is deeply luxurious, one of the top resorts on the island, and without a doubt the place you'll want to come if you've had it with snow drifts, stalled cars, and obstreperous bosses whose idea of a world-class vacation is a visit to the Duckpin Bowling Hall of Fame. The resort, which came under new management in 1996, has been refurbished to the point of shining and now sports new landscaping, an activities center with a conference room, a library, and a small museum. Biras Creek sits on 140 acres and comprises bungalow-type suites and villas—all with bright sitting rooms, separate bedrooms, phones, minibars, a/c, and overhead fans. You won't need the a/c—most face the ocean and are cooled by a constant ocean breeze. Each guest is provided a bicycle in order to get around the sprawling complex, which has its own private beach and beach bar at Deep Bay (the noon barbecues there include exotic cheeses, caviar, and champagne), tennis courts, pool, nature paths with labeled flora, and restaurant. The restaurant, in the main building on a hill with views to the ocean and surrounding islands, serves West Indian and seafood specialties and is one of the finest in the British Virgin Islands. Water sports, including small Boston Whaler boats for trips to neighboring islands and nearby Bitter End, as well as Sunfish, kayaks, windsurfers, and snorkeling equipment, are complimentary for guests. Biras also maintains several yachts and powerboats for charters or fishing excursions. The resort is located in North Sound and can be reached by boat only, which is arranged when you make your reservation. This is a large but intimate resort, with accommodations for only 64 people, providing plenty of room for individual attention and privacy. Boaters can use the small marina and some facilities at Biras for a fee. **Luxury.**

Bitter End Yacht Club (P.O. Box 46, Virgin Gorda, British Virgin Islands; tel. 809-494-2746, U.S. tel. 312-944-5855), another retreat reached by boat only, is also on North Sound. It has 95 rooms, cottages, and villas. The marina here is large, and many of the services are geared toward yacht guests. You'll find a restaurant, beach, shops, and water sports. The complex is sort of a village unto itself, and the atmosphere is all about boats and yachts, but you'll have fun using it as a base to explore the North Sound islands and neighboring Biras Creek resort. **Luxury.**

Leverick Bay Resort (P.O. Box 63, Virgin Gorda, British Virgin Islands; U.S. tel. 800-463-848-7081, Canada tel. 800-463-9396, local tel. 809-495-7421, fax 809-495-7367) is located on Leverick Bay at North Sound. The resort complex features a marina with full water sports, water taxis to Mosquito Island, shops including a Pusser's Company Store, restaurants including a Pusser's, a spa, a pool, and more. You'll even find a small beach fronting the marina. The hotel offers accommodations in 16 modern guest rooms, four two-bedroom condos, and about 30 villas. Expect fully equipped kitchens in the condos and villas and a/c, fridges, and phones in all units. You'll have several different plans to choose from. **Moderate.**

Little Dix Bay Hotel (P.O. Box 70, Virgin Gorda, British Virgin Islands; tel. 800-928-3000 or 809-495-5555, fax 809-495-5661), next to the Yacht Harbor in The Valley, is one of the island's original hotels. Laurance Rockefeller, scion of the one-and-only Rockefellers, who also bought up much of St. John and donated it to the U.S. National Park Service, fell in love with Virgin Gorda in the 1950s and completed Little Dix Bay in 1964. In the process, he also built the Yacht Harbor, which is still managed by the hotel, and the island's airstrip. Today, the grand resort is managed by the Rosewood Company and still exudes old-style elegance. It sprawls over many acres of sculpted land, with a half-mile beach at the door of its 98 rooms—all in villas. The rooms are large, with sitting areas, oversize beds, and rattan-covered closets. This is the kind of elegance it offers: not only do you get a complimentary bottle of rum upon checking in, and not only does your room have everything you'd want including a bathrobe, and not only does a maid come around for turn-down service in the evening, but they've even got a guy whose job it is to deliver ice to the villas. You'll also find a bar, a fine-dining restaurant under a wood canopy, complimentary coffee and scones in the morning, a beach bar, shops, and seven tennis courts on the grounds. **Luxury.**

Mango Bay Resort (P.O. Box 1062, Virgin Gorda, British Virgin Islands; tel. 809-495-5672, fax 809-495-5674) is located a bit more than two miles (under three km) from town, on the Mahoe Bay turnoff. The smallish resort features villas lined along the beachfront, all with kitchens, large fridges, barbecue grills, and one or two bedrooms. The beach here, Mahoe Bay, is wide and long, one of the island's better spots. Also on the lush grounds is **Georgio's Table,** an authentic Italian seaside bistro and one of the island's best ethnic meals. **Expensive-Luxury.**

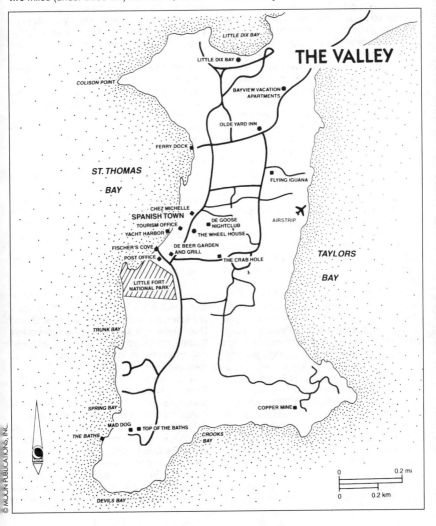

© MOON PUBLICATIONS, INC.

Small Inns and Guesthouses

Bayview Vacation Apartments (P.O. Box 1018, Virgin Gorda, British Virgin Islands; tel. 809-495-5329) are located at the north end of The Valley. Each clean apartment has two bedrooms, two baths, a sitting area, and a full kitchen. The views aren't grand, and you won't find much to do at the apartments, but this is a good place to base yourself, and you can't beat the rates. **Budget.**

Calypso House (P.O. Box 37, Virgin Gorda, British Virgin Islands; tel. 809-495-5367), located at the far end of the Mahoe Bay/Long Bay road, is a small guesthouse and villa, a good deal for those who really want to get out of town—far out (relatively speaking, since we are speaking about Virgin Gorda). The four-room cottage, which can also be rented whole as a villa, sits on the grounds of an old sugar mill at the end of the road above Mountain Trunk Bay. You can still see the old stone mill and slaves' quarters ruins. The building is white with a Spanish tiled roof, and you'll find a small pool in front of the rooms. Some of the rooms have twin beds, all have small kitchens, fridges, and stoves. The ride to town from here is about 30 minutes, and a taxi will be $20 one-way. The beach below is a short hike down the hill. **Budget.**

Olde Yard Inn (P.O. Box 26, Virgin Gorda, British Virgin Islands; tel. 800-653-9273 800-633-7411 or 809-495-5544, fax 809-495-5986), a small, 14-room hotel, sits on the north side of The Valley. The rooms are large with cedar walls and rattan furniture, and all have overhead fans. You'll find a pool, a large library with a piano, a fitness center, and a restaurant on the grounds. This hotel is one of the island's oldest; it opened in 1969 as the Dolphin Hotel, just a few years after the opening of Little Dix Bay. The restaurant is one of the island's more popular eating spots and serves West Indian, French, and continental cuisine. Even if you don't stay here, drop in for lunch or dinner. **Expensive.**

The Wheel House (P.O. Box 66, Virgin Gorda, British Virgin Islands; tel. 809-495-5230, U.S. tel 800-621-1270), formerly the Ocean View Hotel, is located across the street from the Virgin Gorda Yacht Harbor in The Valley. The simple hotel has 12 rooms decorated in bright floral patterns and is clean and comfortable, if not fancy. Rooms have TVs, private baths, a/c, and phones. The restaurant downstairs is pretty good, specializing in West Indian fare and seafood, and the hotel hosts barbecues twice a week. **Moderate.**

EATING AND DRINKING

You won't find a wide selection of restaurants on Virgin Gorda, but you also won't want for new and interesting places to eat if your stay is a week or so. You'll find Italian, French, continental, and West Indian cuisine heavy on stews, *fungi*—a pasty cornmeal starch—and fresh fruits and vegetables. Hotel restaurants often accept credit cards, but don't count on it in every case. Smaller restaurants, particularly beach bistros, are not as likely to accept credit cards. Price categories are based on the cost of an average entrée: **expensive** is $25 or more; **moderate** is $10-25; **inexpensive** is $10 or less.

The Valley

The **Olde Yard Inn** (tel. 809-495-5544) is large on old country charm, romanticism, and French continental cuisine. **Expensive.** At the Virgin Islands Yacht Harbor, the **The Bath and Turtle** (tel. 809-495-5239) is a relaxed and informal pub with light fare, burgers, sandwiches, and more. The pub is full of yachties talking about their boats, which, hey, may be a good thing. **Moderate.**

Chez Michelle (tel. 809-495-5510), on the main road near the Yacht Harbor, serves French and continental food, for dinner only, and is a fine dining experience. **Moderate.** Next door to Chez Michelle is a small lunch counter called **Dixie's,** where you can get great baskets of fried chicken, sandwiches, ice cream, and drinks. **Inexpensive.**

Just south of the Yacht Harbor, stop in at **De Beer Garden and Grill** for drinks and barbecues. Next door is **Friendly Andy's Ice Cream Parlor,** for those in need of the sweet stuff.

The Crab Hole (tel. 809-495-5307), a small bar on a side street (of which there are about three), features light West Indian savories and live entertainment. **Inexpensive.** Also in The Valley's south side is **Fischer's Cove** (tel. 809-495-5328), sort of a basic restaurant with standard continental cuisine and more. Across the street from the Yacht Harbor is **De Goose Nightclub** (tel. 809-495-5641), which serves island fare, including *souse* (spicy pigs' feet), johnnycakes, rotis, fish and chips, and lighter fare such as burgers and dogs. **Inexpensive-Moderate.**

Follow the signs past the police station to the airport and you'll find the **Flying Iguana** (tel. 809-495-5277). This small restaurant, decorated in the light pastels common to the West Indies, serves breakfast, lunch, and dinner daily, brunch on Sunday, and special barbecues on Monday. This is the place for local West Indian cuisine, and you'll find yourself intrigued by the small art gallery here, which features selections of folk art from the Caribbean and Africa. The views are of the airport and open Atlantic. **Moderate.**

Down at The Baths, stop in at **Top of the Baths** restaurant for shopping and refreshments, as well as a dip in the pool. **Moderate.** Behind Top of the Baths is a small bar called **Mad Dog,** which features as a motif T-shirts and mugs and signs from pubs named Mad Dog worldwide. One would have never realized that the name was so popular. The fare is simple and light, and the beers are cold. **Moderate.**

North of The Valley
Up the road and to the left, at Mango Bay Resort, is **Georgio's Table** (tel. 809-495-5684), an Italian alfresco bistro on the ocean serving breakfast, lunch, and dinner. This is a great place to watch the sunset and then stretch the evening into dinner and drinks by the piano bar. **Moderate.** At Leverick Bay, **Pusser's** (tel. 809-495-7369) serves burgers, pizzas, shepherd pies, and famous Pusser's Rum drinks.

Non-guests are allowed to come on up and dine at **Biras Creek** (tel. 809-494-3555), and you won't be sorry you did. Call ahead for reservations and transport arrangements. **Expensive.**

Out in North Sound—and you'll need a dinghy for this—is a small bar located on a very small cay called **Saba Rock.** The bar is easily recognized by the succinct Food and Drink signs in front, but it's actually named **Pirate's Pub.** This is a fun place to stop for a drink as you're buzzing around the sound—just pull in in your small boat, step up, and you're at the bar, just like that. **Inexpensive.**

NIGHTLIFE

Virgin Gorda's nightlife would make a Buddhist monk happy; it can best be described as serene. Some hotels have live bands on weekends, but the common thing to do is find a small pub somewhere and watch the sun set. Then go to bed. If you want to push the envelope, drop in at **Andy Chateau,** a seaside bar and disco with pool tables down by the post office in Spanish Town, in the southern part of The Valley. **De Goose Nightclub** (tel. 809-495-5641), across the street from the Yacht Harbor, has canned and live music, dancing, and dinner nightly.

SHOPPING

Two words: Yacht Harbor. Here, you'll find a couple of gift shops, a supermarket with a newspaper and magazine rack, a restaurant, and more. Other than that, shopping experiences on Virgin Gorda are limited to hotel gift shops.

GETTING AROUND

Virgin Gorda has no organized bus system, and taxis are a good way to get around. You'll pay anything from $3 (from The Valley to The Baths or Spring Bay) to $20 (private taxi from The Valley to Leverick Bay). Most taxi fares hover around $5 if you share with two or more persons. Taxis on Virgin Gorda tend to be of the safari-jitney type—open-air pickup trucks with benches and canopies set up in the back. Taxis are found at the Yacht Harbor parking lot, at the ferry docks, and at the Gun Creek launch slip. If you're staying in a hotel, a taxi service may be affiliated, but that's not always the case. Call **Mahogany Taxi Service** (tel. 809-495-5469) or **L&S** (tel. 809-495-5297) for pick-ups.

It might be more efficient to rent a car. You can't get lost, it'll pay for itself by the end of one day, and you'll have freedom of movement. Rates start at about $40 per day for a Suzuki Samurai, plus $10 for a temporary license. The license will be handled by the rental company. Call **Andy's** (tel. 809-495-5511, fax 809-495-

5162), **Speedy's Car Rental** (tel. 809-495-5240, fax 809-495-5755), or **L&S** (tel. 809-495-5297, fax 809-495-5342). Motor scooters start at about $30 per day at **Honda Scooter Rentals** (tel. 809-495-5212).

Remember, driving is on the left (British style) but cars are left-hand-drive (U.S. style).

For those with a need to get out on the water, you can catch water taxis from Leverick Bay Marina to Mosquito Island and Drake's Anchorage cost about $5.

MISCELLANEOUS

The **Virgin Gorda Yacht Harbor** is sort of a one-stop shopping and taking-care-of-business center, built primarily for sailors in need of provisions, phone calls, somewhere to wash clothes, and a place to have a beer. Consequently, the harbor is the center of activity in The Valley. You'll find a **Barclay's Bank, tourism offices** (tel. 809-495-5181), a laundromat, **Buck's Food Market** (tel. 809-495-5423), the **Bath and Turtle** pub (tel. 809-495-5239), the **Wine Cellar & Bakery** (tel. 809-495-5250), gift shops, taxis, and public toilets here. Down the road south of the Yacht Harbor is the island's main **post office** (tel. 809-495-5224), open Monday through Friday 8:30 a.m.-4 p.m. and Saturday 9 a.m.-noon.

INFORMATION DIRECTORY

Police, Fire, Ambulance, tel. 999

Cable & Wireless, tel. (809) 495-5444

Iris O'Neal Clinic, tel. (809) 495-5851

Virgin Gorda Clinic, tel. (809) 495-7310

Chief Customs and Immigration Officer, tel. (809) 495-5173

Virgin Gorda Airport, tel. (809) 495-5621

National Parks Trust, tel. (809) 494-3904

British Virgin Islands Tourist Board, Yacht Harbor, Virgin Gorda, British Virgin Islands; tel. (809) 495-5181

BOB RACE

soursop

JOST VAN DYKE

If you visit Jost Van Dyke for the day, chances are you'll run into nearly all the 200 residents who live there. The hilly island, a mere four square miles (10 square km), finally received electricity in 1991 and seems to be content with just that and nothing more save several fine beaches and a laid-back lifestyle. Three settlements harbor much of the activity on the island. **Great Harbour,** the arrival point by ferry, sports a church, a few shops, beach bars (including the famous **Foxy's Tamarind Bar**), the police and immigration station, and a dock. Around the corner is the small **Little Harbour,** which is really a dock and a couple of small bars. **White Bay** lies to the west of Great Harbour and is home to Jost Van Dyke's nicest **beach** and only hotel.

SIGHTS, RESTAURANTS, SHOPPING

As you approach the island from Tortola's West End on the M/V *When* ($10 one-way, $15 roundtrip; see appendix "Ferry Schedule"), you'll note a small road that cuts across the top of a large hill looming behind Great Harbour. This is the island's road, and it connects its settlements. You can also get to Little Harbour or White Bay via water taxi from Great Harbour ($5), which is faster and more fun anyway. At Great Harbour, you've got a couple of choices. Its small beach bars and shops are set up on the sand along the waterfront, and you might as well snoop around. Start at **Foxy's Tamarind Bar** (tel. 809-495-9275), to the far right. Foxy Callwoood, the famous island metaphysician and entertainer, started this bar on a lark about 30 years ago and it caught on, mostly by word of mouth among sailors who frequent the island's easy channels and moorings. Today, the bar is wildly popular, especially on New Year's Eve, when its likely to be filled with enough people to triple the population of the island. Business cards from all sorts of visitors are tacked up on the ceiling. If you're lucky, you'll find Foxy himself in attendance. He often picks up his guitar and sings, extemporaneously, calypso tunes. Hope you don't embarrass easily.

Foxy's also serves lunch and dinner and hosts a barbecue on weekends

Along the beach is **Club Paradise** (tel. 809-495-9267), another beach bar and restaurant, with a reputation for a great pig roast on Wednesday night. Next door is **Ali Baba** (tel. 809-495-9280), yet another beach restaurant. Indeed, you can eat and drink your way down the beach if you care, or dare.

Christine's Bakery, near the police station, serves West Indian and seafood specialties for lunch and dinner and reputedly has the best breakfasts on the island.

Around the corner at Little Harbour, you'll find a dockside bar called **Sydney's Peace and Love.** Note the T-shirts visitors have donated over the years, hanging from the rafters. Sydney's has pigs roasts Monday and Saturday and special barbecues Sunday, Tuesday, and Thursday. Standard lunch and dinner fare is West Indian and seafood. To the left is **Harris' Restaurant and Snack Bar** (tel. 809-495-9302), which also has a pig roast, on Monday, and serves West Indian specialties for lunch and dinner. You'll find entertainment at both bars. The Tortola band O-2 plays at Sydney's at least twice a week.

ACCOMMODATIONS

The accommodations listed below are categorized based on the average room rate (some hotels offer a wide range of rooms, from budget to luxury), double occupancy, European plan (no meals), per night, during the 15 December-through-15 April high season, excluding the eight percent room tax. A designation of **luxury** indicates that rooms run $200 or more; **expensive** rooms are $140-200; **moderate** indicates a range of $80-140; and **budget** rooms cost $80 or less.

Hotels and Guesthouses

Sandcastle (6501 Red Hook Plaza, Suite 201, St. Thomas, U.S. Virgin Islands or P.O. Box 540, White Bay, Jost Van Dyke, British Virgin

Islands, tel. 809-775-5262, fax 809-775-3590) consists of four beach cottages and is Jost Van Dyke's only hotel. The rooms sit on a half-mile of white sand, the prettiest beach in these parts. The beach and the luxury of the rooms are the attractions here. Get used to being as far away from the madding crowd, or any crowd, as seems possible. The **Soggy Dollar** beach bar, which claims to be the birthplace of the rum drink called Painkiller, is a hangout for guests and for those who make the trek over the hill or come by boat from Great Harbour. Meals are included in the rates. **Expensive-Luxury.**

Rudy's Inn (Great Harbour, Jost Van Dyke, British Virgin Islands, tel. 809-495-9282) is an apartment located on the top floor of Rudy's home up on a hill in Great Harbour. The two bedrooms, private bath, and kitchenette are clean and comfortable. **Moderate.**

Harris' (Little Harbour, Jost Van Dyke, British Virgin Islands, tel. 809-495-9302, fax 809-495-9296) is a small guesthouse in Little Harbour—just two rooms. **Budget.**

Camping

Tula's N&N Campground (Little Harbour, Jost Van Dyke, British Virgin Islands; tel. 809-495-9302), near Little Harbour, has set up a few platform tents and provides linens. Guests share a bathroom and shower. **Budget.**

White Bay Campgrounds (Ivan Chinnery, General Delivery, West End P.O., Tortola, British Virgin Islands; tel. 809-495-9312). The address is Tortola, but this small campsite is located at White Bay. Accommodations are in platform tents, bare sites, or simple cabins. Mr. Chinnery provides beds and ice chests; toilets and showers are shared. **Budget.**

INFORMATION DIRECTORY

Police, Fire, Ambulance, tel. 999

ANEGADA

From the air, Anegada appears to be little more than a large section of white coral reef that has managed to poke above the surf long enough to gather some shrubbery and sand. And that is, apparently, how the island has formed. The atoll's reef is high, considerable, relatively untouched, and dangerous. An estimated 300 wrecks lie offshore (the roots of the island's name lie in the Spanish *anegar,* to drown or to flood) and provide wide opportunities for divers searching for treasure (unlikely) or pristine environments of fish and coral formations (likely). In 1992, the government released flamingos on the island, with the aim of creating a preserve. Turtles can be seen nesting on the beaches along the north shore during their nesting season. The entire north shore and west end is an extensive, uninterrupted beach, with little shade and few facilities, so bring along hats and sunscreen.

Most of the island's 200 residents live in the sparsely populated and aptly named The Settlement—a dry and dusty town near the airstrip in the south-central section of the island—and concern themselves with fishing, minor building contracting, and servicing the nascent tourism industry.

SIGHTS

The island itself, and the nature at hand, are the attractions here. Your best bet is to rent a car and drive, literally, around the island. If you head west from The Settlement and stay on the road that loops around the island, you'll be back in The Settlement in an hour. Of course, if you stop to eat, swim, take photos, or just loll about, it'll take longer—but you'll be doing precisely what most visitors do on Anegada.

At several points along the straight dirt road that loops the island (it's paved with cement in The Settlement and at a few other places), you'll be able to turn off into the great salt pond and fetid mudflats that occupy most of the interior of the western end of the island. You'll find tracks and tire spores in here, but don't venture too far into the swamp. You never know when the mud will suddenly become unable to support the car. Sinking a rental car in the Anegada

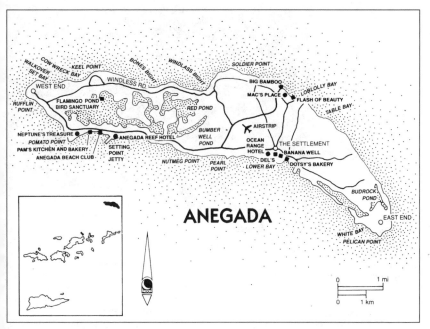

mudflats may not be the end of the world, but it could seem like it for a couple of hours. Keep your telephoto lens or binoculars handy—you may see flocks of flamingos resting in trees or the mud.

RECREATION

Water Sports
The **Anegada Reef Hotel** (tel. 809-495-8002) is the island's center for water sports, with rentals of snorkeling gear, boogie boards, and some diving equipment at its dive shop. (No instruction, just tank rentals and refills.) As well, fishing charters can be arranged here. Bone-fishing is the popular sport out of Anegada. The fish are feisty, tasty, and teem in the eaters around the reef. Deep-sea fishing can also be arranged.

For day charters, fishing trips, and fun, you can charter a 22-foot (seven-meter) powerboat from **Abe & Son Charters** (tel. 809-495-9329).

BEACHES

The island's north shore and much of its south shore comprise long, wide, and mostly deserted beaches. See "Eating and Drinking," below, for places to stop along the beach where you can fuel up on cold drinks, snacks, and find some shade.

ACCOMMODATIONS

Accommodations on Anegada are sparse, to say the least. The choice is limited to one hotel, a guesthouse, and a couple of campsites. Even so, they rarely all fill up.

Nevertheless, the accommodations listed below are categorized based on the average room rate, double occupancy, European plan (no meals), per night, during the 15 December-through-15 April high season, excluding the eight percent room tax. A designation of **luxury**

*Big Bamboo,
Loblolly Bay, Anegada*

indicates that rooms run $200 or more; **expensive** rooms are $140-200; **moderate** indicates a range of $80-140; and **budget** rooms cost $80 or less.

Anegada Reef Hotel (Anegada, British Virgin Islands, tel. 809-495-8002, fax 809-495-9362) is the only hotel on the island and the center for diving, other water sports, chair and umbrella rentals, bike rentals, and more. The 10 oceanview and 10 garden-view rooms are simple, bright, and never more than a few steps from the beach. Rates include all meals. **Luxury.**

Ocean Range Hotel (Anegada, British Virgin Islands, tel. 809-495-8017 or 809-495-2019), more like a guesthouse, is located in The Settlement and is a small, apartment-like building with several single or adjoining rooms, some with kitchenettes, with private baths and hot and cold water. It's a simple enough place and clean, and, if for some reason you prefer to stay in The Settlement, this is the place. **Budget.**

Neptune's Treasure (Anegada, British Virgin Islands, tel. 809-495-9439, fax 809-495-9443) is a small guesthouse and campsite, with a great restaurant, on the south shore of the island on a beach near Setting Point. The four guest rooms are clean and comfortable and have private baths, hot and cold water, towels, and linens. The owners are in the process of adding five more rooms. Tent sites (tents are provided) come with foam mattresses, sheets, blankets, and pillows, but no towels. You'll use a nearby shower and the toilet in the bar. This is highly

recommended for its location and service, and, hey, it's a pretty little spot. Tent sites are $25 d, and the guest rooms, with continental breakfast included, are **moderate.**

Mac's Place (Anegada, British Virgin Islands, tel. 809-495-8020 or 809-495-8022). Mac's is located at Loblolly Bay, a few hundred yards down the beach from Big Bamboo on one side and Flash of Beauty on the other. The site is austere, simple, and cheap. Mac has a large family-style tent ($38), and wooden platforms for your tent ($15), or you can just pitch a tent on a prepared ground site ($8). Showers and toilets are shared, and Mac has a charcoal grill for your use. The beach is at your door. Or flaps. Whatever.

EATING AND DRINKING

Choices are limited here, but you won't starve and that's the beauty of Anegada anyway. It's best to make reservations for dinner. The following restaurants are in the **Inexpensive-Moderate** ($10-25) range, per entrée. The popular **Pomato Point** (tel. 809-495-9466) serves local seafood and drinks on the beach. **Del's** (tel. 809-495-8014), in The Settlement, is good for lunch and local dishes. The **Banana Well,** also in The Settlement, is a popular bar and restaurant. **Dotsy's Bakery** (tel. 809-495-9667), at D&W Jeep Rentals, is well worth the stop for her fresh breads, cakes, and pies, and she also serves lunches and dinners of chicken, seafood, and pizza. For other bakery items, stop at **Pam's Kitchen and Bakery** (tel. 809-495-9237).

Neptune's Treasure (tel. 809-495-9439) on the south shore serves seafood and continental, three meals daily. **The Anegada Reef Hotel** (tel. 809-495-8002), up the road from Neptune's, serves all three meals. Between the two is a small beach bar called the **Anegada Beach Club.** During slow times and off-season, you might find no one at the bar; at such times, it's run on an honor system—prices are posted, and you can help yourself to a drink and leave the money behind.

Anywhere along Anegada's north shore and much of the south shore is a beach, but if you'd like a place to stop with a bar nearby, pull into **Cow Wreck Beach Bar and Grill** (tel. 809-495-9461), at the west end's north shore. The beach here is fine, and the bar provides shade, refreshments, and toilets. Also along the north shore, stop in at **Big Bamboo** (tel. 809-495-2019), at Loblolly Bay. Big Bamboo is a restaurant and beach bar with shaded areas on the beach and some of the finest seafood and lobster dinners on the island. Call ahead, or order and then hit the beach—if you're going to want lobster, it takes some time to prepare. Owner Aubrey Levons can fill you in on just about anything happening on Anegada.

Around the corner from Big Bamboo is **Flash of Beauty,** a small bar and restaurant on the beach where you can get fresh seafood. A gift shop is located here as well. The beach here is good for snorkeling, and you'll find chairs, shade, and toilets at the bar.

SHOPPING

You'll find some shopping in The Settlement, but not much elsewhere. Stop at **Pat's Pottery** and **T-shirts** for, well, Pat's pottery. And T-shirts. A few other small Settlement shops, including **Paris General Store** and **Dotsy's Bakery,** will provide much of anything you'll need. For really living it up, stop in at the **Anegada Reef Hotel.** The gift shop there may be the best shop anywhere on the island. It stocks beachwear and accessories, chic clothing, books, and grocery items.

GETTING AROUND

To get to Anegada, most people fly—a 10-minute flight on Aero Gorda from Tortola's Beef Island. When you arrive at Anegada's small airstrip, the **Captain Auguste George Airport,** you'll find taxis waiting. For the money, an island tour at $45 for three hours seems like a lot, and, unless you have a specific destination in mind, it's better to rent a car. Three outfits do that on Anegada, and if you call ahead they'll have a car waiting for you at the airport. Rentals start at $35 per day, plus $10 for the temporary British Virgin Islands license. Call **D&W Jeep Rentals** (tel. 809-495-8018) for a good selection and rate, or **ABC Car Rentals** (tel. 809-495-9466). **Anegada Reef Hotel** (tel. 809-495-8002) also rents cars and bicycles. Call me overly aware of other people's masochistic tendencies, but Anegada does not seem like the sort of place to ride around on a bike. The dirt roads are dusty and rough, the sun is hot, and it would take much too long—or seem like it—to get anywhere.

INFORMATION DIRECTORY

Police, Fire, Ambulance, tel. 999

NOTICE
DO NOT LITTER THIS PLACE, IT'S OUR LITTLE CORNER OF THE WORLD.
P.H.D.

OTHER BRITISH VIRGIN ISLANDS

COOPER ISLAND

Cooper Island lies in the chain of islands south of Tortola, across the Sir Francis Drake Channel. The island has several good snorkeling beaches and is popular with day-trippers from Tortola or Virgin Gorda and with sailors who pull up to one of its 20 moorings for a day or two of splashing around on its beaches. The island also has a bar and restaurant, the **Cooper Island Restaurant**, and offers accommodations in the small **Cooper Island Beach Club** (Contact Prospect Reef Marina, Tortola, British Virgin Islands; tel. 809-494-3721). The beachfront guesthouse has 12 units. **Moderate.**

GUANA ISLAND

Guana Island is a private 125-acre island with a nature preserve and several fine beaches, located off the north coast of Tortola. The preserve is home to several species of exotic birds. Walking and biking trails meander throughout the island and guests with a yen for exploring the natural aspects of British Virgin Islands flora and fauna will not be disappointed here. Accommodation is at the exclusive **Guana Island Club** (P.O. Box 32, Road Town, Tortola, British Virgin Islands, tel. 800-544-8262 or 809-494-2354), which accommodates guests in 15 villa units. Included in the rates are meals and use of resort equipment. **Luxury.**

MOSQUITO ISLAND

Mosquito Island, just off the Virgin Gorda coast in North Sound, is easily reached by launch from Leverick Bay or the Yacht Harbor in The Valley. The island is a privately owned resort community with walking trails, water sports, a small marina, and miles of beaches. It is an "ultimate escape" sort of place, in the way that only small islands reachable only by boat can be.

The accommodation is **Drake's Anchorage** (P.O. Box 2510, North Sound, Virgin Gorda, British Virgin Islands, tel. 800-624-6651 or 809-494-2254; or contact 1340 Centre St., Newton Centre, MA 02159, tel. 617-969-9913, fax 617-969-5147), a 125-acre resort consisting of two luxury villas, eight rooms, and two suites, a French restaurant, and lots of privacy. Rates include three meals per day, water sports equipment, a small dinghy to get around North Sound, and bicycles to traverse the island. **Luxury.**

NECKER ISLAND

This island, north of Virgin Gorda and on the north side of Prickly Pear Island, is owned and operated by Richard Branson, owner of Virgin Airways and other Virgin ventures. The island features an exclusive and large villa that sleeps up to 20 and is popular with movie stars and jet-set types. No wonder—at about $11,000 per day, only deep pockets need consider it. All amenities, meals, drinks, and sports that you'd even think you'd want are available. Call (800) 926-0636 for details.

NORMAN ISLAND

Uninhabited, this island is widely believed to be the setting that inspired Robert Louis Stevenson's *Treasure Island.* Day trips from Tortola and Virgin Gorda take people snorkeling and lolling about its beaches or exploring its small caves, which are located at several spots along the shore and are often filled with sea water, exotic fish, and other marinelife.

The floating restaurant the *William Thorton* (tel. 809-494-2564), converted from a 1910 Baltic Trading ship, floats off The Bight. To get to the restaurant for dinner, take a launch from the Fort Burt Marina in Road Town on Tortola, which departs every evening at about 5. Call for an exact schedule.

PETER ISLAND

Privately owned Peter Island lies south of Tortola across the Sir Francis Drake Channel. The 1,800-acre island houses the exclusive **Peter Island Resort and Yacht Harbour** (P.O. Box 211, Road Town, Tortola, British Virgin Islands; tel. 800-562-0268 or 809-495-2000, fax 809-495-2500), a sprawling resort comprising 57 oceanview rooms, beachfront rooms (on Deadman's Bay, the island's long beach), and villas, plus two restaurants, a pool, a library, fitness and massage center, four tennis courts (two lighted for night play), a basketball court, a gift shop, a water sports center, and miles of hiking paths, roads, and beaches. This is the sort of place where you'll be hard pressed to find a reason to leave once you arrive; the rooms and villas are large and airy and come with minibars, coffee makers, balconies, double sinks in the bathrooms, a/c, and fans. The center of activity is the beach and the bar and restaurant at Deadman's Bay, but the island is so large that you can grab a bike (complimentary for guests) and zoom off, or hike, to one of four other secluded beaches on the island. Or, head out to Carrot Rock for sunset views. **Dive B.V.I.** has an office on the island and can arrange diving, including trips to the popular diving site, the wreck of the RMS *Rhone* (just offshore). As well, sailing, fishing, boat charters, and more can be arranged by the water sports center. **Solé Spa Services** (tel. 809-494-5999) offers massages, facials, steam treatments, and all those other things you never get a chance to do at home. The hotel's main restaurant, **Tradewinds,** is popular with non-guests, who arrive by complimentary ferry from Baugher's Bay at Wickam's Cay on Tortola for evening dining (the boat leaves about every hour during the day, including 5:30 p.m. and 6:30 p.m. for dinner guests). Non-guests who'd like to come to Peter Island for a day to use beach facilities pay $15 for the 20-minute ferry trip. **Luxury.**

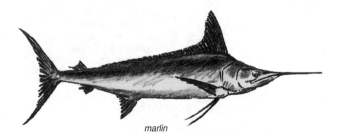

marlin

APPENDIX: FERRY SCHEDULES

Please keep in mind that all departure times and fares are not only *subject* to change, they most probably *will* change. Call the ferry service to confirm information and to make reservations when necessary—say, for large parties. Check in 15-30 minutes before departure time. Unless otherwise indicated, the fares below are for adults.

BETWEEN ST. THOMAS AND ST. JOHN

TRANSPORTATION SERVICES (Tel. 809-776-6282)

Departing Red Hook, St. Thomas, for Cruz Bay, St. John
Adults $3 one-way, children under 12 $1; 20 minutes
Daily 6:30 a.m., 7:30 a.m., then hourly from 8 a.m. until midnight

Departing Cruz Bay, St. John, for Red Hook, St. Thomas
Adults $3 one-way, children under 12 $1; 20 minutes
Daily, hourly from 6 a.m. until 11 p.m.

Departing Waterfront, Charlotte Amalie, St. Thomas, for Cruz Bay, St. John
$7 one-way; 45 minutes
Daily 9 a.m., 11 a.m., 1 p.m., 3 p.m., 4 p.m., 5:30 p.m.

Departing Cruz Bay, St. John, for Waterfront, Charlotte Amalie, St. Thomas
$7 one-way; 45 minutes
Daily 7:15 a.m., 9:15 a.m., 11:15 a.m., 1:15 p.m., 2:15 p.m., 3:45 p.m.

BETWEEN ST. THOMAS AND TORTOLA

Note: Proof of citizenship in the form of a passport, a raised-seal birth certificate, or a voter registration card is required for travel between the U.S. and British Virgin Islands.

**SMITH'S FERRY (U.S.V.I. Tel. 809-775-7292 or 775-5532,
B.V.I. Tel. 809-494-4430 or 495-2355)**

NATIVE SON (U.S.V.I. Tel. 809-774-8685 or 775-3111, B.V.I. Tel. 809-495-4617)

Departing Waterfront, Charlotte Amalie, St. Thomas, for West End, Tortola
Adults $35 roundtrip, $19 one-way; children 6-12 $28 roundtrip, $17 one-way; ages eight months to five years $20 roundtrip, $12 one-way; one hour
Sunday 8 a.m., 8:30 a.m., 2 p.m., 2:30 p.m.
Monday-Friday 8:25 a.m., 8:55 a.m., 12:15 p.m., 12:45 p.m., 2 p.m., 2:30 p.m.
Saturday 8:25 a.m., 8:55 a.m., 12 p.m., 12:30 p.m., 2 p.m., 2:30 p.m.

Departing Waterfront, Charlotte Amalie, St. Thomas, for Road Town via West End, Tortola

Adults $35 roundtrip, $19 one-way; children 6-12 $28 roundtrip, $17 one-way; ages eight
  months to five years $20 roundtrip, $12 one-way; one hour, 45 minutes

Sunday 10:45 a.m., 11:45 a.m., 4 p.m., 5:15 p.m., 5:45 p.m.

Monday-Friday 4:30 p.m., 5 p.m.

Saturday 3 p.m., 4 p.m., 4:30 p.m., 5 p.m.

Departing West End, Tortola, for Waterfront, Charlotte Amalie, St. Thomas

Adults $35 roundtrip, $19 one-way; children 6-12 $28 roundtrip, $17 one-way; ages eight
  months to five years $20 roundtrip, $12 one-way; one hour

Sunday 9:15 a.m., 9:30 a.m., 3;45 p.m., 4:05 p.m.

Monday-Friday 7 a.m., 7:30 a.m., 10 a.m., 10:30 a.m., 3 p.m., 3:30 p.m.

Saturday 7 a.m., 7:30 a.m., 10 a.m., 10:30 a.m., 2:30 p.m., 3 p.m., 5:45 p.m., 6 p.m.

Departing Road Town, Tortola, for Waterfront, Charlotte Amalie, St. Thomas

Adults $35 roundtrip, $19 one-way; children 6-12 $28 roundtrip, $17 one-way; ages eight
  months to five years $20 roundtrip, $12 one-way; one hour, 45 minutes

Sunday 3:15 p.m., 3:35 p.m.

Monday-Friday 6:15 a.m., 6:45 a.m.

Saturday 6:15 a.m., 6:45 a.m., 2 p.m., 2:30 p.m., 5:30 p.m.

Departing Red Hook, St. Thomas, for West End, Tortola

Adults $35 roundtrip, $19 one-way; children 6-12 $28 roundtrip, $17 one-way; ages eight
  months to five years $20 roundtrip, $12 one-way; 30 minutes

Daily 7:45 a.m., 8 a.m., 11:15 a.m., 2:55 a.m., 5:30 p.m.

Departing West End, Tortola, for Red Hook, St. Thomas*

Adults $35 roundtrip, $19 one-way; children 6-12 $28 roundtrip, $17 one-way; ages eight
  months to five years $20 roundtrip, $12 one-way; 30 minutes

Daily 6:30 a.m., 8:45 p.m., 12 p.m., 3:45 p.m.

*Note: On a more limited basis **Speedy's** (B.V.I. tel. 809-495-5240 or 809-495-5235)
  also makes this trip.

Departing Charlotte Amalie, St. Thomas, for Road Town, Tortola

$45 roundtrip, $25 one-way

Tuesday and Thursday 8:45 a.m., 5 p.m.

Saturday 3:30 p.m.

Departing Road Town, Tortola, for Charlotte Amalie, St. Thomas

$45 roundtrip, $25 one-way

Tuesday and Thursday 7:15 a.m., 3:25 p.m.

Saturday 9:15 a.m.

BETWEEN ST. THOMAS AND VIRGIN GORDA

TRANSPORTATION SERVICES (Tel. 809-776-6282)

Departing Red Hook, St. Thomas, for Spanish Town, Virgin Gorda

$35 roundtrip; one hour, 45 minutes

Sunday and Thursday 8 a.m.

Departing Spanish Town, Virgin Gorda, for Red Hook, St. Thomas
$35 roundtrip; one hour, 45 minutes
Sunday and Thursday 3 p.m.

Note: You can also take **Smith's Ferry** (B.V.I. tel. 809-494-4495 or 494-2355, U.S.V.I. tel. 809-775-7292) from St. Thomas to Virgin Gorda, with a stop in Tortola: adults $54 roundtrip, $27 one-way; children $45 roundtrip, $25 one-way

BETWEEN ST. JOHN AND TORTOLA

INTER-ISLAND BOAT SERVICES (U.S.V.I. Tel. 809-776-6597 or 775-7408, B.V.I. Tel. 809-495-4166)

Departing Cruz Bay, St. John, for West End, Tortola
Adults $32 roundtrip, $18 one-way; children under 12 $25 roundtrip, $10 one-way; 45 minutes
Sunday 8:30 a.m., 11:30 a.m., 4:30 p.m.
Monday-Thursday 8:30 a.m., 11:30 a.m., 3:30 p.m.
Friday 8:30 a.m., 11:30 a.m., 3:30 p.m., 5 p.m.
Saturday 8:30 a.m., 11:30 a.m., 3:30 p.m.

Departing West End, Tortola, for Cruz Bay, St. John
Adults $32 roundtrip, $18 one-way; children under 12 $25 roundtrip, $10 one-way; 45 minutes
Sunday 9:15 a.m., 12:15 p.m., 5:15 p.m.
Monday-Thursday 9:15 a.m., 12:15 p.m., 4:15 p.m.
Friday 9:15 a.m., 12:15 p.m., 4:15 p.m., 5:30 p.m.
Saturday 9:15 a.m., 12:15 p.m., 4:15 p.m.

BETWEEN ST. JOHN AND JOST VAN DYKE

INTER-ISLAND BOAT SERVICES (U.S.V.I. Tel. 809-776-6597 or 775-7408, B.V.I. Tel. 809-495-4166)

TRANSPORTATION SERVICES (U.S.V.I. Tel. 809-776-6282).

The ferries below originate at Red Hook, St. Thomas, about 30 minutes before St. John departure times. In other words, you can go roundtrip from St. Thomas to Jost Van Dyke with a stop in St. John.

Departing Cruz Bay, St. John, for Great Harbour, Jost Van Dyke
$32 roundtrip; 30 minutes
Friday, Saturday, Sunday 8:30 a.m., 2:20 p.m., 5:40 p.m. (occasionally, only two runs on Saturday)

Departing Great Harbour, Jost Van Dyke, for Cruz Bay, St. John
$32 roundtrip; 30 minutes
Friday, Saturday, Sunday 9:15 a.m., 3:15 p.m., 9:15 p.m. (occasionally, only two runs on Saturday)

BETWEEN TORTOLA AND VIRGIN GORDA

SPEEDY'S (B.V.I. Tel. 809-495-5240 or 495-5235)

SMITH'S FERRY (B.V.I. Tel. 809-494-4495 or 809-494-2355, U.S.V.I. Tel. 809-775-7292)

Departing Road Town, Tortola, for Spanish Town, Virgin Gorda

$19 roundtrip, $10 one-way; 30 minutes

Sunday 8:50 a.m., 9 a.m., 12:30 p.m., 4:15 p.m., 5:15 p.m.

Monday, Wednesday, Friday 7 a.m., 8:50 a.m., 9 a.m., 12 p.m., 12:30 p.m., 1:30 p.m., 3:15 p.m., 4:30 p.m.

Tuesday and Thursday 7 a.m., 8:50 a.m., 9 a.m., 10:10 a.m., 12 p.m., 12:30 p.m., 1:30 p.m., 4:30 p.m., 6:15 p.m.

Saturday 7 a.m., 8:50 a.m., 9 a.m., 10:30 a.m., 12:30 p.m., 1:30 p.m., 4:15 p.m., 4:30 p.m., 5 p.m.

Departing Spanish Town, Virgin Gorda, for Road Town, Tortola

$19 roundtrip, $10 one-way; 30 minutes

Sunday 8 a.m., 10:15, 3 p.m., 4:30 p.m., 5 p.m.

Monday, Wednesday, Friday 7:50 a.m., 8 a.m., 10 a.m., 10:15 a.m., 11:30 a.m., 2:15 p.m., 3:30 p.m., 4 p.m.

Tuesday and Thursday 6:30 a.m., 7:50 a.m., 8 a.m., 10 a.m., 10:15 a.m., 11:30 a.m., 2:15 p.m., 2:45 p.m., 3:30 p.m., 4 p.m.

Saturday 7:50 a.m., 8 a.m., 8:30 a.m., 10 a.m., 10:15 a.m., 11:30 a.m., 12:30 p.m., 3 p.m., 3:30 p.m., 5 p.m.

NORTH SOUND EXPRESS (Tel. 809-495-2271)

Departing Beef Island/East End, Tortola, for North Sound, Virgin Gorda

Adults $40 roundtrip, $20 one-way; children 6-11 $32 roundtrip, $16 one-way; infant through age 5 $20 roundtrip, $10 one-way; 30 minutes

Daily 6:15 a.m., 10:30 a.m., 3:30 p.m.

Departing North Sound, Virgin Gorda, for Beef Island/East End, Tortola

Adults $40 roundtrip, $20 one-way; children 6-11 $32 roundtrip, $16 one-way; infant through age 5 $20 roundtrip, $10 one-way; 30 minutes

Daily 7 a.m., 12 p.m., 4:15 p.m.

BETWEEN TORTOLA AND JOST VAN DYKE

MV *WHEN* (Tel. 809-494-2997)

Departing West End, Tortola, for Great Harbour and Little Harbour, Jost Van Dyke

$15 roundtrip, $10 one-way; 35 minutes

Sunday 9:30 a.m., 1:30 p.m., 4 p.m.

Monday-Saturday 7:30 a.m., 9:45 a.m., 1:30 p.m., 4 p.m.

Departing Great Harbour and Little Harbour, Jost Van Dyke, for West End, Tortola

$15 roundtrip, $10 one-way; 35 minutes

Sunday 11 a.m., 3 p.m., 5 p.m.

Monday-Saturday 8:30 a.m., 11 a.m., 3 p.m., 5 p.m.

MISCELLANEOUS

A number of special ferry services make specific trips:

FRENCHMAN'S REEF FERRY (Tel. 809-776-8500, EXT. 445)

St. Thomas Marriott Frenchman's Reef Hotel to Waterfront, Charlotte Amalie

$4 one-way; 15 minutes

Daily hourly departures from Frenchman's Reef, 9 a.m. to 4 p.m.

Daily hourly departures from Waterfront, Charlotte Amalie, 9:30 a.m. to 4:30 p.m.

FAST CAT (Tel. 809-773-3278)

Christiansted, St. Croix, to Charlotte Amalie, St. Thomas

Adults $30 one-way, $60 roundtrip, children $20 one-way, $40 roundtrip; one hour, 15 minutes

Departs Christiansted daily 7:30 a.m. and 4 p.m.

Departs Charlotte Amalie daily 9:15 a.m. and 5:45 p.m.

TRANSPORTATION SERVICES (Tel. 809-776-6282)

St. John and St. Thomas to Fajardo, Puerto Rico

$80 roundtrip; two hours

Departs U.S. Virgin Islands twice monthly on Friday afternoons

Departs Fajardo twice monthly on Sunday afternoons

PETER ISLAND FERRY (Tel. 809-494-2561)

Peter Island Ferry Dock, Road Town, Tortola, to Peter Island Resort

$15 roundtrip; complimentary for dinner guests; 30 minutes

Departs Road Town daily 7 a.m., 8:30 a.m., 10 a.m., 2 p.m., 3:30 p.m., 5:30 p.m., 6:30 p.m., 10:30 p.m., 11 p.m.

Departs Peter Island daily 8 a.m., 9 a.m., 12 p.m., 2:30 p.m., 4:30 p.m., 6 p.m., 10 p.m., 11 p.m.

BIRAS CREEK FERRY (Tel. 809-494-3555)

Gun Creek, North Sound, Virgin Gorda, to Biras Creek Resort

Complimentary service for hotel guests; 20 minutes

Departs on as-needed basis

BOOKLIST

The recommended readings represent a small portion of a large and fascinating body of work about the Virgin Islands, the Caribbean region, and its people. Titles have been briefly annotated.

A good source for new, used, and first-edition books about Caribbean issues and by Caribbean writers is West Indies Books Unlimited, P.O. Box 2315, Sarasota, FL 34230 U.S.A.; tel. (813) 954-8601.

BIBLIOGRAPHY

Dance, Daryl Cumber, ed. *Fifty Caribbean Writers: A Bio-bibliographical Critical Sourcebook.* Westport, CT: Greenwood Press, 1986. Presents English-language Caribbean writers from 1700 through the 1980s (Spanish writers, French, Dutch, and others are not represented).

Fenwick, M.J. *Writers of the Caribbean and Central America: A Bibliography.* 2 vols. New York: Garland Publishing, 1992. Recent and thorough collection of titles.

Gordon, R. *The Literature of the West Indies.* 20 vols. Gordon Press, 1977. One of the largest critical and bibliographical works in existence.

BIOGRAPHY

Kennedy, Gavin. *Bligh.* London: Duckworth, 1978. The life and times of Capt. William Bligh, adventurer, dispossessed commander of the fated *Bounty,* and transporter of the lifesaving breadfruit to the West Indies.

Wilford, John Noble. *The Mysterious History of Columbus: An Exploration of the Man, the Myth, the Legacy.* New York: Alfred A. Knopf, 1991. Treatment of the often harsh, vain, and enigmatic man who, through one of the greatest mistakes ever, brought European involvement to the West Indies and changed the course of world history.

CULTURE AND CUSTOMS

Kurlansky, Mark. *A Continent of Islands: Searching for the Caribbean Destiny.* Redding, MA: Addison-Wesley, 1992. Well-regarded treatise on the future of the Caribbean states and their cultures.

MacKie, Christine. *Life and Food in the Caribbean.* New York: New Amsterdam Books, 1991. Life, food, and the Caribbean—a winning combination.

Walton, Chelle K. *Caribbean Ways: A Cultural Guide.* Westwood, MA: Riverdale Co., 1993. More than a list of dos and don'ts, the work discusses the background of cultures and customs.

DESCRIPTION AND TRAVEL

Bastyra, Judy. *Caribbean Cooking.* New York: Exeter Books, 1987. Recipes, terminology, and background information on the cuisines of the West Indies.

The Cambridge Encyclopedia of Latin America and the Caribbean. 2nd edition. New York: Cambridge University Press, 1992. Essential reference work for Caribbean region aficionados.

Dawood, Richard. *Traveller's Health, How to Stay Healthy Abroad.* London: Oxford University Press, 1992. Vaccinations, common ailments, and everything you wanted to know and worry about while traveling.

Dyde, Brian. *Caribbean Companion, the A to Z Reference.* London: Macmillan, 1992. Miniencyclopedia; a good, practical guide to Caribbean terms, issues, history, and personalities.

Foree, Rebecca, ed. *Caribbean Access.* New York: Access Press, 1992. Good photography but light on practical and background information for Caribbean travelers.

Hunte, George. *The West Indian Islands.* New York: Viking, 1972. The author, a former Time/Life writer, is a Barbadian and describes cultures and life in the West Indies as only an insider can.

Lanks, Herbert C. *Highway Across the West Indies.* New York: Appleton-Century-Crofts, 1948. A man travels through the West Indies from Cuba to Trinidad, a distance of more than 12,000 miles, in a car. An interesting and somewhat alarming endeavor.

Showker, Kay. *One Hundred Best Resorts in the Caribbean.* Old Saybrook, CT: Globe Pequot, 1992. Good journalism for an esoteric guide. If resorts are what you want, this is the book.

FICTION, POETRY, ESSAYS

Abrahams, Peter. *Lights Out.* New York: Mysterious Press, 1994. A tale of false imprisonment and skullduggery set against a Caribbean backdrop.

Anderson, John Lorenzo *Night of the Silent Drums.* Charlotte Amalie, U.S. Virgin Islands: MAPes MONDe Editore, 1992. The story of the 1733 St. John slave rebellion, with fascinating lithographs.

Barton, Paule. *The Woe Shirt: Caribbean Folk Tales.* Great Barrington, MA: Penmaen Press, 1980. A collection of regional folk tales from a Haitian goatherd and folklorist.

Brathwaite, Edward. *The Arrivants, A New World Trilogy.* London: Oxford University Press, 1973. This collection of the lyrical and often stark poetry of the Barbadian writer/university lecturer explores issues in the lives of Africans in the West Indies and the cities of Europe and North America.

Burnett, Paula, ed. *The Penguin Book of Caribbean Verse in English.* New York: Viking Penguin Books, 1986. Poets of and from the Caribbean.

Collymore, Frank. *The Man Who Loved Attending Funerals and Other Stories.* Oxford: Heinemann Publishers,1993. A posthumous collection of short stories from the well-known Barbadian writer, who died in 1980.

Cooper, Susan. *Jethro and the Jumbie.* New York: Atheneum, 1979. A children's ghost tale.

Greene, Graham. *The Comedians.* New York: Viking, 1981. Greene's famous novel of Haiti under notorious dictator Papa Doc.

Joseph, Lynn. *Coconut Kind of Day: Island Poems.* New York: Lothrop, Lee & Shepard Books, 1990. Poetry for young adults.

Kincaid, Jamaica. *A Small Place.* New York: Farrar Straus Giroux, 1988. Tales of islanders and tourists from the Antiguan writer.

Kincaid, Jamaica. *Lucy.* New York: Farrar Straus Giroux, 1991. Familiar theme for follower's of Jamaica Kincaid's work: a young girl's life, loves, and travails in the islands.

Lamming, George. *In the Castle of My Skin.* New York: McGraw-Hill, 1954. The Barbadian writer's first novel, a powerful description of island youth and life in the wake of colonialism and pre-independence social awakening.

Markham, E.A., ed. *Hinterland: Caribbean Poetry from the West Indies and Britain.* Chester Springs, PA: Dufour Editions (Bloodaxe, U.K.), 1990. Collected poetry from Caribbean-based and expatriate writers.

McKay, Claude. *Banana Bottom.* This out-of-print work, by the Jamaican poet, was first published in 1933 and is considered by many to be one of the first classic West Indian novels.

Michener, James A. *Caribbean.* New York: Random House, 1989. Michener's epochal and exhausting tale of the settling of the Caribbean from pre-Columbian to modern times.

Murray, John A., ed. *Islands and the Sea: Five Centuries of Nature Writing from the Caribbean.* New York: Oxford University Press, 1991. Collected literature and essays, some turgid and florid, others written by masters.

Naipaul, V.S. *A House for Mr. Biswas.* New York: Alfred A. Knopf, 1983. Reprint of Naipaul's classic tale of Trinidadian society and life as seen through the experiences of an East Indian family.

Ramchand, Kenneth, ed. *Best West Indian Stories.* Surrey, U.K.: Nelson Caribbean, 1982. A brief anthology of lesser-known but admirable Caribbean short-story writing.

Rhys, Jean. *Wide Sargasso Sea.* New York: Norton, 1967. The novel presents the early life and marriage in the post-emancipation West Indies of the mysterious madwoman in Charlotte Bronte's *Jane Eyre.*

Shacochis, Bob. *Easy in the Islands.* New York: Viking, 1985. Collection of short stories of life in the islands; winner of the American Book Award.

Shacochis, Bob. *Swimming in the Volcano.* New York: Scribners, 1993. Novel of political intrigue, expatriate lust, and life on the fictional island of St. Catherine.

Trillin, Calvin. *Travels With Alice.* New York: Ticknor & Fields, 1989. Collection of travel essays from the quirky humorist, including several that deal with Lesser Antilles islands.

Walcott, Derek. *Collected Poems 1948-1984.* New York: Farrar Straus Giroux, 1986. Important introduction to the work of the Nobel prizewinning poet and playwright.

Walcott, Derek. *Omeros.* New York: Farrar Straus Giroux, 1990. Omeros, Greek for Homer, is one character in this ambitious narrative of exile, spiritual travel, and the redemption of place. Considered by many to be one of Walcott's most important works.

Wouk, Herman. *Don't Stop the Carnival.* Garden City, NY: Doubleday, 1965. Wouk's lively, humorous, and often insightful tale concerns a Broadway publicity agent who decides to chuck it all and buy a hotel on a small Caribbean island. Tragedy and farce ensue.

HISTORY

Bourne, Edward G. *Spain in America (1450-1580).* New York and London: Harper & Bros., 1904. History of Spanish influences in North, South, and Central America, as well as the Caribbean.

Burg, B.R. *Sodomy and the Pirate Tradition; English Sea Rovers in the 17th Century Caribbean.* New York: New York University Press, 1984. Male bonding in the pirate tradition reflects the tolerance and attitudes of 17th-century society. Raises questions rarely asked.

Course, A.G. *Pirates of the Western Seas.* London: Muller, 1969. Pirate fun, fact, and fiction.

Cripps, L.L. *The Spanish Caribbean from Columbus to Castro.* Cambridge, MA: Schenkman, 1979. In view of imminent changes in Cuba, parts of the work are outdated, but it's important nonetheless.

Dunn, Richard S. *Sugar and Slavery—The Rise of the Planter Class in the English West Indies (1624-1738).* Chapel Hill, N.C.: University of North Carolina Press, 1972. Details the link between slavery and the sugar economy and culture of the West Indies.

Goldberg, Mark H. *Going Bananas: 100 Years of Fruit Ships in the Caribbean.* Kings Point, NY: American Merchant Marine Museum

Foundation, 1993. Banana boats also brought the first tourists from North America to the Caribbean.

Gosse, Dr. Philip. *The History of Piracy.* New York: Tudor, 1934. Gosse was considered one of the world's foremost experts on the pirates of the Americas.

Gosse, Dr. Philip. *The Pirate's Who's Who.* London: Dulan, 1924. Biographical sketches of major and minor pirates and adventurers.

Klein, Herbert S. *African Slavery in Latin America and the Caribbean.* New York: Oxford University Press, 1986. Sociological study of slavery in the New World.

Knight, Franklin W. *The Caribbean.* London: Oxford University Press, 1978. Basic introductory history of the region.

Knox, John P. *A Historical Account of St. Thomas.* New York: Charles Scribner, 1852. The narrative ends well before the islands became part of the United States but is fascinating for its history of the times.

Lewisohn, Florence. *St. Croix Under Seven Flags.* Hollywood, FL: Dukane Press, 1970. History of St. Croix.

Marx, Jenifer. *Pirates and Privateers of the Caribbean.* Malabar, FL: Krieger, 1992. One of many chronicles of the history of these famed malcontents.

Naipaul, V.S. *The Middle Passage—Impressions of Five Societies: British, French, and Dutch in the West Indies and South America.* New York: Macmillan, 1963. Trenchant observations by the essayist, novelist, and travel writer.

Parry, J.H. and P.M. Sherlock and Anthony Maingot. *A Short History of the West Indies.* London: Macmillan, 1987. Accessible and concise, this is one of the best histories of its kind.

Pickering, V. *A Concise History of the British Virgin Islands.* Falcon Publications, Ltd., 1987. Good development of the early history of the British islands.

Pitman, Frank Wesley. *The Development of the British West Indies, 1700-1763.* Hamden, CT: Archon Books, 1967. Follows the history and influences and consequences of the heyday of British West Indies plantocracy.

Ragarz, Lowell Joseph. *The Fall of the Planter Class in the British Caribbean, 1763-1833.* New York: Octagon Books, 1971. Compelling, if somewhat academic, investigation of the crash of the wealthy British landowner class. Good companion to Mr. Dunn's book, above.

Van Sertima, Ivan. *They Came Before Columbus: The African Presence in Ancient America.* New York: Random House, 1976. Thought-provoking theories of Africans exploring the New World before Columbus.

MUSIC AND ARTS

Burgie, Irving, ed. *Caribbean Carnival: Songs of the West Indies.* New York: Tambourine Books, 1992. Includes music and words.

Ekwene, Laz E.N. *African Sources in New World Black Music.* Toronto, 1972. Traces African influences in black music past and near-present, much of which still holds true today.

Hamelecourt, Juliette. *Caribbean Cookbook.* Melrose Park, IL: Culinary Arts Institute, 1987. Recipes and references.

NATURAL SCIENCES

Allen, Robert Porter. *Birds of the Caribbean.* New York: Viking, 1961 edition. One of the most comprehensive bird guides.

Bond, James. *Birds of the West Indies.* London: Collins, 1960 edition. Author Ian Fleming took the name of this famous naturalist for his super-agent, 007.

Bourne, M.J., G.W. Lennox, and S.A. Seddon. *Fruits and Vegetables of the Caribbean.* London: Macmillan, 1988. Short pamphlet describing major Caribbean species; vivid photographs are its best feature.

Evans, P. *Birds of the Eastern Caribbean.* Hong Kong: MacMillan Education, Ltd., 1990. Birds, birds, and more birds.

Greenberg, Idaz, and Jerry Greenberg. *Guide to Corals & Fishes of Florida, the Bahamas and the Caribbean.* Miami: Seahawk Press, 1977. Waterproof book perfect for carrying to the beach, with illustrations of warm-water coral and sealife.

Greenberg, Idaz, and Jerry Greenberg. *Sharks and Other Dangerous Sea Creatures.* Miami: Seahawk Press, 1981. The authors have photographed sharks for the National Geographic Society, and many startling photos appear here. Excellent illustrations and knowledgeable text.

Hargreaves, Dorothy, and Bob Hargreaves. *Tropical Trees.* Lahaina, HI: Ross-Hargreaves, 1965. Picture guide to tropical trees from Hawaii to the Caribbean.

Honeychurch, Penelope N. *Caribbean Wild Plants and Their Uses.* London: Macmillan, 1986. Uses of wild plants in island folklore, from medicine to magic, with illustrations by the author.

Little, E.L. and F.H. Wadsworth. *Common Trees of Puerto Rico and the Virgin Islands.* Washington, D.C.: U.S. Department of Agriculture, 1964. Targets the trees of the region.

Kaplan, Eugene. *A Field Guide to the Coral Reefs of the Caribbean and Florida.* Princeton, NJ: Peterson's Guides, 1984. This fact-packed guide covers a wide area and is well regarded.

Kingsbury, J.M. *200 Tropical Plants.* New York: Bulbrier Press, 1988. Not 198, not 199, but 200 tropical plants.

Maclean, W.P. *Reptiles and Amphibians of the Virgin Islands.* Hong Kong: MacMillan Education, Ltd., 1982. Complete guide to the scaly and crawly residents of the Virgin Islands.

Seddon, S.A. and G.W. Lennox. *Trees of the Caribbean.* London: Macmillan, 1987. The roots, so to speak, of Caribbean rainforests, landscapes, and gardens.

Stilling, P.D. *Butterflies and Other Insects of the Eastern Caribbean.* London: Macmillan. Photographs and descriptions of buzzing fauna in the Lesser Antilles.

Whetten, John T. *Geology of St. Croix.* The Geological Society of America, Memoir 98, 1960.

SOCIAL ISSUES

Abrahams, Roger D. *After Africa.* New Haven, CT: Yale University Press, 1983. Chronicle of Africans as slaves, citizens, and leaders in the West Indies.

Black, George. *The Good Neighbor: How the United States Wrote the History of Central America and the Caribbean.* New York: Pantheon, 1988. Is the Caribbean's Big Neighbor to the north guilty of wanton adventurism or simple benign regional interest? This is one theory.

Bough, James and Roy Macridis. *The Virgin Islands: America's Caribbean Outpost.* Wakefield, MA: Walter S. Williams Publishing Co., 1970. Analyzes America's role in the U.S. Virgin Islands' past and future.

Creque, Darwin. *The U.S. Virgin Islands and the Eastern Caribbean.* Philadelphia: Whitmore Publishing, 1968.

Ferguson, James. *Far from Paradise: An Introduction to Caribbean Development.* New York: Monthly Review Press (Latin American Bureau, U.K.), 1990. A regional reality check.

Hamshire, Cyril. *The British in the Caribbean.* Cambridge, MA: Harvard University Press, 1972. Historical analysis of the British presence in the Caribbean, to modern times.

Patterson, Orlando. *Sociology of Slavery.* London: 1967. Slavery was the beast that pulled the West Indies economic cart, and its resultant race and class problems are alive today.

Perkins, Whitney T. *Constraint of Empire: The United States and Caribbean Interventions.* Westport, CT: Greenwood, 1981. A history of U.S. interventions, political and otherwise, in the Greater Antilles.

Varlack, Pearl, and Norwell Harrigan. *American Paradise: A Profile of the Virgin Islands of the United States.* St. Thomas: Research and Consulting Services, Ltd., 1992. Profiles the U.S. Virgin Islands history, land, government, and economic future.

Varlack, Pearl, and Norwell Harrigan. "The U.S. Virgin Islands and the Black Experience." *Journal of Black Studies,* Vol. 7, No. 4, June 1977.

PERIODICALS

The Affordable Caribbean. 8403 Colesville Rd., Suite 830, Silver Spring, MD 20910. Published as an adjunct of *Caribbean Travel and Life* magazine, this newsletter lists value-oriented travel destinations throughout the region.

Caribbean Newsletter. Friends of Democracy, Box 8838, Kingston C.S.O., Jamaica, W.I. A 12-page newsletter covering current and controversial Caribbean issues.

Caribbean Travel and Life. Box 6229, Syracuse, NY 13217-7921. A bimonthly glossy magazine devoted solely to travel in the Caribbean.

Caribbean Week. Lefferts Place, River Rd., St. Michael, Barbados, W.I. Monthly newspaper covering Caribbean issues.

Condé Nast Traveler. Box 57018, Boulder, CO 80322. Another glossy monthly, featuring fairly candid reporting and very good photography.

Consumer Reports Travel Letter. Box 53629, Boulder, CO 80322-3629. Unbiased travel reportage covering the world. The report is not inexpensive (more than $35 a year for monthly issues) but is highly regarded for honest nuts and bolts reporting.181

INDEXES
ACCOMMODATIONS INDEX

RESTAURANT INDEX

GENERAL INDEX

Italicized numbers refer to information in a map, chart, or special topic.

ABOUT THE AUTHOR

Karl Luntta lived and worked in Africa, the South Pacific, and the Caribbean before settling in Massachusetts with his profoundly lovely family. He is the author of Moon's *Caribbean Handbook, Jamaica Handbook,* and other travel guides and has published fiction and nonfiction in national magazines and newspapers.

NOTES

MOON TRAVEL HANDBOOKS

THE IDEAL TRAVELING COMPANIONS

Moon Travel Handbooks provide focused, comprehensive coverage of distinct destinations all over the world. Our goal is to give travelers all the background and practical information they'll need for an extraordinary travel experience. Every Handbook begins with an in-depth essay about the land, the people, their history, art, politics, and social concerns—an entire bookcase of cultural insight and introductory information in one portable volume. We also provide accurate, up-to-date coverage of all the practicalities: language, currency, transportation, accommodations, food, and entertainment. And Moon's maps are legendary, covering not only cities and highways, but parks and trails that are often difficult to find in other sources.

On the following pages is a complete list of Handbooks, covering North America and Hawaii, Mexico, Central America and the Caribbean, and Asia and the Pacific. To purchase Moon Travel Handbooks, please check your local bookstore or order by phone: (800) 345-5473 Monday-Friday 8 a.m.-5 p.m. PST. If you are calling from outside of the United States the number is (916) 345-5473.

"Amazingly detailed in a style easy to understand, the Handbooks offer a lot for a good price."
—International Travel News

"Moon [Handbooks] . . . bring a healthy respect to the places they investigate. Best of all, they provide a host of odd nuggets that give a place texture and prod the wary traveler from the beaten path. The finest are written with such care and insight they deserve listing as literature."
—American Geographical Society

"Outdoor enthusiasts gravitate to the well-written Moon Travel Handbooks. In addition to politically correct historic and cultural features, the series focuses on flora, fauna and outdoor recreation. Maps and meticulous directions also are a trademark of Moon guides."
—Houston Chronicle

"Moon Travel Handbooks offer in-depth historical essays and useful maps, enhanced by a sense of humor and a neat, compact format." **—SWING**

"Perfect for the more adventurous, these are long on history, sightseeing and nitty-gritty information and very price-specific." **—Columbus Dispatch**

"Moon guides manage to be comprehensive and countercultural at the same time . . . Handbooks are packed with maps, photographs, drawings, and sidebars that constitute a college-level introduction to each country's history, culture, people, and crafts."
—National Geographic Traveler

"An in-depth dunk into the land, the people and their history, arts, and politics."
—Student Travels

"Few travel guides do a better job helping travelers create their own itineraries than the Moon Travel Handbook series. The authors have a knack for homing in on the essentials."
—Colorado Springs Gazette Telegraph

NORTH AMERICA AND HAWAII

"These domestic guides convey the same sense of exoticism that their foreign counterparts do, making home-country travel seem like far-flung adventure."
—*Sierra Magazine*

Alaska-Yukon Handbook	**$17.95**
Deke Castleman and Don Pitcher	500 pages, 92 maps
Alberta and the Northwest Territories Handbook	**$17.95**
Andrew Hempstead and Nadina Purdon	497 pages, 72 maps,
Arizona Traveler's Handbook	**$17.95**
Bill Weir and Robert Blake	486 pages, 54 maps
Atlantic Canada Handbook	**$17.95**
Nan Drosdick and Mark Morris	436 pages, 61 maps
Big Island of Hawaii Handbook	**$13.95**
J.D. Bisignani	349 pages, 23 maps
British Columbia Handbook	**$15.95**
Jane King	375 pages, 69 maps
Colorado Handbook	**$18.95**
Stephen Metzger	447 pages, 59 maps
Georgia Handbook	**$17.95**
Kap Stann	360 pages, 50 maps
Hawaii Handbook	**$19.95**
J.D. Bisignani	1004 pages, 90 maps
Honolulu-Waikiki Handbook	**$14.95**
J.D. Bisignani	365 pages, 20 maps
Idaho Handbook	**$18.95**
Don Root	582 pages, 42 maps
Kauai Handbook	**$15.95**
J.D. Bisignani	330 pages, 23 maps
Maui Handbook	**$14.95**
J.D. Bisignani	393 pages, 35 maps
Montana Handbook	**$17.95**
Judy Jewell and W.C. McRae	454 pages, 52 maps
Nevada Handbook	**$16.95**
Deke Castleman	473 pages, 40 maps
New Mexico Handbook	**$15.95**
Stephen Metzger	337 pages, 47 maps
New York City Handbook	**$13.95**
Christiane Bird	295 pages, 20 maps
New York Handbook	**$19.95**
Christiane Bird	760 pages, 95 maps
Northern California Handbook	**$19.95**
Kim Weir	779 pages, 50 maps
Oregon Handbook	**$16.95**
Stuart Warren and Ted Long Ishikawa	520 pages, 33 maps

Road Trip USA	**$22.50**
Jamie Jensen	786 pages, 165 maps
Southern California Handbook	**$19.95**
Kim Weir	600 pages, 30 maps
Tennessee Handbook	**$17.95**
Jeff Bradley	490 pages, 44 maps
Texas Handbook	**$17.95**
Joe Cummings	598 pages, 70 maps
Utah Handbook	**$17.95**
Bill Weir and W.C. McRae	456 pages, 40 maps
Washington Handbook	**$19.95**
Don Pitcher	630 pages, 113 maps
Wisconsin Handbook	**$18.95**
Thomas Huhti	580 pages, 69 maps
Wyoming Handbook	**$17.95**
Don Pitcher	581 pages, 80 maps

ASIA AND THE PACIFIC

"Scores of maps, detailed practical info down to business hours of small-town libraries. You can't beat the Asian titles for sheer heft. (The) series is sort of an American Lonely Planet, with better writing but fewer titles. (The) individual voice of researchers comes through."

—Travel & Leisure

Australia Handbook	**$21.95**
Marael Johnson, Andrew Hempstead, and Nadina Purdon	944 pages, 141 maps
Bali Handbook	**$19.95**
Bill Dalton	715 pages, 54 maps
Bangkok Handbook	**$13.95**
Michael Buckley	221 pages, 30 maps
Fiji Islands Handbook	**$13.95**
David Stanley	275 pages, 38 maps
Hong Kong Handbook	**$15.95**
Kerry Moran	347 pages, 49 maps
Indonesia Handbook	**$25.00**
Bill Dalton	1,351 pages, 249 maps
Japan Handbook	**$22.50**
J.D. Bisignani	952 pages, 213 maps
Micronesia Handbook	**$14.95**
Neil M. Levy	311 pages, 70 maps
Nepal Handbook	**$18.95**
Kerry Moran	466 pages, 51 maps

New Zealand Handbook	**$19.95**
Jane King	595 pages, 81 maps
Outback Australia Handbook	**$18.95**
Marael Johnson	424 pages, 57 maps
Pakistan Hanbdbook	**$19.95**
Isobel Shaw	660 pages, 85 maps
Philippines Handbook	**$17.95**
Peter Harper and Laurie Fullerton	638 pages, 116 maps
Singapore Handbook	**$15.95**
Carl Parkes	300 pages, 29 maps
Southeast Asia Handbook	**$21.95**
Carl Parkes	1,103 pages, 196 maps
South Korea Handbook	**$19.95**
Robert Nilsen	824 pages, 141 maps
South Pacific Handbook	**$22.95**
David Stanley	913 pages, 147 maps
Tahiti-Polynesia Handbook	**$13.95**
David Stanley	243 pages, 35 maps
Thailand Handbook	**$19.95**
Carl Parkes	834 pages, 142 maps
Tibet Handbook	**$30.00**
Victor Chan	1103 pages, 216 maps
Vietnam, Cambodia & Laos Handbook	**$18.95**
Michael Buckley	691 pages, 112 maps

MEXICO, CENTRAL AMERICA, AND THE CARIBBEAN

"Travel guides published by Moon Publications are uniformly just as they are advertised: 'informative, entertaining, highly practical.' They satisfy all the needs of travelers on the road. At the same time they are colorful and educational enough to be enjoyed by those whose travel is confined to armchair-bound wishes and dreams." —*Worldviews*

Baja Handbook	**$15.95**
Joe Cummings	362 pages, 44 maps
Belize Handbook	**$15.95**
Chicki Mallan	363 pages, 45 maps
Cabo Handbook	**$14.95**
Joe Cummings	205 pages, 18 maps
Cancún Handbook	**$13.95**
Chicki Mallan	254 pages, 25 maps
Caribbean Handbook	**$16.95**
Karl Luntta	384 pages, 56 maps

Central Mexico Handbook	**$15.95**
Chicki Mallan	391 pages, 63 maps
Costa Rica Handbook	**$19.95**
Christopher P. Baker	750 pages, 74 maps
Cuba Handbook	**$19.95**
Christopher P. Baker	650 pages, 70 maps
Dominican Republic Handbook	**$15.95**
Gaylord Dold	350 pages, 27 maps
Honduras Handbook	**$15.95**
Chris Humphreys	350 pages, 40 maps
Jamaica Handbook	**$15.95**
Karl Luntta	312 pages, 17 maps
Mexico Handbook	**$21.95**
Joe Cummings and Chicki Mallan	1,457 pages, 232 maps
Northern Mexico Handbook	**$16.95**
Joe Cummings	500 pages, 68 maps
Pacific Mexico Handbook	**$17.95**
Bruce Whipperman	483 pages, 69 maps
Puerto Vallarta Handbook	**$14.95**
Bruce Whipperman	285 pages, 36 maps
Virgin Islands Handbook	**$13.95**
Karl Luntta	230 pages, 19 maps
Yucatan Peninsula Handbook	**$15.95**
Chicki Mallan	397 pages, 62 maps

OTHER GREAT TITLES FROM MOON

"For hardy wanderers, few guides come more highly recommended than the Handbooks. They include good maps, steer clear of fluff and flackery, and offer plenty of money-saving tips. They also give you the kind of information that visitors to strange lands—on any budget—need to survive."

—US News & World Report

Moon Handbook	**$10.00**
Carl Koppeschaar	141 pages, 8 maps
Moscow-St. Petersburg Handbook	**$13.95**
Masha Nordbye	259 pages, 16 maps
The Practical Nomad	**$17.95**
Edward Hasbrouck	575 pages
Staying Healthy in Asia, Africa, and Latin America	**$11.95**
Dirk Schroeder	197 pages, 4 maps

WHERE TO BUY MOON TRAVEL HANDBOOKS

BOOKSTORES AND LIBRARIES: Moon Travel Handbooks are sold worldwide. Please contact our sales manager for a list of wholesalers and distributors in your area.

TRAVELERS: We would like to have Moon Travel Handbooks available throughout the world. Please ask your bookstore to write or call us for ordering information. If your bookstore will not order our guides for you, please contact us for a free catalog.

> **Moon Publications, Inc.**
> **P.O. Box 3040**
> **Chico, CA 95927-3040 U.S.A.**
> **tel.: (800) 345-5473, outside the U.S. (916) 345-5473**
> **fax: (916) 345-6751**
> **e-mail: travel@moon.com**

IMPORTANT ORDERING INFORMATION

PRICES: All prices are subject to change. We always ship the most current edition. We will let you know if there is a price increase on the book you order.

SHIPPING AND HANDLING OPTIONS: Domestic UPS or USPS first class (allow 10 working days for delivery): $3.50 for the first item, 50 cents for each additional item.

EXCEPTIONS: *Road Trip USA, Tibet Handbook, Mexico Handbook,* and *Indonesia Handbook* shipping $4.50; $1.00 for each additional *Road Trip USA, Tibet Handbook, Mexico Handbook,* and *Indonesia Handbook.*

Moonbelt shipping is $1.50 for one, 50 cents for each additional belt.

Add $2.00 for same-day handling.

UPS 2nd Day Air or Printed Airmail requires a special quote.

International Surface Bookrate 8-12 weeks delivery: $3.00 for the first item, $1.00 for each additional item. Note: Moon Publications cannot guarantee international surface bookrate shipping. Moon recommends sending international orders via air mail, which requires a special quote.

FOREIGN ORDERS: Orders that originate outside the U.S.A. must be paid for with an international money order, a check in U.S. currency drawn on a major U.S. bank based in the U.S.A., or Visa or MasterCard.

TELEPHONE ORDERS: We accept Visa or MasterCard payments. Minimum order is US$15. Call in your order: (800) 345-5473, 8 a.m.-5 p.m. Pacific standard time. Outside the U.S. the number is (916) 345-5473.

ORDER FORM

Prices are subject to change without notice. Be sure to call (800) 345-5473,
or (916) 345-5473 from outside the U.S. 8 a.m.–5 p.m. PST for current prices and editions,
or for the name of the bookstore nearest you that carries Moon Travel Handbooks.
(See important ordering information on preceding page.)

Name: _____ Date: _____

Street: _____

City: _____ Daytime Phone: _____

State or Country: _____ Zip Code: _____

QUANTITY	TITLE	PRICE

Taxable Total_____

Sales Tax (7.25%) for California Residents_____

Shipping & Handling_____

TOTAL_____

Ship: ☐ UPS (no P.O. Boxes) ☐ 1st class ☐ International surface mail

Ship to: ☐ address above ☐ other _____

_____

Make checks payable to: **MOON PUBLICATIONS, INC.**, P.O. Box 3040, Chico, CA 95927-3040 U.S.A.
We accept Visa and MasterCard. **To Order**: Call in your Visa or MasterCard number, or send a written order with your Visa or MasterCard number and expiration date clearly written.

Card Number: ☐ **Visa** ☐ **MasterCard**

☐ ☐ ☐ ☐ ☐ ☐ ☐ ☐ ☐ ☐ ☐ ☐ ☐ ☐ ☐ ☐

Exact Name on Card: _____

Expiration date:_____

Signature: _____

U.S.~METRIC CONVERSION

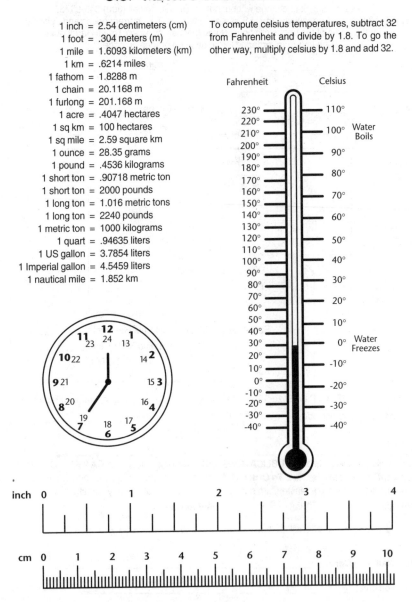

1 inch = 2.54 centimeters (cm)
1 foot = .304 meters (m)
1 mile = 1.6093 kilometers (km)
1 km = .6214 miles
1 fathom = 1.8288 m
1 chain = 20.1168 m
1 furlong = 201.168 m
1 acre = .4047 hectares
1 sq km = 100 hectares
1 sq mile = 2.59 square km
1 ounce = 28.35 grams
1 pound = .4536 kilograms
1 short ton = .90718 metric ton
1 short ton = 2000 pounds
1 long ton = 1.016 metric tons
1 long ton = 2240 pounds
1 metric ton = 1000 kilograms
1 quart = .94635 liters
1 US gallon = 3.7854 liters
1 Imperial gallon = 4.5459 liters
1 nautical mile = 1.852 km

To compute celsius temperatures, subtract 32 from Fahrenheit and divide by 1.8. To go the other way, multiply celsius by 1.8 and add 32.

Fahrenheit   Celsius

230°   110°
220°
210°   100°   Water
200°   Boils
190°   90°
180°   80°
170°
160°   70°
150°   60°
140°
130°   50°
120°
110°   40°
100°   30°
90°
80°   20°
70°
60°   10°
50°
40°   0°   Water
30°   Freezes
20°   -10°
10°   -20°
0°
-10°   -30°
-20°
-30°   -40°
-40°

inch 0   1   2   3   4

cm 0 1 2 3 4 5 6 7 8 9 10